COMING TO CRITICAL ENGAGEMENT

An Autoethnographic Exploration

Frank A. Fear
Cheryl L. Rosaen
Richard J. Bawden
Pennie G. Foster-Fishman

Edited by Patricia P. Miller
Foreword by Jeffrey S. Nielsen

Copyright © 2006 by
University Press of America,® Inc.
4501 Forbes Boulevard
Suite 200
Lanham, Maryland 20706
UPA Acquisitions Department (301) 459-3366

PO Box 317
Oxford
OX2 9RU, UK

Library of Congress Control Number: 2006922455
ISBN-13: 978-0-7618-3470-0 (clothbound : alk. paper)
ISBN-10: 0-7618-3470-2 (clothbound : alk. paper)
ISBN-13: 978-0-7618-3471-7 (paperback : alk. paper)
ISBN-10: 0-7618-3471-0 (paperback : alk. paper)

CONTENTS

Part II – Digging into Engagement

Part III – Making Sense of It All

About the Authors

FOREWORD

At a time of unparalleled crisis and opportunity marking the painful birthing of the twenty-first century, this timely book offers a path to sanity amidst the many voices of acquiescence or dissent. The authors bridge the gap between theory and practice through engaging stories and serious academic analysis. They examine and explore the nature of scholarly engagement at a time when our institutions of higher education are becoming more remote and irrelevant to lives of ordinary citizens. Through their diverse experience in building communities of practice, the authors have developed a transformative model of engagement to assist the concerned academic in serving the public interest and bettering society. I personally found the book meaningful as a guide in my own individual quest, as a philosophy instructor, to make significant contributions and meaningful connections that transcend narrowly defined academic roles.

The openness and transparency advocated in their work is refreshing, especially today in a time of deceptive image wizards, growing social inequities, and secretive rank-based leadership. The practical steps and insights offered by the authors will motivate real change. Specifically, the book reminds us that, in the human sphere, the basic ethical relationship is the face to face encounter between people. When we confront another, we face someone who, like us, possesses certain desires, needs, hopes, and fears. Our initial orientation is biased toward our own pleasure and enjoyment, but we must make the most basic ethical decision—whether to consider the other person as like ourselves, as an equal, or to see the other as different from us, either as our inferior or superior. How we make this most basic of decisions determines whether we enter into a rank-based or a peer-based relationship with the other.

This book will make possible many more authentic peer-based relationships and collaborations, while enriching ourselves and our institutions of higher education.

Professor Jeffrey S. Nielsen
Department of Philosophy, Brigham Young University.
Author of *The Myth of Leadership: Creating Leaderless Organizations*. 2004. Palo Alto CA: Davies-Black Publishing.

ACKNOWLEDGEMENTS

Work on this manuscript was enabled through funding received from the Michigan State University Office of Outreach and Engagement, Assistant Provost for University Outreach & Engagement; and also from the Families and Children Together (FACT) coalition, at Michigan State University. We thank Assistant Provost Hiram Fitzgerald and FACT co-director Janet Bokemeier for their support.

Members of our engagement learning community at Michigan State University contributed significantly to the creation of this manuscript. Participants included Annette Abrams (university outreach & engagement); Marguerite Barratt (psychology and family & child ecology); Hiram Fitzgerald (psychology and university outreach & engagement); John Melcher (urban affairs programs); Joseph Marshall (human medicine); Lee Anne Roman (nursing); Rachel Schiffman (nursing); and Francisco Villarruel (family & child ecology). We also thank graduate assistants Stephanie Jacobson (psychology), Lexine Hansen (resource development), and Sheila Faye Lahousse (psychology) for their dedicated service.

The Authors

AUTHORS' NOTE

Any academic book is the tangible outcome of scholarly inquiry; the last step in the process of what has been "discovered" and created, and is judged to be worth sharing. The production of text is sometimes little more than a reporting process. At other times, it is much more than that. This is one of those "other times."

Writing this book was an inextricable feature of inquiry, serving both as a filter for understanding and as a vehicle for stimulating more ideas, more dialogue, more experimentation, and more writing. Over time, it became clear to us that the medium was indeed the message, and that this book would be an *expression of* engagement, and not simply a *document about* it. We wrote; read what we wrote; talked about the writing; reflected on its transformative powers; and then wrote more. All the while, the rest of our professional lives swirled through and across the writing project. We brought *to* our conversations what we were experiencing in the field and, likewise, we took learning *from* our conversations back out into the field.

The nature of our unconventional yet powerfully transformative undertaking will become evident as the book unfolds. The purpose of this Authors' Note is to focus directly on one dimension of it—the matter of authorship attribution: how our plans evolved in that regard, and where we settled ultimately.

With one or two of us taking the lead in each chapter, we wrote about what we had discovered collectively. But there is more to it than that. Each chapter includes what the writer(s) discovered on his, her, or their own, by investigating topics stimulated through and by our dialogue. Consequently, dialogue and writing are blended in a narrative about a generative, hermeneutic process of individual and collective learning. The iterative nature of this writing process was further enriched by the critically reflexive feature of our time together: we constantly unearthed deeply held and hitherto unexpressed thoughts and feelings about ourselves and our work, as well as our ever-evolving interpretations of "engagement" and its relationships to higher education, in general. As we engaged in dialogue and wrote about our dialogue, we came to live the dialectics of self and other, and of subject and process.

While this book is shared intellectual property, there is diversity of responsibility and expression, just as there is in engagement. None of us could have written any of the chapters without having spent time together. Know also that there are distinct voice changes across chapters, with points of emphasis that are strongly held by one or some of us but not necessarily by all of us. Smoothing out voice changes and purging points of dissensus were never seriously considered; pursuing either option would unalterably and unacceptably change the intent and purpose of this work. In the end, we found coming to critical engagement to be an intensely personal experience: muting or altering individual voice for editorial purposes made no sense.

Toward the end of this book writing project, we made two decisions about how to attribute authorship. First, we decided to order book authorship based on the magnitude of contributions to the overall project. Second, we decided to attribute authorship for each chapter by recognizing specific writer contributions (by chapter) in the Table of Contents.

If those plans had been implemented, there would have been no need for us to write this Authors' Note. Just as we were about to go to press, several reviewers told us they had problems with what we had in mind. First, they raised concerns about claiming credit for the book *and* for chapters, which they believed could be construed as authorship "double dipping." To avoid that outcome, we were advised to pursue one (but not both) of two options: in the co-authored book option, take credit for writing the book together and do not affix authorship to the chapters; in the edited book option, take credit for writing chapters individually or together, and identify an editor (or two) on the book cover. The reviewers also identified a second problem: by attributing authorship for chapters, they felt that we were encouraging readers to cite specific chapters of interest—and not the entire book. That would be fine if this product was an edited volume, but not appropriate if it was a co-authored book.

Receiving this feedback prompted us to revamp our plans for authorship attribution and, in so doing, to be very clear about the nature of this volume. This book was conceived and written together. It is a co-authored book, not an edited volume. And writing it together seemed like the way a jazz quartet performs: within the overarching context of a shared performance each artist takes his or her turn—playing solo, in duets, in trios, and with all others. It is about me and we; and it is also very much about ours.

All of that said we invite you to our coming to critical engagement.

Frank, Cheryl, Richard, and Pennie
East Lansing, Michigan
December 2005

INTRODUCTION

At the interface of expert judgment and community participation stands "engagement," the label currently embraced by colleges and universities to describe activities associated with serving the public interest. What had been viewed by higher education as service *to*, then extension *of*, and still later outreach *from*, is now considered engagement *with*. Today, faculty members, students, and staff collaborate with residents as partners in enhancing community quality of life. The nature of this work makes engagement a complex undertaking, often taking place in contested, messy, and emotionally charged situations.

Reflecting on our experiences as engaged faculty members led us to an undeniable conclusion: if we were going to write a book, it had to be a book about scholarly engagement—exploring issues associated with the underlying nature of engagement. This would not be a book focused solely on how to do engagement, what quality engagement looks like, or how to evaluate engagement's outcomes and impacts. We believe those topics are well attended to and spoken for.[1] This present contribution is our attempt to convey what it means to under-

---

1. There are many publications in multiple fields attending to these matters including: J. Bray, J. Lee, L. Smith, and L. Yorks, *Collaborative Inquiry in Practice: Action, Reflection, and Making Meaning.* (Thousand Oaks, CA: Sage Publications 2000); A. Driscoll, and E. Lynton, *Making Outreach Visible: A Guide to Documenting Professional Service and Outreach.* (Washington, D.C.: American Association of Higher Education 1999); J. Forester, *The Deliberative Practitioner: Encouraging Participatory Planning Process.* (Cambridge, MA: MIT Press 2000); D. Greenwood and M. Levin, *Introduction to Action Research: Social Research for Social Change.* (Thousand Oaks, CA: Sage Publications 1998). B. Holland (2001), Exploring the challenge of documenting and measuring civic engagement endeavors of colleges and universities. Paper given at *The Campus Compact Advanced Institute on Classifications for Civic Engagement.* http://www.compact.org/advancedtoolkit/measuring.html; E. Lynton, *Making the Case for Professional Service.* (Washington, D.C.: American Association for Higher Education

stand engagement intellectually and to offer different expressions and examples of what it looks like when understanding is put into practice. That is not to say ours is a definitive expression. Of course it is not. But it is to say that we believe that faculty members, like ourselves, have much to say about engagement because of our experience with and in it.

It is important to understand the text, subtext, and context associated with this inquiry. The *text* is what we have learned from and about engagement, including what it means in intensely personal terms; the *subtext* is our evolved selves, how we have thought about and practiced engagement over the years; and the *context* is the institution of higher education, the research university in our case. The genre of our written expression is autoethnography, which is a postmodern, evocative form of inquiry, interpreted by Michael Quinn Patton as work grounded in this question: *How does my own experience of this culture connect with and offer insights about this culture, situation, event, or way of life?* (Patton 2002, 84). Autoethnography is an attractive approach when it is less desirable (or even possible) to separate the domain being studied from the analyst studying it, and when "the other," the situation, and self are perceived to be inextricably intertwined (Patton 2002, 84-85). Qualitative researchers Carolyn Ellis and Arthur Bochner define autoethnography as a means to connect the personal to the cultural. "Back and forth autoethnographers gaze . . . focusing outward on social and cultural aspects of their personal experience; then, they look inward, exposing a vulnerable self that is moved by and may be moved through, refract, and resist cultural interpretations" (Ellis and Bochner 2000, 739). In reflexive autoethnography, which is the form of autoethnography used in this work, "authors. . . bend back on self and look more deeply at self-other interactions. . . [such that]. . . personal experience becomes important primarily in how it illuminates the culture under study" (Ellis and Bochner 2000, 740).

What emerged in our reflexive autoethnographic writing, we hope, is a product befitting companionship with Laurel Richardson's evocative *Fields of*

1995); P. Mattessich, M. Murray-Close, and B. Monsey, *Collaboration: What Makes it Work?* (St. Paul, MN: Amherst H. Wilder Foundation 2001); Michigan State University, *Points of distinction: A guidebook for planning and evaluating quality outreach.* East Lansing: Office of the Vice Provost for University Outreach, Michigan State University (1996). http://www.msu.edu/unit/outreach/pubs/pod.pdf; D. Maurrasse, *Beyond the Campus: How Colleges and Universities Form Partnerships with their Communities.* (New York: Routledge 2001); M. Minkler, N. Wallerstein, eds., *Community-based Participatory Research for Health.* (San Francisco: Jossey-Bass 2003); National Association of State Universities and Land Grant Colleges, *Returning to our Roots: The Engaged Institution.* (Washington: NASULGC 1999), a Report of the Kellogg Commission on the Future of State and Land-Grant Universities; S. Smith, D. Wilms, and N. Johnson, eds. 1997. *Nurtured by Knowledge: Learning to do Participatory Action-research.* (New York: The Apex Press 1997); and K. Strand, S. Marullo, N. Cutforth, R. Stoecker, and P. Donohue, *Community-based Research in Higher Education: Principles and Practices.* (San Francisco: Jossey-Bass 2003).

Play: Constructing an Academic Life (Richardson 1997). Among many things, Richardson writes about the value of *crystallization*. How she describes it is how we feel about ourselves, engagement, and our work as engaged scholars:

> The central image is the crystal, which combines symmetry and substance with an infinite variety of shapes, substances, transmutations, multidimensionalities, and angles of approach. Crystals grow, change, and alter but are not amorphous. Crystals are prisms that reflect externalities and refract within themselves, creating different colors, patterns, arrays, casting off in different directions. What we see depends upon our angle of repose. (Richardson 1997, 92)

As our autoethnographic experience unfolded, we *felt* a theme (and title) for this book long before we could put those feelings into words. When the time came, the title seemed obvious, *Coming to Critical Engagement*. The title was inspired by Daniel Yankelovich's thoughtful expression, *Coming to Public Judgment: Making Democracy Work in a Complex Society* (Yankelovich 1991). In that book he extols the virtues of deliberative democracy; critiques the modern preference for what he calls The Culture of Technical (and expert) Control; and decries America's preference for market over communal values. Stimulated by how Yankelovich thought through and articulated his preference for coming to public judgment, our coming to critical engagement is understood as *process*, *text*, and *stance*:

- *coming to* suggests that understanding emerged through an interpersonal process—an intentional journey of collaborative learning
- *critical* conveys the central importance of treating self and subject as a text to be examined
- *engagement* is a stance, which is expressed in answers to core questions: Why do you engage? With whom do you engage? Toward what end do you engage? How do you engage?

By characterizing engagement as process, text, and stance, we came to understand engagement as *opportunities to share our knowledge and learn with those who struggle for social justice; and to collaborate with them respectfully and responsibly for the purpose of improving life.*

How did we come to know this? We began by devoting three months—meeting once a week—to reading and discussing literature selections suggested by group members. The ambiance was seminar-like in nature—seeking to understand, raising questions of clarification, and pinpointing perceived areas of strengths and weaknesses. Functionally, the experience laid the foundation for expanding our collective perspective and vocabulary for engaging in "joint talk."

Immediately after that, and for the ensuing three months, we met in extended dinner (retreat-like) sessions sharing cases from our community work.

Whenever possible, we related our casework to the literature read in the earlier phase. This case-based conversation turned discussion into dialogue; we *really* listened to each other, fascinated by how different group members framed their work, approached it, and struggled with issues and challenges. As we got to know each other and our work better, we asked ever more probing questions. We viewed each case—and the collective set of cases—as a database ripe for analysis. In so doing, we became increasingly analytic about our work.

Our experience brought to life John Bennett's assertion that *conversation is the essential metaphor in the academic life* (Bennett 2003). He writes:

> It is not an esoteric concept, nor are we external to the activity it pictures. Conversation is an ordinary activity, something in which we all participate. It is not a special technique available only to the few nor is it the latest pedagogy, the fad of the moment . . . . The metaphor of conversation suggests that people with different intellectual interests and histories have something important to say to each other. The process is back and forth—comment or question, followed by response, which in turn generates a rejoinder, and so on. One immediate advantage is that conversation identifies the other as a necessary participant in our own learning. Rather than defending turf, faculty learn from each other . . . . Instead of presenting other faculty as competitors and threats, conversation reveals them as genuine colleagues with whom we are linked in the pursuit of greater understanding. (Bennett 2003, 99)

Through disciplined conversation—primarily by analyzing the literature and our field experiences—we began generating insights into community-based practice, new ways (for us) of thinking about engagement. Recognizing that, we started converting meeting notes into text intended for collegial sharing, first, for conference presentations and, soon after, for publication as journal articles.[2] The

---

2. Presentations and publications preceding the publication of this book include:
F. Fear, M. Barratt, and C. Rosaen. "Nurturing the Work: Fostering Scholarly Discovery Though Communities of Practice." Paper presented at the annual meeting of the *American Association of Higher Education*, (Washington, March, 2003). F. Fear, R. Bawden, C. Rosaen, and P. G. Foster-Fishman. "A Model of Engaged Learning: Frames of Reference and Scholarly Underpinnings." *Journal of Higher Education Outreach and Engagement* 7(3) (2002), 55–68. F. Fear and C. Rosaen. "From Ordinary to Extraordinary: Engagement as Transformative Force." Presented at the American Association of Higher Education's *Faculty Roles and Rewards Conference*, Phoenix, (January, 2002). F. Fear, C. Rosaen, P. G. Foster-Fishman, and R. Bawden. "Outreach as a Scholarly Expression." *Journal of Higher Education Outreach and Engagement* 6(2) (2001), 21–34. C. Rosaen, P. G. Foster-Fishman, and F. Fear. "The Citizen Scholar: Joining Voices and Values in the Engagement Interface." *Metropolitan University* 12(4) (2001), 10–29. F. Fear and R. Bawden. "Boyer's Last Word: A Critical Message Overlooked?" Paper presented at *Outreach Scholarship: Learning, Discovery, and Engagement*. The Pennsylvania State University, University Park, PA, (October, 2001). C. Rosaen, M. Barrett, and P. G. Foster-Fishman, "Joining Voices, Values and Visions: Creating a Collaborative Interface." Paper presented at Outreach Scholarship: Learning, Discovery, and Engagement. The Penn-

writing process had an unexpected outcome. We found ourselves engaging in critically reflexive writing by creating understanding *through* writing. In other words, the writing process stimulated fresh ideas and had a generative effect. Writing thus became *part of* the inquiry process, not just an outcome of it.

What emerged over a period of more than three years was an iterative cycle of reading, sharing field experiences, engaging in dialogue, writing, and trying out in the field what we had learned at the table. As we repeated the cycle, the essential nature of our dialogue changed. We began probing more deeply into the substantive and practical dimensions of what we were creating together. Through discourse guided by a stance of criticality, we were able to convert what had been a cycle of tasks—reading, engaging in dialogue about field experiences, and writing—into a routine for transformative professional practice:

- critique your work
- incorporate learning from critique into your practice
- repeat the cycle

Bawden framed well the experience in a letter written to the group as this book was being written:

> For me, the attraction of our work has been the constant flux between practice and theory—between action and informed-reflection, if you will. Our focus has been on scholarly aspects as they play out in practice. I would strongly contend that we have found unity in our diversity by drawing strength from the "tensions of difference" that come with different traditions—different theoretical and philosophical foundations, different areas of concern, and different methodologies.

As time passed and our regular meetings proceeded, we were able to step back from the discourse to ask, "What organizational form have we created?" In the beginning our default (and uncritical) response was, "We are a faculty learning community." As we explored this matter more critically, it was clear that we were generating knowledge by engaging in discourse about existing disciplinary and professional knowledge, including our own practice experiences. That re-

sylvania State University, University Park, PA, (October, 2001). C. Rosaen, P. G. Foster-Fishman, and F. Fear, with F. Villarruel, R. Bawden, A. Abrams, M. Barrett, and S. Jacobson. "The Citizen Scholar; Joining Voices and Values in the Engagement Interface." Paper presented at the University as Citizen Conference. University of South Florida, Tampa, FL, (February, 2001).

sponse caused us to search the literature for placeholders—labels—to better communicate what we were doing together. We found the term *community of practice,* a concept popularized by Etienne Wenger:

> Communities of practice are groups of people who share a concern, a set of problems, or a passion about a topic, and who deepen their knowledge and expertise in this area by interacting on an ongoing basis . . . . These people don't necessarily work together every day, but they meet because they find value in their interactions. As they spend time together, they typically share information, insight, and advice . . . [and]. . . ponder common issues, explore ideas, and act as sounding boards . . . . Over time, they develop a unique perspective on their topic as well as a body of common knowledge, practices, and approaches . . . .(Wenger, McDermott, and Snyder 2002, 4–5)

Communities of practice are grounded in a theory of engaged learning. Learning in them is a social act: members learn *with* others (transcendent learning generated through dialogue); learn *from* others (gaining insights and practice hints from colleagues), and learn *through* others (imagining what it would be like to adopt others' practices in your work). Members negotiate norms of engagement, creating over time a distinctive repertoire of language, activities, patterns, and outcomes as they collectively create value for members. Often, but not always, communities of practice come into being and persist because benefits are not available otherwise.

As self-organizing systems, communities of practice are not easily managed. Members drop in and drop out, as is always the case in voluntary action. In our case, we found episodic participation to be enriching opportunities for testing understandings, for exploring applications and, perhaps, most importantly, for assessing relevance. Because those dropping in were not as deeply involved in the iterative writing process that the four of us had begun, they engaged candidly, embracing and sometimes debunking the prevailing talk around the table. It forced the persisting members to eschew communicating through insider language, which disables transparency and disallows truly collegial engagement.

Practice communities go where they need to go as members collectively decide on directions and learn how to act together. Sometimes communities of practice are characterized by bursts of energy, followed by dormant periods, with organization maintenance issues consuming significant amounts of attention from time to time. Leadership is shared, not controlled by a single person, meaning there is an evolutionary process that is infrequently linear and sometimes unpredictable. Consequently, core virtues—including faith and trust—are required internally and externally. For example, administrators who endorsed and supported our quest did not manage us, preferring instead to be briefed periodically on our progress. High degrees of trust are required that something of value will emerge from the deliberations. Neither members nor external stakeholders can force certain matters or push for specific and preferred outcomes. "The way" is revealed, collegially and naturally.

When practice communities persist over time, a distinct way of thinking about and approaching a matter of mutual interest emerges. Put another way, the group often finds voice amidst the cacophony of other (and sometimes contending) voices that speak to the matter under consideration. When that happens, the group articulates *a discourse*. Maarten Hajer elaborates:

> In everyday speech, discourse is seen as synonymous with discussion, or is at best understood as a 'mode of talking.' Yet from a social scientific point of view it makes sense to reconsider this common-sense of understanding discourse . . . . Discourse is . . . a specific ensemble of ideas, concepts, and categorizations that are produced, reproduced, and transformed in a particular set of practices and through which meaning is given to physical and social realities. (Hajer 1995, 44)

According to Hajer (1995), discourses should be understood not only in substantive terms but also as manifestations of social, cultural, institutional, and other forces that influence how we think about a subject matter in one way versus another way. As a discourse matures, a narrative is constructed by advocates—a "story line" according to Hajer—that serves multiple functions, including a way of conveying a distinct perspective on social reality. There is also the matter of discursive hegemony, that is, reasons why some discourses are preferred to others, and those reasons are political, not just substantive. Embedded in any discourse, as Foucault and others have pointed out, are governing rules, the modes of agreement (often unspoken) that guide how a discourse should evolve and, if need be, change.

This book is an expression of our discourse on engagement. That discourse emerged on its own terms and also in reaction to our interpretation of other discourses on engagement—positions almost never expressed as such—but discourses, nonetheless. In many ways, we do not accept what we consider to be the prevailing discourse on engagement in higher education, which we believe to be instrumental in philosophy, bureaucratic in intent, and promulgated by administrative elites. We do not believe that engagement will prosper as a scholarly expression under its presumed rules. That left us with no option but to articulate our own positionality, and that is what this book is about.

Applying the term discourse in more popular terms, our intent is to contribute to the nascent discourse on the scholarship of engagement. This book describes our journey—our coming to critical engagement—and our insights about the work itself. It also illuminates how these insights influence and inform how we go about our community-based work and learn from it. By offering our perspective we hope to demonstrate how at least one group of scholars understands and practices engagement. *Our goal is to stimulate discourse about engagement praxis, which we see as action connected to critical reflection regarding the practice of social and cultural change* (Freire 1970). We believe this is one of the most important ways to enhance engagement as a scholarly field.

In our journey to critical engagement, we came to appreciate that engagement is not a new idea, although the title is novel. Engaged colleagues are all-around, and they have been there all along, frequently undervalued, often out of the spotlight, and sometimes at professional risk. Rather than act as though this work is something new, it is more a matter of understanding more deeply what is already there, uncovering its distinctive features and, in the process, celebrating its contributions. In the words of Martin Nagler (2001, 12), "The seeds of renewal do not have to be created; they are waiting there in the soil of our own existence—waiting for us to create the conditions to awaken them."

References

Bennett, J. 2003. *Academic life: Hospitality, ethics, and spirituality*. Bolton MA: Anker Publishing.

Ellis, C., and A. Bochner. 2000. Autoethnography, personal narrative, and reflexivity: Researcher as subject. In N. Denzin and Y. Lincoln, eds. *Handbook of qualitative research*. 2nd ed. Thousand Oaks CA: Sage Publications.

Freire, P. 1970. *Pedagogy of the oppressed*. New York: Herder and Herder.

Hajer, M. 1995. *The politics of environmental discourse: Ecological modernization and the policy process*. Oxford UK: Oxford Univ. Press.

Nagler, M. 2001. *Is there no other way? The search for a nonviolent future*. Berkeley: Berkeley Hills Books.

Patton, M. 2002. *Qualitative research and evaluation methods*. 3rd ed. Thousand Oaks CA: Sage Publications.

Richardson, L. 1997. *Fields of play: Constructing an academic life*. New Brunswick NJ: Rutgers Univ. Press.

Wenger, E., R. McDermott, and W. Snyder. 2002. *Cultivating communities of practice*. Boston: Harvard Business School Press.

Yankelovich, D. 1991. *Coming to public judgment: Making democracy work in a complex society*. Syracuse NY: Syracuse Univ. Press.

PART I
A FRAME OF REFERENCE

CHAPTER 1

FINDING OUR VOICE,
LOCATING OUR PLACE

Some things are not meant to be: we never intended to write *this* book. At the invitation of co-author Foster-Fishman, we subscribed to writing a book on good practices in community-based research. That intention expired soon after we began meeting. Something unexpected—different and wonderful—happened. At the beginning of our time together, we allowed ourselves the luxury of drifting into conversation (and it was a real, honest-to-goodness conversation) about the community work each of us has done in the past. We began the conversation as virtual strangers, never having worked on a joint project: we represent different fields, focus on different issues, work in different settings, draw on different theories and methods, and use different language to describe our work. With dissimilarities associated with a shared domain of common interest, we were fascinated to learn about each other's work and surprised (even comforted) to know that we had faced common issues and challenges in the field.

Over time, we migrated from writing a book on how to do community-based research to writing a book on what we learned from being together. We proceeded from one lightly scripted meeting to another, allowing dialogue to inform each step along the way. What did we learn along the way?

Valuing a space for collegial engagement

Our time together was a sabbatical from the daily grind of doing things with precious little time left to reflect with provocative colleagues on topics of mutual interest. Much of our time, and we suspect yours, is spent as workers on an academic assembly line with the ever-present need to complete one project and move to the next. This approach closes out opportunities to critically examine one's work, especially for the purpose of seeing what *new* learning might emerge from engaging in sustained conversation with colleagues who have had similar experiences. With institutional blessing and support, we created an alternative to that assembly line—a space for contemplation—for making sense of big practice issues and challenges faced while on "the assembly line."[1] It was an opportunity to step back, think, reflect, engage, and push ourselves to new levels of understanding about the work we dearly love.

How unpracticed at this we found ourselves to be! The very *first thing* we did was create our own version of the academic assembly line: bring field experiences to the table; mine experiences for "gold nuggets"; document insights; and share insights at conferences, in classes, and in print. Over time, we learned how important it was to refrain from soiling our space that way. We learned to up-shift our thinking by crafting vibrant (rather than linear and mechanical) routines of collegial engagement. We replaced the assembly line with a *dynamic* system by taking knowledge generated by our learning *back into the field* so that, upon returning later to the learning table, we could talk about what it was like to integrate new learning into practice. Then, through dialogue, we would generate new and fresh practice-informed insights about our work. This was not a production system, we slowly realized; it was a *learning cycle*.

---

1. The conventional model in higher education is for the administration to assemble faculty members in task forces or committees for the purpose of analyzing an organizational situation (e.g., service learning) and proposing strategies for addressing that situation (e.g., how to ensure that service-learning work is valued by unit heads during the promotion and tenure process). Perhaps because we are veterans at that sort of work at Michigan State University (MSU) and also because our work is valued, administrators responded with interest when it was clear to them that ours would be an unconventional path. While saying that we were "writing a book" simplified matters considerably, it was abundantly obvious that the administration was willing to experiment. We participated in this work as part of load and central administration provided operating funding (e.g., conference travel) and paid the salary of a graduate assistant. This support says something important about the administrative climate for faculty work at MSU. The university is also recognized nationally for taking intellectual leadership relative to work associated with continuing education, outreach, and now, engagement. Our work was interpreted in that vein.

In recognizing and acting on this realization, we created an alternative to the academic drill we know and do so well. Starting as graduate students (if not before) the drill is presented to us with stealth-like intent. We tend to accept it uncritically as "the way" and are expected to practice it routinely largely because that is the way we are supposed to act (Fear, McCarthy et al. 2003, 34–39). Deviating from the drill requires, first, recognizing that you are in a drill; second, finding the drill to be unsatisfying; and third, having the opportunity (and freedom) to create an alternative reality that involves stepping outside the boundaries of conventional practice. There is power, we found, in discovering that others share similar thoughts and feelings, and that something of value can emerge out of creating a space for collegial engagement.

Doing that requires shedding skin: you start by letting go of sacred practices such as allowing yourself to become comfortable with NOT mapping your journey at the outset. We learned that the learning road will take you "where it will," as long as the journey is undertaken authentically and responsibly, guided by core questions. Doing that allows you to replace the conventional production logic with an alternative logic, *collegial interaction*:

> Ultimately, collegiality requires being open to new possibilities, acknowledging and respecting one another as equals, listening deeply to what others are saying, and slowing down to think about and reflect on what was shared. Above all else, being truly engaged means being open to the influence of others; it requires us to abandon a position of knowing for one of learning. (Fear and Doberneck 2004, 19)

Ironically, in creating our space for collegial engagement we imitated what we nurture in our community work. In that work, we encourage

- *self-determination*, organizing around issues that matter to people
- *open participation and low boundaries*, combining the power of invitation with the virtue of hospitableness[2]
- *ease of operation*, keeping organizational management transactions to a workable minimum
- *decentralized leadership*, encouraging distributive rather than centralized leadership
- *egalitarian ownership*, encouraging an ethic of co-ownership of the process and outcome (Fear and Doberneck 2004, 17–18)

These principles parallel the assumptions that business consultant Jeffrey Nielsen believes are guiding peer-based activity in "leaderless" business operations, namely, that employees are productive; care about their work; bring diversity of perspectives, experiences, and talents to the table; have a good grasp of

---

2. For an eloquent description of the power of hospitality see John Bennett (1998).

what is going on and what needs to happen; and can produce outstanding results with minimal management (Nielson 2004). The emphasis in this way of engaging is *power with* rather than power over. Leadership in a collegial space happens when people—through free will—come together; develop shared norms of engagement; and interact with passion about an issue or topic of importance to them. As organizational scholar Meg Wheatley writes, "We just have to find a few others who care about the same thing. Together, we'll figure out what our first step is, then the next, then the next" (Wheatley 2002, 25).

Recognizing the visceral qualities of engagement

One of the first things we discovered together is that engagement is, above all else, a lived experience, best expressed by what it means to *be* and *feel* engaged. In contrast to some interpretations of engagement—with emphasis on what is done and accomplished by and through its execution—fundamentally, engagement is a visceral expression. "To engage" speaks to us in ways that other words, such as community development, community service, and community research, do not. There is an "outside of oneself" feeling to those words— executing the development *of*, providing service *to*, and conducting research *on*—that contradicts what we found engagement to be, namely, a deep personal expression *with others* in a shared pursuit that is life altering, if not transforming. Because of that, engagement can "grab you" and not let go.

Our reaction is not uncommon among those who have experienced engagement. Images of engagement as a felt experience surfaced through storytelling and metaphor in a study conducted by co-author Fear and colleagues (Fear, Bruns et al 2003, 59–74). Among responses shared were seeing with fresh eyes; understanding the importance of virtue; and recognizing how you are learning and growing. One interviewee observed:

> It was the most uniformly powerful learning experience I have ever observed. The students and their faculty mentors learned an incredible amount about themselves, each other, another community, and the world at large. They observed a number of different leadership styles from the general guiding hands of the building site manager to the committed, visionary leadership of the mission director; the self-taught, inspired leadership of the community pastor; the brave, bold leadership of the local children; and what they could do themselves with hammer and nails and planks and chicken wire. . . . . I think there was a huge unspoken feeling of accomplishment in having done something good, having done it well, and having done it together. We could not find the words to express our feelings. We took pictures. We cried. We sang. And we will remember, always. (Fear, Bruns et al. 2003, 62)

Understanding engagement as lived experience suggests that there is "more to it" than can be captured by the conventional way of Western knowing, propositional knowing, as John Heron and Peter Reason refer to it (Heron and Reason 1997, 274–294.) Put another way, there is a dimension to engagement that cannot be fully appreciated by describing and analyzing a project in terms of what was done, why, how, and with what outcomes. There is another side to engagement, often difficult to put in words, which tells a story about how engagement feels and what it means in personal terms. As physicist David Bohm put it, there is more than an *explicate* order—what we experience explicitly. There is also an *implicate* order, a reality hidden from view that enfolds and unfolds in concert with the explicate order to create a total order, much like what a swimmer experiences when she experiences waves on the lake *and* the current beneath the water's surface (Bohm 1980).

If the explicate order is the text of engagement, then the implicate order is its subtext. When asked to consider this subtext, those interviewed in a study published by co-author Fear and colleagues used imagery to convey their understanding: a blossom; needle and thread; looking in a foggy mirror; freeing a chained child; and waiting to exhale, were among the responses offered (Fear, Burnham et al. 2003, 119–134). Drawing on imagery of the implicate order enabled respondents to explore matters that are often difficult to grasp, let alone discuss, such as, "Don't we often feel lost and confused in engagement?" These conversations helped deepen respondents' understanding of the engagement experience.

As our faculty group engaged in conversations about the implicate order of engagement, especially those times when we felt that our work "really made a difference," we commented on how others have responded to our efforts over the years. Almost uniformly we recollected three simultaneous responses: *affirmation, anger, and puzzlement.* There were those who were exceptionally appreciative and wanted us to know how much our work meant to them. There were also those who were ruffled, if not disturbed by what we were doing, seeing it as wrongheaded and disrupting the status quo. And there was a third group: persons who were perplexed, sometimes mystified, and generally "clueless" about what had transpired. As we reflected on these episodes, we wondered if it could be any other way: affirmation says our efforts resonate in others' hearts; dismay means we are pushing against the grain; and bewilderment suggests our work is beyond convention.

The path to becoming engaged scholars

Creating a space for engagement and, through it, understanding the implicate order of engagement, helped all of us appreciate that this work brings "the true you" to the surface. Working over the years with like minded people enables you to convert common values and beliefs into action. Over time you develop an undeniable and indelible position: understanding what you stand for means being able to articulate preferred outcomes with increasing conviction and clarity.

So, where do we stand? As we reflected together on our years of engagement, it dawned on us how we had become—each in our own way—what organizational researcher Debra Meyerson calls "tempered radicals" (Myerson 2001).

Tempered Radicals are people who find ways to bring about change, but they do so by instigating change through influence and networking rather than by exercising authority vested in organizational positions. By definition, Tempered Radicals are *in* but not *of* the systems in which they affiliate. While they do not leave those systems in their quest to make change, at the same time their ways of thinking and acting are not easily contained in commonly accepted (and expected) organizational and professional routines. Consequently they operate "on a fault line," according to Meyerson, "constantly pulled in opposing directions: toward conformity and toward rebellion." Yet, "successfully navigating the seemingly incongruent extremes of challenges and upholding the status quo helps build strength in and the organizational significance of tempered radicals" (2001, 6–7).

Tempered Radicals will have little influence if they are perceived as malcontents or radicals in the conventional sense. By the same token, in light of their position and reputation they are not close to the organizational core. Instead, they (and often the work they do) are located at *the margins* as defined by prevailing institutional and professional cultures. Yet, the margins are a fertile area, positioned at the interface with other domains, a perfect location for boundary spanning work. The challenge for Tempered Radicals is clear: *to experience the freedom of the margin and the creative possibilities associated with it and, at the same time, to influence the core without becoming co-opted or marginalized by it.*

How do they respond effectively to that challenge? The late Gordon MacKenzie offers a clue. MacKenzie's metaphor of choice (and title of his best-selling book), *Orbiting the Giant Hairball*, came from reflecting on his years of experience working for Hallmark Cards (MacKenzie 1996). He asserts that any large-scale organization is like a hairball, with "hairs" coming in the form of rules, standards, operating procedures, and expected modes of thinking and acting. Over time, and with more and more hairs, a hairball forms. MacKenzie believed that creative people (and we would assert Tempered Radicals) will become trapped unless they learn how to "orbit the hairball." He elaborates:

> To find Orbit around the corporate Hairball is to find a place of balance where you will benefit from the physical, intellectual, and philosophical resources of the organization without becoming entombed in the bureaucracy of the institution . . . . But if you allow that same gravity to suck you into the bureaucratic Hairball, you will find yourself in a different kind of nothingness. The nothingness of a normalcy made stagnant by . . . the nothingness of the Hairball. (1996, 33)

By learning how to successfully orbit the hairball, Tempered Radicals can have the best of both worlds—affiliation without suffocation.

Why not just leave? For us, it was recognizing that being an academic is not simply a way of making a living; it is who we are and all that we have ever wanted to be. The issue, then, is finding a way to maintain identity with integrity *in* academe rather than away from it. We agree with Parker Palmer's interpretation that *identity* lies in the intersection of the diverse forces . . . and *integrity* lies in relating those forces in ways that bring . . . wholeness and life rather than fragmentation and death." For Palmer, integrity also means:

> Determining what is central to one's selfhood, what fits and what does not . . . .
> Do I welcome [these forces] or fear them, embrace them or reject them, move with them or against them? By choosing integrity, I become more whole.
> (Palmer 1998, 13)

The option, then, is to take a stand for something that is full of meaning, worth pursuing, and sustaining. Doing that compels us to embrace engagement, not just as something we do, but also as an ethos that defines our professional being.

Forces for and against the engaged institution

Taking that stand was easy, once we discovered its magnetic attraction. We were pulled toward engagement for obvious reasons: it is why we entered the Academy in the first place. But we also see the ideals of the Academy to which we were drawn slipping away. We did not enter the room the first day with that understanding, but we did enter the room with "a hunch" that required probing, a hunch about what seems to be happening to higher education. Our talk ranged from conversations seeded with incredulity, "How can this be?" to exclamations soaked with anger, "This is not right!" As time passed by, we realized that each of us—for different reasons and through different experiences—had undergone a professional metamorphosis over the years: from embracing the mainstream perspective (the "modern project," as we will it describe later) uncritically, if not mindlessly, to now questioning it, being troubled by it, and picking and choosing ways to speak up and act out against it.

Patricia Gumport's critical analysis of public higher education well describes our sphere of concern (Gumport 2001). Gumport contends that any organized form of social life is grounded in a legitimating idea—what society takes for granted, including the expected activities, approaches, and outcomes associated with a domain of interest. The legitimating idea of a family, for instance, is that it will nurture young people who, as adults, will live responsible personal, professional, and civic lives. As this example illustrates, a legitimating idea serves the public good by enabling prospects for a preferred society.

Gumport believes that public higher education was grounded historically in the legitimating idea of the *social institution* with primary functions that include "the cultivation of citizenship, the preservation of cultural heritage(s), and the formation of individual character and critical habits of mind, as well as economic development functions" (2001, 87). In this view, knowledge is a *public good* because higher education is an expression of social values that are broadly held and firmly structured in society.

Today, Gumport argues, there is a second legitimating idea for public higher education—that of an *industry*, in other words, an economic sector of society. Industry as legitimating idea emphasizes the need of public higher education "to produce and sell goods and services, train the workforce, advance economic development, and perform research" (2001, 87). In this view, knowledge is a *wealth-producing, private commodity*, interpreted largely as an instrument to help individuals and organizations "get ahead." Gumport contends that it is not so much that the image of higher education as industry is misguided, as it holds the prospect of overwhelming (or at least diminishing) higher education's prospects as a social institution.

For this and other reasons, there are obvious tensions between these conflicting legitimating ideas, not just in terms of what public higher education offers to society, but also for how it operates internally. That is because each carries with it a profoundly different logic system associated with leading and managing public higher education. For example, one might conclude by using an industrial sector logic that certain fields—say in science and technology—have more economic value than work being undertaken in the humanities and social sciences. Why not accentuate the applied fields to enable competitive market advantage and consolidate or deemphasize fields with less economic value? From a social institutional perspective, one might counter that argument by contending that society is well served when careful consideration is taken of the social, cultural, and ethical, and moral implications of scientific and technological development.

In addition to the matter of higher education's outcomes, there is the matter of how organizational decisions are made internally. If one subscribes to the social institutional logic, one might conclude that major campus decisions—especially those pertaining to controversial issues—should be vetted broadly among a range of constituencies. Developing skills in public discourse is necessary in a democratic society, the logic would go, and being a model arena for public engagement is vital if higher education is to remain vibrant institutionally. As a counterpoint, one might conclude from the industrial sector perspective that those in authority positions are in charge. They are in a position to have the information, perspective, and acumen to do what is in the best interests of the institution. In the name of effectiveness and efficiency, therefore, those in authority positions should make critical decisions unfettered.

Like many things in life, a prudent path to pursue is both–and rather than either–or, and that is our preference in this instance. Healthy higher education serves society best when it balances its obligations to society as a social institution with efforts that produce outcomes with practical value as an economic sector of society. This happens, for example, when college and university graduates are able to make a good living *and* have a life worth living (Benjamin 1998).

The problem is that higher education seems to be more and more out of balance, with a great appetite for the industrial model and what it affirms. As Canadian educator Edmund O'Sullivan contends, higher education—as an institution—has become an important partner, if not a driveshaft, in the modern project (O'Sullivan 1999). Rather than critique and work aggressively toward alternatives to consumerism, globalization, industrialism, corporate trans-nationalism, and individualism, the institution of higher education—particularly large, public research universities—often aides and abets these efforts. This comes at a time when many and diverse voices challenge the modern status quo, offering compelling evidence of the dysfunctional consequences associated with unbridled emphasis on modernity as the model for world development. Consider, for example, how the environmental domain has been compromised because we now live in a "risk society," as sociologist Ulrich Beck puts it, with industry producing "social and personal bads" (such as in pollution that contributes to health risks) as it produces the goods and services that enable a Western-style life (Beck 1992). And Daniel Yankelovich speaks to the matter in terms of American preferences for market over communal values. He writes:

> In recent years, America has put consumption ahead of production, spending ahead of saving, immediate gratification ahead of working for the future, the welfare of old people ahead of the young, greed ahead of sacrifice, self-interest ahead of loyalty, stockholders ahead of employees, short-term profits ahead of long-term growth, expediency ahead of quality, and the needs of the individual ahead of the needs of society. In the conflict between market values and communal ones, market values have dominated. (Yankelovich 1991, 110)

At issue in response to this backdrop is: "What is the purpose of higher education?" O'Sullivan argues that this is a contested question because there are multiple answers—responses for and against the modern project—each grounded in a different vision of higher education (indeed, society) and informed by different values. Today's educational environment is unstable, O'Sullivan argues, hardly an environment where "the educational and learning tasks are uncontested and the culture is of one mind about what is ultimately important, where there is a kind of optimism and verve about ours is the best of all possible worlds and we should continue doing what we are doing" (O'Sullivan 1999, 4). O'Sullivan believes that just the opposite is the case: the modern project has reached its zenith and that instability is a signal that we are moving into an era of transformative change. At issue is whether higher education will be in the vanguard of change.

We resonate with O'Sullivan's interpretation because we have experienced what he describes, personally. Are we alone in thinking this way? Of course we are not. Of all the literature we have read to help us understand our personal metamorphosis and the situation, generally, the collaborative work of sociologist Paul Ray and psychologist Sherry Anderson is most helpful (Ray and Anderson 2000). The authors share findings from extensive demographic research with the pivot point being how Americans respond to the modern life. Three groups emerged in the research findings: *The Moderns*, which comprised nearly half of American adults at century's end; and two counter groups, each accounting for approximately a quarter of the population, *The Traditionals*, and a growing segment of society that is of particular interest to us, *The Cultural Creatives*.

Ray and Anderson (2000) report that The Moderns buy into the modern project completely and uncritically:

> The simplest way to understand today's Moderns is to see that they are the people who accept the commercialized urban industrial world as the obvious right way to live. They're not looking for alternatives. They're adapting to the contemporary world by assuming, rather than reasoning about, what's important, especially those values linked to economic and public life. (2000, 27)

What values do Moderns embrace? The list includes making and having considerable financial resources; being able to climb the ladder of success; being "trendy" by consuming fashionable goods and services; and obtaining and using new technology. Among other things, Moderns tend to believe that corporations and government operate in the public interest; that bigger is better; what gets measured gets done; science and engineering are models for truth; and efficiency and speed are top priorities (Ray and Anderson 2000, 27–30).

As a counter position to The Moderns, Ray and Anderson (2000) found a group of Americans to which they refer as The Traditionals. Traditionals react against a modern world that they believe opposes their values. They resonate with patriarchal authority, traditional gender roles, and conventional sexual relationships; believe in the centrality of family, church, and local community; and are guided by the wisdom contained in sacred scripts. Traditionals endorse the importance of virtuous behavior, especially when there is acceptance of a uniform value and behavioral system. They believe in hard work, fair play, honesty, integrity, allegiance to God and country, and the ability to live a life without undue government intrusion (2000, 30–32).

In contrast to The Moderns and The Traditionals stand The Cultural Creatives, a segment of society that the authors believe will script a cultural revolution. When asked about various societal issues, Cultural Creatives say they love nature and are deeply concerned about its destruction; give a lot of importance to developing and maintaining relationships; care intensely about psychological and spiritual development; and want politics and government spending to put more emphasis on such domains as enhancing children's well-being, rebuilding neighborhoods and communities, and creating an ecologically sustainable future. Cultural Creatives pay attention to what corporations are doing in the name of making profits and dislike the emphasis in modern culture on success and "making it." Ray and Anderson (2000) comment:

> It is revealing what Cultural Creatives want to replace in conventional American life. They are disenchanted with "owning more stuff," materialism, greed, me-firstism, status display, glaring social inequalities of race and class, society's failure to care adequately for elders, women, and children, and the hedonism and cynicism that pass for realism in modern society. They also reject the

intolerance and narrowness of social conservatives and the Religious Right. They are critical of almost every big institution in modern society, including both corporations and government. (2000, 17)

Ray and Anderson (2000) assert that core characteristics of Cultural Creatives include

- *authenticity* in that action is consistent with what they believe
- *engaged action* where activities are imbued with the "rich, visceral, sensory stuff of life"
- *whole-process learning* involving creating something personally and completely, from start to finish
- *idealism* through commitment to strongly expressed values
- *activism* that puts ideals into action
- *a big picture temperament* by understanding issues in larger systems terms
- *biospheric sensitivity* in the form of attending to ecological responsibility
- *a cosmopolitan mindset* reflected in concern about what is taking place in and around the world
- *a concern for matters of social justice and a caring ethic* with emphasis on the status of persons without ascribed privilege, including women, people of color, children, the elderly, and those with limited resources
- *altruism* that comes in the form of a well-developed social conscience
- *emphasis on self actualization* such that self development is important, especially in terms of becoming a well-rounded person
- *spirituality* by paying attention to one's inner development (2000, 8–16)

Three things strike us regarding Ray and Anderson's findings about the Cultural Creatives. First and foremost, their description helps us more fully appreciate the core attributes of the phenomenon that today we call "engagement." To be and feel engaged—as we have experienced in our work—is captured largely by how the authors' characterize the Cultural Creative mindscape. Second, when we think about the projects in which we are involved and care about the most, it is clear that these are predominantly cultural creative efforts populated extensively by Cultural Creatives. Third, and very importantly, what the authors describe is our preferred image of higher education, how we hope higher education will engage and toward what ends it will strive.

The irony of these conclusions is that we did not begin our careers feeling this way. For a variety of reasons, personally and professionally, we have migrated on our respective journeys. Are we alone? No. This is where Ray and

Anderson (2000) make an enormously important contribution by pointing out that large numbers of Americans are migrating to the Cultural Creative stance. The words they use to describe the metamorphosis speak powerfully to us (and perhaps to you, as well):

> At times the journey feels awkward and perilous; you're asking questions that everyone wishes would go away; you don't know how to put into words what you're searching for; you're wondering just how much of an idiot you really are for leaving what felt sure and safe and comfortable. And at times, the freshness and exhilaration of setting out for new territory are pure pleasure. But whether it's a joy or a trial, the departure from the old worldview and values is fundamentally an inner departure . . . . The change is above all a change in consciousness . . . . (2000, 44)

We believe that the Cultural Creatives in higher education—and we know and work with many of them—participate in a cultural revolution, working diligently to enable a postmodern response to modern realities that they find unacceptable and problematic. These colleagues work side by side with others who speak glowingly about engagement in a modern tongue, accentuating how partnerships with businesses, industry, and the public sector can advance quality of life through jobs and economic opportunity. There is a third group of colleagues, too, who affirm engagement primarily for its human qualities, as an expression of caring, concern, and empowerment, with emphasis on traditional values. For these reasons, we conclude that engagement in higher education is embraced for multiple reasons—as a culturally creative force, as a modern response, and as a traditional value, all at the same time.

We also conclude that higher education remains largely a modern institution in philosophy and practice, most certainly the research university environment that we know well. Will there be a tipping point, institutionally, such that higher education moves from a modern to a culturally creative expression? Are there factors predisposing this shift? Ray and Anderson (2000) say "yes," believing that the flow of cultural change is already taking place largely because it is becoming increasing difficult to justify the modern project. The fault lines are clear: the ill effects of globalization, the recognition that technology is not a cure all to modern problems, the lingering reality of an environmental crisis, the continuing and prevailing gap between rich and poor, and changing preferences for what constitutes "the good life" (2000, 318–320). In addition, Ray and Anderson predict that the number of Traditionals and Moderns will decline and the number of Cultural Creatives will increase.

But will these trends yield an institutional shift in a culturally creative direction? There are certainly pockets of evidence all around in higher education in the form of networked activity and structural nodes dedicated to working in areas that share common values—environmental justice, peace, food security, poverty alleviation, and youth development, to name a few. But we see no evidence of a sea change in how institutions are being led and managed, and higher education, generally, is not taking a public stance against the modern project.[3] Our conclusion: although there are many Culturally Creatives in higher education and there are many culturally creative activities and programs in evidence, higher education remains a Modern institution.[4]

Recognizing multiple discourses in engagement

Contemplating possible shifts in higher education's philosophy and practice made us think more deeply about our personal journeys in engagement and just how different our practice is today from what it was before. What began as a reaching out activity, where we transferred knowledge to those who requested it, evolved over time to include a process specialty where we served as facilitators of others' work. We still engage in each of these pursuits, but our work has evolved beyond knowledge provision or facilitating others' interactions. Today, we are fundamentally in the mix, *a part of* not *apart from* the action. We find the work it to be a complex, interactive, iterative, emotional, and political *border crossing*. We also view it as a moral and ethical commitment, a *stance*, grounded in strongly held values, which include engaging with high professional standards, striving to empower others, seeking justice, and doing the right thing.

As we think about the work we did before—and the way we think about it today—we understand that, over time, our respective practices have gone hand in hand with the prevailing thinking of the times. Certainly, years ago, there were those who thought about engagement as complex border crossing, but it was not the dominant expression then. When we began our careers, the times stressed the act of transferring knowledge to end users and our language, intent, and practices followed suit.

But there is another conclusion, too: that practice preferences are expressions of strongly held value positions with enduring relevance that do not change over time. As just one example, witness the recent exchange about engagement between Mark Wood (2003) and Scott Peters (2003) published in *The Journal of Higher Education Outreach and Engagement*. Drawing from the work of Susan Toton (2002), Douglas Sturm (1998), and Martin Luther King Jr. (1981), Wood asserts the importance of a "relational economy" where

> Our work as socially concerned scholars . . . would be . . . oriented by the goals of democratizing the distribution of wealth and control of productive resources . . . . Working to build a relational economy means working to build institutions that are guided by and reward the values of community, equality and democracy we strive to promote. (Wood 2003, 174)

---

3. We are impressed with some work that is underway. Consider, for example, the character development movement in higher education that is being spearheaded by The John Templeton Foundation. See http://www.collegevalues.org
4. This argument is elaborated in F. Fear and L. Sandmann, (2001– 2002).

Toward that end, Wood (2003) suggests that we reconceive the notion of service, which he believes "assumes the existence of the present social order," to that of *solidarity*, which he believes "assumes the possibility of transforming the present social order. . . and makes it possible for all persons to flourish" (2003, 176.) Given that orientation, Wood resonates with the concept popularized by King (1981), the *transformed non-conformist*, a person who works to transform, not to reform, social institutions and society in general.

Peters (2003) sees Wood's stance as political activism, "more ideological than scholarly, leaving little space for open-minded learning and discovery" (2003, 185). Arguing the centrality of scholarship as an interpretive motif, Peters believes that Wood's presentation generally lacks "serious critical reflection, analysis or evaluation of his work, making it difficult to judge the trustworthiness of his claims, and therefore, the potential effectiveness and promise of his proposal" (2003, 185). Drawing on the work of Thomas Bender (2001) and William Sullivan (1995), Peters argues for another approach to engagement, *civic professionalism*, which he believes meets the goals of an "engaged (academic) institution" as articulated by Barbara Holland.[5] Peters writes: "Civic professionalism places scholars inside civic life rather than apart from or above it, working alongside their fellow citizens on questions and issues of public importance" (2003, 185). Peters believes that civic professionalism requires scholars to "rethink scholarly aims and practices" (2003, 186) which pushes beyond political activism:

> They integrate public work with their scholarship over relatively long time periods with specific publics that are engaged in not only problem solving, but problem setting, an open-ended deliberative, developmental process of coming to understand not just how to solve technical problems, but how to identify, frame and understand civic issues and problems and what ought to be done about them, in pursuit of public values and interests. (2003, 192)

Each of the two perspectives—transformed non-conformism and civic professionalism—is relevant in its own way for engagement. There are different starting points and preferred outcomes, even though there are also striking similarities. Each is a separate container, though, standing as a distinct *discourse in engagement*. As educational theorist James Gee and colleagues put it, a discourse is a way "of talking . . . acting, interacting, believing, valuing . . . so as to display or to recognize a particular social identity" (Gee, Hull, and Lankshear 1996, 10). Adherents make a discourse their own; solicit and socialize newcom-

---

5. According to Holland (2001), an engaged institution "is committed to direct interaction with external constituencies and communities through the mutually beneficial exchange, exploration, and application of knowledge, expertise, and information." "Exploring the Challenge of Documenting and Measuring Civic Engagement Endeavors of Colleges and Universities." Paper given at *The Campus Compact Advanced Institute on Classifications for Civic Engagement* http://www.compact.org/advancedtoolkit/measuring.html

ers; and declare the position publicly, all the while seeking to hone the clarity, coherence, and compelling nature of the message. The problem, as Gee and colleagues point out, is that *all* discourses are

> By definition limited perspectives—limited in that they ignore or denigrate other discourses' perspectives . . . . It is difficult to criticize or change them either from within or from without. And, in any case, what discourse can stand above the others and dictate 'truth' and 'morality'? (1996, 13)

The functional value of discourses in a domain is that they provide, as a set, a more comprehensive view of a sphere of interest. Diverse discourses also help us understand that work in any domain should not be viewed as an "it," understood singularly and practiced uniformly. Certainly, if we like, we can simplify the matter by waging a political contest accentuating the value of a partisan discourse by discrediting or denigrating "competitors." Sadly, that happens all too frequently in higher education. Another approach is to embrace multiple ways of understanding:

> A vibrant Academy, indeed a vibrant society, embraces multiple ways of understanding. A generative Academy, indeed a generative society, encourages people to respect and affirm differences—to listen and learn with, from, and through radically different perspectives, experiences, and approaches. (Fear, Adamek, and Imig 2002, 49–50)

It is in this regard that we suggest adapting for engagement the way researchers Norman Denzin and Yvonna Lincoln evaluate the evolution of qualitative research (Denzin and Lincoln 2000). They use the term *moment* to describe different ways that qualitative work has been undertaken, historically. The authors also contend that moments co-exist and historically overlap.

Consider how this way of thinking applies to the domain of teaching and learning. The lecture was a logical approach to teaching at a time when learning was viewed predominantly as a transfer of knowledge from experts to novices. For many reasons and in response to a variety of circumstances, thinking about teaching and learning has evolved over the years. Today, the lecture form co-exists with a variety of other forms, including Socratic pedagogy, experiential learning, cooperative learning, and collaborative learning, to name only a few. Each form is a discourse in teaching and learning. It grew to prominence for particular reasons, has loyal practitioners, and possesses a distinct rationale, vocabulary, techniques, and preferred outcomes. Certainly we can denigrate lecturing, for instance, showing all the ways that it does not measure up (typically on another discourse's terms). In so doing we accentuate the value of another discourse, say collaborative learning, demonstrating how it addresses the lecture's faults. But the stark reality is that lecturing has its place; the critical issue is not its banishment but, instead, its rightful application, that is, employing it when it makes sense and refraining from its misapplication when another form is better suited to the task. Acting on this way of thinking compels us to find value in the both–and, not the either–or, of learning. We believe that is both a reasonable way of thinking and a potentially effective solution to complex learning challenges.

If we apply this logic to the matter of engagement, we can accommodate both of the two matters considered earlier. First, ways of thinking and practicing engagement have changed over the years—the recent emergence of the term "engagement" suggests that. There is nothing inherently wrong with historical practices, such as knowledge transfer. It, like other approaches, has a place. The problem is that this approach (and others) have been mindlessly applied in the past, often overused and sometimes misapplied, including at times and in places where we simply did not know better. What we need is fitting approach to context so that form follows function. Secondly, we recognize that there are enduring approaches to engagement that reflect strongly held value positions. Rather than pitting one approach against the other and looking for flaws, we recognize that each approach is a discourse with a unique logic system. Each makes important contributions, having value in its own way. We accept each and believe the world is better served by having multiple approaches standing side by side.

Administrative matters as the dominant discourse in engagement

We are trapped by our own logic for reasons that will soon be evident. On the one hand, we affirm the co-existence of multiple discourses and believe an important matter in engagement's scholarly evolution will be for scholars to do for engagement what Denzin and Lincoln have done for qualitative research, namely, define the moments of engagement and describe the multiple discourses across the moments. On the other hand, there is a matter that consumed a considerable amount of our attention, namely, a critique of what we see as the dominant discourse in engagement today. We believe that scholarly discourse in engagement—about what engagement is, how it is undertaken, why, and for what purpose and outcome—is being overwhelmed by an *administrative discourse* pertaining to matters associated with enabling engagement organizationally.

In today's academic environment, engagement is clearly not simply the work that academics do; it has also become an institutionalized expression, what some colleges and universities talk about, stand for, and declare to be a mission-related priority, replete with community engagement programs and offices. Despite this activity and focus, practices undertaken to advance an institutional agenda are not identical with practices undertaken in the name of scholarly inquiry. It is especially troubling when advancing engagement institutionally restrains or confines engagement's progress in scholarly terms. While this seems improbable, consider how an institution's interpretation of "good teaching" can influence the faculty development programs it offers and what it values–rewards in the name of teaching.

We believe the administrative discourse in engagement is *instrumental, reformist,* and *structural* in rhetoric and practice. For one thing, we perceive an instrumental emphasis in the engagement literature; in conference presentations; and what frequently transpires on campuses. How to do engagement, do more of it, and encourage its spread seems to overwhelm what is discussed, written, and undertaken in engagement's name. Lurking beneath this focus are non-instrumental questions, rarely answered and even more infrequently acknowledged, that we believe are at the heart of the engagement enterprise, such as: With whom do we engage? Why and why not? For what purposes do we engage?

In addition to maintaining an instrumental focus, we believe that reformist rhetoric unduly influences conversations about engagement. A reform agenda—to fix what is wrong—enables funding organizations, executive academic officers, outreach administrators, and public officials to occupy, if not own, the engagement space, calling for and crafting agendas of institutional change in ways that parallel a political platform. For example, when engagement spokespersons act as though engagement is automatically "good" and doing more of it is always better, they articulate a stance that flies in the face of contemporary realities. Serious questions are being raised about the dysfunctional consequences associated with *over*-engagement, when higher education becomes a delivery system for partisans with financial and/or political influence (Cranton 1998). When core academic values are exchanged for the benefits derived, at issue is under what circumstances is it better to remain un-engaged.

A reformist stance often carries with it a structural approach to change, that is, "fixing what's wrong" by engaging in the "R's" of change, including Reorganizing, Reinventing, or Reengineering structures and systems. There are ubiquitous discussions about the faculty reward system and unit rearrangement, to name only two items. The problem with this approach is that it misleads us into believing that enhancing and advancing engagement is an organization development matter alone. While organization development can enable engagement, it is not the work itself.

Besides, there is often a Draconian outcome from promoting any organizational platform too vigorously—an inverse relationship between the strength of the promotion and the sustainability of the innovation over time. A considerable amount of political capital is spent introducing an academic innovation, followed by the need to invest substantial administrative time, energy, and funding to diffuse and embed change. Typically what ensues is a burst of activity with significant gains measured by benchmarking followed by periods of unevenness, especially if the champion of change (e.g., a university president) moves on. In a highly contested political environment with many partisan interests standing side by side, there are often demands from those who want to see other agenda items become institutional priorities. Others pass the time on the sideline waiting "for the things to get back to normal." This dynamic can produce the ultimate irony in organizational planned change; that is, the seeds of demise can be sown into an organizational change strategy.

We also know from experience that institutions rarely embark upon multiple paths associated with a single agenda item. For example, the goal of significantly increasing faculty and student participation in study abroad programs is unlikely to be paired at the same institution with a platform for enhancing the pedagogy of study abroad offerings. When applied to engagement, this organizational concept means that with so much emphasis on organization development in engagement it is reasonable to ask, "Where is the scholarship of it?"

Beyond the concerns that we have expressed, there remains the fundamental matter of how the administrative discourse can impede the viability and development of multiple discourses in engagement. Administrative elites typically embrace a particular change platform and then use their authority and influence to diffuse that change through the system. This change typically comes in the form of a "one size fits all" approach, that is, change designed to be accepted across the institution.

In the name of multiple discourses in engagement, we prefer a very different approach. First and foremost, we encourage administrative elites to pay attention to the array of work already happening at their institutions in the name of engagement. That includes work undertaken at the institutional margins, in addition to mainstream expressions. The reframed organization development challenge, then, is to recognize diverse expressions of engagement but, also, to embrace *diversity of interpretation and practice as an institutional platform*. In addition, rather than diffuse one expression of the work up and down "the organizational spine" (the conventional organization development challenge), instead find ways to connect diverse nodes of engagement—the activities and people across the institution who are doing the work. That strategy will strengthen existing webs of relationships and stimulate the creation of new collegial networks.

It seems to us that engagement as a transformative force can be blunted by retreating into conventional modes of thinking about how to create engaged institutions. The work of engagement is happening already. The challenge is less about getting people to embrace a new idea and more about accentuating, promoting, developing, and celebrating the work that is already underway.

Conclusion

The frame of reference shared in this chapter is like peeling an onion; thinking that you have gotten to the core of matters only to discover—with surprise—that there is more to uncover. The purpose, now, in chapter 2, is to give an example of how our work looks in action. Because this work is done collaboratively so, too, is the writing about it; partners join in describing, interpreting, and musing about issues. One of those partners, Séamus Lillis of Dublin Ireland, offers his own story of coming to critical engagement.[6]

Following chapter 2, we reflect more about what this work means to us and how we arrived at it. We entitle chapter 3, "Living our way into a new way of thinking: An exploration of mindful inquiry," adapting the title from a comment made to several of us by humanist Parker Palmer. The chapter is framed as a "mindful" exploration of engagement in the tradition (we hope) of Ellen Langer's work on mindfulness and Valerie Bentz and Jeremy Shapiro's consideration of mindful inquiry (Langer 1989; Bentz and Shapiro 1998). The chapter combines autobiographical narration with critique, necessary for conveying where we stand on engagement and describing how we came to that way of thinking.

---

6. See also S. Lillis, Journeyman. pp. 89-94, in J. McNiff, and J. Whitehead, eds., *Action Research in Organisations.* (London: Routledge, 2000); S. Lillis, (2001), Discernment in Ballintubber. *Céide, a Review from the Margins* 5(3) (2001), 12–14; and S. Lillis, (2001), *An inquiry into the effectiveness of my practice as a learning practitioner-researcher in rural community development through action research.* Thesis submitted in fulfilment of the requirements for the degree of Doctor of Philosophy, National University of Ireland, University College, Dublin.

References

Beck, U. 1992. *Risk society. Towards a new modernity.* Newbury Park CA: Sage.

Bender, T. 2001. Then and now: The disciplines and civic engagement. *Liberal Education* (Winter):6–19.

Benjamin, M. 1998. Making a living and living a life. In *Invitations to learning: Letters to students from the faculty of Michigan State University.* East Lansing MI: Office of the Provost and Board of Trustees.

Bennett, J. 1998. *Collegial professionalism: The academy, individualism, and the common good.* The American Council on Education. Phoenix: Oryx Press.

Bentz, V., and J. Shapiro. 1998. *Mindful inquiry in social research.* Thousand Oaks CA: Sage Publications.

Bohm, D. 1980. *Wholeness and the implicate order.* New York: Rutledge.

Cranton, P. 1998. *No one way: Teaching and learning in higher education.* Toronto: Wall and Emerson.

Denizin, N., and Y. Lincoln. 2000. *Handbook of qualitative research.* 2nd ed. Thousand Oaks CA: Sage Publications.

Fear, F., M. Adamek, and G. Imig. 2002. Connecting philosophic and scholarly traditions with change in higher education. *Journal of Leadership Studies* 8(3):42–51.

Fear, F., K. Bruns, L. Sandmeyer, A. Fields, S. Buhler, B. Burnham, and G. Imig. 2003. Experiencing engagement: Stories from the field. *Journal of Higher Education Outreach and Engagement* 8(1):59–74.

Fear, F., B. Burnham, A. Fields, K. Bruns, and L. Sandmeyer. 2003. Exploring the implicate order: Learning from the theater of engagement. *Journal of Higher Education Outreach and Engagement* 8(2):119–134.

Fear, F., and D. Doberneck. 2004. Collegial talk: A powerful tool for change. *About Campus* 9(1):11–19.

Fear, F., C. McCarthy, A. Diebel, H. Berkowitz, L. Harvey, and C. Carra. 2003. Turning the all around upside down: The graduate classroom as an alternative, self-organizing setting. *Encounter: Education for meaning and social justice* 16(2):34–39.

Fear, F., and L. Sandmann. 2001,2. The 'new' scholarship: Implications for engagement and extension. *The Journal of Higher Education Outreach and Engagement* 7(1 and 2):29–39.

Gee, J., G. Hull, and C. Lankshear. 1996. *The new work order: Behind the language of the new capitalism.* Boulder CO: Westview Press.

Gumport, P. 2001. Built to serve: The enduring legacy of public higher education. In P. Altbach, P. Gumport, and D. Johnstone. *In defense of American higher education.* Baltimore: The Johns Hopkins Univ. Press.

Heron, J., and P. Reason. 1997. A participatory inquiry paradigm. *Qualitative Inquiry* 3:274–294.

King, M. L. Jr., 1981. *Strength to love.* Philadelphia: Fortress Press.

Langer, E. 1989. *Mindfulness.* Cambridge MA: DeCapo Press.

Langer, E. 1997. *The power of mindful learning.* Cambridge MA: Perseus Publishing.

MacKenzie, G. 1996. *Orbiting the giant hairball.* New York: Viking.

Myerson, D. 2001. *Tempered radicals: How people use difference to inspire change at work.* Boston: Harvard Univ. Press.

Nielson, J. 2004. *The myth of leadership: Creating leaderless organizations.* Palo Alto CA: Davies-Black Publishing.

O'Sullivan, E. 1999. *Transformative learning: Educational vision for the 21st century.* London: Zed Books.

Palmer, P. 1998. *The courage to teach: Exploring the inner landscape of a teacher's life.* San Francisco: Jossey-Bass.

Peters, S. 2003. Reconstructing civic professionalism in academic life: A response to Mark Wood's paper. From service to solidarity. *The Journal of Higher Education Outreach and Engagement* 8(2):183–198.

Ray, P., and S. Anderson. 2000. *The cultural creatives: How 50 million people are changing the world.* New York: Harmony Books.

Sturm, D. 1998. *Solidarity and suffering: Towards a politics of relationality.* Albany NY: SUNY Press.

Sullivan, W. 1995. *Work and integrity: The crisis and promise of professionalism in America.* New York: HarperBusiness.

Toton, S. 2002. Liberating justice education: From service to solidarity. *Journal for Peace and Justice Studies* 12(2):231–248.

Wheatley, M. 2002. *Turning to one another: Simple conversations to restore hope to the future.* San Francisco: Berratt-Koehler.

Wood, M. 2003. From service to solidarity: Engaged education and democratic globalization. *The Journal of Higher Education Outreach and Engagement* 8(2):165–181.

Yankelovich, D. 1991. *Coming to public judgment: Making democracy work in a complex society.* Syracuse NY: Syracuse Univ. Press.

CHAPTER 2

STORIES OF CRITICAL ENGAGEMENT

Jerome Brunner understands the central role narrative plays in our lives. He explains that "Story must construct two landscapes simultaneously," the outer landscape of action and the inner landscape of thought (Bruner 1986, 14). This chapter takes up two narratives.

The first narrative describes the outer landscape of action: how an Irish–American collaboration for community development engages people. The narrative is co-authored by collaborators Frank Fear (a professor), Séamus Lillis (an Irish community development consultant), Margaret Desmond (a U.S. graduate student), Maureen Lally (an Irish community development practitioner), and Janice Hartough (an American community development practitioner).

The second narrative examines closely the inner landscape of one of the group's members, Séamus Lillis. He describes his journey to critical engagement.

Taken together, these stories illustrate the collective and individual learning made possible through critical reflection, including re-thinking—if not re-imagining—what engagement work can be.

An Irish–American Collaboration in the Irish West[1]

By

Frank A. Fear, Séamus Lillis, and Margaret Desmond
with Maureen Lally and Jan Hartaugh

The tap-tap-tap of the rain against the windowpane at the Scioból (community center) blends melodically with the clash of teacups and pots, forging an acoustic alchemy so familiar to the American visitors. It is early March in County Mayo, Republic of Ireland, and the Americans are here to work with village leaders in the rural West of Ireland. This is a place they have grown to love, working with people they admire:

> The Tóchar Valley is a beautiful area of rural communities stretching from Balla to Murrisk. Steeped in antiquity the unspoiled countryside is liberally sprinkled with churches, Celtic artifacts and historical sites. The Tóchar Phádraig pilgrim route, which links these townlands and villages, follows a section of the ancient chariot road of the Kings of Connaught which ran from Tulsk in Roscommon to Croagh Patrick, the holy mountain. (From a brochure produced by local people and funded by the South Mayo LEADER Company, 2000)

On this day, community sector board members and their American partners take the next step in their evolving collaboration. Today's plan was crafted the night before over a leisurely meal, emerging from a conversation among the manager of The Tóchar Valley Rural Community Network, faculty members and a graduate student from Michigan State University, and a rural development consultant from Dublin, the instigator of this collaboration. This afternoon board members will be introduced to a development approach called Appreciative Inquiry (Cooperrider et al. 2000). Appreciative Inquiry is both worldview and practical tool, a process in which people discover a common future by affirming the "good things" happening in their lives and, then, envisioning how the future might be if more good things were to happen. Appreciative Inquiry stands in contrast to the conventional approach, symbolized by a glass half empty, which accentuates problems that require fixing. This afternoon's conversation will focus on two questions: What exciting things are happing in the communities?

1. An earlier version of this essay was published in *Céide, A Review from the Margins*, Vo. 5, No. 6, June/July 2002, pp. 24–26. The work described here was enabled with funding from The W. K. Kellogg Foundation; The Michigan Campus Compact; The Kettering Foundation; and Michigan State University through MSU's Extension Leadership Development Network (LeadNet), the Bailey Scholars Program, and the Department of Resource Development.

What compelling things is the Network doing to enable community development? The second question is important. An umbrella organization—The Tóchar Valley Rural Community Network—has been created to undertake rural development in communities that straddle an ancient pilgrim way.

Through Appreciative Inquiry, all involved celebrate the contributions made by a Michigan State University student, Megan, who is spending the academic year working to revitalize youth clubs in several local villages. They wonder, "How might we build on this valuable work?" The conversation turns to the matter of the local secondary school; how wonderful it would be if youth could learn more about local heritage and perhaps undertake service projects as part of the secondary school experience. The Americans introduce board members to the concept of service learning, popular in the U.S. at the secondary and tertiary levels. Service learning is a curriculum strategy that encourages students to "apply knowledge, skills, critical thinking, and wise judgment to address genuine community needs" through experiential learning in community settings (Stowe, Buck, and Martin 2002, 58). A board member suggests that Transition Year might be an appropriate time and place for introducing the idea in County Mayo.[2] Another board member agrees and offers to discuss the concept with the local secondary principal. The Americans meet with the principal before they return to the States. A few months later, Heather—a Michigan State student—arrives in the village of Balla to begin her assignment in the school.

The instrumentality of this arrangement—ideas for joint action—represents only one fruit borne from this collaboration. These partners also learn from each other. On this day, they engage in conversation about the art of managing a community network and how it differs from managing business organizations and public agencies. The conversation spills into the evening over dinner at the pub. The President of Ireland, Mary McAleese, would find inspiration in what is happening here, someone asserts. "What if we were to invite her to visit?" There is mixed response, ranging from strong support to the improbability of it all. Yet, these are moments in which collective dreams are conceived. Three months later the Americans return to Ballintubber and there the President is, addressing a throng.

Emergent action

This Irish–American collaboration is beyond convention for a local development project. There are no predetermined goals; no activities that *must* be undertaken; and no set times that the Americans visit. These Irish and Americans—different in background, experience, and perspective—have a project (if you can call it that) to engage in dialogue (Isaacs 1999). Talk. They trust that joint action will emerge naturally from conversation.

---

2. Transition Year is an applied experience taken voluntarily by secondary school students the year before their graduation.

And it is not as though local development is contingent on joint efforts. Local development continues all the time, much like the daily journey of a regularly scheduled train. From time to time the Americans jump aboard and all passengers continue to a common destination. Initiated by a grant from The W. K. Kellogg Foundation, this collaboration has outlived that funding. What sustains this partnership?

The source of attraction is grassroots development—the coalface of community work—in a country that is experiencing unprecedented economic and social change. The locals are consummate community developers, the fruits of their work hang ripe on the vine. You can see it all around. Some accomplishments are sublime, most notably the refurbished Ballintubber Abbey (1216 AD). Other contributions, less obvious to episodic travelers, have significant local importance—social housing in Belcarra; the community center in Mayo Abbey; and the community park in Ballyheane. This is impressive work—facilitated by retired Téagasc (Extension) staff members and undertaken by myriad volunteers—grounded in a strongly held philosophy of community practice. The Irish speak emphatically about how important it is for projects to reflect and affirm local values. Complex ideas are expressed in lyric voice, rich in metaphor: "The journey is the destination." "The past is our pathway to the future."

Respectful engagement

Working in County Mayo compels the Americans to be clear about their own philosophical moorings. They recognize the potential dysfunctionality of advice offered from the outside, rendered by experts who import trendy techniques and processes. They are familiar with the tyranny of technique; it can displace rather than foster collaborative inquiry and discovery. They are painfully familiar with the tragic outcomes of international development experiences designed to spread the fruits of modernity. They want no part of that and, instead, understand the sanctity of place and recognize the importance of sociohistorical context. The stark reality is that they are not of Ireland and have no vital grounding here. They will never experience being reared, raising a family, and earning a living in the Irish West. They have no frame of reference for how much things have changed in Ireland.

An empathic connection urges them to walk lightly, as any visitor should, with a strong sense of responsibility to and for this place. They do not want local people feeling compelled to act because "the Americans have spoken." A liberating perspective, free of the debilitating force of dependency, is to believe and act as though the Americans are expendable, for indeed they are. The hope is that good things will happen because they are here. If not, at least no harm will be done.

Mooring posts of engagement

What we have here is a form of *autonomous development* that requires loose coupling with outside parties (Carmen 1996). It is classic community development—local people taking control of their affairs. Yet, this Irish–American collaboration is more than that. In form the collaboration represents what Wenger, McDermott, and Snyder call a *community of practice* (2002, 4). A practice community involves people "who share a concern, a set of problems, or a passion about a topic, and who deepen their knowledge and expertise in the area by interacting on an ongoing basis." The parties do not work together on a daily basis, but find great value in creating "a space" to be together. Distributed (and even virtual) communities of practice—experiences that span significant distance and cut across organizational boundaries—are becoming more common.

That is what we have here in the Irish West, a distributed community of practice among diverse parties who share a passion for and experience in local development. Each party benefits uniquely. The American partners bring new ideas, literature, and experiences from development venues around the world. The presence of the Americans affirms the work that the locals are doing. The Americans value the richness of this practice setting as a laboratory for understanding and learning from community development in a dynamic setting. They have an opportunity to work side by side with accomplished practitioners whom they admire. The Irish bring great perceptivity, enthusiasm, and the willingness to try new things. They probe the Americans for new ideas and approaches. But, as experienced hands in local development, they know tacitly whether ideas and suggestions will work in their context.

There is mutuality, then, in this relationship based on respect. As such, neither group seeks to direct, dominate, or overwhelm the other; there is a strong desire to learn with, from, and through the other. This community of practice is an example of what Jean Lave and Etienne Wenger call *situated learning* (Lave and Wenger 1991) and it takes place in what Harrison Owen calls *Open Space* (Owen 2000). For Lave and Wenger, situated learning involves being a co-participant in an action context. In other words, situated learning—unlike learning in the classroom—is "really real." It is immersion in "the work"—in context and in real time. It provokes, evokes, and compels. This learning is raw and real, as much about what is happening in the heart as in the head.

Situated learning in this Irish–American collaboration is unscripted. In Owen's words, it is "Open Space." There is no grand plan or strategic vision. This is an odyssey, going where it needs to go. There is creative energy in Open Space and the experience is full of surprise. Like turning the page in an exciting mystery novel, you never know what comes next. Open Space is grounded in the art of the possible and expressed in the spirit of imagination. It cannot be forced. It must emerge naturally and authentically, always through conversations among those around the table. Just as *the work* is a metaphor for community of practice, *conversations around the table* is a metaphor for Open Space.

Open Space succeeds when participants self-organize in responsible and accountable ways. In other words, they view Open Space as a blessing—a gift—to be treated with profound respect and with great appreciation. It becomes a living expression of collective spirit, embodying what can happen when people are given liberty and license to create their own agenda. Open Space, much like life, is a journey.

An alternative to business as usual

These are radical notions in a development world that demands greater certainty of script. We write funding proposals, describing objectives and procedures in great detail, fooling ourselves into believing that we can predict, if not control, the future. Only the critical eye sees this for what it really is—an epistemology—a way of thinking about development that is inherently mechanistic with emphasis on pulling levers of change. In this worldview, community becomes an object—an "it" to be changed—and development becomes an instrument, a "thing" to make "it" happen.

This Irish–American collaboration represents an alternative. It is also an antidote for poison—the hegemony of development—with people in high places determining what is best for others and, then, using "carrots and sticks" to get their way. Hegemony comes in many and new forms, including what used to be a sacred place—participatory development. Cooke and Kothari (2001) elaborate the challenge: agencies using participatory approaches to co-opt local people into accepting agency-defined goals, approaches, or outcomes. When this happens, the consequences are insidious with local people trapped in a web of deceit.

There are examples all around, if we only take the time to see. There is a reason why it exists. Participation is alluring with magnetic quality, a fundamental feature of the human experience. But the intent can be turned inside out, upside down. Kieran Allen expresses how: "by combining elements in people's experience and reconfiguring them in ways that suits ruling groups" (Allen 2000, 184). Rosie Meade and Orla O'Donovan speak plainly about the matter as it hits home (Meade and O'Donovan 2002, 1–9). "Social partnership" is a common way community development organizations in Ireland interact with the government. How is it working?

> A recurring argument made by the critics of Irish social partnership is that it is a form of corporatism. In this context, the concept of corporatism is used pejoratively to refer to anti-democratic arrangements and foster consensualism, and ensure that policy-making is dominated by the privileged and powerful. (Meade and O'Donovan 2002, 2)

Participation constrained and directed by elites for partisan purposes is an immoral practice. Acting with arrogant intent—believing that one knows best—forecloses openness to learning. The all-knowing live a burdened life, believing as they do that they have arrived at a pinnacle of understanding. As Tobin Hart (2001) suggests, they rely on *will* to get their way. There is much to be said about will; its exercise moves mountains. But will is about right and righteousness, sufficient to begin but not sustain transformation (Hart 2001, 13). Will needs a companion, Hart suggests, and he calls it *willingness*. If will is about agency and the power of intention, willingness lives as submission. Will is what the "I" wants to make happen; willingness connects to something larger than self, the "we." When merged, will and willingness offer a generative opportunity—agency and communion, together.

That is what we have here in the Irish West: will and willingness in the form of a community of practice, situated learning, and Open Space. It is energized by the power of invitation; expressed as a form of the human spirit; and grounded in the enduring values of faith, hope, and love. It is beyond convention.

Apologia pro Vita Mea
(And What Do You Do?)

An individual's story presented in three parts

By

Séamus Lillis[3]

Séamus Lillis' narrative provides a retrospective account of how he came to understand that "learning through conversation" is a central activity in engagement with communities. The narrative is presented in three parts, each illuminating insights gained from Lillis' reflective process. We provide commentary after each part of the narrative for two reasons. First, the commentary illustrates what can be learned when we treat narratives of community life as text to be shared, examined, and critiqued. This process has been a central feature of our faculty learning community's work together. Second, the commentary foreshadows themes and concepts that are embedded in the narrative. These are ideas that will be discussed in more detail and from multiple perspectives throughout this book.

Part 1: Seeking an understanding of "the work"

> To undertake a pilgrimage is to place yourself at risk . . . the risk that you might not return as the same person who set out. The risk that all that you had thought that you knew, understood, had perhaps carefully constructed in your mind, might be blown apart. (Palmer, M. 1997, 8)

The eponymous Ms. Cashman, inspector of taxes, was unrelenting: "Thirty-five years ago, Mr. Lillis, when you first came to our notice, we had you down as an instructor in horticulture and beekeeping; then, in 1982 you began to de-

---

3. Séamus Lillis, a community development consultant, resides in Dublin. He earned a doctorate in agricultural education from University College, Dublin.

scribe yourself as an education officer. From 1991 to 1994, you told us you were a specialist in rural development. You are basically qualified in agriculture. Now you are saying that you are involved in community engagement."

The horn-rimmed glasses flashed under the strong lights.

"Let me quote from your tax return of last year: '. . . in outreach with various communities.' Mr. Lillis, what exactly do you do? Might we describe you as a consultant?"

I thought I would be agreeable. "Well, I was for a while," I answered warily. "Mostly with farmers," I volunteered. That was a mistake. "Yes," said she, "I can see that here from your tax returns. Why did you cease?" The time had come to slander the farming community: "Principally because they are slow to pay," I suggested.

"In your current practice, do you offer advice? Do you train people? Do you educate them? Do you evaluate them? Assess them?"

Ms. Cashman was showing faith in me. She believed me to be an expert with all this potential to improve, reprove, direct, and demarcate. Within her worldview, I showed promise.

Earlier in this interrogation, I had been confronted with an official form, showing a restricted range of boxes that set out to capture the activities of those of the self-employed who engage in pedagogic services. These were empty boxes, needing to be filled. Ms. Cashman was—preferably before her coffee break—determined to pigeonhole my life's endeavours into one (and only one) of the prescribed boxes. These read:

- advisor
- assessor
- apprentice
- consultant
- evaluator
- instructor
- lecturer
- researcher
- student
- teacher

I was being politely maneuvered into selecting one category that best described my livelihood.

Instructing? I started my professional life as an instructor of horticulture. Trained in the late sixties in the positivist scientific tradition of agricultural production, I quickly came to rely on the unwavering principles of technical rationality, particularly in the scientific findings that supported a blueprint approach to crop production. As an instructor, I was expected to instruct, to pass on pertinent research to farmers and growers. I brandished a jug full of horticultural knowledge and doled out appropriate doses to my farmer clients. This communication of knowledge was perceived officially to be a one-way transaction.

Yet, I readily confess that I learned from farmers. Not officially of course; I had to keep the side up. Every crop I observed was a living testimony to its owner's expertise; every farmer I met had experience, knowledge, and skill to impart—but this was not officially acknowledged as a resource. If the crop had performed badly, its testimony was even more eloquent, as the farmer and I jointly brainstormed about what had gone wrong. Of course, I might have decided to satisfy myself alone as to the cause of poor performance. But it seemed feeble if my practice did not include convincing the farmer of my diagnosis.

Teaching? Later in my career, I was put in charge of a wonderful state programme with huge potential, which prepared farm inheritors for their future careers in farming. I was fortunate in that I worked in Ireland's premier horticulture production area and was given a free hand to devise and deliver the programme in horticulture. In the beginning I produced a curriculum that reflected our extension service's preoccupation with passing on information about crop production. In this I emulated the approach of my colleagues who were teaching the programme in agriculture. I would need an even bigger jug for all the extra knowledge this now captive audience potentially were required to absorb.

When I became aware of the disparity of the land resources my students were going to inherit, I questioned the relevance of this approach. Some came from extensive farms; others had less than one acre of protected crops. It made no sense to have them all follow the same curriculum. And when we began to study farm accounts, it became apparent that many horticultural enterprises did not leave a viable return. This was largely due to poor marketing strategies. I determined I should deliver a programme that addressed the challenge confronting these youths, namely, how to make a successful living from their fixed inheritable resources. Crop production know-how alone would not suffice.

Instead of ploughing through a plethora of blueprints for varied crops in the classroom day by day, I gave them all out together, saying that they were background information, to be used as the students saw fit. We began to focus on the lived reality of the constraints that made earning a living in commercial horticulture so challenging. What would have to change to ensure success? The students and I started to think outside the box and to examine alternative opportunities, such as the prospects for new businesses in the adjoining metropolitan city of Dublin, thereby adding value to products and business arising from services.

In due course, I was reprimanded for this approach. My superiors—with one exception—were clear: we were there to impart production knowledge and skills because that was what we had done for a hundred years. It was a sequel to

Harry Chapin's *"Flowers are Red,"* where instead of "the little boy [who] went first day to school" rebelling, it was the teacher who had lost the run of himself.[4]

I persisted, getting external funding for a new "Agribusiness Enterprise Development Programme." With an idea in hand for a viable alternative enterprise, my students would produce a business plan and later start a business. The dynamic changed. I was no longer the pedagogue, the source of expertise. What was striking was how these students took to applied research. They were highly motivated, organised themselves, supported one another and, without exception, delivered the expected outcome. There is nothing more alluring than being invited to make effective plans for one's own future.

I had moved from being a teacher to becoming a facilitator. This shift, had I known it at the time, marked the beginning in the obfuscation of my rapport with the Revenue Commissioners. Responsibility for applicable learning had migrated from me, the former tutor, to the group itself. Sure, there was input on the principles of marketing, accounting, management, but the students were in charge when it came to interpreting relevance to each individual's enterprise. Here were young men and women of mixed ability, addressing future plans, realising that they had to effectively address all the elements that made for a successful business. We had moved a long way from learning how to grow cabbage.

But what did all of this say about my role? I had moved from a centre stage, controlling role to the wings of the stage. In plenary sessions my contributions dropped in duration from a dominant and controlling 70 percent to 80 percent to less than that of the average contributor. I could not say that I was in control; they were. But I could declare that relevant learning was going on. This learning was not unpredictable. Within the elements of the components of a business plan, there were no surprising topics. There was an indicative curriculum. Discussions centered on clarification of the theory and of its application to the individual participants. We had moved from the harassment implicit in the "one size fits all" learning regimen to individual, particularized, and pertinent learning.

The learning differed in another way: it was systemic in the sense that it contributed to the potential creation of a system that was to be a successful business through the means of a business plan. I had little understanding of systems at that time. I vaguely appreciated that unless the students effectively addressed all components of a business plan, there was no prospect of success. As the plans moved from incubation to implementation, the holistic nature of the business system "under construction" dominated. Heretofore I had engaged in the accretion of knowledge, in an eclectic, bit-by-bit approach, which was non-systemic.

But my energies and focus were on ensuring that this initiative would survive within the organisation where I worked. I had to make my case to my supe-

---

4. "Flowers are Red" written by Harry Chapin, Chapin Music, ASCAP. Originally found in *Living Room Suite*, 1978, Electra Entertainment.

riors. My greatest advocates were the graduate students and their enthusiasm. In time, the businesses they set up spoke more eloquently than any sweet-talking memos might.

I freely admit now that I was dependent on my students to support my then primitively understood epistemological and pedagogical stance. The notion that objective evidence—in the form of student testing and examination answers—could eclipse forthright, frank, personal testimony and emerging enterprises was derisory. With hindsight, I realised that the relationship between my students and me had shifted from a controlling me with subordinate students to co-dependence. Evidence of effectiveness of my "teaching" role had moved from the traditional outcome of evidence of examination answers to plans and up and running businesses, from the static to the dynamic, from the subordinate to that of colleague and supporter. Later, I came to understand how the paradigm in use made it difficult for my employers to examine evidence of effective process, unless it came as an outcome (not ongoing process) in a familiar format—examination papers—in line with their expectations and practice.

Specialist? I was appointed as national specialist in Leadership and Community Development in a new Rural Development Division of our extension agency. I expected initially that my role should not change, that I might revert to my original service to my client farmers. I would bring to my new clients in community development sources of well-researched information pertinent to my perception of their needs. My early impulse—a *volte face* back to my conditioning in technical rationality—was that I should scour the latest findings of research, if necessary pre-digest my discoveries, and disperse same to waiting and presumably grateful communities.

It was disconcerting to discover that these communities were not hanging around, waiting for me and my expert guidance. While they were not rude, gratefulness was not their stance. To cap it all, there was very little literature that described the workings of rural communities; there were reports and evaluations aplenty, with descriptions of the outcomes of communities' work, but very little on process. I sought parallel blueprints to my cabbage growing classes, some inspiration on how to "*successfully do*" community development. It did not exist. This was in contrast to my rural development colleagues in farm food development who had no difficulty in devising suitable blueprints in the realms of jam-making, cheese and smoked meats, etc. For them, instruction was still the dependable cornerstone of their extension stance.

One interaction startled me. A colleague reported he had been invited to a monthly meeting of the development association of a small western town. The association had worked hard on plans linked to tourism potential and, to that end, had proposed to enhance the town's amenities; riverside walks, summer bedding plants, signposts, and street seating were among those mentioned. My colleague dismissed these plans; the objective should have been job-creation, and he had told them so. Two months passed and he was invited back to the town to spearhead his job-creation programme. I asked if he had any account of the intervening meeting, where the association's members must have deliberately set aside their plans in favor of his expert view. What were their feelings, I wondered? What kind of paradigm in use were we promoting when community associations were reduced to making proposals to us? Of course, such deferrals to "authority" were flattering, but the basis of decisions seemed entirely unwarranted.

In the meantime, I was coming under pressure for failing to publish guidelines for rural communities on how "to do" community development. My colleagues were conducting training courses in all kinds of alternative enterprises. Classroom materials abounded. Courses were popular. Evaluation reports were being filed and authorities were being comforted that all was in order. My failure to produce parallel documentation and courses was indulgently noted.

Commentary on seeking an understanding of "The Work." We see in the first part of Lillis' narrative that across several years both he and those with whom he worked were struggling not only with the issue of what he does—what is the nature of community-based work—but also how it should be done and what would count as evidence. Embedded in the narrative are key issues related to who he was, what roles he would take on, and how he understood what he was supposed to do—issues that our faculty learning community has grappled with throughout our time together in order to understand "the work" of engagement more deeply. Lillis describes an inner shift from understanding his role as one who "delivers" or "dispenses" knowledge to thinking of his students and community partners as engaging with him as joint problem solvers. He became a "facilitator" as he and his students accepted joint responsibility for decision making. He then helped them engage in clarification of theory and the planned, systematic application of knowledge. This seemed to be a key transition from dispensing knowledge *to* communities to working *with* communities to apply knowledge (as in Boyer's conception of the scholarship of application) (Boyer 1990).

We also see that this shift in thinking and action did not come without a struggle. Institutional norms and expectations were strong forces that tried to push him back into safe and familiar old patterns and habits (technical rationality) and traditional measures of success (concrete outcomes with no appreciation of constructing effective processes). For many, the journey could have stopped there. He had a ready rationale for the need to follow through with his job and just do what was expected of him. Did he?

Part 2: The learning turn

The beginnings of wisdom? Years later, I came to realise there was a "drill": read up on recent research on some aspect of one's brief; produce a blueprint on it; work it into a class (or better still a seminar); disseminate it to involved target audiences; and then produce a booklet or a record of seminar proceedings. But my new professional brief—community development—did not lend itself to fragmentation into fascinating subsections of such opportunities. It was slowly dawning on me that every community was unique, exceptional, and inimitable, both in its context and in its practice. There would be no community perform-ance reports in the sense to which I had once been accustomed to in the world of crop varieties and herbicides, where scientific research had wrested reliable rules with wide—if not universal—application. Science did not get in the door of local communities.

But we had a paradigm for generating research, reliable educational infor-mation, and desirable development, which we had relied on through the three epochs in agricultural development of the last century—the peasant, production, and productivity phases of agriculture. We had now moved into the fourth phase, the postmodern, where products and food sufficiency are now (after over fifty years of concentrated applied research) of secondary concern to crucial is-sues, such as the environment, sustainable systems, self-realisation, and freedom of peoples. We were moving up the pyramid of Maslow's sequence of needs. A new dispensation was coming out of the European Union, which proposed to in-vert the relationship between agriculture and rural development, where agricul-ture would be addressed only as subordinate to rural development, rural com-munities, and the rural countryside. It was shortsighted to cling to technical rationality.

I made two decisions. I enrolled in a programme recently brought from Af-rica to Dublin called "Training for Transformation." This is a foundation course for community workers. Based on the philosophy of Paulo Freire, it seemed to address my needs. It was indeed a transformation, a shift of a lifetime's para-digm. I learned to listen to others, not just hear and not heed, but to attend. A lifetime's experience of being listened and deferred to as an expert was set at naught. Hitherto I would have seen myself as working *for* people. In authentic community development, I had only one option—to work *with* people. This change in prepositions was to have transforming and challenging repercussions. Essentially it was a change of stance. The practice would cease of first drawing up a programme of what would be "good" for others, of subsequently recruiting the participants, confronting them with my acumen and teaching them.

Nothing in my career had prepared me for this. It required a re-evaluation of my philosophy, skills, values, methods, and priorities. Its experiential method, reliance on psychosocial analysis, and emphasis on learners' participation in de-termining what was relevant for them, brought valuable awareness of the poten-tial of these approaches. I questioned my dependence on external expertise.

As a new and fervent convert, I fell into the trap of disparaging technical ra-tional approaches. I was of the "either–or" simplistic school and as yet, unrecep-tive to "both–and." Yet technical rationality had served me well and I could cite reports from that stable that were very influential in facilitating significant rural development initiatives. That was yet another learning point.

My second decision was to conduct three "Training for Transformation" programmes for rural people. Most participants told me privately that the programme was enriching. One member, however, was very upset. The subject of equitable wages for farm labourers was discussed. These wages are notoriously low in Ireland, to the extent that the Government continues to exercise prime responsibility for organising a trade union on behalf of these employees. I was accused of being left wing and of stirring up trouble and threatened with complaints to my superiors. In a way I sympathise because the complainant had dealings with me as an instructor, brandishing my horticultural jug. He felt betrayed by this development of my role.

My earlier interactions with farmers and students were predictable and because they were largely foreseeable, I could confidently expect to control them. This farmer's complaint was symptomatic of the potential discourse of—for me—a new means of engagement. My employers advised caution. It began to dawn on me that my employing organisation was not suited to the cut and thrust of community development, particularly as it would have to cede significant control to participants. Yet all I was offering was more of this kind of discourse and very little by way of their expected—if not by then long overdue—guidebooks, conventional training courses, and job creation.

Reflection

My experience of extension in my public service years taught me that reflective education was rarely a one-way transaction; engaged adults should have a role in determining the curriculum. Once I had vacated the expert's podium and was willing to confer meaningfully with participants on what they wished to learn, I became a learning facilitator within a set curriculum—as in my class on business instigation—creating an occasion where participants could learn in fairly predictable ways. It seemed to me that there was a temptation to abuse one's position if one did not respond and change from the instructional approach. Particularly if one were not truly expert in one's field, the basis of talking down to one's students was questionable, if not deceitful. In my early career I understood the notion of working *for* people as noble; moving to work *with* people—albeit within the confines of an agreed curriculum—was even more splendid, less predictable, and more challenging.

Commentary on the "Learning Turn." By reflecting on and critiquing his work, Lillis gained insights into what made "the work" he began to do different from his early days as an instructor. Two key understandings shaped his thinking. First, he understood that no blueprint could provide "steps to follow" that were so familiar in his previous extension work. Why? Because he realized that each community is unique in its context and practice. Second, and perhaps more importantly, he began to understand the importance of thinking in new ways about what seemed to be familiar problems. The late Donald Schön pointed out that how we name and frame problems shapes what we pay attention to (or not), and problem framing is influenced by our own backgrounds (Schön 1987). Lillis realized that the traditional "problems" of products and food sufficiency in agriculture were no longer center stage. Instead, current critical issues in agriculture demanded attention to more urgent matters such as the environment and sustainable agriculture. As Werner Ulrich says, "making 'the problem' the problem" is an essential part of critical examination (Ulrich 2003, 325–342). In other words, Lillis began to see that a different framing would be needed if community efforts would lead to transformative action.

These insights led Lillis to see the need for new learning. He enrolled in a "Training for Transformation" program that helped him learn to act on his emerging stance. He learned to listen for meaning and work *with*, not *for* the community. Once engaged in listening, further learning about his own thinking emerged as he reflected on his philosophy, skills, values, methods, and priorities. John Heron and Peter Reason refer to these ideas as important epistemological, philosophical, ontological, and axiological questions to consider for engaging in participatory inquiry (Heron and Reason 1997, 274–294).

We also see in Lillis' narrative that change was not easy. In taking first steps at operating within an emerging paradigm, he describes how he made the mistake, at first, of taking an either–or stance toward technical rational approaches. When he tried to engage community members in listening for meaning instead of rushing merely to get things done, he upset community members who saw his actions as only stirring up trouble. Community members, too, need to learn new ways of interacting and understand that engaging in discourse *is* a form of taking action. Finally, as Lillis reflected on his development thus far, he acknowledged that there were limits to his progress. He realized that although he was learning to engage in new practices, he still clung to what he calls a "set curriculum" that bounded what was possible.

Part 3: Discovering the centrality of conversation
     Introducing the unpredictable curriculum. More epiphanies followed. William Kimball's description of community development as "intricate networks of purposeful conversations about the issues that matter most to people" gave a hint as to how communities learn.[5] It also provides a turning point.

If conversation is the key, then the practitioner is challenged to decide how to join the conversation. What is the appropriate and most effective stance? Most experts, no matter how well-intentioned, have the effect of stopping the conversation. If communities learn principally through conversation, persevering in lecturing communities flies in the face of what I now know to be the more effective means of education for this sector. Conversational learning is the key. And we are all familiar with that medium. Conversational learning is the universal experience of all infants in their start in life. The podium was redundant and could be listed for sale.

In Ireland, community development has been colonised by the State as a principal means of addressing the disadvantaged in our society. The State has

---

5. Personal communication.

tended to become prescriptive; it inveigles community groups—the preponderance of which it has itself set up—to do what the State regards as desirable. The State has unwittingly annexed communities' agenda. Mutually respectful conversation about shared concerns among equals is therefore difficult, if not impossible.

But conversational learning is conducted in communities in additional ways that facilitate and accommodate the engagement of inexperienced, new members through a form of apprenticeship. Lave and Wenger (1991) explain this (*italics theirs*):

> Learning viewed as situated activity has as its central defining characteristic a process that we call *legitimate peripheral participation*. By this we mean to draw attention to the point that learners inevitably participate in communities of practitioners and that the mastery of knowledge and skill requires newcomers to move towards full participation in the socio-cultural practices of the community. (Lave and Wenger 1991, 29)

In being a legitimate apprentice, new entrants gain entry to communities with whom they aspire to share interests/concerns. All are called to Kimball's "purposeful conversations," inferring a potential for committed participation in a connected sequence of resulting actions. Pursuing my quest for legitimacy and effectiveness for my contribution as a learning practitioner, these features—conversation, action, and apprenticeship—provide clues for my appropriate, functioning stance. Apprentices are critical to the long-term sustainability of communities. They provide energy as well as new ideas. Their vitality should find expression in both the concerned conversations and in the resultant activity. The question is: "How might I enter into and contribute to these communities' conversations?"

My current thinking is that I join communities with some of the characteristics of apprenticeship. I, like apprentices, gain entry on the basis of becoming a legitimate peripheral participant. I state that I share a concern for the sustained well-being of a community and have some skills that would advance that well-being. Unlike long-term members, I cannot commit to stay in each and every community. I, like these novices, wish to contribute through some parallel route of Lave and Wenger's legitimate peripheral participation, where I have a say, like any other participant and where my opinions are taken on board, as would be the case for any other contributor. Instinctively, I feel my contributions would focus on the broad area of enhancing sustainability, an area of long-term shared—if under appreciated—concern. This includes effectively addressing such questions as, "How can we be more effective?" "How do we know we are doing the right thing?" "How can we show we have made a difference?" These questions strike me as opening an ethical domain of concern, efficacy, and relevance that yields learning and shared understanding that conventional research does not address. Empowering communities to do their own research and evaluation is at the heart of what I would wish to encourage.

I believe that what I am trying to articulate is what Parker Palmer (1990) describes as an expressive act:

> An expressive act is one that I take, not to achieve a goal outside myself but to express a conviction, a leading, a truth that is within me. An expressive act is one taken because if I did not take it, I would be denying my own insight, gift, nature. By taking an expressive act, an act not obsessed with outcomes, I come closer to making the contribution that is mine to make in the scheme of things. (Palmer, P. 1990, 24)

But this could sound pretentious were it not for my conviction that my role in communities is predominantly one of affirmation, support, and encouragement, that is, to walk along side and not take over or dominate. I am conscious of the tendency of some leaders in community development to overshadow community activity to the extent that community activity is dependent on them exclusively and, if they depart, "the centre cannot hold." I am aware, too, of the unproductive practice of some researchers, who conduct their research and evaluations *on* communities, thereby excluding them from participation—and conversation—in any meaningful way other than being the objects of these researchers' attentions. I have heard communities complain how this is unhelpful and how findings take far too long. If a community has a pressing concern, it really cannot wait for two to three years for a scholastically researched recommendation. Communities do not work that way. I believe that communities should direct and manage their evaluation and research. They need to do their own research and evaluation, rather than handing over research and evaluation to external, disengaged professionals.

An emerging mission statement

About three years ago I wrote a mission statement for myself. It read: I wish to help communities improve their effectiveness by helping them

- resource themselves
- plan their future
- do their own research and evaluation
- identify their skills, networks, and assets
- attend to their training needs
- build their community structures to deliver goals
- evaluate programs and progress
- deal with issues of leadership, values, and principles, and
- work more effectively.

In pursuing this mission, I rely on conversations to engage communities from the outset. Conversation will also be a principal means of establishing and advancing the goals I would wish to share with a community. Conversation will also pervade our analysis of the community's performance and when the findings are presented within a cycle of ongoing consultation, conversation will result, will be the ongoing process, and will be a measure of the interest generated. I see my role in these continuing conversations as highlighting achievement, remarking on it, and celebrating it. Conversations will also pervade our analysis of the community's performance when findings are presented within a cycle of ongoing consultation. Under those circumstances, conversations will be three things at the same time: an ongoing process, a measure of interest, and an outcome.

And so what do I know?

I have been criticised for labouring the obvious but I go on doing so, mindful of the Holmes–Watson discourse on the self-evident:

Sherlock Holmes and Dr. Watson went on a camping trip. As they lay down for the night, Holmes said: "Watson, look above you and tell me what you see."

Watson: "I see millions of stars."

Holmes: "And what does that tell you?"

Watson: "Astronomically, it tells that there are millions of galaxies and potentially billions of planets. Theologically, it tells me that God is great and that we are small and insignificant. Meteorologically, it tells me that we will have a beautiful day tomorrow. What does it tell you?"

Holmes: "Elementary, my dear Watson; somebody stole our tent."[6]

The auspices for my future rapport with Ms. Cashman are poor. I wonder if there is any way she might be persuaded to categorise me as an apprentice conversationalist.

Commentary on discovering the centrality of conversation. We see additional discoveries in the final portion of Lillis' narrative. First, he recognized that if learning through conversation—really listening and seeking meaning—is a key to meaningful community engagement, then he needed to figure out how to join it. He describes the process of joining in conversation as an apprentice, which entailed two types of learning—learning to be part of a discourse community and learning from the discourse by reflecting on it. Moreover, Lillis makes clear that he is still in the process of examining and understanding his role and "the work." Through a process of critical reflection and critique, his most recent thinking about his role is quite different from prior years. Instead of being an instructor or teacher in the traditional sense, he currently understands his role as an obligation to *join* a community—temporarily—to learn with them through conversation, not for the purpose of producing measurable outcomes, but for the purpose of empowering the community to do their own research and evaluation. As he "walks alongside" his community partners, he tries to affirm, support, encourage, and celebrate their accomplishments. His mission statement

---

6. I am indebted to Chris Glavey for this anecdote.

is another attempt to understand and newly define "the work" of community engagement. But he is not merely posting it as though he has finally gotten it "right." It guides his work, for now, until his learning through conversation leads him to further insights.

Narratives reveal concepts and themes

The narratives shared in this chapter provide concrete views of two landscapes. From the first story we get a view of the outer landscape of actions—how a community of practice engages in situated learning in Open Space governed by mutuality and respect. It is work that is initiated and pursued by community members while faculty members join them in working side by side. The second story provides a view of the inner landscape of how an individual who participated in various community efforts grew and changed over time.

Both stories introduce us to key themes and concepts—such as mutuality, respect, reciprocity—and reveal how important it is to learn through conversation, respect multiple ways of knowing, and adopt a critical stance. These themes and concepts will reappear throughout the remainder of the book, explored from multiple perspectives—to illustrate the learning process of our faculty learning community, and to tell the story of our coming to critical engagement.

References

Allen, K. 2000. *The Celtic tiger: The myth of social partnership in Ireland.* Manchester UK: Manchester Univ. Press.

Boyer, E. 1990. *Scholarship reconsidered: Priorities of the professoriate.* Princeton NJ: The Carnegie Foundation for the Advancement of Teaching.

Bruner, I. 1986. *Actual minds, possible worlds.* Cambridge MA: Harvard Univ. Press.

Carmen, R. 1996. *Autonomous development, humanizing the landscape: An excursion into radical thinking and practice.* London: Zed Books.

Cooke, B., and U. Kothari, eds. 2001. *Participation: The new tyranny?* London: Zed Books.

Cooperrider, D., P. Sorenson, D. Whitney, and T. Yeager, eds. 2000. *Appreciative inquiry: Rethinking human organization toward a positive theory of change.* Champaign IL: Snipes Publishing.

Hart, T. 2001. *From information to transformation: Education for the evolution of consciousness.* New York: Peter Lang.

Heron, J., and A. Reason. 1997. A participatory inquiry paradigm. *Qualitative Inquiry* vol. 3:274–294.

Isaacs, W. 1999. *Dialogue and the art of thinking together.* New York: Currency.

Lave, J., and E. Wenger. 1991. *Situated learning.* Cambridge UK: Cambridge Univ. Press.

Meade, R., and O. O'Donovan. 2002. Corporatism and the ongoing debate about the relationship between the state and community development. *Community Development Journal* 37:1–9.

Owen, H. 2000. *The power of spirit: How organizations transform.* San Francisco: Berrett-Koehler.

Palmer, M. 1997. Foreword. In *Sacred journeys: Paths for the new pilgrim.* J. Westwood, ed. London: Gaia Books Unlimited.

Palmer, P. 1990. *The active life: A spirituality of work, creativity, and caring.* San Francisco: Jossey-Bass.

Schön, D. 1987. *Educating the reflective practitioner.* New York: Basic Books.

Stowe, D., C. Buck, and S. Martin. 2002. *Generation Y speaks out: Public policy perspectives through service learning.* Lansing MI: Michigan Nonprofit Association.

Ulrich, W. 2003. Beyond methodology choice: Critical systems thinking as critically systemic discourse. *Journal of the Operation Research Society* 54(4):325–342.

Wenger, E., R. McDermott, and W. Snyder. 2002. *Cultivating communities of practice.* Boston: Harvard Business School Press.

CHAPTER 3

LIVING OUR WAY INTO A NEW WAY OF THINKING: AN EXPLORATION OF MINDFUL INQUIRY

We must not cease from exploration
And the end of all our exploration
Will be to arrive where we began
And to know the place for the first time[1]

Each step on the pathway to discovery leads to the next. For us, the question became: How, then, did we get *here*? On the surface it did not compute, arriving at *this* destination, fully recognizing that destination is a poor word choice. But the stark reality is that, today, we have rethought many of our earlier ways of thinking and practicing. And, yet, we understand that all of this was inevitable: we *had* to go through it all without taking shortcuts. The words of humanist Parker Palmer apply in our context: "You can't *think* your way into a new way of living. You *live* your way into a new way of thinking."[2] In our case, the living–thinking connection made the difference.

Through dialogue, we now understand that our work (and approach to it) enables a constant state of becoming—connected inextricably to critical analy-

---

1. T. S. Elliot, "Four Quartets," (London: Faber and Faber, 1960).
2. Comment made during a luncheon conversation during a campus visit, September 20, 2001.

sis—finding the time and making the effort to stand back and inquire into what we are doing, why, and with what outcomes. Engagement in living makes critical analysis worthwhile. Otherwise, as Palmer (1998) avers, it is like trying to think (and perhaps fool) your way into a new way of living.

Mindful inquiry is the name we prefer giving to this way of engaging, adapting its application from the contribution made by Valerie Bentz and Jeremy Shapiro in the research domain (Bentz and Shapiro 1998). Taking this approach puts you and your work at the center of an inquiry process, seeking to avoid making that work "a disembodied, programmed activity." As Bentz and Shapiro see it, mindful inquiry is undertaken with "reflection as to its purpose" and with a clear understanding of your "purpose for engaging in it." Above all else, it is a manifestation of "the way in which you engage with the world" (1998, 4–5). The authors link mindful inquiry to the concept of scholarly practice:

> To us, a scholarly practitioner is someone who mediates between her professional practice and the universe of scholarly, scientific, and academic knowledge and discourse. She sees her practice as part of a larger enterprise of knowledge generation and critical reflection . . . . The awareness of both the nature of knowledge and its limits is, we believe, part of the identity of a mature practitioner who is personally, ethically, and professionally responsible. (1998, 66)

Mindful inquiry is grounded in the general concept of mindful behavior, which psychologist Ellen Langer calls *mindfulness* (Langer 1989). Mindfulness is characterized by *creating new categories* (continually creating new ways of understanding); *welcoming new information* (and seeking out new stimuli); and *affirming different perspectives* (being receptive to different points of view and recognizing the validity of multiple stances) (63–72). On the other hand, "mindlessness is characterized by an entrapment in old categories; by automatic behavior that precludes attending to new signals; and by action that operates from a single perspective" (Langer 1997, 4).

The beginning: looking at service and outreach through an institutional lens

Where do we begin this story? It begins in the early 1990s: looking at public service and outreach (that is what we called it then) through an *institutional* lens. The three main activities in higher education—teaching, researching, and serving through outreach—are largely discrete institutional activities, undertaken and administered separately. At least in a conventional sense, it is clear to most (on-campus and off-) what teaching and research are; they are primary, demonstrable, and familiar activities. Service and outreach are different, the meanings diffuse and status contested. Are they core functions, equivalent to teaching and research? Are they academic functions? If so, why are they? If not, why aren't they?

Caught up in a movement

We stepped to the table to address this challenge. It seemed to us that there were three fundamental tasks: clarify what service–outreach means; reestablish its value in higher education; and enable its capable undertaking. We joined with others at the invitation of executive administrators to chart the territory and soon found ourselves swept into a campus and national movement. The 1990s, we discovered, was a renaissance for those associated with the service–outreach function. What had been historically at the margins of higher education seemed, now, to be moving to the mainstream. Service–outreach was a topic of consideration and conversation: conferences were held; administrators hired; structures formed and reformed; proclamations made; task forces established; strategic planning undertaken; articles published; and journals created. This was a movement, a movement fueled by rhetoric to realign how we value work on campus with historic institutional obligations. Many of us had the feeling that something important would happen as a result.

Inspirational voices and images: the coming of engagement

All movements have primary spokespeople, messengers who have a way of framing and expressing the message in precisely the right way and at the right time. We, as did many others, found Ernest Boyer to be our spokesperson. We read his *Scholarship Reconsidered* with great interest, using it in our teaching and writing, and sharing it eagerly with colleagues (Boyer 1990). We found references to Boyer all around—cited at conferences and discussed at meetings— his words carrying quasi-Biblical quality. The most important quality of his book, as we read it and discussed it with others, was its affirmatory stance. We interpreted Boyer as saying, first and foremost, that our work mattered in the academic scheme of things; and, second, that our work qualified as scholarship. Because the messenger is as important as the message, we understood the enormity of this bearing. This was not just *anybody* talking; it was the president of the Carnegie Foundation.

In addition to the affirmation of our work was the image associated with it. It was a compelling image; here we had painted in words the feelings that drew us to the academic life. Perhaps nowhere was this imagery more vivid and compelling than in Boyer's *Chronicle of Higher Education* essay entitled, "The new American college" (1994). Boyer wrote expressively about what this college would be—a testimony to collegiate engagement in the issues and problems facing society. We not only wanted this work to be higher education's center stage, we wanted to be agents of enablement. That longing—and it was that for sure— fueled our commitment to "the cause."

In 1996, the inaugural issue of *The Journal of Public Service and Outreach* published as its lead article an essay drawn from a speech that Boyer delivered shortly before his death (1996). Entitled "The scholarship of engagement," the article—in title, substance, and direction—captured our full attention. For the first time, there was a name for this movement with galvanizing allure, *engage-*

ment. In a style that we had come to expect, Boyer wrote convincingly and passionately about his vision of engagement:

> I have this growing conviction that what's needed is not just more programs, but a larger purpose, a larger sense of direction . . . . Increasingly, I'm convinced that the scholarship of engagement . . . means creating a special climate in which the academic and civic cultures communicate more continuously . . . what . . . Geertz describes as the universe of human discourse and enriching the quality of life for all of us. (1996, 20)

Engagement had a magnetic quality to it, much more so than Boyer's initial offering of "the scholarship of application," which carried with it a strikingly different image. Application seemed to us to be about mechanically taking something from a prior activity (research in this case) and then using it for some instrumental purpose, much like applying a coat of varnish to a deck. To the contrary, engagement (to us) referred to a fully embodied experience that defied separateness and spoke viscerally to what we had come to know. Put another way, the concept had experiential validity and personal valence. Engagement resonated with us for another reason. For the first time, we felt there was a concept that addressed a troubling subtext in the service–outreach domain—the one way nature of its delivery. The words used traditionally are inherently problematic in that regard: service *to* (audience-centered); extension *of* (topic-centered); and outreach *from* (institution-centered). None of these references is robust enough to capture the essence and scope of what we do, or how and why we do it. However, engagement *with* offers a radically different image and prospect because it is *participant-* and *participation-*centered. Clearly, engagement is not "all about us." It is about what happens when academy and society meet, when they engage for the purpose (as Boyer describes) of "communicating more continuously" with each other.

The journey proceeds: taking action

Through the early to late 1990s, we wove these understandings and connected them to endeavors associated with helping to create what is now referred to as "the Engaged Institution."

Articulating a scholarly foundation

The first contribution was work that several of us undertook at our then-provost's request, work that resulted in creating an intellectual foundation for outreach at Michigan State University and linking that foundation to a set of strategic proposals for institutional change.[3] Of the first order was defining out-

---

3. Michigan State University, "University Outreach at Michigan State University: Extending Knowledge to Serve Society," Office of the Vice Provost for University Outreach, (East Lansing: Michigan State University, 1993). A report prepared by the Pro-

reach. We saw it as work that involves *generating, transmitting, applying, and preserving knowledge for the direct benefit of audiences in ways that are consistent with university and unit missions.* At first glance, it appears that this definition positions outreach as a transcendent and overarching university function, that is, outreach as everything.

The definition actually serves a very different purpose, signaling an understanding of outreach as a *cross-cutting function.* Simply put, there are forms of outreach that involve teaching (e.g., off-campus instruction), research (e.g., applied research for a client), and service (e.g., speaking at a service club on a topic in which one is expert). The next task was to answer the question, "When is outreach a scholarly expression?" Our response: it is scholarship *when it is deeply informed, the outcome of collegial review, using standards that are publicly accepted in the professions, disciplines, and multidisciplines.* Using this logic, the committee established a basis for arguing that there are boundary conditions for work that can (and should) carry the title, "the scholarship of outreach."

What is quality outreach?

Having established an intellectual frame of reference for outreach and for the scholarship of outreach, in particular, several of us began tackling the matter of quality outreach. Again, by provost charge, a task force was created and in 1996 a report was published.[4] Outreach as a scholarly expression was the point of departure for defining quality outreach:

> In order to make a convincing case for scholarship in outreach, one must demonstrate that: 1) the project was *guided by a driving intellectual question* that led to knowledge discovery, integration, application, transmission, or preservation; 2) the *process of project development and implementation occurred in a scholarly fashion* (guided by clear goals, appropriate methodology, and so on); and 3) the project *impacted multiple stakeholders* (such as community members, professional colleagues) *in multiple, relevant ways* (such as by improving community life or creating cutting-edge information).

We asserted that other dimensions of quality outreach included *significance, attention to context,* and *internal* (to the university) *and external* (societal) *impact.* In conceiving our framework for "distinctive outreach," we drew heavily on the work of Ernest Lynton (1995) and on a prepublication version of *Schol-*

---

vost's Committee on University Outreach.
http://www.msu.edu/unit/outreach/missioncontents.html
4. Michigan State University, "Points of distinction: A guidebook for planning and evaluating quality outreach," Office of the Vice Provost for University Outreach, (East Lansing: Michigan State University, 1996), http://www.msu.edu/unit/outreach/pubs/pod.pdf. We are indebted to the leadership and contributions of Lorilee R. Sandmann who served as committee chairperson and lead author of the report.

arship Assessed, the Carnegie Foundation's follow-up to Boyer's 1990 book, co-authored by Charles Glassick, Mary Huber, and Gene Maeroff (1997). The second Carnegie book was especially helpful because the content was based on a cross-disciplinary study: what scholars do when they engage in scholarly activity. In our thinking, the study results could (and should) be transferred to and applied in the outreach domain.

Following the release of the report, several of us began applying the framework to help faculty members plan, report, and evaluate their outreach work. Four MSU faculty members—a professor of veterinary science, an associate professor of landscape architecture, and co-authors Foster-Fishman (psychology) and Rosaen (teacher education)—participated in a pilot effort that was undertaken in conjunction with The W. K. Kellogg Foundation Project on the Documentation and Peer Review of Professional Service and Outreach.[5]

The conversations were so rich that the MSU participants decided to write a manuscript based on their experiences. In 2000, that article appeared in *Change: The Magazine of Higher Learning* (Sandmann et al. 2000, 44–52). The co-authors presented the quality framework and used examples from their work to discuss issues and tensions associated with putting the framework into practice. This was an important step—a bridging function, as we understand it now—associated with writing that article. The authors began shifting the locus of attention from institutional development efforts to inquiring into the essence of the work as a scholarly endeavor:

> In contrast to all the recent publications about 'engagement' from the viewpoint of administrators, this article provides a voice for full-time, tenure-stream faculty actually engaged in university-community partnerships. (2000, 46)

Enabling engagement through institutional development

Although enabling engagement through institutional development and studying engagement are certainly not incompatible, growth in the latter domain seemed stunted by an overwhelming emphasis on institutional matters, from revamping the faculty reward system to restructuring campus systems. It was with this mindset that each of us read the Kellogg Foundation report on the engaged institution, a product of the Kellogg Commission on the Future of State and Land-Grant Universities that was undertaken in conjunction with the National Association and State Universities and Land-Grant Colleges (NASULGC 1999). Again, to a person we found an indelible institutional focus—what public universities need to be and do—and how, in embracing engagement, these institutions can "return to their roots."

---

5. For information about the Kellogg Project, see A. Driscoll and E. Lynton, "Making Outreach Visible: A Guide to Documenting Professional Service and Outreach." (Washington, D.C.: American Association of Higher Education, 1999).

As we read the text, it was clear to us that the conversation about engagement was taken up by institutional elites—university presidents, chancellors, and others (e.g., trustees)—who worked with consultants and held forums. The authors established boundary conditions for engagement, to the point of defining how engagement should proceed. There was a "Seven-Part Test," a manual of sorts, telling readers what should happen in the name of engagement: *responsiveness, respect for partners, academic neutrality, accessibility, integration* (of engagement with teaching and research*), coordination* (of endeavors across the institution), *and resource partnerships.*

It was not a matter of our responding, "Wrong!" It was just very odd to read recommendations authored by presidents and chancellors and directed to people on the firing line about how to do engagement. This, we thought, was akin to hospital administrators writing a report to surgeons about surgical practices. The declaratory form of the report also seemed incompatible with our understanding of engagement. This is not how engaged colleagues go about their work in the field, we thought, telling people what to do and how to do it. Worse yet, the report had a scolding tone to it. There is a section entitled, "a bill of particulars" describing higher education's unresponsiveness. The language in it troubled us:

> It's difficult to get a grip on this institution, understand its points of leverage, and find a way through the academic maze. But even though we, as leaders of these institutions, understand clearly what we want to accomplish, we are sometimes not entirely clear on how to proceed. (NASULGC 1999, 4)

The image of "university as machine" came to us as we read this passage: those in control wanting to pull levers to get certain and specific outcomes. We are cogs in their machine and they are frustrated by the inability to get the machine (and us) to do what they want.

As we thought about this quote, it dawned on us how revealing language can be. Clearly, university presidents and chancellors are making "engagement" their idea, a priority item on a leadership agenda with boundary conditions they manage and with outcomes they prefer. Because of that, it is no wonder that so much of the conversation about engagement pertains to organizational matters. That is the space they can talk about with understanding and for which they have fiduciary responsibility. But what about other matters pertaining to engagement, like the work itself? Rather than open up that space to others, which would seem to make practical sense and the "engaged" thing to do, they seek to colonize that space by declaring engagement's meaning and its proper conduct. This stance has enormous implications because, with authority and power invested in their positions, elites can mandate conformity to the engagement platform as they define it.

Ironically, the approach taken by the report authors runs counter to what researcher Jim Collins discovered and reported recently in his widely read study of exceptional corporate performance (Collins 2001). Among other things, he concludes that:

> When we began the research project, we expected to find that the first step in taking a company from good to great would be to set a new direction, a new vision and strategy for the company, and then to get people committed and aligned behind that new direction. We found something quite the opposite. (2001, 41)
> The good-to-great companies had no name, tag line, launch event, or program to signify their transformations. Indeed, some reported being unaware of the magnitude of the transformation at the time; only later, in retrospect, did it become clear. Yes, they produced a truly revolutionary leap in results, but *not* by a revolutionary process. (2001, 11)

Besides, we thought, one of the restraining matters associated with institutional change is that so much emphasis is placed on the implementation process, that is, on how to "get to" the preferred vision. In academic life, however, there are almost always multiple, diverse, and contested interpretations of the underlying phenomenon. Take, for example, the matter of "good teaching." A mindless activity would be to focus instrumentally on good teaching without, first, taking the time to explore what it means; there is a rich and diverse literature associated with its theory and practice. It makes sense to explore alternative interpretations and understanding of engagement before seeking to create engaged institutions because:

> Change platforms—such as. . .The Engaged University—do not carry automatic and unequivocal meaning. Meaning is a contingent phenomenon. In an academic setting, meaning is gained only partially by communicating clearly and concisely. A concept like 'engagement' is not clarified for scholars by simply defining it. Scholars nest definitions in philosophic and conceptual frames of reference. These frames of reference often connect to profound worldviews. Because of that, to say that engagement means different things to different people obfuscates a fundamental scholarly axiom. Engagement actually means specific things to specific people, who use the concept to refer to specific processes, situations, and outcomes, contingent on their school of thought and practice. (Fear, Adamek, and Imig 2002, 48)

What that means in our case is that there is nothing inherent in engagement that says it can or even should carry singular meaning. It is not an "it" to be understood monolithically, practiced uniformly, and with "tests" to pass. Consequently, any attempt to define boundaries—especially at the early stage of a movement and particularly by people with the power to enforce a particular stance—is anti-intellectual, hegemonic, and likely to constrain the movement's evolution. A leadership issue, then, is whether or not discourse about engagement is encouraged or stifled. One can argue, especially in the case of new ideas, that we need leadership and change platforms that are more *embracing* of diverse perspectives than declarative of a single way of understanding; more *inviting* to an array of stakeholders than restrictive in philosophy, approach, and intent; and more *connecting* across campus divides than partisan to a restrictive subset of stakeholders (2002, 51).

Perhaps that tells us that there is an "engaged" way of leading engagement, a leadership style that befits the qualities that some ascribe to the underlying phenomenon. Acting on that understanding will hasten the prospect of engagement as a transformative force; a means to change how we engage inside the Academy, not just outside of it. We have addressed this matter elsewhere:

> In our estimation, the scholarship of engagement represents a profoundly different way of thinking about and approaching scholarship from business-as-usual academic practices. When institutional change is envisioned and promulgated by central administrators and enacted through systems redesign and the use of incentives and disincentives, we have a misalignment between strategy and outcome: a conventional approach is used to diffuse an unconventional phenomenon, engagement. The irony is that engaged scholars would never use that change strategy in the field because it violates the premises of engagement as participatory and democratic. (Rosaen, Foster-Fishman, and Fear 2001, 24)

Toward an intellectual understanding of engagement

As we have tried to show, there is considerable danger in framing engagement primarily as an institutional development matter and there is much to be gained by developing intellectual understanding and exerting engaged leadership. There is, above all else, the matter of "the work" itself. How might we understand the work? We consider the question from multiple vantage points, starting with the concept of engagement as movement.

Engagement as movement

We should expect diverse voices to be drawn to a movement, especially early on; polyvocality is a *sine qua non* of movements, including circumstances where people "talk past one another." Trite as it seems, the reality is that engagement means different things to different people, and the work has magnetic pull for at least three reasons: as an *ethos* (of collaboration and partnership); for *utilitarian purposes* (as an effective problem solving means); and for *political value* (accruing to those who associate with the engagement movement). Because of these realities, nimble boundary crossing is required *within* the movement: people engage for different reasons and often "talk past one another." Those who embrace engagement as ethos are likely to align deeply held personal values with their professional identity and approach. That is a very different stance from those who see engagement as practical means to "get results" and different, yet again, from those who insert engagement language into a grant proposal for the purpose of impressing a potential funding source.

Understanding engagement as a movement also helps us recognize another dynamic: people believing that, with the current emphasis on engagement, *fi-*

nally "the world is coming to their way of thinking." The problem with this logic is that it is inherently mindless in nature, uncritically relabeling past work as engagement. If engagement and, say, Extension are the same, why do we need a new label for historic work? Another way of thinking about this—again, emphasizing the diversity of players coming to the table—is to consider engagement territory as a complex reality context. Continuing with our example, rather than assume Extension and engagement are the same, those who think that way need to make a public case for drawing that conclusion. Scholars understand that conversations of this sort, although sometimes difficult, are undertaken for the purpose of deepening understanding of the underlying work. Such conversations also help depoliticize circumstances, as can happen when people slap labels on things for partisan purposes and impression management.

Understanding engagement as a movement helps us not only appreciate the different ways in which the idea is interpreted and enacted *individually* but, also, how the idea is interpreted and adopted *organizationally*. This is an important distinction because there is the matter of engaged practice, on the one hand, and the pronounced desire to become "Engaged Institutions" on the other. Parker Palmer speaks directly to the matter of how organizations and movements differ (P. Palmer 1998).

> Organizations and movements both play creative roles, but to quite different ends. Organizations represent the principle of order and conversation: they are vessels in which a society holds hard-won treasures from the past. Movements represent the principle of flux and change: they are the processes through which a society channels its energies for renewal and transformation. (1998, 164)

Palmer (1998) argues that there are different logics—an organizational logic and a movement logic—with each logic serving a different purpose. He warns about the dangers associated with overlaying an organizational logic on movement related ideas:

> The genius of social movements is paradoxical: they abandon the logic of organizations so that they can gather the momentum necessary to alter the logic of organizations. Both the civil rights and women's movement had to free themselves from racist and sexist organizations in order to generate power. Then, with that power, they returned to change the lay, and the law, of the land. (1998, 165)

Palmer advises those associated with movements to understand movement logic (as it differs from organizational logic) so that they can use that understanding to "learn how a movement unfolds, partly so that we can know where we are located within it, partly so that we can help it along" (1998, 170).

What insights regarding engagement emerge from Palmer's interpretation? We believe that all institutions, including higher education, would lead us to believe that *bold ideas* (the province of movements) are incorporated as a matter of course as institutions do their business and evolve. Without question, bold ideas—like engagement—are conceived on a regular basis. Yet, bold ideas represent an alternative to the organization's logic system and, as a result, may threaten the status quo. That is one of the reasons why bold ideas often take root outside the mainstream of institutional life, unencumbered by organizational constraints. When institutions do adopt bold ideas, at issue is whether they absorb them holistically and completely. Frequently, bold ideas are modified and molded to *fit* the prevailing institutional culture and systems architecture. In other words, the institution redefines bold ideas to make them institutionally "digestible." When that happens, institutions experience a paradox of transformational change. One would think that bold ideas have the power to change the way business is done institutionally. However, just the opposite can happen (Barr and Fear 2005, 25).

Engagement as alternative stance

Bold ideas push the boundaries of conventional organizational practices because they represent robust *alternatives* to mainstream ways of engaging. For example, work associated with both conventional and alternative food systems are undertaken at our university. Conventional work focuses on the improving the existing market-based system, including the efficient production and distribution of food, which is designed to provide consumers with accessible, safe, and quality food at affordable prices. In addition to this important work, work is also underway to develop food systems that are locally based. Local food systems are grounded in an ethic that accentuates the importance of "place" as citizens participate in a value-driven, socially conscious form of local development, designed to transform them from consumers to active agents of community development. For example, establishing a cooperative grocery store creates a locally owned, community-based business with the potential of offering high quality and nutritious food, grown with minimal (or no) reliance on chemical inputs. Through investment of local capital and "sweat equity," members co-own the enterprise, deciding on focus and scope, including purchasing decisions. Often this means establishing relationships with local producers, thereby facilitating community access to locally grown food (Fear et al. 2004).

This example puts the spotlight on a major political question, namely, the normative dimension of deciding how higher education will engage and for what purpose. The default option is to take no institutional position or to support any and all work undertaken. It is not that easy, though. Consider our example as a case in point while pondering these questions:

- Does the term "engagement" apply in our instance to work associated with the conventional food system? If so, what makes it so? If not, why not?
- Can you think of an unengaged way to participate in local food systems development?

- Should conventional and alternative work go on at the same institution? If it should, why should it? If not, why not?

Beyond the provocative questions our example raises, there are mundane matters to consider. Consider the reality that higher education institutions purchase food all the time for use in residence hall dining rooms, at conference gatherings, and for a variety of other campus purposes. To what extent, if at all, does a university embrace local food systems practices? In our example, that could mean thinking beyond "best quality food at an affordable price" (conventional logic) to purchasing food from local producers that is grown in an environmentally conscious matter (alternative logic). Doing that would expand the way we often think about the term "Engaged Institution"—where engagement is embraced as an academic practice *and* engagement practices are embraced institutionally.

The flip side of this coin is whether partisans of alternative-to-mainstream ideas want to affiliate with higher education. Capra, for one, believes there is increasing evidence of unengagement, particularly among those working on an activist agenda (Capra 2002). Higher education is seen by many activists as affiliated with and funded by parties that engage in work they oppose (e.g., biotechnology). Capra writes:

> To place this political discourse within a systematic and ecological perspective, the global civil society relies on a network of scholars, research institutes, think tanks, and centers of learning that largely operate outside our leading academic institutions, business organizations, and government agencies. Their common characteristic is that they pursue their research and teaching within an explicit framework of shared values. (2002, 222)

Engagement as "new scholarship"

In making this observation, Capra brings up an extremely important issue, an issue that the engagement movement must address, namely, the matter of underlying frameworks of shared values. Without oversimplifying engagement's reality context, we submit that there are at least two paradigmatic views of engagement.[6] The first way is connected to the grand narrative of the modern world, which we refer to as *the historically dominant paradigm*. In one form or another, this paradigm has been a dominant force for approximately 400 years. That narrative began with the scientific revolution of the seventeenth century, continued with The Enlightenment of the eighteenth century, evolved during the Industrial Revolution of the nineteenth century, and expressed in the rise of transnational corporatism of the twentieth century. This grand shift moved soci-

---

6. The material immediately following is drawn from R. Barr and F. Fear, "The Learning Paradigm as Bold Change: Improving Understanding and Practice." In C. McPhail, (ed.), *Establishing and Sustaining Learning-centered Community Colleges*. (Washington, D.C.: The Community College Press, 2005), 13–31.

ety from traditional authority, humanism, and smaller scale modes of operations to rational administration, technical procedures, and systematic management of large-scale operations with economies-of-scale. The outcomes are manifest in a variety of expressions including the positivist scientific method, behavioral psychology, and the factory model of production, which includes bureaucratic organizational systems, higher education among them.

The late Donald Schön wrote about the historically dominant paradigm, specifically in terms of its implications for the research university, with reference to what he called *Technical Rationality* (1995). We elaborate on Schön's interpretation:

> Technical Rationality is the way that many of us go about the work we do as scholars. It is the use of rigorous and systematically applied procedures. It 'lives' in the form of many of our research designs; the way courses and curricula are typically structured and offered; and how we often design, undertake, and evaluate outreach projects. Technical Rationality is not just the dominant way we go about our academic work, it influences the way academic institutions are designed and operate. For Schön, the Research University values technically rational teaching, research, service, and operations. In his eyes, Technical Rationality is an *institutional* epistemology, that is, a preferred organizational theory of knowledge. (Fear and Sandmann 2001-2, 31)

How does the historically dominant paradigm influence engagement's interpretation? Here is one example:

> The tri-partite mission of a land-grant university is teaching, research, and extension. But the basic business of a land-grant university is knowledge: knowledge that is transferred through teaching, developed through research, and utilized through extension. These three functions represent a dynamic connection of knowledge that connects, or engages, land-grant universities with the people of the state and to the needs of society. Being engaged means that a land-grant university serves as a change agent in society. As faculty members anticipate the issues that will affect individuals, business, and society, they develop the knowledge needed to address those issues. They then share that knowledge with decision-makers in both the public and private sectors. This can lead to the adoption of new management techniques and public policies. (Fischer 2000, 13)

Note how language choices reveal the character of the underlying paradigm: knowledge transfer; knowledge utilization; university functions as separate and discrete enterprises; the university as change agent; faculty members anticipating needs as experts; developing knowledge; sharing knowledge with people; and people adopting what faculty members tell them. This logic is an expression of what Daniel Yankelovich calls *The Culture of Technical Control*, a logic based on objectivism and instrumental rationality—with experts in charge using rules they have created (Yankelovich 1991). It seems odd—but also consistent with the organizational dynamics described earlier in this chapter—that such a way of thinking and practicing would be labeled "engagement." Along that line, Yankelovich asserts that "epistemological anxiety is the feeling that your special way of making sense of the world is being threatened" (1991, 186). One way to reduce anxiety in the engagement domain is to transfer a technically rational philosophy into engagement. But doing so means that engagement loses its transformative power in exchange for becoming an acceptable expression of the prevailing worldview.

There is an alternative to this Technically Rational world view. Many analysts, including Fritjof Capra and Peter Drucker, believe that we have entered a period of epochal change, a time when society literally rearranges itself, organizing around new and different philosophies, values, forms, and goals (Capra 1982; Drucker 1992). This epochal change, called postmodern by some, includes a variety of counter positions to the historically dominant paradigm. Among the core ideas are multiplicity of meaning and interpretation; diversity of expression and form; centrality of interpersonal relationships and connectedness; and recognition of and appreciation for nonlinearity, complexity, and emergence (Barr and Fear 2005). For Capra and others, one of the essential differences in the alternative paradigm is how power is exercised and structured—with less emphasis on authority exercised through hierarchies and more emphasis on discovery mediated through interaction (Capra 1996). This new way of thinking and practicing is embodied in such contemporary expressions as shared leadership, participatory management, and collaborative learning.

Schön (1995) believed that the alternative to the historical dominant paradigm has significant implications for scholarly work. It required a "New Scholarship:"

> . . . if the new scholarship is to mean anything, it must imply . . . norms of its own, which will conflict with the norms of technical rationality . . . . If we are prepared to take it on, then we have to deal with what it means to introduce a new epistemology . . . into institutions . . . dominated by technical rationality. (1995, 25–37 with emphasis added)

Daniel Yankelovich elaborates:

> For purposes of gaining control over people and things, the knowledge of technical and scientific experts has proven superior to other ways of knowing. But for the truths of human experience—learning how to live—knowledge is awkward, heavy-handed, and unresponsive. It fails to address the great questions of how to live, what values to pursue, what meaning to find in life, how to achieve a just and humane world, and how to be a fully realized human person. (Yankelovich 1999, 196–197)

Scott Peters, a faculty member at Cornell University, has articulated an understanding of engagement that we believe reflects the values of the alternative to the historically dominant paradigm (Peters 2000, 23–30). He writes:

> On the surface . . . it looks . . . as if it [engagement] marks a renewal of a robust civic mission . . . with . . . 'two-way partnerships, reciprocal relationships between university and community, defined by mutual respect for the strength of each . . . .' While this view of engagement points to a welcome shift away from the expert-dominated understandings of university outreach work, it does not necessarily represent a shift away from the default mode of instrumental individualism. Unless engagement is tied to a commitment to place social, political, and moral aims on the table as serious and legitimate concerns of scholarly work, 'the engaged institution' idea might simply reinforce the procedural, customer service-oriented politics of the default mode. (2000, 17)

Note several things as you consider Peters' words. First, note how he critiques the words used to describe engagement; he does not accept surface understanding but searches, instead, for deeper meaning. Second, he seeks to reposition engagement—from an instrumentally-focused outcome to something with moral valence. And third, he connects his understanding of engagement to his hope for higher education as an institution with civic virtue and purpose. He does all of this by encouraging engagement's disconnection from *instrumental individualism*, a concept drawn from the work of William Sullivan of The Carnegie Foundation (Sullivan 2000). According to Sullivan, instrumental individualism refers to circumstances when higher education focuses on undertaking "research and disseminating knowledge and skills as tools for economic development and the upward mobility of individuals" (2000, 21).

The analysis offered here helps us make concrete the reality that engagement can be understood and practiced in different and sometimes radically different ways. The historically dominant paradigm and the "New Scholarship" stand side by side. No matter what the preferred stance, constant boundary crossing is required, and little is to be served by combat:

> The Academy is not served by the 'range wars' that seem to characterize much of higher education today. The dance is all too familiar—the repeated assaults on whatever the dominant paradigm might be (it is always flawed and inherently dangerous) and the repeated counterassaults against those who express 'alternative perspectives' (they are always flawed and inherently dangerous). (Fear, Adamek, and Imig 2002, 49–50)

Nothing is served by making definitive pronouncements about engagement. Instead, we need honest and authentic discourse about engagement's meaning and intent, conversations that are guided by evocative questions, such as the ones in which our discourse is grounded:

What is engagement?
With whom do we engage?
Why do we engage?
How do we engage?
Toward what end do we engage?

In our case, we eventually came to a shared understanding about what engagement means to us and, then, we put that meaning in explicit terms: *It is about sharing knowledge and learning with those who struggle for social justice; and collaborating with them respectfully and responsibly for the purpose of improving life.* Perhaps more than anything, we know this is simply *a* way of understanding engagement, and is not *the* way. But making it explicit helped us better grasp the essence of *our* way. More than anything, we began to understand (and appreciate) those circumstances where we had failed to either measure up to our own standards or where we had forced ourselves (for any number of reasons) to strive for a new level of understanding and practice. Perhaps it was those regrettable and often humbling moments that hastened a coming to critical engagement, including thinking about engagement in radically (for us) new ways, a topic to which we now turn.

Revisiting our roots: revising core understandings
When we thought more deeply about the alternative to the historically dominant paradigm and linked that understanding to analysis of our engagement work, there was a surprising outcome: heretofore fundamental views about scholarship did not stand up well.

Boyer's forms of scholarship
Take, for instance, Boyer's conception of scholarship's multiple forms—as discovery, learning, engagement, and integration (Boyer 1990). Earlier, we had accepted this framework uncritically and disseminated it enthusiastically. Political benefits accrued from thinking that way: it put the spotlight on engagement and made this scholarly form equivalent in standing with discovery, for example. Those advantages aside, there were different outcomes when we shifted emphasis from *applying* Boyer's framework to *critiquing* it. For one thing, his categories seem to modernize (rather than transform) traditional academic placeholders—exchanging discovery for research, learning for teaching, engagement for service, and integration for interdisciplinarity—"rearranging the deck chairs," we thought. More importantly, the framework did not help deepen understanding of our work, either descriptively (what we do) or normatively (what we hope and aspire to be and do). That led us to reframing our prior interpretation in four important ways.

First, we view as problematic the concept that there are separate forms of scholarship, namely, that there is a scholarship of engagement that is separate and distinct from, say, a scholarship of discovery. Instead, we see *all* our work as a scholarly expression. With sensitivity to language form, we no longer refer to the scholarship *of* because it conveys a sense of separateness, focusing attention on discrete activities. Instead, we replace "of" with "scholarly," as in *scholarly* engagement. Doing that puts scholarship at the center of the conversation—not the activity undertaken—and signals connections, rather than separations, across scholarly activities. As we have observed elsewhere:

> . . . we [do not wish to] . . . compartmentalize our work and become teaching scholars, research scholars, and outreach-engagement scholars. . . . All we do connects thematically to a larger purpose: to an overarching program of scholarship that is enriched by, but is not restricted to, a single scholarly domain. (Fear et al. 2001, 24)

Second, we conclude that focusing on the activity (rather than the underlying phenomenon of scholarship) has an insidious effect on the way scholarly work is interpreted. While there is an engagement section on academic paperwork (e.g., on promotion and tenure forms) and an organizational domain carrying the engagement title (we have an office of outreach and engagement on our campus), overemphasizing professional activities and the organizational architecture can create "hardening of the academic categories," if not scholarly silos. That happens if form drives function, thereby reifying an activity. That logic goes like this: because there is an activity called engagement (form), there is also a scholarship of engagement (function). To the contrary, we assert that there are transcendent qualities associated with scholarship's undertaking that can not be fully described (let alone completely understood) by focusing on any scholarly activity without considering all scholarly activities. An example is the quest to become deeply informed about a subject of interest. The way we see it, the quest to be deeply informed (function) enables all sorts of scholarly activities (form).

Third, Boyer's categorization did not apply well when we discussed scholarly episodes that were particularly exhilarating and meaningful. We found—time and time again—that these were often cases of the "and's," that is, experiences that cut across and connected two or more of activities, such as engagement *and* discovery. More than finding these experiences meaningful, we found them to be regular occurrences. It made sense, as we thought about it, because of the self-serving need to have coherent, connected programs of scholarship: teaching, research, and service activities connected dynamically.

Fourth, is all of our work described well by categorizing it? Take discovery for example. Is there a scholarship of discovery that exists apart from our other scholarly endeavors, including engagement? Certainly, we can think of episodes where the primary purpose has been to generate knowledge—to discover—when we can unequivocally say we are participating in a formal, discrete activity—a process of discovery. But there are also instances where knowledge discovery takes place *when* and *as* we engage. That means engagement includes, but is more than, what takes place in a location (context); engagement includes, but is more than, an axiological stance (ethos); engagement includes, but is more than, a way of interacting with collaborators (process); and engagement includes, but is more than, work associated with practical outcomes (instrumental value). Engagement can also be a form of, and an opportunity for, discovery; just as we have found that it can be a form of, and an opportunity for, learning and integration. For example, while fully recognizing learning as a formalized for-credit activity that takes place in a campus classrooms, off-campus locations, and virtual settings, in our work there are marginal differences between how we approach formal learning with collaborators in the field *vis-à-vis* with "students" in the undergraduate–graduate classroom. Because of that, learning and engagement are interactive and symbiotic activities. Rather than view scholarly learning as a separate and distinct quest, we found it to be an inextricable feature of scholarly engagement and, likewise, we found scholarly engagement to be an inextricable feature of scholarly learning.

Scholarship as process?

After critiquing Boyer's framework, we turned attention to the follow-up book published by The Carnegie Foundation, *Scholarship Assessed*, co-authored by Glassick and others (Glassick, Huber, and Maeroff 1997). Without question, there is value to framing scholarly endeavor in process terms, as Glassick and his colleagues have done, including *setting clear goals, being prepared adequately, selecting appropriate methods, obtaining meaningful outcomes and impacts, sharing the results with others,* and *engaging in reflective critique.* This is a sound planning model.

The challenge, as we thought about it, is the image that framing reveals: work undertaken in a stable environment with those responsible in control. This does not well describe our engagement experiences and, more so, seems to be a Technically Rational perspective on scholarship. Those conclusions reminded us of a topic treated years ago by Abraham Kaplan in *The Conduct of Inquiry* (Kaplan 1964). In that book Kaplan discusses the matter of *reconstructed logic*, the way group members convey understanding of what is involved when undertaking their appointed task (e.g., what architects do as they engage in building design). To understand reconstructed logic, Kaplan suggests, "it is not a question of whether the facts *can* be so construed, but whether it is still worthwhile to continue to throw light on the sound operations actually being used" (1964, 10). That is another way of saying that reconstructed logic is an idealization that may be worthwhile even if the characterization does not actually reflect what happens in practice. Kaplan warns that

> The idealization may be carried so far that it is useful only for the further development of logic itself, and not for the understanding and evaluation of scientific practice. Reconstructions have been so idealized that, as Max Weber wryly observed, 'it is often difficult for the specialized disciplines to recognize themselves with the naked eye.' At worst, the logician becomes so absorbed with enhancing the power and beauty of his instrument that he loses sight of the ma-

terial with which it must work. At best, he commits himself to a questionable Platonism: that the proper way to analyze and understand something is to refer it to its most ideal form, that is, its form abstracted from any concrete embodiment. There is *a* way but it not the only way; and I am far from convinced that it is always the best way. (1964, 11)

In a practical vein, we face this dilemma all the time when teaching research methods classes and advising graduate students in their research. Time and again, we advise students (and they soon discover) that the research process "isn't exactly" the way it is described in methods texts. Rather than accept everything they read as gospel with the intent of implementing it precisely, students find how important it is to view reconstructed logic as an interpretive frame of reference. They discover this by experiencing the research process themselves, through what Kaplan calls *logic in use.*

We do not question the validity of the Glassick et al. framework as reconstructed logic. It seems to be a reasonable description of what scientists do when they engage in the scientific process. What concerns us is how readers may interpret and apply it. First, there is risk in reifying a reconstructed logic as "the way it is," such that the framework is accepted uncritically and then replicated. We did that and suspect that others may have done so, as well. Second, we hypothesize that the Glassick et al. framework applies exceptionally well to certain inquiries and perhaps not as well to others. At issue, of course, is how well the framework applies to our understanding and experience with engaged inquiry. To assess that matter, we interpreted the framework in relationship to personal engagement experiences that we found to be especially provoking, those that pushed us to new levels of understanding. We selected those experiences for analysis because, as persons who are especially interested in transformative change, we were curious about its logic in use. Here is what we discovered:

> We find it impossible to describe our compelling outreach experiences in a linear, phase-driven way. For example, more than once we have found ourselves in the middle of an outreach experience and in over our heads. We were unprepared, not because of oversight, but because outreach is in reality a border crossing. We have found ourselves working in community contexts that were new to us, and with partners whose ways of knowing and operating were distinctly different from our own. We have been propelled beyond the realm of prior experience and stretched outside our comfort zone. In these situations, we gained knowledge and skill on the fly . . . . At the same time, we cannot deny the truth: these experiences extend our reach, professionally and personally, changing the way we work, how we understand and act on societal issues, and how we view our professional *raison d'etre.* If these experiences had been designed and undertaken with preplanned certainty, we doubt they would have had such an impact. (Fear et al. 2001, 24–25)

What this says more than anything else is that understanding scholarship as process—as happens if we apply the Glassick et al. framework—misses the contextual richness of engagement. Adopting the framework would emphasize attributes of preparedness, organizational acumen, systematic and responsible action—the planning, execution, and reporting of engagement—(all important in one sense) in exchange for more fully understanding the profoundly contextually embedded dynamism that we have discovered in engagement. Besides, it places undue emphasis on the expert partner's judgment about what constitutes quality engagement, raising (among other things) questions about the "knowledge" resulting from the process. We agree with Frank Fischer's assessment:

> What we call 'knowledge' of the social world is the outcome of a negotiation between those with more 'expert knowledge' and the actors in the everyday world . . . . For this reason, the process of investigation necessarily involves the expert in the normative understandings and processes of everyday life. As such, the process of knowing cannot be understood as the exclusive domain of the expert. (Fischer 2000, 74)

Engagement as collaborative inquiry

Thinking about this made it clear to us that there is a difference between outreach and engagement. We can think of many times when we have been asked for, and when we respond with, expert knowledge: knowledge that we offered others. The Glassick et al. framework seems to be perfectly reasonable for the outreach function, but not for engagement as we interpret it. Engagement to us is a participatory and collaborative process as expert and local knowledge systems merge to address compelling issues located in time and context. Embracing that stance involves, first and foremost, respect for people and place, followed by understanding one's responsibilities as a participant–collaborator in an engaged relationship.

An understanding like this emerges, we believe, from mindful inquiry and the reflection associated with it. Reflecting on practice, we contend, is a critical element in Schön's "New Scholarship." It is also an example of what John Bray and colleagues refer to as *collaborative inquiry,* which "is a process consisting of repeated episodes of reflection and action through which a group of peers strives to answer a question of importance to them" (Bray et al. 2000, 6). Beyond the essential *instrumentality* of answering questions of mutual importance (its first characteristic), collaborative inquiry is a *stance* (its second characteristic). Collaborative inquiry takes seriously the concept of "peers," meaning that participants are colleagues in a jointly defined and undertaken enterprise. Being collegial means that power is distributed equitably among the partners; there are open and honest transactions; there is sincere, authentic desire to learn from and with each another; and all involved "honor a holistic perspective on the construction of valid knowledge." Finally, collaborative inquiry holds the *prospect of personal transformation* (its third characteristic). Engaging in it can affect participants deeply, as long as "there is authentic reflection on the interests that motivate participation." Bray et al. continue:

As they (participants) make meaning from their experience, their personal horizons and the horizons of their life-world under investigation become merged into a new understanding of their world. Usually this new understanding is more comprehensive and more integrated than was their previous understanding, a marker of having experienced transformative learning. (2000, 24)

We suppose this is what happened to us: by reflecting together on engagement, we developed a new and more comprehensive understanding. What emerged is a phenomenon called *Engaged Learning*, a topic we now consider.

Engaged Learning

Engaged Learning is a practice associated with the alternative to the historically dominant paradigm. It is also a form of Schön's "The New Scholarship." We define it thusly:

Engaged Learning is grounded in an ethos of mutuality, respectfulness, and stewardship; it proceeds through dialogue; and fosters inclusive well being. It is an approach; an expression of being; a leadership and management ethic; and a way for scholars to connect otherwise diverse activities thematically, coherently, and meaningfully. (Fear et al. 2002, 66)

In the material below, we analyze Engaged Learning in six interrelated ways: as a *thematic, connective expression*; as *an ethos*; as *action-based learning*; and as a scholarly stance toward practice that is *informed conceptually, grounded philosophically,* and *undertaken with normative intent.*

As thematic, connective expression. Influenced by viewing outreach as a cross-cutting function—with outreach expressed as teaching, research, and service—we see Engaged Learning as a thematic, connective expression of scholarly work. Engaged Learning is a transcendent stance and approach, permeating everything we do in the name of engagement:

In the undergraduate and graduate classroom, in research, and in service, our work looks and feels very much the same. The cornerstone of engaged practice is practice is co-participation . . . . We engage with collaborators in co-envisioned and co-constructed episodes of mutual learning, discovery, and action. Issues are identified jointly, agendas for action are co-created, and evaluation is undertaken collaboratively. (Fear et al. 2002, 56)

In taking this position, we join others who—in stance and action—embrace participatory processes with emancipatory outcomes. Drawing on the work of Jurgen Habermas (1987), public health educators Nina Wallerstein and Bonnie Duran provide a rationale:

For Habermas, capitalist societies have created two distinct worlds: the systems world of highly differentiated, legal, economic, and political systems; and the life world, the resource in which individuals form their identity and reproduce their culture. As the life world has increasingly become colonized by the systems world, people begin to define themselves by their role within systems. They become objects—clients and consumers—rather than subjects or democratic members of civil society who reproduce themselves as social and cultural beings. The manifestation of this colonization is seen in anomie, powerlessness, dysfunctional behaviors . . . and the overall decline of civil society. (Wallerstein and Duran 2003, 32–33)

Thinking this way has led us to reorient and restructure the places and forms of our engagement. Our campus classrooms are now examples of engaged pedagogy, illustrative of concepts and practices associated with collaborative learning (Bruffee 1999) and our research endeavors are now influenced by the tradition of action and participatory research (Greenwood and Levin 1998). More so, we fuse collaborative learning and participatory research in Engaged Learning, such that there is commonness across what had heretofore been distinct and discrete activities—teaching, research, and service—activities that we worked hard "to integrate." Today, we celebrate being "divided no more" (following Parker Palmer's advice) because there is seamlessness in our work. Everything is about what happens *"at the table."* We co-create episodes of engagement—in teaching, research, and service—with those who join us there. This inherently democratic and connective work begins when we get there and it proceeds based on what happens there.

As ethos. Engaged Learning is a profound expression of personhood. Because of that, it cannot be fully understood by describing only how it is practiced and what it produces. Understanding also requires recognizing why one would want to engage and, just as importantly, what it means "to engage" and to "be engaged." By exploring the felt and relational dimensions of engagement, we articulated a set of *norms of engagement* (influenced largely by Yankelovich's work cited earlier), which "include respectfulness, collaboration, mutuality, and dedication to learning with emphasis on the values of community, responsibility, virtue, stewardship, and a mutual concern for each other" (Fear and Sandmann 2001-2, 31). We elaborate:

> Our use of the word 'ethos' tips our hand (as language always does) about how we see engagement—as a deeply personal stance. Embracing engagement as an ethos keeps us from objectifying engagement as a strategy . . . . We believe that engagement norms are relevant for all forms of academic work—from how project teams operate to how institutions of higher education function altogether. (Fear et al. 2002, 59)

It dawned on us at that point that the *form* in which engagement is undertaken speaks volumes to the way engagement is *interpreted.* In our case, the community of practice form of engagement (as described in the Introduction) enables exercising the norms of engagement as we have described, a medium (in this case) for helping scholars across fields advance understanding of engagement in theory and practice.

As action-based learning. Why engage? Our answer: to enhance understanding and the *capacity for action through learning.* We view ourselves as engaged learners and believe that our work is best captured through the image of people engaging each other and learning together. For this reason, and others we shall now describe, Engaged Learning (not engagement) is our concept of choice:

- Engagement carries multiple and extraneous (to our purpose) meanings—used also to describe a social commitment, an impending marriage, and a battlefield skirmish. Engaged *Learning*, on the other hand, contextualizes engagement in terms of how we seek to use it—for educational purposes.
- Engagement has a "thing" quality to it, harkening reference to a space or time when an activity or action took place. Conversely, Engaged *Learning* characterizes the active nature of the underlying phenomenon; learning is dynamic, not static. It also conveys a progressive image, as in "The more we learn, the better we will be able to engage."
- As discussed earlier, we prefer disconnecting conversations about engagement from historically understood organizational functions–activities. We are disinclined to see outreach, service, or Extension understood *as* engagement. We also do not see engagement as a separate feature of higher education's mission, such that what had been previously described as teaching, research, and service now becomes learning, discovery, *and* engagement. These are distracting images that carry an organizational management quality to them. They also give the impression that "things have really changed" when that matter is open to debate. Interpreting engagement (or our Engaged Learning) in either of these ways places the work in a sealed box, limiting its scope and restricting its influence: growth stunted and future constrained by definition.

Informed conceptually. Engaged Learning involves learning in context, an experience described by Jean Lave and Etienne Wenger as *situated learning.* Consider this interpretation by William Hanks, which was published in the Preface of Lave and Wenger's 1991 book, *Situated Learning*:

Learning is a process that takes place in a participation framework, not in an individual mind. This means, among other things, that it is mediated by the differences of perspective among the co-participants. It is the community, or at least those participating in the learning context, who 'learn' under this definition. Learning is, at its core, distributed among co-participants, not a one-person act. (1991, 14–15)

If situated learning describes the learning context associated with Engaged Learning, then *dialogue* describes the learning process (Ellinor and Gerard 1998). Dialogue enables learning from, with, and through others by enhancing understanding of complex issues and situations:

> It reflects a respectful stance: people listening to what others have to say about matters of importance—'engaging' for the purpose of understanding and taking action. Situated learning *through* dialogue differs remarkably from learning *from* experts in non-action contexts and then applying learning at a later time. Although that is an important way of learning, we do not see it as Engaged Learning. (Fear et al. 2002, 61)

Dialogic understandings and practices were evident in the good-to-great companies identified by Collins in the study cited earlier. Collins found that great companies "lead with questions, not answers" and "engage in dialogue and debate, not coercion." Collins elaborates:

> There's a huge difference between the opportunity to 'have your say' and the opportunity to be heard. The good-to-great leaders understood this distinction, creating a culture wherein people had a tremendous opportunity to be heard . . . Leading from good to great does not mean coming up with the answers and then motivating everyone to follow your messianic vision. It means have the humility to grasp the fact that you do not yet understand enough to have the answers and then to ask the questions that will lead to the best possible insights. (Collins 2001, 74–75)

We have confronted many challenges associated with using dialogue in practice. In our instrumental society—where moving quickly toward problem resolution is part and parcel of "strong leadership"—some either find dialogue to be a waste of time or do not know how to engage in it effectively. Among other things, effective dialogue requires listening rather than promoting one's point of view; suspending judgment rather than imputing motives; and being open to having one's position challenged rather than challenging others' positions. As we have commented elsewhere:

> For starters, conversations have a tendency to devolve into debates. . . . We must abandon the fundamental academic position of proving intellectual competence, by seeking to influence others by the power of our words. We also must be willing to acknowledge one another as equals by listening—really listening—to what is being said. As William Isaacs, organizational scholar, urges in *Dialogue and the Art of Thinking Together*, for dialogue to work, we must 'relax our grip on certainty and listen to the possibilities that result simply from being in a relationship with others—possibilities that might not have occurred otherwise.' (Fear and Doberneck 2004, 19)

With experience, we have learned how important it is to recognize the complexities associated with who comes to the table; why; how they prefer to interact; and how willing they are to put their beliefs (and themselves) "out there" for consideration. We have found that some are enriched by dialogic interactions while others feel dominated, even oppressed, by the experience. Trust is a key factor, as is the willingness to engage others authentically in public situations.

As grounded philosophically. Engaged Learning is philosophically grounded in what John Heron and Peter Reason refer to as a *participatory worldview* (Heron and Reason 1997, 274–294). A participatory worldview is different from the worldview embodied in Technical Rationality. An example of a technically rational approach to engagement would be to assert that "higher education has knowledge and communities have problems." A participatory worldview, on the other hand, lodges responsibility for learning in the hands of those who are most affected—people in context—by repositioning knowledge as a commodity produced by experts to a shared responsibility that is contextually grounded. A participatory worldview is the foundation for many forms of participatory inquiry, including collaborative inquiry, collaborative learning, and participatory (and action) research, as discussed earlier in this chapter. This work is inherently experiential, interactive, and iterative such that, as Heron and Reason assert, "all involved engage in democratic dialogue . . . to define the questions they wish to explore and the methodology for that exploration" (1997, 288).

A participatory worldview enables mindful inquiry because it lifts up and reframes the level of discourse, ensuring that the questions "what and how" (endemic in instrumental outreach) never overwhelm the questions "why and for whom" (central to emancipatory engagement). Consequently:

> A participatory worldview is not about 'quick fixes' and settling for the greatest gains in the shortest possible time. It emphasizes an 'oneness ethic' that urges us to recapture a sense of wonder and awe with and of the world. It seizes our sense of responsibility for all living things, not just for people. This philosophy stands in stark contrast to the 'people first' ethic of modern society where resources have been exploited to maintain and sustain elite lifestyles. (Fear et al. 2002, 63)

As undertaken with normative intent. All work undertaken in the name of outreach and engagement is undertaken for a purpose. At issue is the question, "What is that purpose?"—a question that seems to be getting lost in the engagement shuffle. Asking the question causes discomfort because it suggests that there may be unacceptable reasons for engaging. Our purpose here is not to fix boundary conditions in that domain (it is not our place) other than to say that the alternative of concluding that "anything goes" is just as undesirable:

> We do not view engagement as a catch basin for all applied work. For example, we exclude from engagement an effort made by faculty and students to design more comfortable airline seats for transcontinental travel. This is important work, certainly a contribution to society, but it should be called outreach, corporate consulting, or an internship, not engagement. Calling it engagement trivializes what we believe to be the essential attributes of Engaged Learning. (Fear et al. 2002, 63–64)

As we see it, one of the most important contributions made in the name of Engaged Learning is joining with people as they make informed decisions, particularly in circumstances that are ambiguous, uncertain, and risky. Guided by a participatory worldview, it means that we will not exert influence in a partisan way and that we will champion inclusivity; foster appreciation for considering multiple ways of valuing and knowing; and pay special attention to who is likely to be affected by an action and how much.

However, Engaged Learning involves more than attending to matters of process and participation. There is temptation in development work today to capitulate to technically rational thinking. It strikes us how much of our work has been evaluated on the grounds of its economic utility and political acceptability. These are certainly important characteristics, but from our standpoint there *must* be more to engagement. Engaged learners understand the importance of ecological responsibility, ethical comportment, cultural respectfulness, and spiritual attentiveness. Consequently, Engaged Learning complicates the nature of engagement but, by complicating it, it aligns well with the reality context of a postmodern world.

The engagement interface

Engaged Learning practices take place in what we call *the engagement interface* (Fear et al. 2001), a place where community members and academics work to address pressing social issues and problems. The engagement interface is a "dynamic, evolving, and co-constructed space—a collaborative community of inquiry—where partners work together with an activist orientation to seek transformative ends for both the community and the academy" (Rosaen, Foster-Fishman, and Fear 2001, 10).

The engagement interface demands attention because it is the place where engagement occurs. Because we see engagement as a unique expression in community work, we likewise interpret the engagement interface as a unique setting. Engaged Learning in the engagement interface is different from activities that take place in conventional approaches to community work, which include serving a community, extending to a community, disseminating information to a community, and transferring innovations into a community. While each is a valuable approach appropriate in certain circumstances, in nature and quality each is different from the dynamics associated with establishing and sustaining collegial relationships in the engagement interface.

The engagement interface as alternative setting

In light of its unique nature in community work we consider the engagement interface as a *form of alternative setting*. According to community psychologists Kanter and Zuercher, alternative settings are established because existing social structures do not satisfy core requirements associated with preferred ways of valuing, thinking, and practicing (Kanter and Zuercher 1973). The research on alternative settings suggests that alternative settings are most effective when they are environments "that promote mutual support and trust, encourage democratic decision-making processes, have a sharp focus on purpose, and include undifferentiated member roles and responsibilities" (Rosaen, Foster-Fishman, and Fear 2001, 24).

While these characteristics are exactly what we experience in engaged learning, the literature also points out that alternative settings are fragile in nature, especially susceptible to external influences that work to align the alternative setting with how business is done in conventional settings. They are also vulnerable to internal dynamics—difficult to create because they push against the grain and are hard to sustain, as happens when there is leadership and member succession (Cherniss and Deegan 2000).

Having experienced these external and internal tensions personally prompted co-author Fear to convey his thoughts and feelings about alternative settings in lyric form (Fear 2001).

"Just Like All the Rest"

Step by step . . . inch by inch
*   You pick the way.*
Why does it always seem to slip away?
*   Before your eyes, through your voice, and sometimes*
*   by your hand.*

What happens when we ask today:
*   Has it been worth the fray?*
Of risks taken and challenges met.
*   Such pain and joy!*
Will these be memories of what once was,
*   and not of what will be?*

Challenges within!
*   Challenges without!*
Why not retrace our way and walk a normal path?
Look! See it there? It's not far from here.
*   It's not too late! If we only take the time*
To talk that talk and walk that walk . . .
*   Ah, to feel normal again!*

Now I feel unsure of me and certainly of we.
        After all we've done, I still don't know:
"Will we make it? Will we make it?"
        That's all I hear all over here
        Drums playing on our fear.

Many once fought the fight, but now have left my side.
Many stay to fight the fight, but seem to take both sides.

Am I up to it? Do I want it? What is 'it' anyway?

Tired of being sick
        Sick of being tired.

I'm afraid. And I'm scared.

To be of the pack, in the current, and with the grain

I know how to play that game!
        I know those rules!

I know the way!
        Books and workshops, too!
Now all I have is people games,
        and the over and over and over again.
Of two steps up and ten steps back, all the ups and downs.

I long to go to work today with none of that around.
        Oh how grand it would be,
        for you and for me

To be just like all the rest!

Dynamics in and of the engagement interface

Analyzing and comparing case examples of our work led us to conclude that engaged learning in the engagement interface is not about first-order change, what Canadian educator Michael Fullan refers to as doing things *better* (Fullan 1991). Rather, engaged learning is an example of what Fullan calls second-order change, namely, doing *better* things. Toward that end, engaged learning in the engagement interface represents a profoundly philosophical position:

- with respect to *ontology* (its perspective on the nature of reality), engaged learning is inherently subjective and intersubjective, such that reality is co-created by the mind and in a given environment
- with respect to *epistemology* (its perspective on the nature of knowing), engaged learning is informed by multiple ways of

knowing that does not privilege one form of knowing (or knower) over another

- with respect to *methodologically* (its rules of conduct), engaged learning proceeds collaboratively, rather than unilaterally or dictatorially, under rules that participants define
- with respect to *axiologically* (its conclusion about what is intrinsically worthwhile) engaged learning is grounded in empowerment practices with social justice as a goal (Rosaen, Foster-Fishman, and Fear 2001, 13–14)

How does engaged learning look like in the engagement interface?

The process becomes an educational and developmental endeavor that brings both sets of expertise—the insiders' and the outsiders'—to bear on the questions under investigation or the project under development. From the residents' perspective, academic knowledge becomes woven into local knowledge and they become informed consumers of research and science. From the faculty's perspective, local experiences and priorities enhance the validity, utility, and meaning of the work. (Rosaen, Foster-Fishman, and Fear 2001, 15)

For this to happen (and again drawing on case experiences), we suggest that attention needs to be paid to *essential practices* of engaged learning, which constitute creating a shared culture of engagement at the interface between community and Academy (Fear et al. 2001, 27–29). The first practice—*constructing joint purposes*—is connected to a bilateral requirement, grounding work in community relevance *and* linking that work to intellectual question(s) of scholarly relevance. The second practice—*developing shared norms*—requires listening to and respecting diverse voices of those participating *and* proceeding always with skills grounded in an informed practice of dialogue and discourse. The third practice—*bringing unique perspectives and skills to bear*—means integrating participants' knowledge and abilities in the work *and* viewing the practice arena as a formal learning laboratory for learning with, from, and through one other. The final practice—*engaging in shared appraisal of outcomes*—means taking time to assess the quality, outcomes, and impact of the work *and* doing that in ways that conform to recognized and accepted forms of evaluative inquiry.

Although it is possible to view engaged learning at the engagement interface in terms of processes to be undertaken and techniques to be employed, we do not. As important as process and techniques are to community work, success cannot be reduced to picking the right tool. We have experienced that approach on many occasions and it almost always exchanges transformative possibilities for applying prefabricated inventions. What we suggest is something much more than that. Engaged Learning in the engagement interface is an emergent experience. You bring what you know and who you are, engage with diverse others deeply, and figure out directions as you go. It is synonymous with what it means to be and feel engaged.

Conclusion

What we have found engagement to be and not to be, as well as the journey that brought us to those conclusions, are certainly a personal expression. And that is our reason for sharing it. If the understanding and practice of scholarly engagement is to evolve and prosper, we believe those with experience need to share what they have learned. John Forester, an urban planning professor from Cornell University, has a magnetic way of expressing the value of this approach. In his book, *The Deliberative Practitioner,* he writes expressively about "learning from friends" (Forester 2000).

> We learn from friends because they do not typically offer us simplistic cure-alls or technical fixes. They do not explain away, but rather try to do justice to the complexities we face. They do not reduce those complexities to trite formulas . . . . Friends recognize complexity, but as pragmatists concerned with our lives, our practice; they neither paralyze us with detail nor hide details from us . . . . Instead, they help us see more clearly, to remember what we need to, to see in new ways, perhaps to appreciate aspects of others, or ourselves, or our political situations, to which we have been blind . . . . [And] we learn from friends because they present us with a world of experience and passion, of affect and emotion . . . [including]. . . the academic undiscusssables of fear and courage, outrage and resolve, hope and cynicism too . . . . (2000, 32–35)

Forester's interpretation tells us that mindful inquiry cannot be a solitary act. It must also include social exchange, engaging with others in conversations about "the work." There is no question that no one of us could have created what we have shared here. We required each other and, just as importantly, needed the diversity of background, perspective, and experience to get it done. That says there is something to the notion of the strength of weak ties (Granovetter 1973). But our story of engagement aside, there is also the matter of the "ethnos" of autoethnography, higher education in our case. In earlier chapters, we spoke of our changing interpretations of engagement in higher education. In the next chapter we delve into that subject more deeply.

References

Barr, R., and F. Fear. 2005. The learning paradigm as bold change: Improving understanding and practice. In C. McPhail, ed. *Establishing and sustaining learning-centered community colleges*. Washington D.C.: The Community College Press.

Bentz, V., and J. Shapiro. 1998. *Mindful inquiry in social research*. Thousand Oaks CA: Sage Publications.

Boyer, E. 1990. *Scholarship reconsidered: Priorities of the professoriate*. Princeton NJ: The Carnegie Foundation for the Advancement of Teaching.

Boyer, E. 1994. The new American college. *The Chronicle of Higher Education* 9, March:48.

Boyer, E. 1996. The scholarship of engagement. *The Journal of Public Service and Outreach* 1(1):11–20.

Bray, J., J. Lee, L. Smith, and L. Yorks. 2000. *Collaborative inquiry in practice: Action, reflection, and making meaning*. Thousand Oaks CA: Sage Publications.

Bruffee, K. 1999. *Collaborative learning: Higher education, interdependence, and the authority of knowledge*. 2nd edition. Baltimore: The Johns Hopkins Press.

Capra, F. 1982. *The turning point: Science, society, and the rising culture*. New York: Bantam Books.

Capra, F. 1996. *The web of life*. New York: Anchor Books.

Capra, F. 2002. *The hidden connections: Integrating the biological, cognitive, and social dimensions of life into a science of sustainability*. New York: Doubleday.

Cherniss, C., and G. Deegan. 2000. The creation of alternative settings. In J. Rappaport and E. Seidman, eds. *Handbook of community psychology*. New York: Plenum.

Collins, J. 2001. *Good to great: Why some companies make the leap. . .and others don't*. New York: HarperBusiness.

Driscoll, A., and E. Lynton. 1999. *Making outreach visible: A guide to documenting professional service and outreach*. Washington D.C.: American Association of Higher Education.

Drucker, P. 1992. *Managing for the future*. New York: Penguin Books.

Ellinor, L., and G. Gerard. 1998. *Dialogue: Rediscover the transforming power of conversation*. New York: Wiley and Sons.

Fear, F. 2001. A conversation about transformational change in higher education: The unique situation of 'the alternative setting' and its relevance for Olivet College. Seminar presented to the Olivet College Executive Leadership Team. Olivet College. Olivet MI. July 25.

Fear, F., J. Adamek, and G. Imig. 2002. Connecting philosophic and scholarly traditions with change in higher education. *The Journal of Leadership Studies* 8(3):42–51.

Fear, F., R. J. Bawden, C. Rosaen, and P. G. Foster-Fishman. 2002. A model of engaged learning: Frames of reference and scholarly underpinnings. *Journal of Higher Education Outreach and Engagement* 7(3):55–68.

Fear, F., N. Creamer, R. Pirog, D. Block, and L. Redmond, with M. Dickerson, D. Baldwin, and G. Imig. Higher education-community partnerships: The politics of engagement. *Journal of Higher Education Outreach and Engagement* 9(2): 139–156.

Fear, F., and D. Doberneck. 2004. Collegial talk: A powerful tool for change. *About Campus* 9(1):11–19.

Fear, F., C. Rosaen, P. G. Foster-Fishman, and R. J. Bawden. 2001. Outreach as a scholarly expression. *Journal of Higher Education, Outreach, and Engagement* 6(2):21–34.

Fear, F., and L. Sandmann. 2001-2. The 'new' scholarship: Implications for engagement and extension. *Journal of Higher Education Outreach and Engagement* 7(1 and 2):29–39.

Fischer, F. 2000. *Citizens, experts, and the environment: The politics of local knowledge.* Durham NC: Duke Univ. Press.

Fischer, J. 2000. The idea of a land grant university. President's Colloquium. Nov. 9. Clemson SC: Clemson Univ.

Forester, J. 2000. *The deliberative practitioner: Encouraging participatory planning processes.* Cambridge MA: MIT Press.

Fullan, M. 1991. *The new meaning of educational change.* New York: Teachers College Press.

Glassick, C., M. Huber, and G. Maeroff. 1997. *Scholarship assessed: Evaluating the professoriate.* San Francisco: Jossey-Bass.

Granovetter, M. 1973. The strength of weak ties hypothesis. *American Journal of Sociology* 78:1360–1380.

Greenwood, D., and M. Levin. 1998. *Introduction to action research: Social research for social change.* Thousand Oaks CA: Sage Publications.

Habermas, J. 1987. *The theory of communicative action. Vol. 2. Lifeworld and system: A critique of functionalist reason.* T. McCarthy, trans. Boston: Beacon Press.

Heron, J., and P. Reason. 1997. A participatory inquiry paradigm. *Qualitative Inquiry* 3(3):274–294.

Isaacs, W. 1999. *Dialogue and the art of thinking together.* New York: Random House.

Kanter, R., and L. Zuercher. 1973. Concluding statement: Evaluating alternatives and alternative valuing. *Journal of Applied Behavioral Science* 9:381–397.

Kaplan, A. 1964. *The conduct of inquiry.* Scranton PA: Chandler Publishing.

Langer, E. 1989. *Mindfulness.* Cambridge MA: DeCapo Press.

Langer, E. 1997. *The power of mindful learning.* Cambridge MA: Perseus Publishing.

Lave, J., and E. Wenger. 1991. *Situated learning: Legitimate peripheral participation.* Cambridge UK: Cambridge Univ. Press.

Lynton, E. 1995. *Making the case for professional service.* Washington D.C.: American Association for Higher Education.

National Association of State Universities and Land Grant Colleges. 1999. Returning to our roots: The engaged institution. A report of the Kellogg Commission on the Future of State and Land-Grant Universities. Washington D.C.: NASULGC.

Palmer, P. 1998. *The courage to teach: Exploring the inner landscape of a teacher's life.* San Francisco: Jossey-Bass.

Peters, S. 2000. The formative politics of outreach scholarship. *Journal of Higher Education Outreach and Engagement* 6(1):23–30.

Rosaen, C., P. G. Foster-Fishman, and F. Fear. 2001. The citizen scholar: Joining voices and values in the engagement interface. *Metropolitan Universities* 12(4):10–29.

Sandmann, L., P. G. Foster-Fishman, J. Lloyd, W. Rauhe, and C. Rosaen. 2000. Managing critical tensions: How to strengthen the scholarship component of outreach. *Change* 32 Jan/Feb:44–52.

Schön, D. 1995. Knowing-in-action: The new scholarship requires a new epistemology. *Change* Nov/Dec:27–34.

Sullivan, W. 2000. Institutional identity and social responsibility in higher education. In T. Ehrlich, ed. *Civic responsibility and higher education.* Phoenix: Oryx Press.

Wallerstein, N., and B. Duran. 2003. The conceptual, historical, and practice roots of community-based participatory research and related participatory traditions. In M. Minkler and N. Wallerstein, eds. *Community-based participatory research for health*. San Francisco: Jossey-Bass.

Yankelovich, D. 1991. *Coming to public judgment: Making democracy work in a complex society*. Syracuse NY: Syracuse Univ. Press.

Yankelovich, D. 1999. *The magic of dialogue*. New York: Touchstone Books/Simon and Schuster.

CHAPTER 4

HAVE WE *EVER* BEEN CRITICALLY ENGAGED?

From time to time throughout their history, there have been calls for American universities to be much more responsive to the direct needs of society and to be more relevant to the lives of the citizenry. This is ironic because, historically, U.S. universities have been among the most applied institutions of higher education in the world. David Jordan, president of Stanford University, wrote at the turn of the twentieth century that the American contribution to higher education has been "toward reality and practicality" (Veysey 1965). Jordan's interpretation was certainly reflected in the quintessential American philosophy of pragmatism of those times, expressed explicitly in the work of Charles Sanders Peirce, George Herbert Mead, William James, and John Dewey. While there were significant disagreements among these early philosophers, as well as many variations on the "pragmatist theme" that continue to this day, the central concern was with fresh ways (for the times) of looking at "truth" and the process of human judgment from the perspective of experience. Akin to Socratic logic, pragmatism holds that "while one judgment cannot be truer than another, it can be better, in the sense of better consequences" (Russell 1961, 164). Such a context provoked Dewey's opinion about the discipline of philosophy itself: "[b]etter it is for philosophy to err in active participation in the living struggles and issues of its own times than to maintain an immune monastic impeccability without relevancy and bearing in the generating of ideas of its contemporary present" (Dewey 1908, cited in McDermott 1981, xli).

There are differing interpretations of what constitutes "betterment," including who gets to decide, upon what assumptions these decisions are made, and of the nature of the processes that are adopted. These interpretations have been major sources of criticism regarding why universities have not been as responsive as they might to the everyday problems facing the citizenry. Coupled with that matter is the inherent nature of the Academy, an institution that is notoriously slow to adapt to changes in the world about it (Keller 1983), conservative, and generally non-innovative in the manner of its responses. At the heart of the matter lies an apparent reluctance among academics to bring scholarship to bear on to both the substance of issues and the processes by which those issues are addressed as they are experienced by people. Another way of saying this is "to bring conceptual order to the perceptual order of experience," to paraphrase William James (1940).

Land-Grant universities as institutions of social enhancement

Despite the range of different and significant impediments to the goal of social enhancement, the Academy has also demonstrated its commitment to what we now call engagement. No better example can be found than the establishment of the "land-grant" colleges in the nineteenth century. These institutions were established with an unequivocal mission to educate "an uneducated populace that was, at the same time, the principal resource of the society and its principal challenge" (Gordon 1992). In a very real sense, the land-grant university was "christened as an agent of social change and economic development" (Schuh 1984). These schools were designed to be centers of innovation in the service of society, just as they themselves were manifestations of societal innovativeness—or at least of the institutions charged with the governance of society. Their establishment was all the more poignant because of the historical context: the Morrill Act of 1862, which established this "service-focused" branch of the American Academy, was passed at the height of the Civil War—a monumental example of a "living struggle," if there ever was one. Inherently populist in design—with emphasis on access, opportunity, and relevance—these institutions were designed to function as a microcosm of society as well as a primary source of its transformation. Smith (1990, 62) captures their essence at their foundation:

> Different as they were in many ways, the emerging state universities shared with places like Johns Hopkins and Clark University the exhilarating sense of a great new venture. They also shared the vision of mind as being in the service of society, although they were also more practically oriented in terms of careers.

While the initial emphasis in the land-grant colleges was on education, over time two additional functions were added to the explicit missions of these institutions—problem-oriented applied-scientific research and extension/outreach. These initiatives formalized and galvanized the notion of what has been referred to as the "ideal of public university service to community and nation" (Kellogg Commission 1999). For example, the enactment of the Hatch Act in 1887 enabled the establishment of research stations at locations distant from campus; and the Smith Lever Act in 1914 allowed the university—in close cooperation with federal, state, and county agencies—to educate practical people in the "ways of science," even when they lived in remote corners of the nation. In so doing, these institutions urged everyday people to adopt science-based technologies as a means for "social improvement" and, through that work, land-grant institutions became a prominent partner in the process of "modernization."

Land-grant institutions quickly developed into socially networked institutions that were firmly connected to people and communities, especially to people without influence and to communities that heretofore had been "left behind." They stood in stark contrast to the public image of medieval universities and to the American "Ivy League" analogs of the day, which were seen as "ivory towers" operating in deliberate isolation from society. The land-grant mantra of "bringing academic scholarship to the issues of day" was reinforced by another role that American academics began to assume, that is, serving as "expert specialists" in the process of public policy making (Damrosch 1995). Adoption of this role extended the reach of the Academy's practical arm, going beyond the individual in need of advice to organizations in all sectors, including units of government at all levels.

Reframing the matter of engagement

With such a rich heritage of involvement with societal issues and cultural development, it is difficult at first blush to reconcile today's call for American higher education to be *more* engaged with society, a call that comes in a variety of hues and colors—to be a more "vigorous partner" in the resolution of "the most pressing social, civic, economic, and moral problems" (Boyer 1996); to change its fundamental mission to be more "development-focused" (Bawden, Busch, and Gagni 1991); to "reinvent itself" as a problem-focused institution (Sinnott and Johnson 1996); to "return to its roots" (Kellogg Commission 1999); and to "renegotiate its social contract with the people" (McDowell 2001). But what if one asserts that American public universities (and land-grant colleges in particular) by and large *have* retained their commitment to actively participate as agents of social change? With that reframing, the question is "not whether universities need to concern themselves with society's problems, but whether they are discharging this responsibility as well as they should" (Bok 1990). Put another way, it is not a matter of *should* they continue to participate in the affairs of the citizenry—for that moral imperative continues to exist—but rather *can* they be better at it.

As Boyer (1996, 3) queried, "[C]an America's colleges and universities, with all the richness of their resources, be of greater service to the nation and the world?" Boyer's belief was that the relatively low-level and quality of "engagement" of the Academy with the pressing problems of the day lay with the "priorities of the professoriate," which, as he saw it, is dictated by a limited view of the nature of scholarship. He argued for a broader conceptualization of it, a need to embrace with equal vigor and resolve four dimensions of inquiry—discovery, teaching, integration, and application. His essential concern was the need to re-define scholarship in ways that enable academic work to "respond more ade-quately to the urgent new realities both within the Academy and beyond." Later, he was to refer also to "the scholarship of engagement" (Boyer 1996), which he associated with the development of what he referred to as a "universe of human discourse," attributing that connection to the work of Clifford Geertz. While Boyer's untimely death prevented further elaboration of the concept through his voice, the inference was that the process of "engagement" itself—of the Acad-emy with the citizenry—deserved and demanded urgent and scholarly attention.

Purpose of this chapter

If Boyer had lived, he might have elaborated his interpretation of Geertz by making the case for a particular form of engagement—the form we address in this book—because that form is *not* reflected in the tradition of American higher education. Put more specifically, academics rarely engage *with* the citizenry in full appreciation for all the dimensions implicit in what Yankelovich (1991) re-fers to as "coming to public judgment." In the past, we have routinely brought our "expert" discourses of rationality and scientific objectivism to bear on to matters of "public concern." The point here is that more instances of expert knowledge transferred in public settings are not likely to satisfactorily address the complex realities in society. More so, it will certainly not lead to societal transformation.

While traditional and conventional connections between higher education and society have resulted in immense benefits to human well-being, it also has notable limitations. Its application creates an asymmetric relationship between academics as "expert specialists" and citizens as "passive recipients of expert knowledge." Because of these twin dynamics, society is more and more depend-ent on science and technology to "solve its problems" and expert knowledge has assumed a position of privilege—as *the* superior way of knowing and under-standing.

Accordingly, as it will be argued here, the scientific and expert discourses are singularly inadequate to address contemporary circumstances both at home and abroad. Furthermore, while there is certainly no shortage of examples of academics working in close participation with citizens in the pursuit of "better-ment," rare, indeed, are illustrations of commitment to the multi-faceted, critical, and reflexive discourses as called for in this book. Worse yet, while there is little indication of a strong commitment to rectify that situation in the Academy, there do seem to be many impediments to its actualization. The very nature of univer-sities today—including the way they are organized and governed, and the pre-vailing non-reflexive intellectual discourses—militates against reform, if not transformation.

By focusing explicitly on the institutional environment in which critical en-gagement is exercised, this chapter builds on the ideas presented in earlier chapters and also serves as a connecting rod to case examples that will be presented in Part II of this book. Special attention is given in this chapter to describing and critiquing the techno-development paradigm of modernity and, with it, the prevailing institutional epistemology in higher education. Considerable attention is then given to the "challenge of change," that is, moving beyond the confines of what has become familiar in mainstream practices. This requires a "learning turn," a notion that will be explored at chapter's end.

The challenge of change: beyond the techno-development paradigm of modernity

The involvement of land-grant universities in the development of scientific agriculture offers a rich illustration of these contentions. The claim of influence could also legitimately be extended to embrace much more inclusive issues of the use of land and other natural resources and, in an even broader context, to the nature of human relationships with the entire biophysical environment of "nature" writ large. Indeed, it can be argued with considerable justification that, from its inception, the land-grant Academy has not only represented the very essence of modernization, it has played a leadership role in the evolution of the industrial, techno-scientific epoch of modernism.

But times are changing, and herein lay the rub: Fundamental to the whole enterprise of modernity has been the acceptance by the citizenry of the logic and means of science. With that, it is assumed that people will accept in good faith not only the benefits of science-based technological innovations but that they will also put their trust in scientists whom they assume will act in their best interests. To satisfy their part of this bargain, academics have embellished and promulgated what might be called the *techno-development paradigm of modernity* and its associated techno-scientific discourse.

This paradigm displays all three characteristics that Fairclough (1992) ascribes to discourses: it helps establish social identities; enables social relationships; and contributes to "the construction of systems of knowledge and beliefs." This last dimension has had a particularly profound influence on what people believe actually constitutes "the pressing issues of the day," as well as on the most appropriate actions they take to deal with them. Essentially, it is these systems of knowledge and understandings that generally constitute the way people view the world about them which, in turn, provides the epistemic perspectives that guide their actions—whether they realize it or not. For it is *how* we see the world about us that determines, in large part, what we do in it, as well as how we do what we do.

The importance of these three characteristics in the modernist discourse—in the constitution and social structure of the state, as well as a determinant of people/environment inter-relationships within it—cannot be overestimated. In essence, they represent what might be seen as the expressions of the "paradigms-of-the-everyday" and the reflections of the life-world of citizens. They exemplify, just as they profoundly influence, the manner by which people live their everyday lives in response to those features of it that they regard as demanding of their attention. They also provide a central focus for diagnosing what might be done to facilitate the next generation of cultural change or transformation associated with the challenges of what has been referred to by Beck (1992) as the "risk society." In the risk society, the march of modernization not only leads to the globalization of the flow of intentionally traded "goods," but also produces the unintentional and global circulation of "bads," that is, the undesirable side effects of industrial production. As Beck avers:

> With the advent of risk society, the distributional conflicts over 'goods' (income, jobs, social security) which constituted the basic conflict of classical industrial society and led to attempted solutions in the relevant institutions, are covered over by the distributional conflicts over the 'bads.'(Beck 1994, 6)

The challenges of the new, emergent phase of modernity, therefore, must include concerns for the very process of modernization itself, including its dominant discourse; and that has truly transnational dimensions in an era of globalization, in which the focus of issues increasingly transcends those of individual nation states and national cultures.

Readings (1996) presents a provocative thesis with respect to the impact that the decline of the nation state is having on the Academy, which has, as he suggests, the potential to leave "the university in ruins." He argues that because the Academy has spent the past 100 years or so serving the nation-state through the promotion and protection of the national culture, the demise of the latter will see redundancy for the former. He also provides further historical context to university/state relationships—to the evolution of national culture and also to the nature of the discourse that has developed in consequence—which he traces back to the influence of the German Idealists at the beginning of the nineteenth century. Readings is particularly impressed by the vision of Wilhelm von Humboldt with his focus on the role of the Academy in the development of national culture, and Readings recognizes this as a vital influence on the development of the American Academy. Humboldt, as the rector of the University of Berlin, argued that the social mission of the university was neither thought nor action, but rather *thought as action*. Under his plan, the university would become much more than either a site for contemplation or a center for abstract thought disengaged from the issues of the day. It would become an *active agent in the cultural transformation of the nation state*. With this momentum established, the university would become "the primary institution of national culture in the modern state." In Readings' interpretation, state and university would become inextricably interconnected and mutually engaged with the affairs of each other. He elaborates:

> The university seeks to embody thought as action toward an ideal; the state must seek to realize action as thought, the idea of a nation. The state protects

the action of the University; the University safeguards the thought of the state. And each strives to realize the idea of a national culture. (1996, 69)

There are, of course, those who have argued for the opposite—that the Academy should be as remote from society and its "ills" as it possibly can be. This was certainly the view espoused by an English contemporary of Humboldt, namely, John (Cardinal) Newman. His "idea of the university" was "a place detached from society, uncontaminated by its worldly values, and undistracted by pursuits other than the search for greater knowledge and understanding" (Bok 1990). And there is no doubt that there are some in the contemporary Academy who continue to commit to such an ideology.

The call for a "scholarship of engagement" then, (Boyer 1996) can be interpreted as a focus on intellectual activity that is essentially oriented to public judgment and social action. In this context, *engagement with* equates to *participation in* a "universe of human discourse" which appreciates, embraces, and reflects the wide range of different "ways of knowing and valuing" that includes different aspirations, internationalities, and epistemologies that are activated and energized in the process of coming to public judgment. It is thus a call for profound transformation of a culture where all too often, "like blacksmiths, cowboys, and bookstore proprietors, university scholars tend to be in society but not really part of it" (Keller 1983, 34). And this suggests not just a reluctance to heed societal calls for change, but perhaps also an impotence and/or reluctance by those within the Academy to *really* engage with the citizenry in a manner that extends beyond the conventions of the present and the past.

Critical engagement

It is not that the Academy is disengaged from the issues of the day. Historically, academics have engaged with the issues of the day in their own ways—tackling problems that have been identified and approached from perspectives that reflect the particular world views and rationalities of the techno-sciences as, indeed, they continue to do so today. However, examples of engagement in issues with the citizenry in ways that appreciate, encourage, and facilitate the emergence of new rationalities and critical discourses are much more difficult to cite. Accordingly, the Academy is seen by the citizenry all too often as being "out of touch and out of date" (Kellogg Commission 1999).

The establishment of non-inclusive partnerships between universities and other institutions (including corporations in the private sector) also represent potential impediments to coupling with the broader community because the obligations inherent are not always perceived as being in the public interest. At issue here is the integrity of the institution of Academia as a whole, which compounds matters that pertain to trust in the integrity of scientists, as well as with the credibility of science and technology. Even where significant connections do exist between the Academy and the citizenry, the quality and nature of the relationships of the engagement are all too often distorted by a power divide that reflects differences between expert and lay knowledge. As Habermas (1979) has emphasized, there is the matter of the interests, intentions, and dispositions of those involved in any communal relationships. Well-being is sought for its own sake or leads to informed consensual action and desirable situational transformation.

To be critical in this complex situation, then, is to be concurrently concerned about

- knowledge-based power relationships between "experts" and the "lay citizenry"
- conflicts built into the very structure of society
- the "boundaries" of societal issues and how these come to be established
- the cultivation of emancipatory interests in the process of change, and
- the nature and significance of diverse processes of knowing and forms of knowledge.

Attempts to truly engage within such a context, then, call for critical scholarship in all of its diversity and with particular regard to the quality of the relationship between academics and the citizenry.

Regrettably, while the theme of multiple aspects of scholarship has been pursued with some vigor since Boyer first introduced the concept, the focus of concern all too frequently has been what might be termed "academy-centered" and instrumental. For example, in an attempt to bolster a broader conception of scholarship, Glassick and his colleagues at the Carnegie Foundation have paid considerable attention to the articulation of standards "that can be applied to each kind of scholarly work, that can organize the documentation of scholarly accomplishments, and can also guide a trustworthy process of faculty evaluation" (Glassick, Huber, and Maeroff 1997, 5).

While there is little doubt that incentives for faculty play an important function in constraining engagement by the Academy, there is much more to the situation than that. First, there are a number of relatively instrumental organizational and structural matters of the Academy. These matters reflect and influence the internal cultures of universities in ways that are antithetical to engagement— and this includes prevailing interpretations of the nature of the pedagogical processes of education, as well as the characteristic conventions of research and "extension." Second, there are concerns associated with the nature of the contemporary problematique and the role of techno-science and technical control as amplifiers of it. Put simply, society faces challenges that require new ways of thinking and approaches—more and better application of past approaches will not always work. And, third, there are issues to do with the nature of the paradigms and perspectives that prevail within different epistemic communities, both within and beyond the Academy. These world views represent significant impediments to a universe of human discourse and, overall, to the maintenance and sustained development of extramural participatory relationships. For one thing, prevailing academic discourses often dismiss and view as inferior other frameworks of knowing and understanding.

The organization and conventions of the academy

In general terms, there is still a strong espousal of the classical trinity of functions—of teaching, research, and public service—as the stated missions of the Academy. Having said that, there is a tendency—especially within universities—for research as scholarship to dominate the academic landscape. In ruing this tendency, Smith (1990) opines that such work is all too frequently "mediocre, expensive, and unnecessary," which serves not to "push back the frontiers of knowledge" but only "to get professors promoted." While this clearly overstates the situation and undervalues the contributions that researchers make to society, a primary emphasis on research does significantly influence the way that universities are organized, the mission they perform, and, to a very significant degree, the characteristics of the culture that they self-nurture.

This drift *to* discovery has not only meant a drift *away* from involvement in relationships with extramural communities (save where they function as a source of research subjects), it has also resulted in a profound change in the relational aspects of life and work within the Academy itself. Kerr (1982) is among those who believe that faculty have become noticeably more self-preoccupied and less committed to the common good. The consequent loss of focus on citizenship amounts to what he sees as an "ethical disintegration within the Academy." This results in what Bennett (1998) refers to as "insistent individualism" as a prevailing ethos, which is expressed as an internal culture increasingly characterized by "competition and isolation" with the inevitable "diminishment of intellectual community." So not only are faculty losing connections with those in their extramural communities, they are also losing connection with each other, not just through the "insistent individualism" induced by competition, but also through the specific characteristics of the particular epistemic cultures in which they find themselves: "Those amalgams of arrangements and mechanisms—bonded through affinity, necessity and historical coincidence—which, in a given field, make up *how we know what we know*" (Knorr Cetina 1999, 1). The Academy has become characterized not by a single culture or epistemic community, but by a multitude of them with few opportunities for integration, and this is especially so where discipline-based research and academic specialization within the curriculum are privileged over other activities. While epistemic communities are plentiful, the reductionist/objectivist paradigm of scientific research continues to colonize academia.

Another outcome of the increasing primacy of research within the Academy is that researchers turn increasingly to non-traditional and often corporate sources for research funds and contracts. With that, the university starts to assume characteristics of an industrial organization. In this manner, "the university and segments of industry are becoming more and more alike" (Kerr 1982) with concomitant risks to the integrity and independence of the Academy, and to its role in the service of the public. Readings (1996) goes so far as to suggest that universities are actually *becoming* transnational corporations.

With these changes in focus, emphasis, and prevailing discourse, the mission of the Academy in general is becoming increasingly unclear and, thus, demanding of urgent attention. As Readings (1996, 2) suggests, "[i]t is no longer clear what the role of the university is within society nor what the exact nature of that society is, and the changing institutional form of the university is something that intellectuals cannot afford to ignore." This loss of clarity of mission is particularly evident in the land-grant universities where there is clear public perception that these institutions are not well organized to bring the resources and expertise available on their campuses "to bear on local problems in a coherent way" (Kellogg Commission 1999). Accordingly, there is a strong sense—from at least some within the institutions themselves—that land-grant universities "have lost their way" (Schuh 1984).

The industrialization of the Academy produces other regrettable outcomes, including fragmented and atomistic organizational structures (the disciplinary "silos"); an emphasis on hierarchical and administrative control; and contests about the ownership of intellectual property. At risk is the very issue of academic freedom and the potential loss of hard-won principles and practices of democratic governance. The erosion of institutional democracy *in* the Academy is a particularly damning blow at a time when concerns are being voiced about the erosion of the ability of the "American public to participate in political decisions that affect their lives" (Yankelovich 1991). If fateful decisions are being made "in Washington, in corporate boardrooms, on Wall Street, in state legislatures, and in city halls" as Yankelovich claims, with the loss of democracy in the Academy an important question is: "Who will encourage public judgment and the exercise of self-governance that are central aspects of democracies?"

There is further irony, and indeed tragedy in this regard. Giddens (1991) argues that individuals within society have come to rely on knowledge and information generated by specialists, which they routinely interpret and act upon as they live their everyday lives. But experts do not always agree on matters of mutual interest, which often leaves citizens in the position of not knowing whom to believe. This circumstance is exacerbated when experts are hired by advocates who support a particular position. Consequently, "to engage" all too often means "to invite conflict" between and among contesting groups. As Yankelovich (1991) observes, over the years the nature of the relationship between experts and public "has grown adversarial rather than mutually supportive," with the progressive development of a very significant "gap that separates the public from the experts." The distance between the world of expert policy making and the world of public opinion is growing ever greater, and the result includes a continuing decline in the quality of public participation in their own affairs and the erosion of self-governance.

Yankelovich is certainly not alone in expressing concerns about the expert/lay divide, particularly with respect to specialist knowledge and the potentially distorting impact on governance. As is becoming increasingly obvious to anyone involved with the domain of environmental and technology public policy, for instance, the entire matter of the "possibility of participatory democracy" in a world of technical and social complexities depends upon the generation of a practical discourse that involves appreciation of the connections between the technical data of scientists, "and the particular social situation, the societal system, and the way of life" (Fischer 2005, 65). There are, it is claimed (Plough and Krimsky 1987), two often opposing rationalities involved here, a *technical rationality* that emphasizes "logical consistency and universality of findings" and a *cultural discourse* that privileges "personal and familiar experiences rather than depersonalized technical data." Defining lay resistance to scientific expert opinion as ignorance or irrationality understandably alienates the public even further and also reinforces "tacit public ambivalence about being dependent upon social actors (experts) who engender such alienation, and social control" (Wynne 1996, 68).

Fuller (1988) applies a vital epistemological perspective to issues pertaining to the expert/lay knowledge divide, including what he refers to as the "problem of cognitive authoritarianism." His explorations into the "lures and avoidance" of this phenomenon reveal some of the paradoxes in situations when the "layman" refuses to defer to the "expert" even when this is apparently justified, and alternatively, does defer under circumstances where it is clearly not warranted. There are, he suggests, rational epistemological explanations behind these apparent irrationalities that provide not only explanations for them, but also provide "considerations against adopting a general policy of deferring to the authority of experts." Issues of significance here include differences between the epistemic goals of the layman and the expert; lay perceptions about the reliability of expert knowledge and the epistemic significance of reliability thresholds; and differences in the context for which knowledge is being sought.

With the danger of "cognitive authoritarianism" ever-present, we in the Academy all too often find ourselves caught in a paradoxical and unhealthy double bind: "at once imagining ourselves as alienated exiles from society at large and yet also continually trying to recreate society in our image" (Damrosch 1995). This leads to the situation where the university "persistently embodies a profound ambivalence toward society," reproducing many of the organizational and cultural features of society which, at the same time, "it most wishes to oppose."

It can be argued that the opposite situation is not only equally true but also equally problematic for the Academy and civil society alike. While the trend in the Academy is the ever-greater disciplinary fragmentation and associated epistemic isolation of specialists (with its concomitant loss of community and collegiality), the trend in society is for greater communal collaboration as society faces ever-more complex risks and hazards. These challenges demand collective, consensual action in an era of sustainable development or, perhaps better stated, within a developmental ethos of "sustainabilism" (Bawden 1997). There are no simple answers and even the questions are elusive. Indeed, as some see it, one of the great strengths of the emerging concern for sustainability is that it gives rise to an agenda of good, practical, and essentially normative questions that evoke responses that are inevitably contestable. This demands "not categorical certainty, but the capacity to articulate what we feel to be most worthy of being sustained in our lives" (Davison 2001, 213). This circumstance brings into question the very essence of modernity and the processes of modernization.

Reflexive modernization and the contemporary problematique

A growing preoccupation with risk and hazard is seen to now characterize the emergence of a new modernity—a *risk society*—the entry into which "occurs at the moment when the hazards, which are now decided and consequently produced by society, *undermine and/or cancel the established safety systems of the provident existing state's risk calculations*" (Beck 1996–emphasis in the original). A major contributor to this emerging epoch has been the unintended, but nonetheless, ubiquitous side effects of industrial production: the unanticipated negative consequences of actions that were designed to be beneficial.

Technological modernization has rarely been without its degrading consequences, and the paradox is that much of the risk that this represents to the citizenry can only be identified by the very techno-scientific expertise that was in many ways responsible for its occurrence in the first place. Meanwhile, that same techno-science is limited in its response to such situations by its own logic and paradigmatic limitations. This demands that the agenda of technical development must change, as Beck asserts:

> We are concerned no longer exclusively with making nature useful, or with releasing mankind from traditional constraints, but also and essentially with problems of techno-development itself. Modernization is itself becoming reflexive; it is becoming its own theme. (Beck 1992, 19)

By "reflexive" Beck means a stance that is self-*referential* and critically self-*confrontational* which, as he is at pains to emphasize, must address the consequences "of risk society which cannot (adequately) be addressed and overcome in the system of industrial society that is measured by industrial society's own industrialized standards" (Beck 1996, 28). To many, this shift towards reflexivity is a reaction to growing skepticism that experts are generally insensitive to the consequences of innovations and slow to respond to concerns when the extent of hazards are revealed. By their very nature, however, the issues that attract attention are essentially non-amenable because of their sheer complexity, multi-dimensionality, and unpredictability to the classical approaches of techno-science. Typically, they are neither limited in time or place nor are they accountable according to the established rules of causality (Beck 1996). But, of course, this does not silence the critics of those institutions that are perceived to be those that should be responsive—including, and especially, the Academy—or does it excuse their lack of responsiveness.

Of particular significance here, given its heritage of a philosophy of pragmatism, is the apparent lack of concern within the techno-scientific discourse about the consequences of actions. As Dewey asserted, an essential difference between pragmatism and the historical empiricism from which it was extended was that "it does not insist upon antecedent phenomena but on consequent phenomena; not upon the precedents but upon the possibilities for action" (Dewey 1922, 50).

To respond adequately, then (as the argument goes) the Academy must, too, become more self-reflexive and confrontational because it is a partner in the techno-science project. An example with respect to the land-grant universities is apposite: such has been the level of complaint at the lack of responsiveness regarding negative social and environmental impacts of agricultural technologies. The concerns have reached a veritable "Greek chorus of criticism," according to Bonnen (1983) and include the extrusion of smaller family farms from agriculture; environmental degradation; animal welfare; impacts on the health and safety of farmers, agricultural workers, and consumers; adverse nutritional effects of production and processing technologies; the decline of rural communities and the concentration of agricultural production and economic wealth; and commercial exploitation of fragile lands that should not be in cultivation.

While there have been significant and commendable attempts within land-grant universities to address many of the issues of the risk society—often in concert with citizen stakeholders and under a rubric of sustainability or sustainable development—it would be true to conclude that the general state of the system is generally the same. Moreover, with the passage of time since the "Bonnen critique," a number of highly contentious and systemic issues have been added to the agenda. These include the globalization of what might be referred to as national agri-food systems, as well as the emergence of a new generation of bio-technologies whose significance is greatly amplified by both their global reach and the global penetration of transnational agro-industries. The development of these bio-technologies, which typically involve the use of genetically modified organisms (GMOs), finds strong support among many who are involved in agriculture, both within and beyond the Academy. Yet, to the concern of many others, there are potential risks. Theoretically, transgenic technologies can revolutionize agriculture and transform the agri-food industry because bio-engineered crop plants can be endowed with resistance to pests and pathogens; tailored with dietary nutrient or pharmaceutical profiles; and grown with reduced reliance on material inputs, such as fertilizer and water. An equally impressive range of possibilities applies to the case of livestock animals.

Notwithstanding these advantages, grave concerns persist about the potential risks inherent in technologies based on "altered genes" (Hindmarsh and Lawrence 2001). The spectrum of the concerns is broad and eclectic, ranging from concerns about impacts of bio-engineered food on human health; threats to the diversity of life forms; and intrusion into the entire nature of nature as we now know it. "Genetic engineering confronts us with a new medium by which to imagine a future nature, one very different to the nature we have known for millennia" write Hindmarsh and Lawrence (11). Here, then, we have a novel situation—with "culture" suddenly assuming the ability to transform "nature" using technologies, most especially those of recombinant DNA (rDNA), which themselves represent culturally-transformed nature. The attendant advantages and risks reinforce the pressing need to reestablish the "broken circle of ecology, economics, and ethics" (Bormann and Kellert 1991).

The challenges here are profoundly systemic, both in the sense of being globally pervasive and by the complex and often dynamically unpredictable interconnections between the whole of culture and the whole of nature. A further aspect of these biotechnologies is that many of the concerns are prospective rather than retrospective; and there are appeals to the Academy to contribute constructively to debates that are, in large part, conjectural. This represents a very significant issue, for as Yankelovich (1991) has claimed, there are all too few contemporary institutions devoted to helping the public form considered judgments.

Indeed, all of these matters bring into stark relief the truly global scale of the challenges and risks of technological modernization, as well as the interconnectedness across different domains of human endeavor. What happens in agriculture not only mirrors the universal impacts of industrialization, but plays a very significant amplifying effect within it. Agrarian and industrial life are essentially inseparable; changes in agriculture are rarely, if ever, isolated from other aspects of either the general socio-cultural or bio-physical environments in which they are embedded.

The agricultural example provides poignant reinforcement of the broad claim that

> . . . the transformation of the unseen side-effects of industrial production into global ecological trouble spots is therefore not at all a problem of the world surrounding us—not the so-called 'environmental problem'—but a far reaching institutional crisis of industrial society itself. (Beck 1996, 32)

An important point to be reinforced here is that this crisis transcends national borders, which adds enormously to the complexity of the situation. Witness the case of global climate change and the complex interconnections between the use of hydrocarbon fuels by individuals as they go about their daily lives and the impact that fuel emissions have on the accumulation of the greenhouse gases. What happens locally has the potential to seriously impact globally and vice versa. This reality raises exceptionally difficult challenges with respect to making informed judgments across the entire spectrum, from the individual level to global institutions.

As these examples illustrate, the great majority of the most pressing problems in today's society are indeed amazingly complex and multidisciplinary. Latour (1993, 2) refers to them as "hybrids" that represent lived experiences of "mixed-up affairs." Such is the level of this mixing that "all of culture and all of nature get churned up again every day" in stark contrast to the situation within the Academy where culture and nature are conventionally held apart as profoundly different intellectual domains. The university, with its "silo-ed" compartmentalization of disciplines and distinct epistemic cultures, is not well positioned to deal with hybrid issues and is not always able to respond sensibly to concerns expressed by the citizenry about them. These are systemic matters that demand connections between and across disciplines. In addition, these complex and hybrid issues demand, if not deserve, forms of action-focused inquiry that are systemic, deliberative, democratic, and sustainable. That sort of response is itself an individual/socio-cultural "hybrid," blending complex aspects of human nature (including primal survival instincts and reflexes) with moral values to do with "good" and "bad"; with "rights" and "wrongs"; with aesthetic and spiritual beliefs that distinguish the sacred from the profane; and with onto-epistemological beliefs about the "nature of nature," the nature of knowing, the nature of emotions, and so on. Individuals are influen*ced* in the manner of the expression of these characteristics and by the socio-cultural environment in which they are embedded, just as they are capable—under particular circumstances—of themselves influen*cing* that environment.

While there is clear evidence that multi-disciplinary and inter-disciplinary approaches are on the increase in the Academy, there is also clear evidence that many of these initiatives are "prisoners" of a dominant reductionist/objectivist paradigm that privileges scientific inquiry over all other ways of knowing and scientific knowledge over all other forms of knowledge: What is needed is a type of systemic inquiry that enables the quest for "systemic betterment," an approach that inevitably involves aspects of both intellectual and moral development (Bawden 1995). The challenges to transformation, then, are fundamentally paradigmatic. As Grove-White (1996, 221) has asserted about modern environmentalism, it has evolved "not simply in response to damaging impacts of specific industrial and social practices, but also, more fundamentally as a social expression of cultural tensions surrounding the underlying ontologies and epistemologies which have led to such trajectories in modern societies."

The hegemony of the dominant paradigm

As Kuhn (1962) defined them, paradigms are "constellations of beliefs, values, techniques and so on, shared by the members of a given community." They can be formally characterized by reference to the key criteria of epistemology, ontology, methodology, and human nature (Burrell and Morgan 1979) or axiology (Guba and Lincoln 1994). Paradigms are held and expressed collectively by groups of people who, following Wenger's logic (1998), might be termed communities of practice; or borrowing from Norgaard (1989), would be seen as "epistemic communities."

Whatever the label, members act in ways that reflect and reinforce shared assumptions and values, based on ways they see and experience the world— their "life-worlds," as it were. While members rarely critique and reflect on the nature of these profoundly held philosophical positions, they do often embrace their positions with ferocious loyalty, such that any changes in them are tantamount, as Kuhn portrayed it, to "revolutions." That said, paradigmatic revolutions do occur from time to time, triggered by the recognition that prevailing worldviews are inadequate in the face of what appear to be anomalies that somehow violate "paradigm-induced expectations." Kuhn's concern and focus was science itself, and as he presented it:

> Scientific revolutions are inaugurated by a growing sense . . . often restricted to a narrow subdivision of the scientific community, that an existing paradigm has ceased to function adequately in the exploration of an aspect of nature to which that paradigm had previously held sway—the sense of malfunction that can lead to crises is prerequisite to revolution. (Kuhn 1962, 92)

Characteristic of such crises is that which manifests itself in the ontological/ epistemological tensions that lie between objectivism and contextual relativism—with the former representing the classical position within normal science and the latter threatening to usurp that position. Further exacerbating the tensions are growing doubts about the whole matter of the foundational beliefs about the nature of nature *and* the nature of knowledge about it. As Bernstein (1983, 19) opines:

> [T]he primary reason why the *agōn* between objectivists and relativists has become so intense today is the growing apprehension that there may be nothing— not God, reason, philosophy, science, or poetry—that answers to and satisfies our longing for ultimate constraints, for a stable rock upon which we can secure our thought and action.

But for all that, paradigmatic changes have occurred within science—often with the new and the old persisting incommensurably side-by-side—but at considerable distance from, and invariably in energetic opposition to, each other.

To extend the paradigmatic concept beyond science, we can generalize that any particular collective of people therefore can, and sometimes will, change the worldview that has previously prevailed. And this, in turn, can and sometimes does lead to changes in the way things are done collectively. What this means is that communities of practice, or epistemic communities, can assume fresh and new ontological/epistemological/axiological positions which, in turn, support the adoption of fresh and new methodological practices. However, such shifts will certainly not be without angst and typically include episodes of individual transformation and public displays of paradigmatic disagreement.

Actually the notion of *communities of praxis* is perhaps a more appropriate focus than either communities of practice or epistemic communities. The notion of informed practical action implicit in praxis is *intentional, informed, reflective action as a dialectical way of being in the world.* This way of thinking transcends the mere application of "science to technical tasks," which as Gadamer (1975) argues, "degrades practical reason to technical control." Freire (2003, 66) captures well the dialectic nature of reflection and action as praxis when he posits that

> The insistence that the oppressed engage in reflection on their concrete situation is not a call for an armchair revolution. On the contrary, reflection—true reflection—leads to action. On the other hand, when the situation calls for action, that action will constitute an authentic praxis only if its consequences become the object of critical reflection.

Jurgen Habermas has written extensively on matters that are pivotal to understanding the nature of praxis; of its significance to democracy; and to discourse related to the consensual judgment upon which it depends. One of his provocative observations is that knowledge is always linked to purpose. Because of that, we need a *variety* of different ways of knowing so that *multiple and different* purposes can be accommodated. Initially, he described three categories of knowledge that reflected what he saw as three different forms of knowing and reason—the *technical* that concerns itself with empirical scientific knowing about the natural world; the *practical* that is associated with clarifying the "inter-subjective understanding" associated with the motives, character, and world-views of people; and the *emancipatory* that focused on freeing people from prejudice, ideology, and most significantly, mental coercion (Habermas 1971). After reorienting his ideas from the purpose of knowing and knowledge, and also to notions concerning language and consensual action, he later synthesized these three categories into two—*instrumental rationality* and *communicative action* (Habermas 1984). From an initial concern with the individual searching to understand the world of nature, Habermas shifted his starting point from

> . . . the solitary individual in his own interior subjectivity and searching for reliable ways to have knowledge of the outside world, the starting point is the social act of language, the dialogue of people attempting through language to communicate with one another to achieve mutual understanding (Yankelovich 1991, 218) and consensual action.

In the end, as Habermas has recently argued, it comes down to common sense, which

> . . . being full of illusions about the world needs to be informed the sciences. The scientific theories that intrude upon the lifeworld however, do not essentially touch on the *framework* of our everyday knowledge, which is linked to the self-understanding of speakers and actors. (Habermas 2003, 105)

This search for "informed common sense" should be the objective of the quest for public judgment. With that, it represents a noble goal for engagement with the citizens as they seek responsible actions for dealing with the pressing, systemic, and hybrid issues of the day.

The separation of knowledge and ways of knowing draws attention to a second aspect of the dominant techno-scientific paradigm, namely, reductionism, which is certainly of equal paradigmatic significance to the objectivism that continues to prevail. The foundations of reductionism can be ascribed to Descartes who, with the second and third of his four rules of logic, posited the need "to divide each problem or difficulty into as many parts as possible" and to "commence my reflections with objects which were the simplest and easiest to understand, and rise thence, little by little, to knowledge of the most complex" (Bronowski and Mazlish 1960, 220). He was also, of course, the source of the separation of "mind from matter," the "Cartesian split" as it is known. This "split" has been associated (justifiably or otherwise) with so many different "divides," including nature from culture; the objective from the subjective; the empirical from the normative; science from ethics; and rationality from emotions. It is divides like these that pose potent barriers to dealing with Latour's "hybrid issues" and also reinforce the need for a synthesis of ways of knowing which, by design, are intended to "get beyond the dichotomies" and contribute to situation improvement within complex problematiques.

The challenge of change here should not be underestimated, for these again are nothing less than paradigmatic matters: positional shifts are only achieved after considerable resistance and, then, are rarely complete in the sense of universal adoption. Indeed, by definition, universality is undesirable. What is sought in a world of multi-dimensional issues is a multiplicity of perspectives and practices, which is a "mature" way of engaging.

As Churchman (1971) sees it, maturity is a function of the *ability of individuals to hold different worldview perspectives at one and the same time.* Maturity, as we see it, is a requirement for dealing with problematic situations because it demands appreciation for the benefits of *paradigmatic pluralism,* a step toward moving "beyond the divides," as Bernstein (1983) put it. He cites the "Cartesian Anxiety" that is sometimes expressed as a function of the paradigmatic clash between objectivism and relativism, which he argues is "misleading and distortive":

> It is itself parasitic upon an acceptance of the Cartesian persuasion that needs to be questioned, exposed and overcome. We need to *exorcise* the Cartesian Anxiety and liberate ourselves from its seductive appeal. (Bernstein 1983, 19)

Bernstein goes on to support the appeals of Habermas, and others, to view knowledge and action from perspectives beyond those of conventional paradigms. Yet, in a somewhat paradoxical way, Habermas is himself guilty of persisting with the Cartesian divide between nature and culture. In the face of circumstances where nature and culture not only get "churned up everyday" but also become increasingly embedded within each other, they are essentially impossible to sensibly separate. Communicative action has as its purpose the search for *mutual, rational understanding*—a means to realize common goals that embrace the values, intuitions, and assumptions that concern a culture. On the other hand, instrumental rationality—with its objectivist, scientific foundations—has as its fundamental purpose understanding nature as the basis for its control. In public dialogue, the latter discourse is likely to singularly distort the former, and thus assure the maintenance of the hegemony of technical control and the objectivist/reductionist paradigm.

A good example of this dilemma is the public debate around the intentions, processes, and outcomes of bio-technologies in agriculture. These debates illustrate the expert–lay divide as expressed in the growing loss of trust by the public in the expertise of the specialists. In the first place, instrumental rationality, upon which the public has been so reliant, is clearly beginning to show its inadequacies. It is becoming increasingly obvious, for instance, that

> [B]iotechnology is not just a scientific issue, raising questions of interest only to scientists. It is a subject capable of generating considerable controversy and has the potential to throw up a host of what are often referred to as 'moral and ethical concerns,' about which it seems difficult if not impossible to reach any substantial degree of consensus. (Straughan 1995, 163)

Furthermore, technologies such as recombinant DNA present potential risks that are virtually incalculable currently and may ultimately prove to be essentially unknowable.

At the heart of the issue lie concerns about the risks to safety that bio-engineered agriculture represents to the consumer of its products; to the users of the field applications; to the general citizenry; and to the environment at large. As illustrated by different perspectives on safety, there are two matters of concern: first, the probability of an insult or injury as a consequence of an action or practice; and second, the feeling of confidence or a sense of well-being regarding one's situation, activities, and outlook (Thompson 1998). As Sandman (1992) puts it, risk is a function both of hazard (that is, the probability of insult and/or injury) and outrage (that is, the challenge to the sense of well-being). Where instrumental rationality is entirely appropriate for dealing with the former, it is inappropriate for dealing with the latter. Indeed, outrage can be easily fueled under circumstances where this distinction is lost. A lack of public trust in existing techno-scientific rationality is perfectly justified under circumstances where "moral judgment has seemingly been eliminated from prevailing concepts of rationality as far as they are actually manifest in the scientific and systems paradigms that currently prevail" (Ulrich 1988).

Within science, and hence within the prevailing techno-scientific discourse of modernization, the normative has been overwhelmed by the empirical, triggering calls for profound changes in paradigmatic emphasis within the Academy. As Wilshire (1990, 80) submits, "We have powerful means of altering the earth and ourselves, but only a fix on goodness could give our means their aim, support, and meaning." Bio-technological interventions provide substance to the call for "fixes on goodness." The embrace of moral judgments thus becomes an imperative for a paradigmatic reform within science itself—marked by a synthesis of the normative with the empirical as two different but complementary "cognitive interests" into what has been referred to as a "systems science" (Alrøe and Kristensen 2002).

Discourse and judgment

Where scientific discourse has an essential role to play in the establishment of the probabilities of risk associated with, say, the use of rDNA technologies in the production and processing of food products from agriculture, it is to *moral discourse* to which we must turn if we are to explore the ethical implications of their use. These are difficult and complex challenges. In addition to ethical concerns about the potential harmful consequences of such technologies on a wide range of stakeholders (including nature itself), there also is the matter of the rights and privileges of an equally broad spectrum of characters (again including nature itself). Recent initiatives by the Danish government illustrate this complexity associated with developing a code of practice that is based on the four ethical principles of autonomy, dignity, integrity, and vulnerability (Kemp 2000). While it is not overly difficult to accord these four features to a policy that applies to human beings, it is much more conjectural to apply them to other living beings and to nature as a whole.

This matter provides another powerful illustration of the interdependencies between agriculture and the rest of society:

> Moral discourse is essential to agriculture insofar as people's willingness to recognize morally valid rights, privileges, and constraints shapes agricultural practices, and agriculture is essential to moral discourse to the extent that practices for producing and consuming food are sources of conflict, interest, and loyalty. (Thompson 1998, 204)

A potential source of conflict is the increasing involvement by the Academy in bio-technological research and development, an act that is often undertaken with corporate interests and with considerable financial interests at stake. This activity can diminish the integrity and dignity of the Academy, while at the same time it can increase the prospects of public scrutiny. With respect to community engagement, this is a source of conflict between private gain and public good because the issues of truth, trust, and integrity are matters of concern. There can be instances when the authority of expert knowledge is greatly dented, not just by assurances from different expert sources of different facts of the matter, but also by the misrepresentation of factual reports from some experts.

A cogent illustration of the latter is provided by Jones (2000) in his searching review of the machinations of a public hearing instituted by the Canadian government. The focus of attention is the application by a transnational corporation to import a product of recombinant technology (Bovine Somatotrophin rBST) for use in the dairy industry, a product that is freely available commercially in the United States. The spectrum of issues invoked in this case range from concerns about human health, animal health, and environmental residues; through to the concentration of wealth; and on to the differential distribution of economic gains.

The hearings were characterized by conflicting responses to a host of different issues of concern from different, yet appropriately qualified, professionals. Each claim about benefit, safety, or ecological benignity made by expert specialists was met by a counter claim offered by an equally qualified specialist. Such differences in the "truth" were seriously disturbing to many involved in the hearings and beyond. In addition, certain evidence was suppressed by several professional scientists, who were less than honest about what they knew about the nature and scale of the risks involved with the importation of rBST into Canada.

The apparent inability of the specialists to agree about the potential risks to people and nature, alike, was further exacerbated by concerns about the truthfulness and integrity of the specialists who provided evidence though their "expert" submissions. Implicitly, all four of the claims for validity that Habermas (1979) attaches to communicative action were invoked and, indeed, could be shown to have been violated: (1) much of what was said was *not mutually comprehensible;* (2) with such differences in the dispositions, some of what was said was clearly *not empirically true* or at least not accurate; (3) some of those who testified were *less than truthful* and thus morally suspect; and (4) some of what was said was *not stated sincerely.*

As the hearings progressed, it was little wonder that public outrage increased and that response inflicted considerable damage on the reputations of many "expert specialists." By extension, the episode invoked doubts about the trustworthiness of the entire techno-scientific enterprise and its foundational paradigm.

Citing the circumstances of potential hazard and potent outrage, the Canadian government—acting both as the guardian of public interest and as the essential decision maker—rejected the application; enacted legislation that disallowed the importation of the particular product in question; and placed a five-year ban on the importation of any commercial product that was an analog of it.

While highly specific in nature, this particular bio-technological case reflects the key elements of the contemporary problematique, in general, and illustrates the nature of the discourses that increasingly prevails around it. The issue was certainly hybrid and systemic in its character; as well as complex in the sense of the multi-dimensionality—both of the matter itself (with "nature and culture truly churned up") and of the interests of various stakeholders. It was also characterized by a number of different and asymmetric discourses that were grounded in different validity claims. Furthermore, the case aroused considerable public passions with respect to matters of ethics, aesthetics, and economics.

An orientation to potential future risks set within a broad global objective is becoming an increasingly significant facet of the new modernity. This interest is well expressed in the discourse on environmental sustainability and development. Consider, for example, the most commonly accepted definition of sustainable development as drawn from the report of the First International World Commission on Environment and Development (Brundtland 1987): "Development that meets the needs of today without compromising the needs of tomorrow."

The Canadian rBST "bio-technological case" might also seem somewhat unusual in that a single decision maker, in the form of the government, could be clearly identified. Yet this, too, represents a realization of reflexive modernization: it is increasingly apparent that aspects of the modern problematic have global implications and that clearly includes the potential environmental impacts of modern technologies and the corresponding "call for decisive political interventions" (Hajer 1996). This is not to say that governments, or other institutions of governance, always act in the citizen's best interests when faced with potential risks to public safety—even when they apparently act to facilitate the necessary interactions between the discourses of experts and lay citizenry. There is much to understand yet about the necessary synthesis between the empirical and the normative, and how it might be achieved. However, it would seem that of all social institutions the Academy is best positioned to take the lead in addressing epistemic challenges. But if that is to happen routinely, there is another challenge to be met: institutional transformation. As Wynne (1996) asserts, the modern project has brought us to the point where there are "crises of legitimacy of modern economic, scientific-technical, and political institutions." The new modernity thus requires the Academy to change at the most essential level.

Consideration of the Canadian example allows the identification of the key elements that characterize what ought to be present at the *engagement interface* (Fear et al. 2001) with the citizenry, the Academy, and other socio-cultural institutions *if* such fundamental transformations are to be achieved. Six such characteristics suggest themselves:

1. a *cast of appropriate stakeholders* that includes citizens, experts, decisions makers, witnesses, actors or enabling agents
2. a *clear indication of the objectives being pursued* in the name of improvements
3. an *articulation of the worldviews* that provide the support for the objectives as improvements
4. a *critical discourse* that is minimally distorted by the influence of power and where claims to validity are transparent and intrinsic

5. an *appreciation of the nature and dynamics of the environmental conditions that surround the situation*—both natural and cultural

6. some understanding of the *range of such environmental conditions that can be considered plausible in the future*

As we envisage it, the engagement interface is most essentially a milieu for transformative learning. And the only sensible way to deal with the modern problematic, particularly within the context of the sustainability of life on Earth, is to "learn our way out," as Milbraith (1989) has posited. This form of learning must be self-reflexive and adaptive to accommodate the new complexity.

Consequently, a case needs to be made in support of a *learning turn* within the Academy if it is to respond appropriately and innovatively to the Boyerian call for it to be "of greater service to the nation and the world" (Boyer 1990). This is especially relevant given the environment in which contemporary engagement must take place, that is, an age of reflexive modernization and socio-cultural and bio-physical sustainability. If, as citizens of the world, we are to become significantly more competent at dealing with issues that are complex and messily unpredictable—and also *learn our way* to Milbraith's vision of a sustainable society—considerable attention will need to be paid to the issues of the nature of *learning* itself and the process of *learning how to learn*. In essence, the issues we face dictate the need for *systemic ways* of learning and knowing. An important and primary focus of such learning will be on the features, dynamics, and designs of innovative systems of learning, or "inquiring systems" as Churchman (1971) named them.

The promise of a learning turn

It is perhaps more than provocative to suggest that there should be a "learning turn." From the time of its very establishment in medieval Europe, the university has claimed (with some considerable justification) to be the quintessential seat of learning with "an historical background of reflection that goes back at least to Socrates" (Gaita 1997). The university, by its very name and traditional nature, is the one institution that has been dedicated historically to the pursuit of the truth for its own sake, as well as for the generation and conservation of knowledge as truth through the ages.

However, preoccupation with the activities of research, teaching, and extension/outreach—and preoccupation with higher education as a "knowledge institution" for generating, transmitting, and preserving knowledge—has deflected attention from *learning* as the foundation of all of it activities. This is especially odd in light of the contemporary emphasis on the "learning communities," "learning organizations," "learning society," and even to "learning nations" (Unnikrishan Nair 2001). Witness the pervasiveness of learning as the theme in "Higher Education in the Learning Society"—Report of the National Committee into Higher Education in the United Kingdom (Dearing 1997); "Learning for Life"—Report of the West Committee into Higher Education in Australia (West,

1998); and "Learning: The Treasure Within," Report to UNESCO of the International Commission on Education for the Twenty First Century (Delors 1996). Even in the face of such language and activity, evidence suggests that the Academy has not changed significantly since Simon (1967) charged over a quarter century ago that that in our colleges we make "no use of any learning principles in a considered, systematic, professional way."

There are legitimate concerns that a lack of emphasis on learning *per se* is a prime illustration of what is often perceived from outside the Academy, that is, that higher education is generally self-centered and isolated. It is also testimony to the prevailing approach to education: where students are taught a lot about a subject but know little beyond telling and/or showing what they have been taught. They also do not learn much about dealing with the messy problematics of everyday experiences and how to deal with them, collectively and comprehensively. Indeed, there is very little explicit attention at all paid to the connections between experience and the learning process—a subject that so long ago attracted the scholarly attention of John Dewey with his acceptance of the principle that

> . . . education, in order to accomplish its ends both for the individual learner and for society must be based upon experience—which is always the actual life-experience of some individual. (Dewey 1963, 38)

As Dewey saw it, experience had metaphysical dimensions:

> Like its congeners, life and history, it (experience) includes *what* men (*sic*) do and suffer, *what* they strive for, love believe and endure, and also *how* men (*sic*) act and are acted upon, they ways in which they do and suffer, desire and enjoy, see believe, imagine—in short, processes of *experiencing*. (Dewey 1929 and McDermott 1981, 257, emphases in original)

As argued in this book, engagement is a meta-physical stance; it requires learning your way forward through the complex challenges of contemporary life. And yet, as Reason and Rowan (1981) contend, the current accent in the Academy is placed primarily on propositional and practical learning—learning by knowing and by doing respectively—over the experiential *learning by being*. The conventional pedagogies within the Academy (both in the curricula for campus students and the process of undertaking extension-as-education) neglect the epistemological nature of knowledge and disrespect unconventional paradigmatic assumptions and beliefs. This pedagogical neglect and disrespect is further fueled by the pervasiveness of a techno-scientific paradigm that, by its very nature, is not only inherently unreflective, but is notoriously resistant to external critique. While those of us in the Academy might be reflective in the sense that we transform both observations and thoughts into knowledge, nonetheless, we also seem to be less committed to being reflexive in Beck's sense of being critically self-confrontational. In other words, *we have been reluctant to address two issues—the consequences of what we know, and the ways, means, and perspectives through which we come to know what we know.*

Most of our critical competence is associated with scientific observations of natural phenomena and socio-cultural experiences and what we know from theories that frame our interpretation and understanding of the world around us. On the other hand, very little critical attention is accorded the essential *processes* of observation and interpretations, including *how* we come to know how we know. For all the knowledge that has been generated over the eons, for all that has been learned, and for all that is now known, there are those who argue that "the core of all the troubles we face today is our very ignorance of knowing" (Maturana and Varela 1987). By extension, it can be argued that is equally true for *learning*, the cognitive foundations of which still remain a mystery to the majority of those within academia who teach, research, and/or "reach out."

Applying a theory of cognitive processing proposed by Kitchener (1983), it can be contended that academics focus most of their attention on *first-level* cognition, which deals with *knowing about the matter at hand*. There seems to be passing interest in *second level* (meta-cognition), which deals with *knowing about knowing;* or in *third level* (epistemic-cognition), which deals with *knowing about the nature of knowledge*. Yet it is through these higher-order levels of knowing that we come to know how to transform our ways of knowing as well as how to challenge and change the assumptions we hold about knowing and the learning process. As Salner (1986) submits, "[e]pistemic cognition is Kitchener's term for the capacity to think epistemologically . . . and evaluate the foundations of thought itself." As these foundations find their expressions in the paradigms that we live by, epistemic challenge is equivalent to paradigmatic challenge or, as Mezirow (1991) argues, challenges to "meaning perspectives," which he defines as "habits of expectation" that are essentially "rule systems governing perceptions and cognition."

This notion deserves further elaboration, for, as Kolb (1984, 31) persuasively argues

> . . . to learn is not the special province of a single specialized realm of human functioning such as cognition or perception. It involves the integrated functioning of the total organism—thinking, feeling, perceiving, and behaving.

Echoing Dewey, Kolb submits that "learning is the process whereby knowledge is created through the transformation of experience" (1984, 38) as a continuous, "holistic process" of adaptation to the world that involves constant transactions between people and their environments.

Drawing key ideas from the "Theory of Logical Types" of the philosophers Alfred North Whitehead and Bertrand Russell, as well as from the science of cybernetics, Bateson (1972) emphasizes the significance of "difference" as either a stimulus or response for learning. He is especially interested in differences in context that reflect particular sets of premises and expectations that frame the learning at different levels. He presents a hierarchy of logical types of learning from Zero Learning to Learning III (and, indeed, beyond to a hypothetically possible Learning IV, which "probably does not occur in any adult living organism on this earth.") The series reflects the following logic:

> Stimulus is an elementary signal, internal or external. Context of stimulus is a *meta*message which classifies the elementary signal. Context of context of stimulus is a meta-metamessage which classifies the metamessage. And so on. (Bateson 1972, 289)

In this manner, each level of learning in the hierarchy represents a change in the process of the level that precedes it, a notion that is also clearly reflected in Mezirow's scheme. It can also be seen in the scheme of Cell (1984) who also recognizes four levels of change: response learning, situation learning, trans-situation learning, and transcendent learning.

Given the significance that has been attributed to the concept of praxis earlier, it is important to emphasize the commitment here to the synthesis between knowing and doing and also to illustrate how this particular dichotomy can be overcome. From their position as biologists concerned with the biological foundations of cognition, Maturana and Varela (1987) submit that "all doing is knowing and all knowing is doing." To these writers, the everyday world that each of us experiences is a world that we ourselves bring forth through the process of living itself. In a glorious circularity, the world we come to know through personal experience is the world we personally create (bring forth) through our knowledge.

Language is absolutely central to the connection between cognition and action; we do not simply use language to communicate, we are immersed in it, and we build relationships through the process of "languaging." As Fell and Russell (2000, 37) contend: "Our ever-changing present reality consists of how we describe our experiences to ourselves and one another and we are always explaining and reporting our experience. Furthermore, we act according to our current view of the world," which means that what we do in this world reflects how we see it, and how we see the world reflects what we do in it.

Maturana and Varela include emotions as elements of this process of seeing and doing, and Maturana (1988) has presented the idea that "emotioning" is a "bodily predisposition to action." These are matters of great significance to the way people act together and, by connection, to the issue of engagement with others in issues of mutual concern. Similar to other ideas presented in this chapter, this discourse not only challenges conventional views of the biology of cognition, it also challenges the conventional paradigm that frames them.

A synthesis

The arguments developed here suggest the need for a critical rephrasing of Boyer's call for the Academy to become "a more vigorous partner in the search for answers to our most pressing social, civic, economic, and moral problems and must affirm its historic commitment to what I call the scholarship of engagement" (Boyer 1996). There are at least two elements in that rephrasing.

In the first place, the most pressing issues of the day (from the public perception, at least) are not experienced as "neat" and discrete social, civic, or moral problems for which equally neat and discrete "answers" might be found. Rather, they are complex, systemic, and "hybrid" problematiques: best understood as "imbroglios of science, politics, economy, law, religion, technology, fiction" (Latour 1993, 2) that demand continuous attention as well as the adoption of new, universal multi-faceted discourses, which are systemic in nature and inclusive in intent. These characteristics and "intentionalities" defy the conventional discipline-based and essentially techno-scientific rationality of the prevailing discourses and methodologies of academia.

In the second place, it is contentious to claim that there has indeed been an "historic commitment" to a "scholarship of engagement." There is no doubt that American universities have played vitally significant roles in the "service" of the development of the nation and beyond through their educational, research, and extension/outreach activities, including the many instances where they have vigorously addressed social, civic, economic, and moral challenges. But that is not the same as claiming that "engagement" itself has historically been the focus of scholarly work, and it certainly does not say that this work has been considered as a historically "legitimate" domain of scholarly inquiry. Indeed, if a tradition of engagement is emerging, then it is a tradition of valuing engagement's exercise, that is, "the doing of it." That tradition does not automatically include advancing the scholarly underpinnings of engagement. Indeed, it can be argued quite vigorously that despite enthusiastic response to Boyer's call for engagement, the primary focus of attention is on reforming academic institutions to be more engaged. While this is an important, perhaps a necessary objective, it is an organization development matter. What is also required is a corresponding intellectual commitment to understand what it means "to engage" in an era of "reflexive modernity" (Beck 1992).

Moving forward

All of this is to say that there needs to be the sustained pursuit of a particular form of engagement, what we described earlier as "scholarly engagement," one that focuses on what it means to engage in comprehensive, inclusive, and responsible human/environment "betterment." Without that work, there is no possibility of coming to critical engagement. At the same time, this work can (and should) be integrated into a "universe of human discourse" that Boyer valued as engagement. Without that integration, there will be no sustained discourse in the Academy about what it means to engage.

In a real way, we (the authors of this book) represent a microcosm of what has just been described. Each of us works in different fields and focuses on different problematiques. Coming together represented a decisive turning point in our coming to critical engagement and, with that, a deeper understanding of what it means to engage. In Part II, and specifically in chapters 5–7, there are examples of our work in field settings. These are interpreted stories, loaded with critique. Then, in chapter 8, we end Part II just as we ended Part I. We ask ourselves what it all means, especially in terms of our evolving understanding of engagement.

References

Alrøe, H. F., and E. S. Kristensen. 2002. Towards a systemic research methodology in agriculture: Rethinking the role of values in science. *Agriculture and Human Values* 19: 3–23.

Bateson, G. 1972. *Steps to an ecology of mind: A revolutionary approach to man's understanding of himself.* New York: Ballantine Books.

Bawden, R. J., L. Busch, and A. Gagni. 1991. The agricultural university for the twenty-first century. *Impact of Science on Society* 164: 353–366. Adapted from keynote paper for workshop on Agricultural Universities for the Twenty-first Century. Reston VA. Oct. 1988.

Bawden, R. J. 1995. I as in Academy: Learning to be systemic. *Systems Research* 12: 229–238.

Bawden, R. J. 1997. Learning to persist: A systemic view of development. In F. A. Stowell, R. L. Ison, R. Armson, J. Holloway, S. Jackson, and S. McRobb, eds. *Systems for sustainability: People, organizations, and environments.* New York: Plenum Press.

Beck, U. 1992. *Risk society: Towards a new modernity.* London: Sage Publications.

Beck, U. 1994. The re-invention of politics: Towards a theory of reflexive modernization. In U. Beck, A. Giddens, and S. Lash, eds. *Reflexive modernization: Politics, tradition and aesthetics in the modern social order.* Stanford: Stanford Univ. Press.

Beck, U. 1996. Risk, society, and the provident state. In U. Beck, B. Szerszynski, and B. Wynne, eds. *Risk, environment and society: Towards a new ecology.* London: Sage Publications.

Bennett, J. B. 1998. *Collegial professionalism: The academy, individualism, and the common good.* American Council of Education. Series on Higher Education. Phoenix AZ: Oryx Press.

Bernstein, R. J. 1983. *Beyond objectivism and subjectivism: Science, hermeneutics, and praxis.* Philadelphia: Univ. of Pennsylvania Press.

Bok, D. 1990. *Universities and the future of America.* Durham NC: Duke Univ. Press.

Bonnen, J. T. 1983. Historical sources of U.S. productivity: Implications for R&D policy and social science research. *American Journal of Agricultural Economics* 65: 958–966.

Bormann, F. H. and S. R. Kellert. 1991. *Ecology, economics, ethics: The broken circle.* New Haven: Yale Univ. Press.

Boyer, E. L. 1990. *Scholarship reconsidered: Priorities of the professoriate.* The Carnegie Foundation for the Advancement of Teaching. San Francisco: Jossey-Bass.

Boyer, E. L. 1996. The scholarship of engagement. *Journal of Public Service and Outreach* 1:11–20.

Bronowski, J., and B. Mazlish. 1960. *The western intellectual tradition: From Leonardo to Hegel.* New York: Harper Torchbooks.

Brundtland, G. H. 1987. *Our common future. Report of the World Commission of the Environment and Development (WCED)* Oxford: Oxford Univ. Press.

Burrell, W. G., and G. Morgan. 1979. *Sociological paradigms and organisational analysis.* London: Heinemann.

Cell, E. 1984. *Learning from experience.* Albany: State Univ. of New York Press.

Churchman, C. W. 1971. *The design of inquiring systems.* New York: Basic Books.

Damrosch, D. 1995. *We scholars: Changing the culture of the university.* Cambridge: Harvard Univ. Press.

Davison, A. 2001. *Technology and the contested meanings of technology*. Albany: State Univ. of New York.

Dearing, R. 1997. Higher education in the learning society. Report of the National Committee into Higher Education in the United Kingdom. http://www.leeds.ac.uk/educol/ncihe Accessed 03/28/05.

Delors, J. 1996. *Learning: The treasure within*. Report of the International Commission on Education for the 21st Century. Paris: UNESCO Publishing.

Dewey, J. 1908. Does reality possess practical character? In J. L. McDermott, ed. 1981. *The philosophy of John Dewey*. Chicago: Univ. of Chicago Press. (1)

Dewey, J. 1922. The development of American pragmatism. In J. L. McDermott, ed. 1981. *The philosophy of John Dewey*. Chicago: Univ. of Chicago Press.

Dewey, J. 1963. *Experience and education*. New York: Macmillan Publishing. First published 1938, Kappa Delta Pi.

Fairclough, N. 1992. *Discourse and social change*. Cambridge UK: Polity Press.

Fear, F., C. Rosaen, P. G. Foster-Fishman, and R. J. Bawden. 2001. Outreach as scholarly expression: A faculty perspective. *Journal of Higher Education Outreach and Engagement* 6:21–34.

Fell, L., and D. B. Russell. 2000. The human quest for understanding and agreement. In R. L. Ison and D. B. Russell, eds. *Agriculture and rural development: Breaking out of traditions*. Cambridge: Cambridge Univ. Press.

Fischer, F. 2005. Are scientists irrational? Risk assessment in practical reason. In M. Leach, I. Scoones, and B. Wynne, eds. *Science and citizens*. London: Zed Books.

Freire, P. 2003. *Pedagogy of the oppressed*. 30th anniversary edition. New York: Continuum.

Fuller, S. 1988. *Social epistemology*. Bloomington: Indiana Univ. Press.

Gadamer, H. G. 1975. Hermeneutics and social science. *Cultural Hermeneutics* 2:312–321.

Gaita, R. 1997. Truth and the idea of a university. *Australian Universities Review* 40:13–18.

Giddens, A. 1991. *Modernity and self-identity*. Cambridge UK: Polity Press.

Glassick, C. E., M. T. Huber, and G. I. Maeroff. 1997. *Scholarship assessed: Evaluation of the professoriate*. An Earnest L. Boyer Project of The Carnegie Foundation for the Advancement of Teaching. San Francisco: Jossey-Bass.

Gordon, J. C. 1992. The environmental curriculum: An undergraduate land grant future. In National Research Council, Agriculture and the Undergraduate. Washington D.C.: National Academy Press.

Grove-White, R. 1996. Environmental knowledge and public policy needs: On humanising the research agenda. In S. Lash, B. Szerszynski, and B. Wynne, eds. *Risk, environment, and modernity: Towards a new ecology*. London: Sage Publications.

Guba, E. G., and Y. S. Lincoln. 1994. Competing paradigms in qualitative research. In N. K. Denzin and Y. S. Lincoln, eds. *Handbook of qualitative research*. Thousand Oaks CA: Sage Publications.

Habermas, J. 1971. *Knowledge and human interests*. Trans. Jeremy Shapiro. Boston: Beacon Press.

Habermas, J. 1979. *Communication and the evolution of society*. Trans. Thomas MacCarthy. Boston: Beacon Press.

Habermas, J. 1984. *The theory of communicative action. Vol. 1. Reason and the rationalization of society*. Cambridge UK: Polity Press.

Habermas, J. 2003. *The future of human nature*. Cambridge: Polity Press.

Hajer, M. 1996. Ecological modernisation as cultural politics. In S. Lash, B. Szerszynski, and B. Wynne, eds. *Risk, environment and modernity: Towards a new ecology.* London: Sage Publications.

Hindmarsh, R., and G. Lawrence. 2001. Bio-Utopia: Future natural? In R. Hindmarsh and G. Lawrence, eds. *Altered genes II.* Melbourne: Scribe Publications.

James, W. 1940. *Some problems with philosophy.* New York: Longmans.

Jones, K. 2000. Constructing rBST in Canada: Biotechnology, instability, and the management of nature. *Canadian Journal of Sociology* 25:311–341.

Keller, G. 1983. *Academic strategy: The management revolution in American higher education.* Baltimore: The Johns Hopkins Univ. Press.

Kellogg Commission. 1999. *Returning to our roots: The engaged institution. Kellogg Commission on the Future of State and Land-Grant Universities.* National Association of State Universities and Land-Grant Colleges.

Kemp, P. 2000. Bioethics in law and biolaw in ethics. In P. Kemp, J. Rendtorff, and N. Mattsson Johansen, eds. *Bioethics and biolaw. Vol 1. Judgment of life.* Copenhagen: Rhodos International Science and Arts Publishers and Centre of Ethics and Law.

Kerr, C. 1982. *The uses of the university.* 3rd Edition. Cambridge: Harvard Univ. Press.

Kitchener K. S. 1983. Cognition, meta-cognition, and epistemic cognition: A three level model of cognitive processing. *Human Development* 26: 222–232.

Kolb, D. A. 1984. *Experiential learning: Experience as the source of learning and development.* New Jersey: Prentice Hall.

Knorr Cetina, K. 1999. *Epistemic cultures: How the sciences make knowledge.* Cambridge MA: Harvard Univ. Press.

Kuhn, T. 1962. *The structure of scientific revolutions.* Chicago: Univ. of Chicago Press.

Latour, B. 1993. *We have never been modern.* Trans. C. Porter. Cambridge MA: Harvard Univ. Press.

Maturana, H. 1988. Reality. The search for objectivity or the quest for a compelling argument. *Irish Journal of Psychology* 9:25–82.

Maturana, H., and F. Varela. 1987. *The tree of knowledge—The biological roots of human understanding.* Boston: Shambala Publications.

McDowell, G. R. 2001. *Land grant universities and extension: Into the 21st Century.* Ames: Iowa State Univ. Press.

Mezirow, J. 1991. *Transformative dimensions of adult learning.* San Francisco: Jossey-Bass.

Milbraith, L. W. 1989. *Envisioning a sustainable society: Learning our way out.* New York: State Univ. of New York Press.

Norgaard, R. B. 1989. The case for methodological pluralism. *Ecological Economics* 1: 37–58.

Plough, A., and S. Krimsky. 1987. The emergence of risk communications studies: Social and political context. *Science, Technology, and Human Values* 12:4–10.

Readings, B. 1996. *The university in ruins.* Cambridge: Harvard Univ. Press.

Reason, P., and J. Rowan. 1981. *Human inquiry: A sourcebook of new paradigm research.* Chichester: Wiley.

Russell, B. 1961. *History of western philosophy.* 2nd Edition. London: George Allen and Unwin.

Salner, M. 1986. Adult cognitive and epistemological development. *Systems Research* 2: 225–232.

Sandman, P. 1992. Hazardous vs outrage: Responding to public concerns about the risk of industrial gases. IOMA Broadcaster. Jan–Feb. pp. 7–17.

Schuh, E. 1984. Revitalizing the land grant university. Colloquium. Strategic Management Research Center. Univ. of Minnesota.

Simon, H. 1967. The job of a college president. *Educational Record* 58: 68–78.

Sinnott, J., and L. Johnson. 1996. *Reinventing the university: A radical proposal for the problem-focused university.* Norwood: Ablex Publishing.

Smith, P, 1990. *Killing the spirit of higher education in America.* New York: Viking.

Straughan, R. R. 1995. Ethical issues of crop biotechnology. In T. B. Mepham, G. A. Tucker, and J. Wiseman, eds. *Issues in agricultural bioethics.* Nottingham: Nottingham Univ. Press.

Thompson, P. B 1998. *Agricultural ethics: Research, teaching, and public policy.* Ames: Iowa State Press.

Veysey, L. R. 1965. *The emergence of the American university.* Chicago: Univ. of Chicago Press.

Ulrich, W. 1988. Systems thinking, systems practice and practical philosophy: A program of research. *Systems Practice* 1:415–428.

Unnikrishan Nair, K. 2001. Adaptation to creation: Progress of organizational learning and increasing complexity of learning systems. *Systems Research and Behavioral Science* 18:505–521.

Wenger, E. 1998. *Communities of practice: Learning, meaning, identity.* Cambridge: Cambridge Univ. Press.

West, R. 1998. Learning for life. Report of the West Committee into Higher Education in Australia. Department of Employment, Education, Training and Youth Affairs (DEETYA). Canberra: Commonwealth of Australia.

Wilshire, B. 1990. *The moral collapse of the university: Professionalism, purity and alienation.* New York: State Univ. of New York Press.

Wynne, B. 1996. May the sheep safely graze? A reflexive view of the expert–lay knowledge divide. In U. Beck, B. Szerszynski, and B. Wynne, eds. *Risk, environment and society: Towards a new ecology.* London: Sage Publications.

Yankelovich, D. 1991. *Coming to public judgment: Making democracy work in a complex world.* Syracuse: Syracuse Univ. Press.

PART II
DIGGING INTO ENGAGEMENT

CHAPTER 5

LEARNING THROUGH DISCOURSE

Despite their best efforts, many faculty members who have done community-based work have experienced "it." It begins with earnest intent and proceeds with diligent effort—forging ahead with a group of stakeholders, a group that is committed to making significant change and to improving the ways things are done. After months (and sometimes years) of meeting, planning, thinking, rethinking, and designing, a nagging question surfaces: Is this work *really going* to change things? Unfortunately, the answer is often, "No." Although a community of committed community and academic folks have enabled a solution that makes things better for a few and/or for a limited period of time, transformative change is elusive because an ordinary solution was created for a circumstance that required extraordinary means. At issue, then, is: *What does it take to move community processes from the safe territory of what is already known (and what feels comfortable and familiar) to the territory of extraordinary change?*

In our faculty community of practice, we discovered that although solutions may appear to be clear and straightforward, they actually are quite difficult to create and execute. We have learned that a transformative change process requires, first and foremost, *learning through dialogue*—not just any type of learning, but significant, deep, and structural learning that leads to new understandings; new ways of thinking about organizational or community life; and new ways of conceptualizing and enacting solutions. In many ways, this learning is similar to the emancipatory knowledge and action described by Habermas (1984), the sort of knowledge and action that move us closer to social justice and social change.

By examining critically our own community-based work, we have found that we are most successful at fostering this learning when we generate and sustain critical dialogic processes for the purposes of discovering, understanding, and taking action. We have also discovered that opportunities for critical dialogue are created within what we think of as an *engagement interface* (Rosaen, Foster-Fishman, and Fear 2001), a co-constructed space where collaborative work unfolds through sustained interactions between community and academic partners (Springett 2003). While ultimately the desired outcome of work in the engagement interface is often a new approach, program, or intervention, the *value* of what emerges is influenced by the quality of the dialogue. How the dialogue proceeds—what is allowed to be discussed; what is considered taboo; which realities and perspectives are emphasized; and how much the status quo can be questioned—sets the stage for whether or not learning will inform extraordinary change.

Chapter overview

In this chapter we shall discuss how to elevate everyday conversations—that is, how we can transform the typical dialogue that occurs naturally and often within community-based settings—to co-construct a space where critical thinking and situated learning have the potential to bring about radical change. We begin by presenting a case study, an effort by a faculty-community group to address the problem of obesity in a county setting. The case, "Discovering Discourse," illustrates the nature of work that takes place at the engagement interface, work that is often uncertain, messy, and challenging. It also demonstrates the importance of what can happen when a group of people evolve their interaction from "talking and listening" to engaging in dialogue, that is, when they start to *really* listen and hear one another.

Following the presentation of the case, we shall introduce the concept of *critical Discourse* (emphasis added). We explain how criticality enables learning from multiple perspectives. As Gee (1992) views it, discourse is a complex set of social practices. We use Gee's interpretation to analyze the social practices revealed in the case material. We argue that learning through critical Discourse is an essential way of engaging in praxis, which we see as necessary for pursuing transformative ends in the engagement interface. Recognizing that this type of discourse is difficult to achieve, we believe new roles and relationships are necessary if critical Discourse is to occur.

In sum, this chapter is a call for a *certain kind* of engagement work, work that requires a particular set of social practices. In doing so, the chapter also illustrates the kind of critical analysis manifest in our faculty learning community of praxis. We began our learning journey by analyzing critically our own work by examining community-based efforts that did and did not result in transformative outcomes. Finally, the chapter provides essential background for understanding other essential aspects of an approach to engagement that emerged through conversation in our learning community and will be discussed in Part II of this book. That approach includes capacities necessary for building social capital (chapter 6); two strategies for co-empowerment (chapter 7); and an understanding of what it really means to engage in work with transformative outcomes (chapter 8).

Introduction to a case example: discovering Discourse

It was not supposed to be this difficult. Our group of committed faculty and community leaders had been meeting for more than two years with the goal of developing a comprehensive plan to address the problem of increasing rates of obesity in a county. The talent in the room was extraordinary: we were all bright, well read, and eager to learn. Many of us had years of experience addressing similar issues and we all knew how to work collaboratively with others; how to tap into the knowledge at the table; and how to design programs and processes that could make a difference. And yet, this time we could not make it work. The plan and processes we prepared to release to the community were neither expressions of our best work nor would they create the social change desired. Many involved in this effort acknowledged as much behind the scenes. As a community leader put it, in our two years of working together we had "simply worn ourselves out with many difficult conversations laced with tension and sometimes even conflict." So, without conscious intent, we ended up designing something "easy;" something to which we could all agree; and something that would at least get an initiative started in the community.

What follows is a story that illustrates how it took the thoughts, experience, and words of those community members *not* initially at the table to shift the discourse and perspectives necessary for creating a vision of what could and should happen. What resulted initially in "doing *things* better" was later expressed as "doing *better* things."

The beginning: through the looking glass

In the fall of 2000, the Director of the Department of Community Services in a local county (an alias and hereafter referred to as "department") approached faculty at Michigan State University (MSU) and invited them to join a recently formed local coalition. The goal was to find a way to address the rising rates of obesity in a nearby community. The community had received several substantial grants from state agencies and local foundations to address this issue and had recently created a coalition of key organizational leaders. Coalition members wanted faculty to partner with them during the initial two-year design and planning phase. Among other things, it was expected that faculty would provide support, consultation, and information to inform the decision making and planning process.

Four faculty members with experience in health issues and community change joined the coalition and began meeting with the group on a bi-weekly basis. Most of the influential organizations in this community were present at the table, including representatives from key human service organizations; the educational system; civic institutions; and local business leaders. All involved were perceived to be dedicated to creating a healthier community and establishing programs that "worked."

In our initial meeting with the coalition, we (the faculty) were struck with the energy around the table and the conviction to do things differently. As background, this community had been working on the issue of obesity for more than a decade with modest success. Now, with millions of dollars at stake, they wanted to achieve results and the principals involved felt that a different strategy was required to accomplish that end. Several community leaders had attended a national conference on community health partnerships and obesity reduction and were introduced there to community-building approaches, including the strategies of resident empowerment, community organizing, and creating durable and effective partnerships across diverse community segments. Local leaders thought partnership development would be a powerful way to address chronic issues in their community. The invitation for faculty to join this planning process came, in part, because the academicians had knowledge about this strategy and success working with communities elsewhere.

Many of us (the faculty) left early meetings convinced that this was the opportunity we had been waiting for. On car trips back to the university, we talked enthusiastically about how we felt the conditions fostering transformative change were in place: a group of powerful stakeholders were committed to the issues; there was evidence of innovative thinking at the table; the resources to make a difference were available; local participants seemed committed to enabling the empowerment processes that we had seen work successfully elsewhere; and there seemed to be a plan in place to create inclusive decision making and governing processes among residents from all sectors of the community.

Overall, we were optimistic and excited. So, too, were our organizational partners. Individuals spoke with passion and conviction at initial meetings. They were committed to the vision and seemed convinced that a comprehensive, grassroots approach was necessary for addressing obesity problems. The early meetings were filled with language that confirmed that everyone at the table thought this initiative was on the right track. Comments made reinforced this belief: "This time we have it right." "We really are going to make a difference this time." Participants exuded excitement and energy; they would arrive early or stay late, to talk about what was and might be.

But the excitement soon waned. Within six months, conversations became cumbersome and far less enjoyable. They were dominated more by rhetoric than by an examination of the real issues, including why obesity rates seemed to be intractable in this community. When issues surfaced or disagreements emerged, they were either dropped altogether or put into the ubiquitous "parking lot" of ideas to be discussed later (but never). We didn't have time or wouldn't take the time for discussion; at each meeting there was a "packed agenda."

Before we knew it, this coalition—the group in which faculty members and community partners had invested considerable hope—began looking no different from prior efforts in this community. Yet, we continued to meet because there was work to do: funds needed to be spent, and plans and processes needed to be implemented. For the next year, we worked on creating a plan of work. While considerable debate and heated discussion occurred often, very little dialogue took place.

Who's on first?

While everyone at the table was invited to be there as a partner in the process—and initial conversations supported the notion that we were all equal participants—it soon became painfully clear that this was not a *true* partnership. The department set the agenda despite representatives stating otherwise initially. The gap between reality and intent was partly a function of accountability: the department was ultimately responsible to the funding agencies. But the emergent power dynamic in this case was also embedded in the community structure: many organizations worked on other projects with the department and some received sub-contractual work from it. Given this politics of circumstance, a group norm developed—group members asking department representatives what they thought about an issue before offering their personal opinions.

In reality, then, the department led this effort even though many members felt that it had the least knowledge (among organizations represented in the group) about matters pertaining to health and obesity. As the months went by, it also became clear that the department's position on two important matters was inconsistent with how other partners felt: it did not support the initiative being defined as a grassroots mobilization effort and also preferred to defer action until the coalition had "everything figured out." Moreover, working in collaborative partnership arrangements seemed to be an anathema to the department's organizational culture. All of this added up to a situation where collaboration became a concept whereas unilateral control became the practice.

The department's need to control this process as much as possible became more direct and explicit over time. Early in the effort, representatives said: "We are here to listen to you and to support your decisions. You are the decision makers here, not us." Later they said: "These decisions are ours. We need to determine the parameters of this effort because we are the primary recipients of funds. This coalition is not a decision making body; it is advisory in nature." With this shift in stance, a plan of work that was supposed to have been designed collaboratively by the partners became a document that was authored solely by the department. For sure, coalition members saw drafts and were allowed to provide input and feedback, but they were also told explicitly what issues were and were not "up for negotiation" from the department's perspective.

At least for faculty members at the table, this shift from partnership to a nominal advisory council made us less vested in the process; the value of our input seemed to matter less. As a result, we found ourselves agreeing to things in which we did not believe and refraining from bringing up issues with which we knew the department would disagree. If we were to be truthful about what happened, we would have to confess that we had allowed ourselves to be co-opted by the power vested in the department. We, too, were recipients of their funds, just as were many of the community partners.

"I am expert," hear me ROAR?

This narrative "points a finger" at the department's need to control the process, but the faculty also played a role in impeding "real" conversations. Faculty members were caught in what could be called an "experting problem." We were initially brought to the table because of our "expertise" in the issues and on the processes being considered. Our expertise was lauded by partners and our formal accomplishments and successes were mentioned frequently and publicly. We were expected to deliver this expertise by informing our partners about matters pertaining to best practices, process strategies, and program design. With expectations for us to be experts, experts we became.

Very early in the process we began sharing what we thought *should* happen. Feeling the pressure to help the coalition meet its self-imposed timeline to launch this effort within eighteen months, we became less concerned about HOW we communicated information and more concerned about WHAT we said and if we really shared all of the "expertise" we possessed. Upon reflection, we realized that we became quite prescriptive in our communication: "This is what you need to do." "This is what should be done." "This is how it has succeeded elsewhere."

So, while we really wanted to generate a *dialogue* about ideas, we had instead contributed to the creation of culture of *monologue*. We put forward our expertise and expected the community to listen. And as we watched the department take control of the process, we made matters worse: rather than encouraging the group to shift from a receiving to a dialogic culture, our pedantic tendencies increased. We became concerned about the decisions that were made, as well as the processes that were being ignored (particularly community resident involvement), so we prescribed more insistently. Although we saw agreement with our ideas as we presented them, we saw fewer and fewer of the ideas actually informing the decision making and the plans. We saw members *listening to* us less and less and, in response, we *talked at* them more and more.

As we reflect on the way we contributed to closing down the conversation, it became evident that we, the faculty, had identified the *wrong* problem. The problem wasn't, "They (people at department) are not hearing us and our ideas." They weren't supposed to hear US. Instead, they were supposed to hear each other (and community members) and discover a new understanding, that is, *a new way of thinking* about the issue of obesity. These prescriptive statements—the brilliant nuggets we felt compelled to share—had not opened their minds but, instead, had shut them down. (We could almost hear the coalition members say, "Here they go again.") We had merely succeeded in crafting another ordinary "plan" to solve an extraordinary problem, *when what was needed was a pathway to transformative change within community.*

Opening up the dialogue: moving toward Discourse

When it came time to launch the project plan in the community, the faculty remained significantly concerned about the proposed plans and, in fact, met privately with several departments to share this concern, explaining why we felt the plans would not deliver what had been proposed and expected. Department leaders listened and then restated that this was *their* initiative, and that they had their reasons why the plan was designed the way it was. No changes were made.

The department decided they wanted to first share their plan with a small group of resident leaders who had been sitting on an advisory board for the local Public Health Department and working on other community health concerns. This meeting was designed as a time for the department to meet with residents, share their plan, and get resident reactions. To our distress, it was also decided by the department that the plan was a "final document." As such, revisions could not and would not be made. Getting resident reaction was designed primarily to gather input that would be used to frame the upcoming media campaign.

The meeting began according to script: department leaders began their presentation—presenting their ideas with passion; emphasizing how obesity rates must decline; and sharing what the department was committed to doing on the community's behalf. When they finished, they asked the resident leaders for reactions. What happened next was a surprise. Speaking from their hearts, the leaders rejected many pieces of the plan and explained why they felt the ideas would not work. Among other things, they spoke directly about the need for resident empowerment and control. If the department went forward with their plan (a plan the residents had been excluded from) they argued, trust between the residents and department would erode. They asked the department to work WITH THEM to design a better plan.

Those of us observing the meeting held our collective breaths. We had been told, just hours before, that this plan was final—no changes could be made—and a media campaign to launch the plan would begin within days. How would the department leaders respond? They responded with open hearts and minds saying "okay." They admitted that their plan was no longer useful and that they needed to work with the residents to create a plan that would really work. That very night, plans were made for the department to begin working with the residents to redesign the initiative. Within three days of this critical meeting, a governance body with real authority was created, a body that included key local organizations and fifteen residents who participated in this first meeting. This new governance body now meets monthly with leaders from the department to discuss obesity issues and to consider what really needs to be done to "fix" the obesity problem. While this governance body is still in its infancy, it is already deemed a success: for the first time in the history of the department, this unit is engaging local organizations *and* residents in an authentic decision making role.

What was most surprising to the faculty who observed the meeting was the stark reality that they had delivered the same message to department representatives frequently and earlier. Why did the department pay attention this time? Conversations with several department representatives, coalition members, and residents are the basis for offering possible explanations:

- Department leaders were *now ready and able to hear this information.* In the past two years, department leaders and staff attended many conferences, read many books, and consulted with many experts around the country to learn about how others had addressed the issue of obesity. This capacity-building work may have helped them reach a place where they, themselves, were able to engage as *informed* partners in the process. The information we provided during this capacity-building phase was *not* as accessible to them because they were not yet ready to listen, understand, and dialogue—in an informed way—about the topics discussed. By the time the resident meeting was scheduled, department leaders may have felt comfortable enough with their own knowledge and understanding to participate in dialogue about the issue.

- There was *over-emphasis on "doing" within the coalition.* A process–product tension was evident from the very beginning of the coalition's time together. Department leaders repeatedly communicated a desire to "get it right this time" and the department put pressure on the group to get the effort "rolling." Over time, the desire to get the project started won out over the need to *really* process and learn about how to proceed. As a result, little if any time was spent reflecting on our own process and decisions, despite the acknowledgement by all that such time was needed. Even though two two-day retreats were organized each year for just this type of reflection, the need and pressure to make decisions and design programs were so strong that the retreats became places where decision making and program design work occurred.

- Residents were the *appropriate ones to have the conversation with.* Simply put, one could argue that the department should have been engaging with residents in this process from the beginning. They heard the residents because they represent a primary stakeholder audience—a group whose voice really matters.

Commentary: criticality in Discourse

Many who write about participatory approaches (e.g., Jason et al. 2004; Minkler and Wallerstein 2003) have found that sometimes even recruiting individuals to come to the table may be difficult. While we certainly agree, the "Discovering Discourse" case illustrates a greater challenge that exists within community-based work. That challenge is creating a climate and establishing norms to *promote mutual understanding.* This case illustrates a familiar pattern where faculty talked to many different individuals, engaged in many conversations, and fostered frequent group discussions. Yet, merely having good conversations is insufficient because it lacks *criticality,* an element that is central to engagement. Even though the group recognized that they needed to transcend the status quo—to get beyond what they already knew and what was comfortable in order to really address the issues being targeted—the real issues within the community did not surface and, because of that, deeper meaning was left unexplored. While disagreements emerged, the conflict that occurred was either tabled or side-stepped at the expense of developing mutual understanding. In the end—despite the activities and projects that were pursued—significant change was elusive *until* there was a turning point in the dialogic experience.

Bringing a case like this to our faculty community of practice helped us realize that we are more likely to be successful in our work when we foster a climate and establish norms that *value engagement as an ongoing discovery process* (Wallerstein 1992). Engagement as discovery mode can help faculty and community participants get out of their respective "conceptual ruts" (Wicker 1985), meaning that we need to examine underlying assumptions about community problems; assess old roles and relationships; critique joint work; and identify common ground, language, and goals. Examination of this sort was generally lacking in the "Discovering Discourse" case. Discovery is most likely to happen when conversations in the engagement interface move beyond conversation, discussion, or debate, and migrate to *critical Discourse.*

We purposely use the term Discourse with a capital *D* to draw upon Gee's (1992) notion that each socio-culturally defined group of people has its own social practices, or, its own Discourse. As we discussed in chapter 3, social practices include "ways of talking, acting, interacting, valuing, and believing" (1992, 107). A Discourse also includes "words, acts, values, beliefs, attitudes, social identities, as well as gestures, glances, body positions, and clothes" (1992, 107). Gee explains that in addition to acquiring a primary Discourse through immersion within a socio-culturally defined group, such as a family or neighborhood, we also learn *secondary* Discourses that enable engagement in social practices with other groups (e.g., school, church, sports teams, people with whom we work). Moreover, Gee points out that when we have a meta-cognitive awareness and understanding of the secondary Discourses, we are more empowered as learners and participants to engage in, examine, and change the social practices that are in place. Through participation in our faculty practice community, we have learned to think of a critical Discourse *as a set of social practices that can guide the dialogical process within the engagement interface.*1 Accordingly, we define critical Discourse in three ways—as a *stance, a relational process,* and a *text*:

- *As a stance*: A critical Discourse demands that participants adopt a normative stance where they value critical inquiry as a means to seek betterment. Participants recognize that transformative change will occur only if real issues are examined and understood (Habermas 1984) and when dialogue is intentionally directed toward learning (Burbules 1993). As such, this stance raises epistemological questions (Freire 1985) because language and meaning are viewed as social constructs, requiring all participants in the engagement interface—including those from the Academy—to treat themselves as subjects and as topics of critical inquiry. Adopting a stance of *criticality* means participants rigorously examine and re-examine the taken-for-granted assumptions, habits, and perspectives, as well as the conditions (e.g., historical forces and structures) that give rise to them (Ulrich 2003).

- As a *relational process:* When Discourse is intentionally directed toward learning, participants enter into a relationship where they commit to ongoing introspection and the cooperative pursuit of knowledge (Shor and Freire 1987). A relationship of reciprocity, one that is based on mutual concern and respect, enables participants to engage in social practices that include ongoing cycles of critical inquiry that can lead to mutual understanding (Burbules 1993; Habermas 1984). As Burbules (1993, 47) contends, dialogic relationships are developmental and diachronic in nature: "Dialogues change over time; they move through different phases or

---

1. Our thinking has been influenced by many scholars including Bakhtin, 1981; Bohm, 1996; Burbules, 1993; Dewey, 1916; Flick, 1998; Freire, 1985; Habermas, 1984; Schoem and Hurtado, 2001; and Yankelovich, 1999, who use terms such as "dialogue" or "public discourse" or "communication" to describe social interaction that seeks mutual understanding through shared inquiry. Our choice of "critical Discourse" is intended to reflect a complex set of social practices that makes explicit the central role of criticality as a specific value that guides relational processes and self reflection.

stages; they take shape gradually as the participants discover more about the communicative process, about each other, and about the topic at hand."

- *As a text:* Those participating in critical Discourse recognize that the underlying meaning and experience within a community will shift only if the narrative about community life is examined and open to change. Similarly, the covenant called "engagement" requires individuals to recognize that the texts they generate must be examined and altered if life within the community is to shift. As Bruner (1986, 14) reminds us, both speech and story have narrative functions, so that "story must construct two landscapes simultaneously," the outer landscape of action and the inner landscape of thought. The narratives that unfold through sustained Discourse within the engagement interface create the text for investigating what can and should be transformed. When narratives are treated as texts to be shared, examined, and critiqued, participants are more likely and able to uncover implicit knowledge; make explicit their governing theories and intentions; and gain insight into their life perspectives, values, and emotions.

When pursuing transformative ends, learning through critical Discourse is an *expression of praxis* (Burbules 1993). But critical Discourse is not a method in a "follow these steps" kind of way. Rather, learning through critical Discourse emerges from evolving norms and relationships, together with a shared commitment to seek transformative ends. Whether it be in the context of collaboration, university–community partnerships, community-based participatory research or evaluation approaches, or a community of practice, it is essential that relationships of mutual concern and respect are created in a trusting environment where critical, ongoing reflective inquiry occurs. Such inquiry is more likely to be pursued, and learning is more likely to emerge, when engagement participants embrace a stance with three interrelated attributes:

- Criticality is viewed as essential.
- Cycles of inquiry are pursued with participants committed to learning.
- New narratives about community life are encouraged to emerge.

With all of this as background, we shall now use the concept of critical Discourse—elaborated as a stance, relational process, and text—to analyze the narrative as it unfolded in the "Discovering Discourse" case. We shall also describe why and how Discourse as an expression of praxis can foster essential dynamics within the engagement interface.

Discourse as a stance: the importance of making learning central
Transformative community work requires more than the application of known expertise. It also requires an inquiring stance, as well as willingness and the ability to "think outside the box," where partners—university and community members alike—have the courage to let go of well understood ways of thinking and commonly accepted modes of approaching and solving problems. As Schön (1987) reminds us, the act of naming and framing problems defines what we do and do not pay attention to, and our own backgrounds influence how we frame problematic situations. All of this was amply illustrated in the case of "Discovering Discourse." The possibility of transformation was enabled only after stakeholders shifted their attitudes and practices (Foster-Fishman, Perkins, and Davidson 1997).

Because Discourse involves joint exploration in a way that fosters co-learning, local community capacity-building, and participant empowerment (Israel, Schurman, and Hugentobler 1992), in "Discovering Discourse," authentic dialogue took place only after participants spoke the truth. To do that, residents had to overcome years of having their voice ignored. Consequently, they came to the meeting fully expecting it to "just be another meeting" with community leaders pretending that the residents' voices mattered. As one resident put it:

> I have been to meetings where . . . people said, "We wanna hear what people have to say," and then they make their own decisions. You have people that speak out boldly and are adamant and angry about the decisions that the leaders are bringing to the table, but they'll go out and do just that! What is the purpose of the meeting? I saw nobody agree with what you just did, but you did it anyway. What was the purpose? It was a front, and . . . when you do that enough times you definitely disconnect from the people, and it's like whatever. Like why should I get involved with something when you're gonna do what you wanna do? You know that's like a parent asking their child what do you want for dinner tonight, and they say hamburgers; and you say "no" we're gonna have green beans and spinach. Why did you ask me then? Don't ask me if you're gonna do what you wanna do anyway. What was the purpose? You just frustrated me. (Community town hall meeting resident)

Department staff created an opening for trust to be established with residents the moment they acknowledged that their plans were inappropriate for this context and recognized that they should have been engaged in dialogue with residents from the beginning. As one resident acknowledged:

> I've been here [in this city] long, and I've been very disgusted and very put out, and last month, well that meeting with Community Services . . . that was the best meeting, getting people on one accord and not at each other's throats. It was like, we all, you know, we all care about the same things, and we're willing to work this out. Let's, you know, let's do this. It was almost like a family

atmosphere versus the political pulls . . . . There's just too many wounds, and in order to heal them you're gonna have to have somebody listen in order to get them to trust. That happened that night. We said "no" to their plans and they listened. (Community town hall meeting resident)

In turn, by responding the way they did, residents enabled dialogue. They responded with care, not contempt, and proposed thoughtful solutions rather than simply demeaning the department's ideas or attacking the staff.

The shifts in attitude and behavior by both parties enabled the partners, together, to explore new meanings. By "speaking for themselves" in a participatory, democratic environment (Dewey 1916; Ulrich 2003; Yankelovich 1999), they started the process of shaping a new reality (Freire 1985; Habermas 1984) which, in this case, meant the possibility of thinking about and approaching matters of obesity in a radically (for them) new way.

All of this activates what Greenwood and Levin (1998) refer to as *co-generative learning*. Co-generative learning is based on the assumption that *all* forms of knowledge are valued and recognized, including what is often referred to as more *practical* knowledge held by community members about the everyday workings of community life, as well as the more commonly accepted *scientific* knowledge held by faculty. When discourse practices focus on learning, then attitudes of respect and trust enable acknowledgment of differences in knowledge, insight, and expertise without reifying them into inflexible and calcified status or role identities (Burbules 1993).

Co-generative learning also assumes that transformative problem solving and action require an iterative learning cycle. Participants in the engagement interface need to continually examine, critique, and elevate not only individual understandings but also evaluate routine and collective definitions of how to frame and solve problems. As bell hooks (1994) reminds us, transformative work requires all participants—including faculty—to become transformed Without this mutuality of revealing and learning, faculty risk becoming "all knowing silent interrogators" (hooks 1994, 21). As we learned in our faculty practice community, work in the engagement interface can be enhanced by dialogic learning processes *if* participants—including ourselves—examine critically our own and each other's attitudes, values, and relationships; and, then, *learn our way* (mindfully and intentionally) into developing new methods and approaches.

A critical step enabling transformation in the case of "Discovering Dialogue" was the department's willingness to ignore plans it had constructed over a twelve-month period. Doing that changed fundamentally *whose* judgment would be included in the decision making process and *how* they positioned themselves relative to community participants. These were critical steps, steps that enabled co-generative learning. For example, department leaders believed that a critical change required improving the food options associated with school lunches. Because most children qualify for free or reduced lunches, shifting to more healthy food options could be an important step in establishing a community norm for healthy eating. Despite numerous complaints by parents to the school district about the current food options, no changes had yet occurred. But what if residents and various representatives of civic organizations had invited parents, teachers, and school administrators to talk about what it means to eat healthy and, then, invited a dialogue about the implications of that meaning for school lunch choices? Suppose, further, if this group had questioned why only schools in wealthier districts had healthy food options? At issue, then, might be how schools can promote healthy eating and how parents can support healthy eating options. When given an opportunity to appraise current practices, a group like this has the power to "learn their way" into creating and implementing new methods and approaches.

The challenge of adopting a stance of criticality

As we have seen, individuals in the case example came together because of their commitment to changing or improving something within their community; there was an urgent need to address issues of obesity in the county. While engagement participants often share a commitment to improving (which means changing) their community, they may not be committed equally to, and sometimes do not recognize the need for, changing themselves, including their own attitudes, perspectives, or practices. Yet, intrapersonal change is a necessary component in transformative work. Emancipatory knowledge (Habermas 1984) will not happen if engagement participants are unwilling or unable to engage in an exploration process. In other words, they *must* recognize that changing their own internal representations of community life is a necessary component of engagement work.

For example, although at the beginning of the case, department leaders said they wanted to be partners (not leaders) with others in designing the new program, over time, their "old way of doing business" dominated. Conversations with them about how this approach was contrary to their desire to partner had no effect on changing the decision making landscape. As a result, a year into this initiative the department failed to enable general community ownership. Instead, they controlled the project. This shows that when participants do not believe that intrapersonal change (for themselves and other engagement participants) is feasible and desirable (Armenakis, Harris, and Mossholder 1993), and fail to "unfreeze" their old attitudes and perspectives (Lewin 1951), then emancipatory knowledge is less possible and transformative change is unlikely (Bartunek and Moch 1987).

Having said all of that, making inquiry and learning central to the dialogic process is not easy. We live in a society where funding agencies, institutions (e.g., schools, hospitals), and other community agencies prefer instrumental approaches to solving complex societal problems. In our case example, instrumentality was manifest in several ways: product was valued over process, and preference was given to achieving efficient, concrete, and pre-established outcomes. There was little room for "time-consuming" dialogic processes because "too much talking" was viewed as a waste of time. Moreover, with the current societal tendency to seek a single, correct answer (that is, to find and act on "the truth") even when dialogue is affirmed it is very difficult to put into practice: people are more practiced at promoting one's point of view than listening; imputing motives than suspending judgment; and questioning others' positions than challenging their own position.

New understandings are also difficult to create if there is a history of mistrust, especially if there are preconceived notions of others' intentions and actions, if previous efforts have failed to create radical change, and if there have been negative prior experiences with university collaborators (Brown and Garg 1997). In many ways, the community in our case example experienced all of these dynamics. For example, significant disparities in wealth existed across racial lines, and community leadership solely represented what most people considered to be "the wealthy white majority." African-Americans felt that their perspective on issues and needs was either not heard or thwarted, sometimes even violently opposed. For example, requests by poor renters to have street lights placed in their neighborhoods and to live in sufficiently heated buildings were either delayed or ignored. Some complainants had their tires slashed and fires were set outside of their buildings. Moreover, "promising" programs— previously funded and viewed positively by residents in "the Projects"—were terminated prematurely with no explanation offered.

Overall, through examination of this case and other cases from our own work, we have found that we are most successful at making criticality a part of engagement work when we work with engagement partners to intentionally construct and establish a set of norms of engagement. Questions for exploration include: Why hasn't the community succeeded in the past at addressing this problem? How will our work together have to be different to overcome these barriers? Guiding values that have been particularly helpful to maintaining a stance of criticality include the understanding that no stance is sacred; that all perspectives are valid; and that we will never know (about a circumstance or position) unless we inquire.

One way to think about guiding social practices in a *learning-ful* dialogic relationship is to use implicit *rules of dialogue* as signposts of progress (Burbules 1993). Burbules nominates three such rules, but also cautions that they are subject to flexible interpretation and judgment. The first rule is the *rule of participation*. This means that discourse for learning requires voluntary, active involvement, where "any participant should be able to raise topics, pose questions, challenge other points of view, or engage in any of the other activities that define dialogic interaction" (80). The second rule is the *rule of commitment*, where participants pursue "intersubjective understanding, which may or may not result in agreement" (80). Without a commitment to see the process through to some meaningful conclusion—to stay with the process over time—communicative interaction will be distorted or cut short. The third rule is the *rule of reciprocity*, meaning that dialogue needs to be "undertaken in a spirit of mutual respect and concern, and must not take for granted roles of privilege or expertise" (82).

Discourse as a relational process: pursuing cycles of inquiry

A dialogic relationship requires a commitment among participants to pursue honest, frank, and sometimes uncomfortable discussions that are intended (and necessary) to generate new understandings about community life. Assumptions must be revealed; multiple, competing realities and solutions need to be explored and debated; and all forms of knowledge need to be valued (Greenwood and Levin 1998). Through Discourse, deeper meanings are sought as participants explore the "what's and why's" of community life. That means participants must routinely ask one another: "What do you mean?" We see this question as fundamental, as a habit of living and working together, because it is the primary avenue to sense making.

However, as our case example illustrates, sometimes "real issues" surface before shared meanings can be explored. One of the ironies of our "Discovering Discourse" case is that great lengths were taken to introduce coalition members to "best practices"—publications were purchased; nationally known experts were flown in to consult with the group for days at a time; and coalition members were sent to conferences across the country. Yet, critical learning processes did not emerge as an outcome of those efforts, at least not directly. While most coalition participants publicly acknowledged that their own personal capacity and knowledge about the issue of obesity had increased significantly, the group—together—was not able to establish an environment where knowledge was examined, and ideas, assumptions, and values were critiqued. Because of that, they did not develop a collective understanding about why obesity was a chronic problem in their community, and what might be done to change that reality.

Why did this group fail to get at the real issues? One explanation is that the coalition meetings became places where individuals focused more on crafting solutions than learning about the issue at hand. Coalition members spent meeting time "positioning themselves": many participants, including faculty members, used the meetings to convince others (mostly the department) that their partisan ideas and approaches were "best." As a result, the issue of obesity and the matter of how it played out contextually were under examined. However, in the breakthrough meeting with the department, residents focused on why previous attempts had failed in their community. And, by responding as they did, department representatives began treating residents with the respect needed for both parties to participate as co-inquirers of a complex matter.

The cycles of inquiry

Critical analysis of our own work—and examination of our interactions within our faculty learning community—have led us to understand that Discourse is a dynamic social practice that evolves (and changes) over time. It starts with critical reflection, but cannot end with a single and dramatic moment of honesty. Ongoing attention is essential, given that previously emerged understandings may no longer represent the most recent iterations of community life. Learning through Discourse unfolds through iterative cycles of inquiry. For each essential issue or understanding that emerges in the engagement interface—and for every solution or program that is proposed—participants need to *examine, critique, elevate,* and *repeat the process.*

Examine it: Participants need to understand the meaning, purpose, and potential impact of the issues they are addressing or solutions they are considering. Participants start by asking questions aimed at articulating underlying assumptions, eliminating misunderstandings, and revealing "naked truths." These questions are framed to uncover what Sackman calls "dictionary or descriptive knowledge," such as: Why is this issue or solution important? What does this mean for the community? How does or will this play out in the community? Who benefits? Who is at risk? In one sense, this involves "making 'the problem' the problem" throughout the examination process (Ulrich 2003). Participants also need to examine the underlying conditions that influence their thinking by asking questions such as: What are the historical forces that have shaped our ideas? What institutional structures have made things the way they are today? This part of the cycle continues until all participants come as close as they can to understanding the topic or issue under consideration. This requires taking time to examine different perspectives represented by people at the table and, in so doing, to suspend judgment and strive for mutual understanding.

Critique it: There are at least six interrelated dimensions to critique: information quality; evaluation of fit; feasibility; consideration of impact; commitment to continuous learning; and questioning the innovativeness of thought and action. After generating a common (albeit tentative) understanding of an issue or solution, participants *need to assess the value and quality of the information at hand.* How do we know the information is valid, up-to-date, and historically accurate? Are there information gaps? They must also consider whether the proposed way of comprehending or approaching the issue *fits the context.* Fit in this sense is a multidimensional concept—fit with respect to circumstances, values, intentions, and goals. Next, comes the matter of whether the preferred problem framing or approach is as *meaningful and relevant as the group perceives it to be.* This automatically involves comparing the preferred option to alternative options. Considerations of *impact* also need to be raised: Will anybody be affected negatively if we pursue this solution? If so, who? The need for *continuous learning* is also important, embodied in a commitment to asking: Are we missing something? What else do we need to know? Finally, because groups often "believe themselves" into thinking that their creation is new, different, and compelling, it is important to ask: Are we really doing anything new? Even if we are, does it really matter? Is it worth the time and effort?

Elevate it: After seeking understanding and assessing, the next step in the inquiry cycle involves applying the lessons learned. This process often requires further learning, such as obtaining additional information to make an informed decision, revising inaccurate understandings, or altering a solution to accommodate community circumstances. Questions that guide this phase of the inquiry process include: Where can we find the information we need to fill in the gaps? How can we improve upon the proposed solution, given what we just learned? Finally, new insights must be fed back into the dialogic process to guide future action: What does this all mean for understanding the issue in this community?

Repeat it: Learning through Discourse requires repeated cycles of inquiry. Community life is dynamic and it requires a constant focus on the question: Is what we are thinking and doing still relevant and worth doing? In addition, each new frame and proposal needs to be examined, critiqued, and elevated. When community processes create static outcomes they are less likely to result in transformative change.

Importance of democratic discourse processes
    For co-inquiry to happen in the engagement interface, learning requires democratic processes where all members are valued participants. In our experience, it is important to distinguish between democratic *participation* and democratic *processes.* Democratic *participation* suggests an egalitarian structure: power is shared equally. This may or may not be feasible because there is great variety in individual experience in decision making. In our case, in addition to the obvious power differences associated with large, public sector organizations, coalition members had differential decision making backgrounds and experiences. There were several new organizational leaders, individuals who had never been in a leadership position, and their active participation had to be groomed. At the beginning it was evident that they felt uncomfortable, as they often spoke tentatively, even sometimes apologetically. This limited participation was particularly concerning because they represented the organizations most closely linked to the needs and desires of the groups targeted by this effort.
    As the case illustrates, the expectation of immediate and full participation by all participants, without first working to develop new leadership within a group, runs the risk of merely maintaining the status quo (Constantine-David 1982). Creating egalitarian structures may be insufficient when power differentials produce inequalities of roles, responsibilities, and resources, such as

knowledge, educational expertise, and control of whether decisions are implemented (Gruber and Trickett 1987).

Alternatively, democratic *processes* include and embrace the viewpoints, knowledge, needs, and purposes of community partners (Ansley and Gaventa 1997; Heron and Reason 1997). The aim is to involve directly the people who are concerned with an issue and whose life chances are affected by it (Dewey 1916; Ulrich 2003). We saw the emergence of democratic processes at the end of our case example, processes that Habermas refers to as "language for reaching understanding," as opposed to "the instrumental" or "strategic" use of language" as Dibos (2002, 14) describes it. With democratic processes, there exists

> . . . the possibility for discussing crucial issues of our life in common (conflict, violence, justice, rights, needs, recognition, identity, inclusion, affection, and so forth), in order to reach understanding and agreement to coordinate our actions. . . . Democracy means that there is always the space or possibility to contest, to question, or to say "no" to what is in place, or to what happens to be the case. Democracy is the space and place where we express and exchange our thoughts, concerns, feelings, alternatives with regards, especially, to the issues that are very important to our lives. Democracy means enough openness to enable transformation and change to be initiated by responsible citizens, protagonists of their life in common. (2002, 15)

In our case example, community members finally found a space to communicate their concerns and worries and, with that space, had an opportunity to take charge of personally relevant solutions. Moreover, deliberative democratic processes were in play, processes that have implications for forming judgments about desired ends as well as the means for attaining them. Put another way, community members were in a position to begin applying good judgment to human conduct. For example, they began asking questions like: Who else should be at the table? How can we make all participants feel valued? How might those people not at the table be engaged in the work? Who should be leading the discussion? When questions like these are at the forefront, critical Discourse is a form of deliberative democracy where reasoned discussions about issues involving the common good take place. Deliberative processes have epistemic value as well, because those making decisions must justify their views to all involved, including those who will be most affected by the decision (Habermas 1984; Gutmann and Thompson 2000).

Discourse as text: paying attention to language and narratives
The pursuit of learning through Discourse requires attending to the language we use, especially the language we use to define a problem or to describe a desired outcome (McLeroy et al. 1988). Careful examination of language has the potential to uncover matters of community dynamics, including issues of power. For example, there was significant diversity represented in our case in

terms of levels of education, race, position affiliation, and class affiliation. Differences may cause participants to reveal only what is safe and easy to talk about, what James Scott (1985) refers to as the "public discourse." This communication form lacks criticality because it reveals only what is assumed to be common knowledge. It becomes a predominant form of discourse when participants are concerned that others might use information against them (Chavez et al. 2003) or when participants frame what they say based on assumptions that they have about what others know, expect, or prefer them to say (Bourgois, Lettiere, and Quesada 1997).

The turning point in our case example seemed to occur when the possibility of a trusting environment emerged. When trust is established and sustained, inquiry is possible, which enables group members to purposively examine not only what is said but who speaks and who is silent. Such examination makes it possible to discover the more meaningful and often "hidden transcripts" about community life (Chavez et al. 2003). Certainly, at times, disclosure of these transcripts takes place informally and outside of a larger group context, especially when the knowledge or information involved could put others at risk. For example, the faculty in our case were invited into numerous and private one-on-one discussions with coalition participants. It was in those private meetings that the faculty learned about concerns that members had about the coalition's status, progress, and prospects, and also became familiar with racial issues in the community and how members felt that those issues were playing out as the coalition's work unfolded.

As these transcripts are revealed in a community episode, discomfort often increases, making formal conversations, inquiry, theorizing about local matters, and the search for meaning all the more challenging, yet all the more essential, too. For example, after one of the faculty members heard about the possible undercurrent of racism—learning that the department rejected a request from two African-American leaders to join this coalition—she called the department and requested a private meeting with them. Representatives requested that she describe the concerns (and what she had heard) at the next coalition meeting. While coalition members were impressed with the willingness of the department to have the concerns raised in public, the public airing of this matter had a reverberating effect. Department leaders responded defensively to the accusations made and questions raised, and then simply suggested moving off the subject to the next agenda topic. As often happens, though, rather than viewing an action as conclusive, raising a sub-textual matter to the surface often is akin to planting seeds in the spring. In this case, four months after the meeting, the department reframed their vision for this initiative and, in so doing, reduced inequities across racial lines.

As this example illustrates, as individuals uncover, discover, and bring uncomfortable issues to the surface—whether they be matters associated with racism, inequitable distribution of resources, or institutionalized oppression—

conflict of some magnitude is almost guaranteed (Gutierrez and Lewis 1997). Having said that, the presence of conflict is often an indication that transformation is possible; an important first step has been taken—the unspoken has been spoken and, with that, discourse is possible.

Engaging with a community to make public a more complete narrative about community life is a powerful attribute (Rappaport 1998) of the engagement interface. When hidden transcripts are revealed, an opportunity exists to explore fundamental issues, such as why and how these transcripts came to be (i.e., understanding critical community history); what these transcripts mean in and for community life (i.e., the reality context); and the implications these transcripts have for community development (i.e., the future possibilities) (Habermas 1984). In many cases, the prospects of creating novel narratives about community life, which is another way of talking about community development, are contingent on the prospects of developing new roles and relationships.

Exploring narratives to construct new roles and relationships

Learning within the interface is an evolving, ambiguous endeavor (Perkins et al. 1994) often requiring examination of the narratives we hold about existing roles and relationships so that new ones can be created. As we described earlier, collaborative endeavors may provide some participants with their first opportunity to assume a decision making position in their community. In our case example, new roles for community members may require powerful partners (such as foundation leaders and public sector leaders) to share authority and control with others. When stakeholders hold personally restrictive role definitions and prescribe narrow roles for others, they are unlikely to adopt or enact these new roles. For example, community members often hold narrow role prescriptions for individuals or groups who have been traditionally excluded from positions of power and privilege. In our case, many community leaders were hesitant to have resident leaders from "the projects" participate in the coalition because they felt these individuals did not have the skills to fully engage in this complex work.

While the very process of collaborative inquiry is one in which roles are redefined and opportunities are made available, stakeholders must first perceive the possibility before enacting or supporting these new roles. When these behaviors are viewed as illegitimate or when stakeholders fear the potential loss of political power (Frost and Egri 1990) collaboration and learning are less viable.

In our work, we have used a range of formal and informal techniques, such as Blake and Mouton's imaging exercise, stakeholder analyses, and story telling over lunch. These techniques represent different approaches to a mutual discovery process, where university and community partners disclose their personal and professional experiences, values, motivations, and expectations for the joint endeavor (Maton 2000). Sharing and examining personal narratives provides a critical context from which to understand individual comments and action; to reduce misinterpretation; and to mitigate interpersonal conflict. Ultimately, such sharing can be intra- and interpersonally transformative for all participants, university and community alike.

Discovering and sharing of narrative histories need to continue throughout the collaborative learning process. Personal and professional situations are constantly shifting and these shifts can have dramatic impact on one's behavior and on the emerging culture of engagement at the interface. Through the construction of new and expansive roles for community members, new forms of discourse—and new insights and better outcomes—are more likely to emerge.

Conclusion

To this point we have portrayed a particular type of dialogic interaction—critical Discourse—that takes place in the conceptual space we call the engagement interface. We have taken the position that critical, deliberative Discourse is an essential mode of engagement that enables participants to learn and discover approaches to seeking transformative ends. We have also argued that by changing the way faculty and community partners interact and communicate it is possible to move the focus of community work from *doing things better* to *doing better things*.

In the three chapters that follow, we shall focus on three interrelated matters, namely, using social capital to leverage change, enabling co-empowerment, and achieving transformative outcomes.

References

Ansley, F., and J. Gaventa. 1997. Researching for democracy and democratizing research. *Change* Jan/Feb:46–53.

Armenakis, A. A., S. G. Harris, and K. W. Mossholder. 1993. Creating readiness for organization change. *Human Relations* 46(6):685–703.

Bakhtin, M. 1981. *The dialogic imagination.* Austin: Univ. of Texas Press.

Bartunek, J. M., and M. K. Moch. 1987. First-order, second-order, and third-order change and organizational development interventions: A cognitive approach. *Journal of Applied Behavioral Science* 23:483–500.

Bohm, D. 1996. *On dialogue.* London: Routledge.

Bourgois, P., M. Lettiere, and J. Quesada. 1997. Social misery and the sanctions of substance abuse: Confronting HIV risk among homeless heroin addicts in San Francisco. *Social Problems* 44:155–173.

Brown, P., and S. Garg. 1997. *Foundations and comprehensive community initiatives: The challenges of partnerships.* Chicago: Chapin Hall Center for Children.

Bruner, J. 1986. *Actual minds, possible worlds.* Cambridge MA: Harvard Univ. Press.

Burbules, N. 1993. *Dialogue in teaching: Theory and practice.* New York: Teachers College Press.

Chavez, A. F., F. Guido-Cibrito, and S. L. Mallory. 2003. Learning to value the 'Other': A framework of individual diversity development. *Journal of College Student Development* 44(4):453–469.

Constantino-David, K. 1982. Issues in community organization. *Community Development Journal* 17(3):190–200.

Dewey, J. 1916. *Democracy and education.* New York: Macmillan.

Dibos, A. 2002. Democracy as responsibility, meaning and hope: Introductory reflections on a democratic project in education. *Journal of Thought* 37(1):11–24.

Foster-Fishman, P. G., D. Perkins, and W. Davidson. 1997. Developing effective evaluation partnerships: Paradigmatic and contextual barriers. *Analise Psicologica* 3(15):389–403.

Flick, D. L. 1998. *From debate to dialogue: Using the understanding process to transform our conversations.* Boulder CO: Orchid Publications.

Freire, P. 1985. Reading the world and reading the word: An interview with Paulo Freire. *Language Arts* 62:15–16.

Frost, P. J., and C. P. Egri. 1990. Influence of political action on innovation. *Leadership and Organization Development Journal* 11(1):17–25.

Gee, J. P. 1992. *The social mind: Language, ideology, and social practice.* New York: Bergin & Garvey.

Greenwood, D. J., and M. Levin. 1998. Introduction to action research: Social research for social change. Thousand Oaks CA: Sage Publications.

Gruber, J., and E. J. Trickett. 1987. Can we empower others: The paradox of empowerment in the governing of an alternative public school. *American Journal of Community Psychology* 15(3):353–371.

Gutierrez, L. M., and E. A. Lewis. 1997. Education, participation, and capacity building in community organizing with women of color. In M. Minkler, ed. *Community organizing and community building for health.* New Brunswick NJ: Rutgers Univ. Press.

Gutmann, A., and D. Thompson. 2000. Deliberative democracy beyond process. Paper prepared for the Conference on Deliberating about Deliberative Democracy. Austin: Univ. of Texas.

Habermas, J. 1984. *Theory of communicative action. Vol I. Reason and the rationalization of society.* Boston: Beacon Press.

Heron, J., and P. Reason. 1997. A participatory inquiry paradigm. *Qualitative Inquiry* 3(3):274–294.

hooks, bell. 1994. *Outlaw culture.* New York: Routledge.

Israel, B. A., S. H. Schurman, M. K. Hugentobler. 1992. Conducting action research: Relationships between organization members and researchers. *Journal of Applied Behavioral Science* Vol. 28(1) Mar. 1992:74–101.

Jason, L., C. Keys, Y. Suarez-Balcazar, R. Taylor, and M. Davis, eds. 2004. Participatory community research: Theories and methods in action. Washington D.C.: American Psychological Association.

Lewin, K. 1951. *Field theory in social sciences.* New York: Harper.

Maton, K. I. 2000. Making a difference: The social ecology of social transformation. *American Journal of Community Psychology* 28(1):25–57.

McLeroy, K. R., D. Bibeau, A. Steckler, and K. Glanz. 1988. An ecological perspective on health promotion programs. *Health Education Quarterly* 15:351–377.

Minkler, M., and N. Wallerstein. 2003. Introduction to community-based participatory research. In M. Minkler and N. Wallerstein, eds. *Community-based participatory research for health.* San Francisco CA: Jossey-Bass.

Perkins, D. F., T. M. Ferrari, M. A. Covey, and J. G. Keith. 1994. Getting dinosaurs to dance: Community collaborations as applications of ecological theory. *Home Economics FORUM*/Spring.

Rappaport, J. 1998. The art of social change: Community narratives as resources for individual and collective identity. In X. B. Arriaga and S. Oskamp, eds. *Addressing community problems: Psychological research and interventions.* Thousand Oaks CA: Sage Publications.

Rosaen, C. L., P. G. Foster-Fishman, and F. Fear. 2001. The citizen scholar: Joining voices and values in the engagement interface. *Metropolitan Universities* 12(4):10–29.

Schoem, D., and S. Hurtado. 2001. *Intergroup dialogue: Deliberative democracy in school, college, community, and workplace.* Ann Arbor: Univ. of Michigan Press.

Schön, D. 1987. *Educating the reflective practitioner.* San Francisco: Jossey-Bass.

Scott, J. 1985. *Weapons of the weak.* New Haven CT: Yale Univ. Press.

Shor, I., and P. Freire. 1987. What is the 'dialogic method' of teaching? *Journal of Education* 169:11–31.

Springett, D. 2003. An 'incitement to discourse': Benchmarking as a springboard to sustainable development. *Business Strategy and the Environment* 12(1):1–11.

Ulrich, W. 2003. Beyond methodology choice: Critical systems thinking as critically systemic discourse. *Journal of the Operation Research Society* 54(4):325–342.

Wallerstein, N. 1992. Powerlessness, empowerment, and health: Implications for health promotion programs. *American Journal of Health Promotion* 6(3):197–205.

Wicker, A. W. 1985. Getting out of our conceptual ruts: Strategies for expanding conceptual frameworks. *American Psychologist* 40:1094–1103.

Yankelovich, D. 1999. *The magic of dialogue.* New York: Touchstone Books.

CHAPTER 6

FROM BUILDING CONNECTIONS TO DEVELOPING SOCIAL CAPITAL TO LEVERAGE CHANGE

A hallmark of community-based work—and work within the engagement interface—is that it pulls together people from different contexts to work toward shared purposes. Take, for example, a community struggling with high levels of child abuse. As community leaders and faculty members identify whom to engage in a development effort associated with this problem, they note that individuals representing a wide range of contexts should be included, such as representatives from public and private service delivery organizations, family homeless shelters, child advocacy agencies, parent training centers, and the judicial system. It is not unusual, then, for lawyers, parents, child advocates, nonprofit executives, elected officials, case workers, and faculty from the local university to find themselves—perhaps for the first time as a group—at community meetings to discuss the problem of child abuse. While the targeted issue and the players involved may vary, it has become commonplace for diverse groups to come to the table for the purpose of identifying shared goals and developing plans to address them.

Despite the popularity of bringing diverse stakeholders together to address significant issues, there is a growing body of empirical literature and anecdotal "stories on the street" to convince even the most committed collaborator that such efforts represent hard and difficult work. Why? For one reason or another, diverse groups often share a history of conflict, misunderstanding, and distrust, as well as represent power imbalances and competing priorities. These factors, coupled with the reality that some stakeholders have limited experience working collaboratively (Bartunek, Foster-Fishman, and Keys 1996; Wischnowski and McCollum 1995), impede collaborative processes and action (Foster-Fishman, Perkins, and Davidson 1997). Consequently, a critical part of the work at the interface—and an important part of Discourse processes as they unfold—is the creation of a new form of relational community.

This chapter discusses the importance of promoting connections and positive relationships among partners at the interface. It highlights what is gained when critical Discourse plays a central role in the process of building these connections and helping them evolve into more sustainable relationships. The central focus in this chapter is what we call *the development of social capital to leverage change.*

We start with a description about why connections need to be fostered and follow with a description of a community project undertaken by Foster-Fishman and others that was designed intentionally to foster connections. We then consider how a concern for social capital augments the connection process. Strategies for promoting discourse in the process of building connections and social capital are highlighted at chapter's end.

The value of connectivity

Involving multiple and diverse stakeholders in community-based work is an engagement staple. For one thing, it is widely believed that the involvement of different stakeholders at the interface—and access to diverse perspectives, ideas, solutions, and resources—can strengthen a group's capacity to address an issue of common concern (e.g., Allen 2005; Foster-Fishman et al. 2001a; Israel et al. 1998; Lasker and Weiss 2003; Kelly et al. 1988). In addition, the active involvement of multiple stakeholders in the problem-solving process can provide a broad base of support for interventions (Altman 1995; Lasker, Weiss, and Miller, 2001). Involvement in community decision making processes is also believed to increase the commitment of those involved to change efforts (e.g., Kelly et al. 1988). Recent evaluations of multiple stakeholder effectiveness suggests that more diverse groups—as interpreted in terms of diverse representation of community sectors and in racial composition—are perceived to be more effective (Allen 2005) and often have greater impact (Hays et al. 2000).

While inviting a diverse and representative group of stakeholders to the table is an important part of engaging community members in shared efforts, work at the interface will not proceed successfully unless participants develop strong connections and vibrant social relationships (Foster-Fishman et al. 2001a). Stakeholder relationships not only provide the medium for collaborative work, they also enable access to needed resources (Lin 1999); promote stakeholder commitment, satisfaction, and involvement (Butterfoss, Goodman, and Wandersman 1996); Sheldon-Keller, Lloyd-McGarvey, and Canterbury 1995) and increase the likelihood that collaborative efforts will be sustained in the long term (Chavis 1995). In other words, work at the interface often requires participants to broaden their relational networks and find new ways of interacting with current contacts.

However, achieving positive relationships with strong connections among partners is a necessary, but not sufficient, factor for enabling transformative change. If we want our work to lead to transformative ends, then emerging community connections must enable the exchange of information, resources, and ideas needed for collective action. In addition, these connections must yield the sort of trust and social cohesion that makes it possible for collaborative efforts to unfold naturally and sustainably.

When partners at the interface develop inter-group processes based on mutuality—and when partners also make available to each other the resources that exist in those networks—then collaborative efforts not only foster connections, they build *social capital*. Social capital is a critical currency for communities and groups: it fosters the flow of resources, opportunities, and information required for groups of people and individuals to take action effectively.

Working to build connections: the role of discourse

During our faculty learning community meetings we shared "war stories" about the challenges associated with building social capital in organizational and community settings. Irrespective of scale or scope of context, we found that our partners often described themselves as relatively disconnected from each other—often unfamiliar with the work, values, background, and priorities of others at the table—even if they had collaborated previously.

What have we learned from experience? First of all, diverse collaborations seemed to work more effectively when we took the time to help strengthen connectivity between and among participants (Bartunek et al. 1996; Foster-Fishman et al. 2001a). As a result, in past work we have worked hard to help partners learn more about each other; discover what they have in common; and gain insights into and about their connectedness and interdependence. From experience we also recognize that connectivity comes in many forms and across multiple dimensions: sometimes as personal connections, as members discover shared life histories and/or overlapping social networks; and sometimes as substantive commonalities, as partners discover they share values, worldviews, and similar thoughts about issues at hand. Finally, we have learned that commonalities represent the heart of connectivity, stimulating participants to *want* to work together, especially when they begin to see "all the possibilities" that may be enabled by joint activity. When that happens, members invariably recognize each other as assets (Maton 2000) and, with that, start envisioning all the things it may be possible for them to accomplish together.

How does Discourse play a part in the process of building connections and creating social capital? Transforming relationships at the engagement interface requires, first, learning why and how relationships exist as they do and, then, reflecting critically on how new relational forms might lead to transformative processes and ends. In many ways, Discourse at the interface creates a subtext where—as part of the process of critical inquiry—partners begin to discover, then understand, and finally act, in new and transformed ways. For this to happen, the norm of criticality must be in play, meaning that the climate must be hospitable to examining assumptions; analyzing habits of past interactions; and critiquing historical and social/political factors (including critical incidents, episodes, experiences, and personalities) that have influenced the current reality.

The goal of building connections and the desire to foster Discourse are interdependent, symbiotic processes. Building connections without Discourse can result in *under*whelming outcomes, as members fool themselves in thinking transformation is taking place. By the same token, engaging in Discourse without building connections can have disastrous outcomes, giving those involved plenty of reasons for wanting to *stay away* from the table. From our experience, we have found that it takes strong connections for Discourse to be sustained: individuals are not likely to engage in authentic reflection and critical inquiry unless they know and trust their colleagues. And Discourse helps unlock transformative possibilities, enabling participants to see the past and the future with "fresh eyes" as they engage in interpersonal give and take.

Of central importance is not using "the table" as a staging ground for getting others to accept one's way of thinking and agenda but, rather, seeing the table as an opportunity field for changing one's way of thinking and, then, crafting with others an agenda that emerges through interpersonal exchange and public insights. When all of that happens, Discourse is far from a sterile, analytic, intellectual experience. It helps build trust, the glue that keeps connections solid and helps them grow into social capital. Discourse emerges *through* connections in the form of norms of engagement, which is another way of referring to the culture of the engagement interface—a culture centered around the *mutual* learning that happens through dialogic processes and in the form of cycles of learning as described earlier in this book.

Emphasizing connections in our work: a case example

We now move to a case example from Foster-Fishman's work: how Discourse processes helped promote connection, and ultimately social capital, in a community-based effort. We describe initial attempts to foster connections across diverse stakeholders, and then comment about how participants, over time, recognized the central role of building social capital in the quest to achieve transformative outcomes. The role of Discourse is highlighted throughout.

Phase 1: Addressing a history of disconnection

The field of disabilities is plagued with considerable dissent and disagreement: primary stakeholders—including people with disabilities, family members of individuals with disabilities, and human service delivery professionals—often disagree on basic issues, including what issues to prioritize, how services should be delivered, and how resources should be expended. Even among people with disabilities, significant disagreement exists concerning these issues. These disagreements have often impeded the disability community's ability to mobilize different constituencies around shared policy goals. For example, during legislative hearings different disability advocacy groups sometimes argue for different (and sometimes competing) policy and resource allocation goals.

While efforts have been made to foster collaboration across disability groups and organizations—and important steps have been made in that direction—many disability advocates acknowledge that mutual understanding and agreement on appropriate future courses of action do not exist currently. Some policy makers have claimed that progress will be impeded unless and until the disability community unites around shared understandings and goals.

Perhaps in response to this circumstance, many federal agencies require key disability organizations to engage multiple and diverse stakeholders in state-level planning and program design. In Michigan, for example, disability organizations work together periodically to craft a strategic plan for independent living, services, and supports. Known as the "State Plan for Independent Living" (SPIL), the plan is intended to guide decision making and action regarding policy development, program design and selection, and resource allocation, among other things. However, the SPIL in Michigan had been seen by some stakeholders as an ineffective tool for promoting organizational collaboration and systemic change.

In 2000, the organization responsible for leading the SPIL planning process—called the State Independent Living Council (SILC)—recognized that a more strategic effort was needed to foster meaningful change. Toward that end, SILC hired Foster-Fishman and one of her graduate students to improve collaborative relationships. The first step was to organize a strategic planning process designed to promote broad scale buy-in for SPIL across a range of disability focused organizations. Some of these organizations had not been involved in previous planning processes, including organizations representing people who are blind and deaf; have developmental disabilities; experience mental illness; suffer from spinal cord injuries; and live with cerebral palsy.

During this initial effort—and throughout the duration of her time with SILC and its partners—Foster-Fishman's primary role was to facilitate processes that nurture learning through critical dialogue. Put more directly, this meant encouraging opportunities for enabling dialogic conversations about assumptions, issues, and perspectives that had not heretofore been a central feature of SILC's strategic planning efforts. In addition, because this assignment unfolded in parallel to the faculty learning community effort as described in this book, the experience offered Foster-Fishman a robust opportunity to explore and apply ideas that were under scholarly consideration. Specifically, she used the "examine, critique, elevate" framework presented in this book to guide her work with SILC.

Examine it. SILC asked Foster-Fishman to design a retreat that would excite state and regional disability leaders about the potential impact of a statewide plan. Of particular interest was using the retreat to galvanize commitment to the belief that all disability groups should work together to craft shared goals, including those that had not been involved in prior SPIL-related processes. In practical terms, achieving this vision required giving affirmative responses to two core questions: *Is it possible to establish and sustain (in meaningful, and not just in "on paper" terms) an inclusive network of disability organizations? Once established, can members of this network discover common ground?*

Because Foster-Fishman had prior experience working in the disabilities arena, she knew that past efforts had failed to achieve compatible goals. In fact, in Michigan these failed attempts have become "urban legends," dominating conversations about future prospects. Because of that, she knew it was essential to reframe the new effort, not simply try to do a better job at what had been attempted previously. The approach undertaken this time would be an inquiry process: collaborators were asked to share their vision for inclusion and also to articulate the meaning, purpose, and potential of collaboration in the disabilities domain.

Because of known conflicts among some stakeholders (which Foster-Fishman believed would mitigate the prospects of having successful conversations in group settings), she and her graduate student solicited initial input in the form of personal interviews from among about forty individuals who were identified by SILC as key disability leaders in Michigan. These interviews served multiple goals, including learning about the stakeholders' perceptions of SILC; their interest in supporting inclusion; and what they saw as priorities and preferred change strategies. Respondents were also asked to provide input on planning retreat goals, offer their interpretation of past efforts to work together more effectively, and suggest what they saw as the likely future for collaboration in Michigan. As described in the previous chapter, the interviews were designed to uncover what Sackman (1991) calls "dictionary" (or descriptive) knowledge.

Following the personal interviews, Foster-Fishman and her student coded the interview data, culling from responses themes related to these questions:

- What are the goals and preferences of different stakeholder groups?
- To what extent is there agreement or disagreement?
- Do partners feel that collaboration is an important part of achieving these goals?
- What is required for collaboration to succeed?
- Can SPIL play a prominent role in fostering new connections and collaborations?

Responses were then shared with SILC leaders and the meanings were interpreted in collaboration with Foster-Fishman and her student. The ultimate task before the group was to determine by mutual agreement whether or not the data suggested that collaborative goals and processes should be pursued as part of the SPIL process.

Much to the surprise of all involved, most stakeholders said that collaboration was absolutely essential and acknowledged that—under the *right* circumstances—SILC might succeed at building the sort of connections that had failed to materialize in the past. When asked about those conditions, respondents felt that previous efforts had failed because of perceptions of mistrust, skill limitations, and exclusion. Specifically, conveners were not fully trusted; they were not perceived to have the leadership skills necessary to realize collaborative outcomes; and past efforts had excluded (perhaps unintentionally) a variety of groups in the disability community. In contrast to the negative perceptions associated with past efforts, most respondents acknowledged that SILC was in a unique position to succeed at collaboration. The reasons given align with what we know from the literature about what it takes to convene a successful, collaborative effort in a multi-stakeholder environment, namely, that the convening organization is seen as legitimate; is prepared to identify and involve all relevant stakeholders; and is perceived to be trustworthy (Wood and Gray 1991).

Critique it. Emboldened by the emphasis stakeholders placed on collaboration and the support for SILC's role as a catalytic force, organizational leaders invited the Foster-Fishman team to design a year-long process. The goals were to facilitate inter-organizational collaboration and foster stakeholder buy-in to the mission of inclusion. This follow-up effort was launched with a two-day retreat.

To create common understanding, Foster-Fishman began the retreat by sharing the interview findings. Participants were then asked to critique the findings, first, by assessing face validity (that is, to determine if the findings were trustworthy) and, second, by evaluating usefulness (that is, to determine if the findings were helpful given the task at hand). At issue were two prominent matters: whether collaboration was perceived to be critical for achieving the goal of inclusion for people with disabilities; and, if it was, whether the participating organizations would be willing to engage in a deliberate, sustained effort to strengthen connections across disability organizations, services, and interest groups.

An important step toward addressing those matters was helping retreat participants learn more about the efforts and priorities of the organizations represented in the room. To create awareness and nurture mutual understanding, Foster-Fishman and her student created a wall-size matrix listing every organization participating in the retreat. Organizational representatives were invited to list their respective goals, key programs, and to identify the disability groups with which they work. When all the information was on the wall, participants were able to see the real context of the disability domain in Michigan, including (for example) a list of all the organizations in the state that provide job employment services. Once the matrix was completed, participants were asked to study it in terms of these questions:

- What are you learning by looking at this matrix?
- What does the information tell you about the services and supports that are offered to people with disabilities?
- Which services are missing/not represented?

The usefulness of this matrix was obvious: many retreat participants spent break time seeking out representatives from various organizations to explore matters of mutual interest. And because of its immediate and longer-term value, an electronic copy was created and distributed to all participants within a week of the retreat.

As the two-day retreat proceeded, Foster-Fishman and student engaged the stakeholders in a futuring process informed by the work of Weisbord and others (1995). By the end of the retreat, participants decided on themes associated with the new SPIL, including vision, strategies, and obstacles. As part of this process, Foster-Fishman encouraged participants to examine the vision critically:

- Who might be impacted negatively if we pursue this path?
- Is there something we are missing here?
- Is there something that we do not yet fully understand?
- What else do we need to know?
- Does this vision and emerging plan offer anything new to people with disabilities in Michigan?

At the end of the retreat, multiple action teams were organized around core strategies. The action teams were expected to develop detailed implementation plans that could be incorporated into the SPIL and, later, to make a three-month progress report to SILC.

Evaluation results drawn from responses to an exit questionnaire suggested that participants were generally "enthused" about the vision and also believed that, this time, "our efforts at collaboration will really work!" Participants left the retreat excited about the potential for successful collaboration, and plans were made to meet again as a group.

Elevate it. Within two weeks of the retreat, Foster-Fishman and her student met with SILC leaders to evaluate the retreat. Overall, SILC leaders felt that the process was particularly successful at promoting a new awareness of, and commitment to, collaboration across an expanded group of disability groups. Feedback from the field supported that perception: there was anecdotal evidence that participants were "talking up" the value of the experience, saying how excited they were about the prospects for the SPIL. In addition, SILC leaders had received calls from disability organizations asking to be involved in the next meeting.

To deepen their understanding of the retreat experience, Foster-Fishman asked SILC leaders to engage in dialogue with her on the following questions:

- Did we achieve what we expected to achieve?
- Did we really establish a new norm for collaboration?
- Did the retreat contribute to the development of the SPIL? What else is needed to complete the SPIL?
- What else can be done to move forward this collaborative effort?

The conversation that followed focused on two matters: first, how to provide action teams with the support they need to complete plans and implement outcomes; and, second, how to strengthen the spirit of cooperation fostered by and at the retreat.

Following the retreat, the action teams were also asked to elevate their work. First, teams were encouraged to seek feedback about their emerging plans from additional groups and to revise their respective plans based on that input. In addition, teams were invited to reflect on lessons learned about collaboration from previous, failed efforts and, then, to share with SILC how those lessons might be used to improve the current round of work.

Some reflections on this stage of the work

As SILC leaders reflected with Foster-Fishman about this first stage experience, themes emerged from the learning experience.

Creating multiple opportunities for reflection. Critical examination and reflection were means to promote a shift in stakeholder relationships during the initial part of the learning cycle. Three strategies in particular improved the quality and outcome of phase-one activity.

First, respondent feedback during and after the interviews made it clear how important it was to begin the process with personal interviews: points of view conveyed in a private setting would not have been shared in a group setting. Clearly, personal interviews allowed interviewees to "say what they had to say" without being concerned that their opinions would be used against them.

Second, in feeding back the interview results at the retreat, the Foster-Fishman team not only emphasized points of convergence but also noted the range of responses offered to various questions. Doing that promoted dialogue by, first, giving participants a sense of things they had in common and, second, making it clear to them what issues required collective attention. With trust an issue, publicly acknowledging the range of responses validated the opinions of respondents who might otherwise have been perceived by colleagues as obstructionists.

Third, as important as it was to promote individual learning and shared understanding, there were two other key aspects associated with the first-phase activity: organizational learning for SILC and the application of that learning to design a SPIL. To accomplish those goals, the Foster-Fishman team built into the process repeated check points—multiple breaks from "the doing"—to examine progress toward achieving elevated standards.

Establishing a norm for critical reflection WITH democratic processes. From the beginning, the Foster-Fishman team emphasized how important it would be to establish and maintain expectations for reflection, dialogue, and democratic processes. Although it is easy to see how these activities are connected dynamically, less apparent are the challenges involved, especially in a situation characterized by issues of trust and voice, together with a track record of limited success. Norms of engagement in this circumstance would need to be established collectively, understood publicly, practiced routinely, and reinforced through success. Especially difficult would be breaking from tradition and, in effect, setting aside previous norms "without making a big deal about it." This is a palpable example of a point made thematically in chapter 3: that is, how individuals and groups often need to "live their way into a new way of thinking."

By starting the retreat with the presentation of interview data, and then engaging the group in a conversation about these findings, those involved practiced the art of listening carefully, responding critically, and engaging respectfully in a public setting. An important feature of this dialogue was the contextual tone—the need to establish mutual understanding in a collaborative environment with an elevated goal in mind, namely, how and what to do differently this time to make significant improvements statewide. To accomplish that goal, the group needed to critically examine past processes—and do that without attributing blame—as a means to move forward on a new path.

By engaging in dialogue about their perceptions of the findings and, then, locating intersections of understanding, the group began building the type of "communicative context" (Kelly and Van Vlaenderen 1995) needed for successful and sustainable collective social action. Especially important in this regard is the need to create what Habermas (1984) refers to as the "speech conditions" for discourse. For example, no single stakeholder group, organization, or individual was permitted to dominate the conversation. To ensure that would not happen, attention was paid to three critical matters: (1) seeking the input of those whose voices had not yet been heard (encouraging diversity of perspective); (2) asking the group to constantly assess what had been offered (not accepting a dominant voice's perspective as "the truth"); and (3) inviting additional perspectives or opinions about an issue under discussion (avoiding premature closure).

In all of these ways, those involved made progress toward creating a discourse community, a community that operated democratically and respectfully. The challenge, of course, was to avoid constant monitoring by "discourse police." A discourse community matures when group members engage naturally and spontaneously, without being told when and how. Along that line, consider the relevance of this observation made toward the end of the retreat: "*Wait! Be-*

fore we make any decisions we need to hear from the deaf community. They ha-ven't yet had a chance to share their perspective."

Avoiding premature consensus. Sometimes groups are so hungry to find common ground that the quest for consensus can become an end in itself. If that happens, the desire to agree can obscure authentic disagreement. A false consensus then emerges, only to be uncovered later. If that happens, groups find themselves no better off (perhaps even worse) than before. Being able to work through disagreements toward authentic consensus is particularly challenging in situations where stakeholders have differential access to power and resources (Kelly and Van Vlaenderen 1995) and when they feel pressure to support the collective plan and move the process forward (Foster-Fishman et al. 2001b). These pressures are particularly present when decision making and dialogue occur only at the large group level.

For these reasons, Foster-Fishman and team engaged participants in a variety of ways—through individual input and reflection, small group interaction, and large group discussion—at each step of the way. For example, at each decision point during the futuring process, individuals were given worksheets as a means to capture personal thoughts, concerns, and ideas about the issues under consideration. For example, during the section on "Identifying Potential Challenges" participants were asked to reflect on the following: Given your experiences in your local community and in this state, what are some real obstacles and barriers that might get in the way of this vision becoming a reality? Individuals were then asked to share their ideas in small, diverse groups of approximately five to six persons. Significant time was allotted in group time so that each participant could share ideas and, then, all members could engage in conversation in a small group setting.

To ensure that group ideas were represented in large group discussions, each group shared with the entire audience consensus themes that emerged during the small group discussion. To ensure that individual perspectives were not lost—and a false consensus did not emerge—each list had to include ideas from multiple group members AND each item on the list had to be supported by all group members. In the large group dialogue, each group posted ideas—first pasting them on the wall using 5" x 8" cards (one card for each idea), and then describing each idea to the audience. The large group task involved identifying what was common and unique across the groups, with similar issues then clustered together. Once this phase of the process ended, the group was asked to reflect on what they had created. To reduce the likelihood that a false consensus was emerging, participants were asked to uncover dissonance and/or disagreement: Can you find your voice here? Are your concerns represented? What is missing? What do we need to add? Whose perspective might be missing here?

This step was especially important because it led to dialectical exchange—a robust give and take, where different participants and sub-groups presented contrasting viewpoints about the issues discussed. Through this process, two outcomes were observed: a deeper understanding of issues began to unfold and bonds of community among the participants deepened.

Addressing the challenge with retreats. Immediately after the retreat there was a relatively high level of energy around the vision. However, energy created in ad hoc settings is hard to sustain in daily work settings. Faced with the reality of workloads—and with long-standing obstacles to collaboration—individuals and teams struggled to meet their retreat commitments. The result: within six to nine months, most of the action teams had dissolved.

Reflecting on this process—and the successes and failures of it—Foster-Fishman and SILC leaders recognized that the retreat involvement accomplished a number of important things. Among others, it enabled initial contacts; nurtured inter-group awareness; and identified possible nodes of connection across partners. However, when undertaken as a stand-alone intervention, a retreat experience will not help participants overcome—once and for all—a pre-existing and pervasive culture of distrust. For trust to be sustained, individuals need to, first, interact over long periods of time and, then, see benefits accrue from those interactions (Putnam 2000). By working together over an extended period of time, individuals begin to understand one another. That, in turn, strengthens interpersonal connections and facilitates the flow of resources between partners (Fountain 1998). As relationships develop, trust continues to build and social capital expands. Trust is central to fostering and maintaining sufficient levels of social capital (Mandell 2001); and social capital is ultimately needed if a network is to sustain a new way of working together.

While the retreat fostered connections as measured by increased awareness, understanding, and a belief in mutual goals, it did not engender the sort of reciprocity, trust, and resource exchange characteristic of strongly cohesive networks—where social capital flourishes. Along this line, Das and Teng (2001) distinguish between two types of trust: *goodwill trust* and *competence trust.* Goodwill trust pertains to the intentions of partners to get things done and carry out joint efforts. Competence trust, on the other hand, refers to the ability and capacity to actually complete agreed-to work. Although the retreat created high levels of goodwill trust, there remained the unvarnished reality of needing to work together in the weeks and months to follow. Because trust is a multi-level phenomenon—functioning at the personal, organizational, and inter-organizational levels—building trust at all levels is needed for social capital to flow.

For SILC to succeed at building a stronger and expanded network, it needs to help partners work together effectively. Toward that end, it cannot be assumed that once partners agree on shared goals that they will: (1) know how to accomplish those goals; (2) have the ability to do what needs to be done; and (3) be able to work through the inevitable challenges of group work. Overall, the development of trust across partners activates the potential for significant social transformation. Because trust facilitates the flow of skills, knowledge, and resources available across a network, it influences the level of social capital that ensues.

Thinking about the case in broader terms: the value of social capital

Why is social capital so critical to the work in the engagement interface? Social capital refers to the processes of building social relations, accessing resources within those social relations, and using those resources and relations for specific benefits or outcomes (Lin 1999). As it relates to the work at the engagement interface, social capital emerges when the necessary norms and interpersonal and inter-organizational networks are built so that partners can work effectively to pursue shared objectives (Gittell and Vidal 1998). Put simply, when norms are in place that promote the establishment of social networks, relationships become resources for sharing knowledge, skills, and the other resources. Over time, as network members have multiple opportunities to share and gain access to resources, they become accustomed to exchanging what is needed to "get the job done." It is our belief that social capital at the interface demands high levels of trust, support, belongingness, and cohesiveness (Lin 1999). It also needs to unfold in a discourse community. These are factors, we believe, that contribute to positive socio-emotional and behavioral outcomes (e.g., Maton 2000).

Overall, there are two main types of social capital: *bonding capital* and *bridging capital* (Putnam 2000). Bonding capital strengthens the relationships between people who are connected with each other already; and bridging capital links individuals and organizations that have not been heretofore connected. Both forms are critical to the work at the engagement interface: bonding capital nurtures and sustains social cohesion within existing networks; and bridging capital expands capacity through diversifying involvement and opportunities. Collaborative efforts with high levels of both bonding and bridging capital are more likely to achieve sustained social change (Bourdieu 1986; Portes 1998).

A challenge at the interface is avoiding the trap of believing that more levels of one form of social capital, especially bonding capital, can replace lower levels of the other form. Take, for instance, a project that focuses on improving quality of life in poor neighborhoods, specifically seeking to enhance residents' educational and economic standing. This effort will inevitably involve local residents, representatives from neighborhood associations, and leaders from key public and nonprofit organizations that provide resident services. The development challenge this group will face is clear: residents in poor neighborhoods often have less robust social networks (Wacquant and Wilson 1989) with limited access to expanded resources and opportunities (Sampson and Groves 1989).

With the strong link between social capital and a variety of positive outcomes for individuals and communities (e.g., Goddard 2003; Hawe and Shiell 2000; Ream 2003), wise action requires not focusing exclusively on strengthening existing inter-organizational networks but, rather, using development efforts to recalibrate, if not fundamentally redesign, the landscape of participation in development efforts. The sobering reality is that development efforts are not likely to be transformative when the goal is expanding bonding capital primarily or exclusively. The missing ingredient is often bridging capital, namely, including in the development effort individuals and groups previously not involved in decision making processes, especially partners that enable access to networks that are not accessible in the network as it exists currently. That means success is more likely to occur when efforts are made to build diverse connections than when efforts are made to enhance existing connections alone (Altman 1995). Because different stakeholders bring different ideas, connections, and resources to a partnership, more diverse groups have an edge in organizational and community problem solving vis-à-vis less diverse groups (Kelly et al. 1988).

But paying attention to type of social capital says nothing about how to access social capital when it is available. For that to happen, organization and community developers need to be adept at three tasks: (1) identifying the types of resources embedded within social structures; (2) learning how to access those resources; and (3) knowing how to apply resources for different purposes (Lin 1999). Clearly, the resources embedded within social structures can significantly influence network outcomes (Lin 1999). Collective efforts are more likely to succeed if a network possesses the resources necessary for achieving the desired change. If it does not, then the task is to construct network bridges to obtain needed resources (Coleman 1988; Lin 1999; Woolcock 1998).

Because building social capital involves forming new stakeholder relationships, new inter-group understandings, and new strategies for problem resolution, these efforts often lead to creating a reformulated relational community. For example, Bartunek, Foster-Fishman, and Keys (1996) describe the development of a highly successful coalition, which credits much of its success to the formal and informal efforts made to promote positive and expanded stakeholder relationships. Coalition organizers employed a variety of techniques to foster inter-group relationships, value stakeholder diversity, and access resources. Outcomes lead to enhancing the access to resources among stakeholders who had difficulty in that regard previously.

Returning to the case: Phase 2—a journey from forging connections to building social capital

While the first phase of work with SILC improved inter-organizational awareness and understanding, it did not move the disability community to a new level—a level where collective action is undertaken for the collective good. For example, a shared goal was articulated at the retreat—to increase public understanding of people with disabilities. Central to achieving that goal was designing and implementing a social marketing campaign. At the retreat, participants spent time identifying how to develop a marketing campaign and a task force was created to do necessary follow-up work. A task force goal was securing the assistance of public relations experts who would contribute skills and materials pro bono or at reduced cost. Securing resources this way is especially important in the disabilities field where funding is always in short supply. Despite the shared goal of educating the public, the task force failed to secure the necessary resources and plans for launching the social marketing campaign were aborted.

As this example shows, creating connections is only a start, a start that often results in the articulation of good intentions. But there is also the matter of being able to actualize those intentions, and this is where social capital plays a critical function. Building social capital is a potential outcome when efforts are taken to promote inter-group trust; develop new norms for interaction; and create opportunities for organizations and individuals to work together, especially when the goal is expanding existing networks of relationships.

To enable those possibilities, SILC leaders continued their emphasis on the importance of critical dialogue but, at the same time, shifted the scale of engagement: embarking on a systematic effort to involve small groups of diverse stakeholders in a variety of discussions and collaborative projects. With trust built and accomplishments made on a smaller-scale, successes were parlayed into a large-scale undertaking—the goal of preparing for the Michigan State Legislature a White Paper that lawmakers could use in making funding and programming decisions. Entitled "Disability Agenda," the report was co-sponsored and co-written by more than twenty-five disability organizations. The creation of the "Disability Agenda" was heralded as a hallmark event: for the first time in history, a common agenda existed in Michigan for disability advocacy efforts.

Over time, through persistent effort, and with the support of key disability leaders, SILC was able to unite stakeholders around a common agenda. For that to happen, members of disability organizations participated in repeated cycles of learning: they examined, critiqued, and elevated their thinking, learning all the time. This learning rendered changes in norms, ways of thinking, and outcomes. What began as an effort to forge connections later evolved to an effort to build social capital—a process that required multiple learning cycles and spanned four years.

Using social capital to leverage transformative social change

In interpreting this case, especially note Foster-Fishman's insistence on embedding critical reflection in the planning process. Because practitioners are by definition instrumentalists (that is, doers), critical interpretation is not always a commonplace practice and is seen as "too academic" for the tastes of some. Yet, criticality—especially when it becomes embedded as a cultural attribute— enables those involved to "upshift" their level of understanding, which involves recognizing subtle distinctions and fostering an overall elevated way of thinking about practice. For example, it became clear to participants that they were making a problematic "we–they" distinction: efforts were routinely targeted at changing the way that outside groups think and act (e.g., the general public, policy makers). It became clear, with time, that truly meaningful (if not transformative) change begins by making changes from within.

Constant and critical interpretation may have been one of the reasons why an historic pattern of failure was broken in this case. Another reason may have been the decision to interpret the project through a social capital frame. Given the problem facing Foster-Fishman at the outset—working with a considerably fragmented stakeholder community—she could have recommended a conflict resolution approach to SILC or treated the problem through any number of organization development approaches. When combined with criticality, the social capital frame enabled SILC leaders to more readily *see* the distinction between forging connections and building social capital and, more so, to recognize the relevance of making that distinction in relationship to achieving preferred outcomes.

As we shift the lens to what is happening today in Michigan's disability advocacy community, criticality within a social capital frame is enabling stakeholders to explore issues more deeply (and less superficially) and also to have the confidence to engage in transformative change (as compared to systems reform). For example, SILC's leaders now agree that transformation change will only occur if new levels of trust and relationships result in dramatic shifts in how service-delivery organizations work together, provide services, and engage consumers in their work. While it is too early to tell if transformation will be realized, discussions at the most recent retreat had a significantly different "flavor" from the one held nearly four years ago. For one thing, member organizations are more willing now to commit resources to collective efforts. In addition, they are better able to identify what shifts need to be made in their own organizations if local work is to align with a shared, collective vision.

None of this would have been possible had time not been spent on building trust, cohesion, and connections. Among other things, the investment enabled conversations that helps clarify the "I" in change: *This is what I do (and my organization does) that helps and hinders system improvement; and this is what I (and my organization) can do to enable constructive change.* And it helps clarify the "we" in change: *This is what we (the disability community writ large) do that helps and hinders system improvement; and this is what we can do to enable constructive change.* Such conversations promote the "presence" of the self and the collective in the change process (Senge et al. 2004).

As the case of SILC illustrates, the processes of building social capital and engaging in discourse are mutually reinforcing and beneficial. SILC partners began by examining underlying assumptions, their history together, the need for collaboration, and what they could collectively tackle. Through a series of activities (some more successful than others), they learned, refocused, and engaged in increasingly sophisticated ways. They moved from accentuating the need to change others, to honestly and authentically exploring how they—together and as a system—might transform. They came to critical engagement.

Final thoughts

Engagement requires a special way of being together at the engagement interface. It involves becoming embedded in social networks, some overlapping and some not, and takes place through various activities and in the form of myriad formal and informal processes. Understood as a discovery process, engagement proceeds through inquiry. So, it is our habit to spend time talking and listening, learning with and from partners, and paying attention to what is happening around us. Although we never deny the relevance of our knowledge, we are more apt to understand the importance of being inquisitive, of taking the posture that engagement is more about being a learner than it is about being a knower. Having said that, we fully recognize the gifts we (and our partners) bring to the interface, such things as knowledge, experience, understanding, perceptivity, and ideas, among other things. But the bottom line is that important learning emerges, sometimes mysteriously, from being together. The act of learning together promotes insights, and almost always increases personal and collective commitment to "sticking with" the matter at hand. The learning is energized and extended through discourse processes.

Through engagement, we often attend to two needs: sometimes *we* need to become more embedded in community networks; and, at other times, our *partners* need to become more connected to each other and also to others who will become their future partners. Openness to the reciprocal nature of our being together (an attribute that does not always come naturally) allows us to accomplish more together than we might accomplish alone (Rosaen and Hoekwater 1990). Through constant scanning and assessment of the relational nature of community work, it is possible to become more practiced at intervening appropriately to address relationship challenges, if and when such action is needed. Doing that makes it possible to more successfully build a social infrastructure that promotes shared understanding, shared responsibilities, and shared outcomes. When all of that transpires, an interesting thing can happen along the way: outsiders take note of the work, recognizing that "something important" is happening—new ideas, new practices, and new things are taking place (Burkhardt 1994).

But the driveshaft of critical engagement—Discourse—places demands on participants, requiring an acceptance of often unfamiliar attitudes and a willingness to form a different type of relationship. For those reasons, critical engagement requires a *safe space*, a space flush with empathy, trust, and support (Bartunek and Louis 1996). Participants must feel, authentically and without reservation, that the interface is a space where they can discuss matters openly and without the risk of unfair judgment or criticism. The interface must also be a place where individual and collective growth are not only encouraged, but are also supported. This is especially important when delicate issues are the focus of attention. The cruel story line is that often "the more things change, the more they stay the same." Ironically, at the very time when critical engagement can be most worthwhile—when intervention participants should be digging deeply to uncover why things are as they are; when they should be honestly critiquing past efforts; and when they should be thinking creatively about possible options—often, just the opposite happens. There are many explanations for why this is so; some are political and others are cultural. Standing upright in this field of reasons is a perception rarely spoken: if certain actors have intervened in the past and failed, then *they* must be part of the problem today.

Suppose, for example, that a community is interested in reducing infant mortality rates with any eye toward reducing the disparity between black and white infant mortality rates. This is a not a new circumstance for them; there have been prior attempts to tackle the problem. If critical engagement is undertaken in this example, it is important to enable a safe space where discourse can flourish. Actualizing that intent almost never begins by simply sitting down at the table and talking about solutions. It almost always begins by thinking carefully and strategically about how to proceed (such as starting with individual interviews as in the SILC case, followed by group feedback), to discover relevant approaches that ensure safe and authentic engagement. In our experience, at least, the quest for critical engagement almost always begins with becoming immersed in the community context—learning about history, past project experiences, interpersonal relationships, agency involvements and relationships, and becoming familiar with "hot buttons" that lurk beneath the surface.

Critical engagement, then, begins by taking time to understand how and why it might *not* proceed constructively; and, then, considering what needs to be done to make critical engagement possible. Rather than believe that this information is something for academic partners to discover alone, time and time again we have found how revealing it can be for local partners to participate in this inquiry process; they often "see" their context with fresh eyes.

What proceeds from that point is almost always the creation of the "operating principles" of engagement, the norms of engagement as we call them, that define in practical terms how, what, when, who, where, and with what preferred outcomes. These norms of engagement are more than mere statements of goals; they are pledges of allegiance, proclamations of a way of being together. And they cannot be norms that are imported from other places and other times, including uncritically applying expert ideas. They must be living, breathing expressions of what makes sense, here and now. Of utmost importance is avoiding the undeniable urge to apply past experience, thereby seeking to avoid in this circumstance something "bad" that happened somewhere else. After all, the engagement interface is very much about learning in real time, which means paying attention and making adjustments as needed.

Whether to call these agreements norms, or anything at all for that matter, brings up the important matter of language. Whatever language is used, it should be language that promotes understanding and learning—for the group involved and others. For example, an inevitable decision involves determining the type of intervention structure (e.g., advisory group, coalition, task force) and giving the group a name. Rather than view these decisions as necessary inconveniences or routine practical matters, we have found enormous learning to be associated with "getting to" those decisions. And they contribute enormously to relationship building. For example, conversations at informal venues (e.g., having coffee or lunch together, meeting at each others' homes) gives those involved space and opportunity—such critical matters—to ask clarifying questions, express strongly felt points of view, and mull over options "out loud" and with others.

Ultimately, it is all about building relationships and creating spaces for honest and authentic discourse. Of utmost importance, though, is ensuring that the quest for creating a positive working climate does not stifle a group's ability to surface and consider contested issues. If that happens, critical engagement becomes a shadow of itself, a category without meaning. The erosion of purpose is easily seen when, for example, conversations that might engender conflict are avoided because disagreements might compromise relationships. The value of critical engagement is tied to the possibility of high quality decision making and knowledge creation. Those outcomes are products of critical inquiry (Meyers and Seibold 1989; Habermas 1990). What all of this means is that the generation of social capital—and the prospects for transformative change that come with it—requires participants at the interface to nurture deep connections *and* engage in deep conversations, simultaneously.

References

Allen, N. 2005. A multi-level analysis of community coordinating councils. *American Journal of Community Psychology 35*(1–2):49–63.

Altman, D. G. 1995. Sustaining intervention in community systems: On the relationship between researchers and communities. *Health Psychology 14*(6):526–536.

Bartunek, J. M., P. G. Foster-Fishman, and C. B. Keys. 1996. Using collaborative advocacy to foster intergroup cooperation: A joint insider-outsider investigation. *Human Relations 49*(6)70:1–73.

Bartunek, J. M., and M. R. Louis. 1996. *Insider/outsider team research.* Thousand Oaks CA: Sage.

Bourdieu, P. 1986. The forms of capital. In *Handbook of Theory and Research for the Sociology of Education.* J. G. Richardson, ed. New York: Greenwood Press.

Burkhardt, M. E. 1994. Social interaction effects following a technological change: A longitudinal investigation. *Academy of Management Journal* Vol. 37(4):860-898.

Butterfoss, F. D., R. M. Goodman, and A. Wandersman. 1996. Community coalitions for prevention and health promotion: Factors predicting satisfaction, participation, and planning. *Health Education Quarterly 23*(1): 65–79.

Chavis, D. M. 1995. Building community capacity to prevent violence through coalitions and partnerships. *Journal of Health Care for the Poor and Underserved 6*(2):234–245.

Coleman, J. S. 1988. Social capital in the creation of human capital. *American Journal of Sociology* 94:S95–S111.

Das, T., and B. S. Teng. 2001. Trust, control, and risk in strategic alliances: An integrated framework. *Organization Studies 22*(2):251–283.

Foster-Fishman, P. G., S. Berkowitz, D. Lounsbury, S. Jacobson, and N. A. Allen. 2001a. Building collaborative capacity in community based coalitions. *American Journal of Community Psychology 29*(2):241–262.

Foster-Fishman, P. G., D. Perkins, and W. Davidson. 1997. Developing effective evaluation partnerships: Paradigmatic and contextual barriers. *Analise Psicologica 3*(15):389–403.

Foster-Fishman, P. G., D. A. Salem, N. A. Allen, and K. Fahrbach. 2001b. Facilitating interorganizational exchanges: The contributions of interorganizational alliances. *American Journal of Community Psychology 29*(6):875–905.

Fountain, J. E. 1998. Social capital: Its relationship to innovation in science and technology. *Science and Public Policy 25*(2):103–115.

Gittell, R., and A. Vidal. 1998. *Community organizing: building social capital as a development strategy.* Thousand Oaks CA: Sage Publications.

Goddard, R. D. 2003. Relational networks, social trust, and norms: A social capital perspective on students' chances of academic success. *Educational Evaluation and Policy Analysis* Vol. 25(1). Spring 2003:59–74.

Habermas, J. 1984. *Theory of communicative action vol.1.* Boston: Beacon.

Habermas, J. 1990. *Discourse ethics in moral consciousness and communicative action.* Cambridge MA: MIT Press.

Hawe, P., and A. Shiell. 2000. Social capital and health promotion: A review. *Social Science and Medicine 51:* 871–885.

Hays, C. E., S. P. Hays, J. O. Deville, and P. F. Mulhall. 2000. Capacity for effectiveness: The relationship between coalition structure and community impact. *Evaluation and Program Planning 23*:373–379.

Israel, B. A., A. J. Schulz, E. A. Parker, and A. B. Becker. 1998. Review of community-based research: Assessing partnership approaches to improve public health. *Annual Review of Public Health 19*:173–202.

Kelly, J. G., N. Dassoff, I. Levin, J. Schreckengost, and B. E. Altman. 1988. A guide to conducting prevention research in the community: First steps. *Prevention in Human Services 6*(1):174.

Kelly, K., and H. Van Vlaenderen. 1995. Evaluating participation processes in community development. *Evaluation and Program Planning 18*(4):371–383.

Lasker, R. D., and E. S. Weiss. 2003. Broadening participation in community problem solving: A multidisciplinary model to support collaborative practice and research. *Journal of Urban Health 80*(1):14–47.

Lasker, R. D., E. S. Weiss, and R. Miller. 2001. Partnership synergy: A practical framework for studying and strengthening the collaborative advantage. *The Milbank Quarterly 79*:179–205.

Lin, N. 1999. Building a network theory of social capital. *Connections 22*(1):28–51.

Mandell, M. P. 2001. Collaboration through network structures for community building efforts. *National Civic Review 3:279–287.*

Maton, K. I. 2000. The social ecology of social transformation. *American Journal of Community Psychology 28*(1):25–57.

Meyers, R. A., and D. R. Siebold. 1989. Perspectives on group argument. *Communications Yearbook 1:268–302.*

Portes, A. 1998. Social capital: Its origins and applications in modern sociology. *Annual Review of Sociology vol. 24*:1–24.

Putnam, R. D. 2000. *The collapse and revival of American Community.* New York: Simon & Schuster.

Ream, R. K. 2003. Counterfeit social capital and Mexican-American underachievement. *Educational Evaluation and Policy Analysis* Vol. 25(3). Fall 2003:237–262.

Rosaen, C. L. and E. Hoekwater. 1990. Collaboration: Empowering educators to take charge. *Contemporary Education 61*:144–151.

Sackman, S. A. 1991. *Cultural knowledge in organizations: Exploring the collective mind.* Newbury Park CA: Sage Publications.

Sampson, R. J., and W. B. Groves. 1989. Community structure and crime: Testing social disorganization theory. *American Journal of Sociology* Vol. 94(4) Jan. 1989:774–802.

Senge, P. M., C. O. Scharmer, J. Jaworski, and B. S. Flowers. 2004. *Presence: Human purpose and the field of the future.* Cambridge MA: SOL.

Sheldon-Keller, A. E., E. Lloyd-McGarvey, and R. J. Canterbury. 1995. Assessing organizational effectiveness in higher education drug prevention consortia. *Journal of Drug Education 25(*3):239–250.

Wacquant, L. J. D., and W. J. Wilson. 1989. The cost of racial and class exclusion in the inner city. *Annals of the American Academy of Political and Social Sciences 501*:8–28.

Weisbord, M. R., and S. Janoff. 1995. *Future search: An active guide to finding common ground in organizations and communities.* San Francisco: Berrett Koehler Publishers.

Wischnowski, M. W., and J. A. McCollum. 1995. Managing conflict on local interagency coordinating councils. *Topics in Early Childhood Special Education 15*(3):28:1–295.

Woolcock, M. 1998. Social capital and economic development: Towards a theoretical synthesis and policy framework. *Theory and Society vol. 27.* no. 2:151–208.

Wood, D. J., and B. Gray. 1991. Toward a comprehensive theory of collaboration. *Journal of Applied Behavioral Science* 27(2):139–162.

CHAPTER 7

CO-EMPOWERMENT AND WORKING TOWARD BETTERMENT

As we have seen in chapter 6, expanded and strengthened social networks are essential for engaging in transformative work. The metaphor of *voice* is often associated with another key aspect of transformative community-based work: empowering others to gain control over resources in ways that will improve their lives, especially among those who have traditionally lacked influence (Cornell University Empowerment Group 1989; Fawcett et al. 1995). This approach makes intuitive sense. In our efforts to effect change, why not include the people whose lives will be changed? (Dewey 1916; Ulrich 2003). It also makes sense to bring into consideration multiple viewpoints and realities because each person's unique position influences what she/he brings into view or screens out (Bond and Pyle 1998; Gomez, Stone, and Kroeger 2004).

Empowerment and co-empowerment are important concepts and refer to the matter of going beyond the status quo; like social capital, they are resources or outcomes that can leverage further change. As Bond and Keys (1993) contend, co-empowerment and collaboration are synergistic, helping people to undertake significant work. Empowerment enables people to engage more effectively in organizations or communities; grow in understanding (Zimmerman 1995); and feel more and better connected with others (Bond, Belenky, and Weinstock 2000). When empowered, people not only are better able to participate, they often have the will to follow through and the inclination to reflect on the past and future (Gutierrez 1990; McMillan et al. 1995).

Organizations also help empower individuals and groups. They do so by providing mechanisms for groups with differing agendas to mutually influence the direction an organization takes (Bond 1999; Peterson and Zimmerman

2004). As an outcome, empowered organizations influence the larger system of which they are a part (Peterson and Zimmerman 1995). Within communities, empowered individuals can form social networks that become a political force (Stall and Stoecker 1998).

But as Gruber and Trickett (1987) remind us, there is a paradox associated with empowering others "because the very institutional structure that puts one group in a position to empower also works to undermine the act of empowerment" (353). As we learned in our faculty community of practice, empowerment is not something that takes place only within individuals or groups; it is *situated in social context*. Because of that, empowerment inherently involves how power is both understood and negotiated (Trickett 1994). Moreover, as Reissman (1993) points out, "we cannot give voice, but we do hear voices that we record and interpret" (as cited in Casey 1995, 223). In other words, the power others hold is, in part, dependent upon what *we* do when they speak. Casey (1995) explains it this way: "The problem is, after all, not with the voices that speak but with the ears that do not hear" (223). All of this says that empowerment and co-empowerment—as appealing as they are to those who seek transformative outcomes—are complicated and multilayered concepts that cut across the domains of individual, organizational, and community participation.

In this chapter, we discuss what we have learned in our faculty learning community about empowerment and co-empowerment processes and outcomes. The chapter begins with the presentation of a detailed case that focuses on what can be learned by critically examining a narrative of engagement practices. In this instance, the effort was designed to make improvements in approaches and outcomes over time. Following the case example, we discuss what it takes to foster empowerment, that is, to enable the development of structures and spaces where voices can be heard and multiple ways of seeing can be fostered. All of this is required to influence dialogic processes aimed at transformative ends.

Introduction to a case example: learning to support novices in educating all children

These days it is hard to pick up a newspaper, turn on the radio, or watch television without learning something about the educational crisis in American schools. We are reminded constantly that today's teachers serve an increasingly diverse population; U.S. school-aged children represent a range of languages, cultures, ethnicities, abilities, and socio-economic realities. But what scholars tell us about school outcomes is sobering: student progress as measured by student achievement data is unacceptable, especially among students from poor families across racial and ethnic groups.[1]

While some people think that federal laws, such as the *No Child Left Behind Act* (2002), provide the necessary goals and supports to make key improvements

---

1. See, for example, the work of Darling-Hammond (1991), Liston and Zeichner (1991), Villegas and Lucas (2002).

in literacy instruction, many legislators, policy makers, and educators contest the effectiveness of top-down mandates. Critics contend that these initiatives are underconceptualized and underfunded, nothing more than "carrot and stick" approaches to a complex and enduring problem. Efforts to educate *all* children bump up against a harsh reality, namely, that too many American students have unequal access to a high-quality education.

Teacher educators, in particular, are raising questions about how best to prepare novice teachers to teach *all children well* in an environment characterized by testing and accountability, teacher shortages, and high attrition among beginning teachers. There is growing recognition of the need to move beyond "tinkering around the edges," which all too often results in simply doing teacher education *better*. The counterpoint is that contemporary challenges demand dramatic improvement in teacher preparation—a transformation that obliges teacher candidates to do *better* teacher education. Doing that requires teachers who can teach effectively in a variety of settings and also requires them to be committed to and capable of continuous professional improvement.

The case example presented below illustrates how Rosaen and her colleagues are seeking to transform approaches to teacher preparation. It tells the story of co-empowerment at the individual and organizational level—an attempt to bring together faculty and collaborating teachers to reshape learning opportunities for novice teachers. Overall, the narrative and interpretations are intended to illustrate one way that educators are trying to *learn their way* to the goal of "doing better things" in teacher preparation.

Part 1: the journey begins with co-designing a practicum

About ten years ago, Michigan State University's (MSU) teacher preparation program underwent a complete redesign, a transformation that resulted in extending the teacher certification program from four to five years. In the new design, target areas for improvement included increasing the depth of subject matter preparation for beginning teachers and providing extensive school-based experiences for them. Overall, the new program was designed to produce "well-started novices" and to instill in them the capacity to sustain professional learning throughout their careers. Rosaen's role in this effort included serving as Faculty Leader of one of three elementary teacher preparation teams.

In the new program, teacher candidates complete a baccalaureate degree; engage in a year-long internship to earn certification; and take four Master's-level courses during the year. In this "field based" program—from their junior year on—teacher candidates participate on a regular basis in elementary or secondary classrooms. Because the program is large (almost 600 interns per year are certified), the demand for high-quality field placement sites is great.

The new program was not designed by MSU alone. Drawing upon a long tradition of collaborative work with schools, faculty worked with collaborating teachers to develop the new program design. Structures were formed, including representative teacher groups (e.g., a Teacher Education Liaison Group) and principal groups. Because those participating in this work aspire to engage as learners to enable continuous improvement, deliberations among faculty and school personnel typically focus on key questions:

- How are we doing?
- How can we do things better?

As an example of a mutual commitment to learning and improvement, at one point Rosaen and her school- and campus-based colleagues noticed that interns were struggling to implement the research-based literacy and mathematics practices that they had learned about during their senior year. They observed a disconnection across critical domains—learning about literacy and math practices; implementing those practices (fall of senior year); and developing their own practices in a supportive context (spring semester of internship year).

In analyzing what they were doing, the collaborators recognized that attention during the fall months of the internship focused on supporting planning and teaching of science and social studies, the foci of the interns' fall semester Master's level courses. To address the circumstance, they convened a task force of about fifteen collaborating teachers, colleagues who were selected because they were providing strong mentoring for their interns in a number of ways. It seemed important to involve them: as a group, they not only had knowledge and experience in guiding the learning of novice teachers, they would also be able to offer important insights necessary for redesigning field-based learning experiences.

The group worked for several months to identify key mentoring practices that would enable novices to work more directly on specific aspects of their practice across the internship year. The result of the deliberations was a design for a Mentoring Guide that outlined "phases" of the internship and specific types of mentoring support needed during each phase. The plan included a description of the "Literacy and Mathematics Practicum," which is a set of experiences for interns in the fall semester (e.g., observing mentors' teaching, assessing, and learning about the curriculum). All of these experiences were designed to help interns use their prior knowledge of literacy and math practices; to make sense of their internship classroom; and to provide a bridge from the more theoretical course work (senior year) to the practical work of teaching (intern year). The Practicum is followed up in the spring semester with, first, coursework in literacy and math methods; and, second, with an extended period of "guided lead teaching," where interns put their ideas into action with the support of their collaborating teacher and a field instructor.

The design group knew that it would be important for implementation purposes to include key players in a review of the Practicum redesign. Therefore, the design was discussed and reviewed by course instructors and field instructors who work with interns in schools, and also by members of the Teacher Education Liaison Group. Those teacher representatives were asked to discuss the ideas with other collaborating teachers in their respective buildings and then bring ideas back to us. The final plan incorporated feedback from all groups and was implemented the following fall.

Those involved fully recognized that a new plan needed to be reviewed thoroughly and revised over time. Over a four-year period, the coordination staff surveyed collaborating teachers and interns to learn about their reactions to the Practicum experiences, and also interviewed a small sub-set of interns and collaborating teachers to gain deeper perspectives on their collective experiences. Each year, the group used the information gathered and analyzed to work with course instructors to modify (with the intention of improving) the content and structure of the Practicum.

Over the years, interns' response to the Practicum and their perceived value of it steadily improved. With that outcome, it might be concluded that this is an example of a group "getting it right." There is more to be done, though. For example, while the approach has helped interns learn to teach literacy and math to a *particular* group of children (namely, those who were in their classrooms that school year), it has not necessarily helped them prepare for the *range of grade levels and diversity of students* they are likely to face in their early years of teaching. Moreover, while there appears to be increased ownership among the interns in Practicum work, there has been a range of responses among collaborating teachers: some embrace assigned activities as opportunities to talk with interns about key practices through observing and debriefing, while others leave it up to the intern to make the events happen. That is somewhat disappointing because one of the goals of the Practicum design was to get *all* collaborating teachers more involved in active mentoring in literacy and math during the early months of the school year. Clearly, "tinkering" has not led to transformation in learning opportunities for our interns.

The story of how the redesign unfolded suggests several questions to explore for further learning:

- If the design of these experiences was based on the "wisdom of mentoring" found in the Task Force group, why isn't this working differently or better?
- What type of collaborating teacher participation would be necessary to generate more ownership and enthusiasm for supporting the interns' learning?
- What should happen next?

Commentary: learning from the practicum narrative

Important lessons are revealed by examining the Practicum experience. First, there is the matter of *inclusiveness*. While a reasonable number of collaborating teachers (n=15) were empowered to share their expertise and influence the Practicum design, how do we know they were actually empowered? We might argue that they were empowered because the Practicum requirements were designed following their advice regarding the types of experiences interns need. However, that number represents only about 15 percent of the eighty-five to ninety teachers who typically participate in the collaborating teacher group. If we include the regular representative group of Teacher Education Liaisons (about twenty-five teachers)—colleagues who also had significant opportunities to discuss the ideas directly with our faculty—the participation in deliberations increases to a little more than 40 percent. Are these numbers sufficient for inclusiveness to be in place?

Another matter to consider is *what it meant to be included*. In this case, while the initial fifteen teachers had opportunities *to generate* ideas, the second group of teachers (N=25) were invited *to react to others' ideas*. Whereas the remaining collaborating teachers (N=~50) were asked by their representatives to react to ideas, it is likely that they had little understanding of the real intentions for the design; they were removed from naming and framing the problem(s) that the core group was trying to address. Even if they did offer input, their ideas were communicated through an intermediary (i.e., another colleague) and not voiced directly. Consequently, at issue is how much "real input" did these teachers have in the redesign process?

To better understand the issues under consideration, it may be useful to revisit our earlier discussion (chapter 5) regarding the distinction between democratic processes and participation. *Democratic participation* requires creating egalitarian structures that enable a range of people to engage in decision making. By contrast, democratic processes are those that embrace participants' diverse viewpoints, knowledge, needs, and purposes (Ansley and Gaventa 1997; Heron and Reason 1997). In these ways, participants are involved directly in shaping the course of events that affects their future (Dewey 1916; Ulrich 2003). *Democratic processes* require engaging in discourse as a means for reaching mutual understanding. In our case, the full range of teachers had minimal opportunities to *participate* in redesigning the Practicum. Specifically, their participation was limited to offering input as part of the decision making process. Because of that, it is doubtful that they had genuine opportunities to engage in *democratic processes*, that is, in discourse about the purposes and design of the Practicum.

Moreover, another group of key players—the interns—was excluded from either democratic participation or processes regarding the Practicum redesign. While faculty and collaborating teachers certainly had the interests of the interns at heart and in mind, rather than include them explicitly in the deliberations, the group redesigned the Practicum with what they "thought" interns needed. However, interns were not excluded altogether. At the end of each year, interns and collaborating teachers are invited to offer comments and suggestions about how to improve the program. Still, this activity is not undertaken using a democratic process: Rosaen, as editor of the Internship Handbook and with input from the course instructors, maintains control over the text that describes the rationale and requirements for the Practicum. We all know how powerful the control of words can be in any decision making or design process.

The Task Force was never reconvened even though ongoing input was so-licited. Approaches to soliciting feedback were designed, redesigned, tallied, and interpreted by the course instructors and Rosaen *without* the Task Force's continued input. Similarly, although collaborating teachers and interns were asked regularly to be *respondents* to the survey, they did not have input into the design of information sought or interpretation of results. Because questions asked are as important as responses given, diverse stakeholders (e.g., those who work at MSU and in the schools) are likely to ask different questions and offer different interpretations of answers given. Thus, by restricting the approach in this case, valuable resources were not incorporated into the learning cycle.

The critical examination of this case illustrates how hard it is, even with the best of intentions, to form productive and imaginative collaborations between two institutions—the university and public schools. Because of that, the out-come is often doing no more than "tinkering around the edges." In this case, empowering one group of teachers (the Task Force) may actually have disem-powered others in the decision making process (Rich et al. 1995). However, it is also important to note that critical examination of this case has led to insights that are informing ongoing collaborative work. The work in that regard will be described in the second part of the case.

Part 2: the learning cycle continues—from inclusiveness to co-empowerment in the co-teacher education project

In 2002, MSU became involved in the *Teachers for a New Era* initiative, a five-year, university-wide endeavor funded by the Carnegie Corporation de-signed to make significant improvements in teacher preparation. Teacher prepa-ration in this instance begins in the teacher candidates' freshman year and spans the first two years of induction into the profession. Among the many areas tar-geted for improvement is the clinical component, that is, the field-based experi-ences in which students engage during their junior, senior, and internship years.

Carefully designed classroom-based experiences have the potential to help novices go beyond *having experiences* to helping them *learn from them*. This is accomplished by helping them develop abilities to perceive and assess a class-room situation, make judgments, formulate goals, choose a course of action, and reflect on consequences (Dewey 1904, 1964; Kennedy 1987, 1999; Kessels and Korthagen 1996; Schön 1983, 1987). In this perspective, concepts and theories are not learned discretely as ends in themselves; rather, novices use concepts and theories interpretively to explore their perceptions, generate questions, ex-amine points of view or arguments, and make judgments about means and ends. To learn robustly from experience, novices are encouraged to see the connection between analysis and action (Kennedy 1987).

Overall the goal of this approach to teacher preparation is to create powerful clinical experiences that help teachers become "transformative intellectuals"

(Giroux 1988), that is, professionals whose practice is designed and redesigned to go beyond the status quo. That intent—defined specifically in terms of outcomes sought in the teacher preparation field—aligns precisely with what the co-authors of this book seek in their respective domains of work. As learned in our faculty learning community, achieving the preferred outcome requires *examining* and *critiquing* prior work as the basis for *elevating* future work in transformative directions. As described below, that is exactly what Rosaen and her colleagues did in the Co-Teacher Education Project, an initiative in which Rosaen served as co-leader of the Literacy Team.

While the Practicum work described previously focused on making improvements in clinical experiences during the internship, in the Co-Teacher Educator Project participants are working to transform clinical experiences during the senior year. The journey began by asking some former interns to visit with the team about their experiences in the program and to talk about what additional experiences are needed to strengthen their preparation for teaching literacy. At the same time, a group of collaborating teachers identified specific areas that needed improvement in senior year preparation A common issue emerged from these conversations: how to improve the "field work" or ways seniors participate in elementary classrooms to complement their course work.

Rather than asking collaborating teachers and former interns to help them with an idea that they had already defined, the team worked together with them to develop a shared understanding of whether and how the clinical experience needed to be enhanced. The team purposely facilitated small group discussions (versus a whole-group format) to assure that they heard each voice and gained ideas from multiple perspectives. They also organized those discussions by grade level so that teachers could look deeply into their teaching practices and think about how, as a group, each teacher's unique expertise could be tapped. Subsequently, a series of planning sessions were organized where collaborating teachers would work alongside the team in designing, planning, and implementing "Partner Classroom" visits for seniors.

The concept of Partner Classrooms was suggested as a means to stimulate thinking (certainly not as an exact plan), as an image of how the group might improve the regular field placement in which seniors typically participate (i.e., observing, tutoring, teaching small- and whole-group lessons). For example, small groups of seniors might make a planned visit to a first grade classroom and observe the teacher conducting a guided reading lesson (while also reading and discussing that approach in their course work). They not only observe the teacher, but also talk with her beforehand and afterward to learn more about a critical area that can be missing from classroom participation—thereby learning about the teacher's thinking as she conducted the lesson. In this way, even those students who were placed at different grade levels for their own field placement could see effective practices at a grade level different from their own. Moreover, these experiences could take place in classrooms that represent a range of student diversity.

By presenting the idea as an "image" to stimulate conversation; then writing up some possible (and varied) scenarios; and, finally, accompanying the image with a series of questions (not answers) about what a Partner Classroom visit might entail, the team hoped to engage in what Greenwood and Levin (1998) have described as *co-generative learning*. That is, they hoped to tap into the expertise and insights of all participants—teachers and faculty alike—to achieve more than what could by accomplished by working independently (Gomez, Stone, and Kroeger 2004; Rosaen and Hoekwater 1990).

Interestingly, some collaborating teachers decided to observe each other's practice (between planning meetings) to help identify interesting Partner Classroom ideas and to learn from one another. To the team, that revealed their engagement in addressing the problems identified with seniors' clinical experiences and, more importantly, illustrated their empowerment to honor their own expertise as well as to learn from one another. They were also delighted to find out that some teachers were eager to return to their buildings to find colleagues who would be interested in opening their classrooms for this new type of field experience. Some teachers worked with those present from their buildings to plan ways in which seniors could experience visits in a variety of grade levels and instructional approaches.

Many ideas were exchanged about how to handle logistical challenges of adding as many as five to ten adults to already-crowded classrooms. Ideas abounded about what background materials would be necessary to help seniors prepare for the visits and approaches for creating them. Teachers emphasized the importance of providing materials that would help seniors tap into their thinking (e.g., lesson plans, discussions of ways they have changed their practices over time). The group played with the idea of creating "chat rooms" and other electronic venues that would extend the seniors' experiences beyond the physical visits. The teachers also requested copies of course syllabi and texts so they could design experiences that connect well with course content.

Overall, there was a sense of "we're in this together" as the group generated ideas and worked through logistical details (Bond 1999). It was truly exciting to see the conversations unfold. There was genuine wondering and also, at times, disagreement. Perhaps most importantly, throughout the conversations, teachers *and* teacher educators were equally responsible for maintaining the momentum!

The group is still in the midst of designing the first visits, and they plan to pilot them in fall 2005. It seems critical that the teachers play a significant role in preparing materials and making the events happen (versus leaving it up to the course instructors to make arrangements). Once the plans are implemented, however, the work will not be finished. The group will need to design ways to find out from the seniors what they are experiencing and learning; get their advice for improvements; and track their progress throughout the remainder of the program. All of this will help the group better understand the impact these innovations are having on their overall preparation to teach literacy to today's diverse student populations. The group also needs to think about what has been achieved through this "border crossing" from the university to public schools, and to explore what might be gained by crossing borders in the other direction, from schools to the university.

As the teachers become more empowered to voice their ideas and contribute their expertise to ongoing design revisions, there is also the potential to draw upon their know-how in more direct ways in our classes. The group might also consider the value (and feasibility) of holding courses in Partner Classroom schools as a means to help seniors find increasingly meaningful ways to make the theory–practice connection.

The work described is an attempt to reinvent ever more powerful clinical experiences that are needed to better prepare teacher candidates for teaching and assuming leadership roles in today's schools. The effort has generated much enthusiasm for new ideas and it appears the work is heading in transformative directions. At the same time, there is the need to be open to new ways of thinking. For example, clinical experiences do not have to take place only in public schools, and that recognition raises all sorts of questions to explore:

- What if teacher educators were able to collaborate with the teachers to connect with community programs for children and youth?
- What if the group could tap into parent and community involvement to engage the seniors in a range of experiences and help them learn about the role of families and communities in children's education?
- What if the group engaged the seniors in co-constructing some new clinical experiences that take advantage of their creativity and expertise?
- What will it take to engage additional collaborating teachers in joint design and decision making to transform clinical experiences?

This recent progress is certainly encouraging, but the learning journey has only just begun.

Co-empowerment processes and outcomes

The "Learning to Support Novices" case illustrates some of the ways in which empowerment is a complicated manifestation of how social power is exercised at individual, organizational, and possibly even at the community levels (Speer and Hughey 1995; Perkins and Zimmerman 1995). According to scholars who engage in community-based work, empowered individuals increase personal, interpersonal, or political power so they can take action to improve their life situations (Gutierrez 1990). In an institutional context, such as a teacher preparation program in partnership with public schools, there is the potential to improve the "professional lives" of school and university faculty through empowerment processes. At the organizational level, co-empowerment enables multiple groups with divergent agendas to mutually influence the direction of an organization (Bond 1999). While teacher education faculty try to support teacher candidates in developing theoretical knowledge that will guide their practical work, classroom teachers play a vital role in helping teacher candidates make connections between theory and practice.

Scholars also know that empowered community members work intentionally and take collective action. In that way, those who generally lack access to power and resources have opportunities to gain greater access to both (Cornell University Empowerment Group 1989). However, organization and community empowerment do not happen only when a collection of individuals are empowered (Perkins and Zimmerman 1995). There is a reciprocal or dialectic feature to the empowerment process, and individual development is necessary in order to hasten transformation (Speer and Hughey 1995). As Darlington and Mulvaney (2002) explain from a feminist perspective, "reciprocal empowerment" is:

> . . . a discursive style of interaction grounded in reciprocity which is initiated by people who feel a sense of personal authority. The personal authority aspect of reciprocal empowerment provides an individual with a level of knowledge necessary to develop a heightened self-confidence that can then lead to action. This action can in turn facilitate movement of dialogue from the private to the public sphere. Reciprocal empowerment enables people with mutual self-interests to rise above obstacles based on social and political structures and to use personal authority to discuss issues openly and honestly in order to effect change. (2002, electronic resource)

Change, in this view, involves more than satisfying one's own needs. Instead, it means capitalizing on the strengths of the individual or group to work toward the "common good" (Darlington and Mulvaney 2002). In the "Learning to Support Novices" case, we saw that including only a "representative" group of teachers in the design of the Practicum tended to empower one group of teachers (the Task Force) while potentially disempowering another (i.e., all mentor teachers who work with interns). It seems apparent that there is more work to be done in developing the Partner Classroom concept so as to avoid the same pitfall.

Bond, Belenky, and Weinstock (2000, electronic resource) emphasize personal and interpersonal development that prioritizes "growth in connection" with others and skills to cultivate and maximize the development emerging from such growth." In describing a women-centered model of organizing, Stall and Stoecker (1998) point out that issues that are typically considered to be private, such as violence against women or toxic waste, become public issues "committed to democratic goals and supportive of humane ends." There is a parallel to this way of understanding in the educational community: the continuing struggle to honor teachers' and teacher candidates' current expertise while, at the same time, expecting them to continue to grow during their careers so that they will not become complacent with the status quo.

As our faculty learning community examined and critiqued our own practices, we began to understand the multilayered nature of individual empowerment and co-empowerment within organizations and communities; and we also began to critically examine these concepts as both processes and outcomes. In doing so, we learned that although participation is necessary, it may or may not lead to empowerment: that outcome depends on whether participation is meaningful (Itzhaky and York 2000; Rich et al. 1995). Given that understanding, we shall now consider three areas of influence on empowerment processes and outcomes: the approaches and supports available to develop individuals' skills, self-knowledge, and self-perception; the nature and strength of the relationships being cultivated; and the attention paid to context. These areas of influence cut across individual, organizational, and community empowerment endeavors.

Individual empowerment as a developmental process and targeted outcome
This chapter began with the claim that empowerment is not something that one person "gives" to another person. Rather, individuals must develop specific skills, capacities, self-knowledge, and self-perceptions so they can act on opportunities to exercise control over their lives. Along these lines, Zimmerman (1995) developed a conceptual framework of psychological empowerment that is based on three assumptions: psychological empowerment takes different forms for different people; different contexts may require different skills; and empowerment is a dynamic trait and can change over time. According to Zimmerman, psychological empowerment is in place when

> . . . a person. . . believes that he or she has the capacity to influence a given context (intrapersonal component), understands how the system works in that context (interactional component), and engages in behaviors to exert control in the context (behavioral component). (1995, electronic resource)

Spear and Peterson (2000) refer to these as the *emotional, cognitive, and behavioral* dimensions of empowerment. Accordingly, McMillan et al. (1995) use a multi-level approach to understand psychological empowerment, which at the individual level includes perceived knowledge and skill development; perceived participatory competence; and expectancies for future individual contributions. Put in colloquial terms, these aspects are internalized when a person believes: "I have been given what I need to do it." "I can do it." "I will do it." For the authors, empowerment is actualized at the group level when participants affirm the prospects of current and future group/organizational accomplishments. In other words, empowerment is actualized when, as a collective, individuals believe, "We have done it"; and "We will do it."

Given this background, at issue are important questions: How are these capacities developed? What types of support and experiences are needed?

Skill development through repetitive cycles of reflection and action

Stall and Stoecker (1998) argue that people become empowered through a developmental process that includes repetitive cycles of action and reflection that foster new skills and understandings, which are then followed by new and more effective actions. As illustrated in the case example presented first in this chapter, one problem with the approach taken in the design of the Practicum was that forming a task force was a short-term strategy to design a set of assignments. It could have been designed to achieve teacher empowerment as a desired outcome, a goal that would have required repetitive cycles of action and reflection over time. Arguably, the approach taken in the case seems parallel to what Chavis and Florin (1990) describe as *community-based* work, which they believe happens when problems are defined and solved primarily by outside professionals. By contrast, the authors define *community development* as work that takes place when community members participate in problem definition and solving.

To stimulate a community development approach in the "Learning to Support Novices" case, teachers were encouraged to take active and long-term roles in designing and implementing field-based experiences. In addition, efforts were made to build participants' skills and to expand the number of teachers involved. All of this activity is consistent with the recommendations made by Wolff (1992), who asserts that if coalitions are serious about empowerment, they "will include empowerment in the goals and objectives, and will clearly and specifically define both what they mean by empowerment and who will be empowered" (7).

Identifying and using untapped knowledge and skills

Feminist community organizers have described the empowerment process as developing what Payne (1995) refers to as "developmental leadership." This approach draws upon the types of leadership that women typically display at home with family and friends, and for forming relationships with neighbors and in the community, such as nurturing others, listening to multiple voices, and creating an inclusive setting (Bond, Belenky, and Weinstock 2000). Processes include having small group discussions to foster epistemological growth or "ways of knowing"; developing skills and confidence to question authority and name unjust social situations; reflecting on and learning from their experiences; refining, testing, and critiquing their own and others' ideas; and stretching their thinking about how people's ideas develop (Bond et al. 2000). In a similar vein, Rappaport (1995) emphasizes how important it is to listen to the voices of people, as those voices inform others about what it means to be empowered in particular contexts.

Consistent with this thinking, and in their work in foster home-school connections, Cochran and Dean (1991) operate under the assumption that much of the most useful knowledge about issues, such as child rearing, can be found within the community itself. Consequently, important activities in their community work include making home visits and forming neighborhood groups for particular purposes (e.g., to carry out a plan for neighborhood improvement). Activities, such as simulating parent-teacher conferences through role playing and visiting classrooms, were designed to help build parents' confidence and skills.

These examples suggest that many community participants, particularly those who are typically excluded from such processes, are often unaware of their own expertise. For this reason, it is critical to engage in processes that value indigenous knowledge and uncover untapped skills. With this in mind, in our faculty learning community we have shared with each other strategies that have activated local understanding and stimulated skill development. An example is undertaking a knowledge and skill audit to identify what community members currently know about community life and to learn more about what values they hold, hobbies they pursue, and other talents they possess. Audit outcomes are used to identify individuals who possess the skills and information needed to achieve goals. When partners get to know each other well, they are able to recognize and tap talents to get specific tasks done such as: "Andre has artistic talent. Maybe he could design the logo."

In this type of work, it is important to recognize that a main purpose for listening to one another and sharing stories is to create venues for recognizing multiple and unique realities, as well as for acknowledging differences. These activities create spaces for marginalized groups to define their own realities, rather than having others name and define "realities" for them (Bond 1999; Bond and Pyle 1998). If change in the status quo is to occur, it is also important to engage in discourse that fosters understanding of the forces that make some perspectives less visible, and often less legitimate, than others (Bond 1999; Ulrich 2003). Moreover, dominant groups must be responsible for deconstructing their own dominance and understand that *they* need to hear the perspectives of marginalized people. That is the only way they will know if and when others experience their actions as oppressive. As Bond argues:

> Prevailing beliefs about fairness emphasize sameness—so much so as to be a barrier to the meaningful involvement of diverse participants. . . . Sameness is acontextual; difference frameworks are contextualized. . . when difference is posed as the opposite of equality, it presents an impossible choice. (Bond 1999, electronic resource)

At the same time, if those who have been marginalized want to change their sense of self, they sometimes find comfort, as well as support, in joining with a group of people in co-constructing a new community narrative. In that way, sharing personal stories and constructing collective narratives (shared through dialogue, texts, pictures, performances, and rituals) become empowering activities (Rappaport 1995).

Creating safe spaces to include multiple voices

Recognizing multiple realities through sharing personal stories and recognizing collective narratives require the creation of safe spaces that grow out of mutual respect and trust (Bartunek and Louis 1996; Bond, Belenky, and Weinstock 2000; Stall and Stoecker 1998). These activities also require different types of informal participation and multiple opportunities for meaningful sharing (also see chapter 6 on building social capital), such as listening circles, journaling, and engaging in informal dialogues that take place over coffee or dinner. More formal approaches are also useful, such as focus groups, interviews, concept mapping, values clarification, photo-language, and surveys. To enable these opportunities, outside support (e.g., providing child care, transportation, translation services) and technical assistance (e.g., training in group decision making) are often needed for individuals to participate meaningfully (Campbell, Copeland, and Tate 1998).

An example from the "listening partners" peer groups (Bond, Belenky, and Weinstock 2000) illustrates a way of promoting sharing and understanding multiple realities. Peer groups met weekly for three-hour sessions across an eight-month time period in a comfortable neighborhood setting, such as a church basement. Professional women (social workers, educators, health service providers) acted as facilitators, which meant they provided encouragement and guidance to help women identify personal and group strengths, needs, and priorities. Each sharing session was audio-taped to enable further reflection. Key approaches in this project included engaging in reflective dialogue, creating a safe space for conversation, "re-presenting" the women's words through tape recording, transcribing, and summarizing activities, and reflecting on the roles of women as thinkers and problem solvers. Ultimately, small and large group venues promoted the creation of "'growth stories'—stories of personal vision, strength, and accomplishment that had gone unnamed and unrecognized within the narrow definitions of our gender- and class-based value systems" (2000, electronic resource). In addition, children's growth stories were written and published, and graduation ceremonies were held. Embedded in inclusive processes like these are attempts to ensure what Guba and Lincoln (1989) term "educative authenticity," which refers to helping individuals develop an enhanced understanding of and appreciation for the perspectives and values of others. A wide range of involvement options, as well as a variety of ways to elicit and listen to diverse voices, are pursued not only as means of inclusion, but also as channels for developing mutual awareness.

Sometimes, however, mere "sharing" is not enough; group differences must be confronted as well. Imaging exercises (Blake, Mouton, and Sloma 1965) can be used to achieve awareness of perceptual differences. In this approach, different organizational groups generate self-portraits and then discuss those images with members of other groups. The ensuing dialogue becomes a first step in addressing group differences (Bartunek, Foster-Fishman, and Keys 1996).

If individual empowerment is aimed at working toward the "common good," as Darlington and Mulvaney (2002) contend, then strategies are needed for mobilizing social capital and leveraging change. In this regard, Stall and Stoecker (1998) describe the importance of "centerwomen" or "bridgeleaders" who use existing social networks to connect people and groups with similar concerns for the purpose of

> . . . transform[ing] social networks into a political force and help[ing] translate the skills that women learn in their families and communities (e.g., interpersonal skills, planning and coordination, conflict mediation) into effective public sphere leadership. (1998, 744)

This approach is an example of community development (versus community-based development) as interpreted by Chavis and Florin (1990) and organizing community (versus community organizing) as understood by Stall and Stoecker (2000). In both ways of understanding, emphasis is placed on empowerment as both a process and as an outcome.

The nature of relationships and the importance of context

Just as one cannot "give voice" to another, power cannot be "given" to others. Rather, there are variations in ways that power is understood and negotiated as people interact in local contexts (Speer and Hughey 1995; Trickett 1994). The language of "co" is often used to indicate the roles that partners share, with each partner contributing specific expertise and particular perspectives (Lee 2001; Zimmerman 1995). Co-equal partners engage in shared decision making and shared leadership (Perkins and Zimmerman 1995). However, as Bond and Keys (1993) point out, although co-empowerment enables more than one group to have significant influence on decision making in an organization, empowered groups do not necessarily have equal influence on every decision. That is, specific groups within an organization engage in a fluid process of moving in and out of exercising power at different times, in a range of contexts, and around different topics without homogenizing or diluting the difference among those groups (Bond 1999). In fact, the use of differences as a resource has the potential to enhance problem solving and decision making (Larson, Foster-Fishman, and Keys 1994).

Issues of power and reciprocity

At the organizational level, it is important to note that there are instances where managers and employees must change their beliefs about whether shared decision making can take place among individuals who are hierarchically unequal (Labianca, Gray, and Brass 2000). The change process may require devoting time and support to multi-dimensional objectives, such as helping individuals feel motivated to change their perceptions; working with them to "unfreeze" (Lewin 1951) their current views; providing opportunities to compare and contrast their old views with newer views of how decision making can take place; and helping them stabilize a new way of looking at their own and others' participation (Labianca et al. 2000).

Ironically, we have also found that including multiple groups in decision making processes can sometimes lead to "group think," which occurs when individuals are wary of conflict and (because of that) focus more time and attention on building consensus than on valuing and engaging in critical dialogue about issues. In our experience, we have found it helpful to discuss this risk openly with participants to emphasize the natural and important role conflict can play in group work (Chavis 1999). This includes nurturing the development of group norms where dissent is not only expected but also encouraged.

For example, an explicit effort of voicing dissent was embedded into the monthly agenda in an advisory group with which Foster-Fishman worked. At some point in every discussion, group members were asked to identify reasons why they disagreed with the consensus opinion that was emerging. This process was particularly important within the community in which efforts were under way; a community in which leaders were known for supporting efforts during meetings and sabotaging efforts later. An explicit norm was adopted that required participants to voice *dissent in* meetings and voice *consent outside* of meetings. In the "Learning to Support Novices" case discussed earlier, the Practicum design work may have focused prematurely on coming to a consensus about effective mentoring practices. Planning outcomes might have been enhanced had group members taken the time to consider approaches that other mentors might value.

A related approach to promoting critical thinking that leads to mutual understanding is to adopt the norm of engaging in what Elbow (1986, 254) terms "methodological doubting and believing." Methodological believing includes the disciplined procedure of not only listening to, but genuinely trying to believe, a view or idea that someone else has advanced. This stance enables listeners to think about what is interesting, new, or helpful about a viewpoint; to consider whether an idea addresses matters that the listener might not have noticed (especially in relationship to the listener's preferred way of thinking); and to consider in what sense or under what conditions an idea might be true. The second process—methodological doubting—involves learning to question (rather than unquestionably accept) an idea, especially an idea that is routinely taken for granted. By doubting, one takes an inquisitive if not a critical view. As Elbow puts it, "Epistemologically, doubting reflects the trial-by-fire foundation of knowledge whereby we feel no position should be accepted until it has withstood the battering of our best skeptics" (1986, 266). He argues further that these deliberate processes—methodological belief and doubt—represent centerpieces of critical thinking. Put in the language used repeatedly in this book, processes such as these help in efforts devoted to examining, critiquing, and elevating one's work, essential practices for coming to critical engagement.

The issue of doubting often extends beyond an idea to include faith in a proposed effort. This happens frequently in community development work, especially when historically excluded community members question whether their participation will represent something other than token involvement (Bartunek, Foster-Fishman, and Keys 1996). The stark reality is that community groups sometimes experience tokenism and, with that, resist joining new partnership efforts (Hogue et al. 1995). Although resistance in those instances should be expected, it does not necessarily mean the end of organizational or community engagement. In fact, as we discussed in our faculty learning community, it can represent a dialogic opportunity: participants talking about what genuine inclusion *really* means and analyzing episodes of inauthentic engagement.

For example, in a project associated with Foster-Fishman's work, a key community leader refused to participate initially, citing as his rationale frustration over failed attempts to improve the service delivery process. Slowly and over time, this person was "courted" by several community members. They reminded the skeptic of his important role in the process; described how this project could be different; and suggested that he play a "devil's advocate" role to mitigate the prospects of history repeating itself in his community. After a month of conversations with a variety of stakeholders, the individual decided to join the effort. As time passed and as he participated on his terms, the heretofore skeptic became an outspoken champion of the project.

This story reinforces of importance of what Darlington and Mulvaney (2002) describe as "reciprocal empowerment" for fostering and sustaining egalitarian environments of engagement:

> Reciprocal empowerment combines the attributes of self-determination, independence, knowledge, choice, and action embodied in personal authority with the early empowerment attributes of compassion, companionship, collectivity, community, cooperation, communion, consensus, and competence to enhance oneself and others, thereby creating an egalitarian environment that fosters equality, mutual respect, mutual attention, mutual empathy, mutual engagement, and mutual responsiveness. (2000, electronic resource)

The concept of reciprocal empowerment carries with it a distinctive notion of what it means to exercise power—one that relies on nurturing relationships versus exercising authority—in a context created for purposes of developing mutual understanding. Starhawk names this interpretation of power as "power-with":

> The source of power-with is the willingness of others to listen to our ideas. . . . Power-with is more subtle, more fluid and fragile than authority. It is dependent on personal responsibility, on our own creativity and daring, and on the willingness of others to respond. (Cited in Darlington and Mulvaney 2002; Starhawk 1987, 10–11)

Stall and Stoecker (1998) argue that the strengths of a women-centered model of community organizing are in "building relationships that can sustain over the long haul" (749). However, once private sphere issues move into the public sphere, ". . . their resolution is subject to the competitive, masculine, zero-sum processes of that sphere" (750). That tells us that no one type of relationship works in all contexts, and that individuals and groups that have learned to work together successfully in one context may need to redefine those relationships and take different approaches as they move into other contexts.

Knowing and responding to the context

The importance of context has been a central theme in our faculty learning community's reflections on our work (Speer and Hughey 1995; Stall and Stoecker 1998; Trickett 1994). From experience, we have learned to pay attention to the interplay between individuals and their settings to understand the potential for empowerment processes and goals to succeed. For example, Foster-Fishman and Keys (1997) argue that pre-conditions exist for employee empowerment at the organization and individual levels. Organizationally, employees need ample control in situations that they think are important, which includes having access to resources and opportunities to exercise their rights. Moreover, the organization must have formal and informal norms that promote inclusion and participation. Peterson and Zimmerman (2004) refer to these organizational qualities as the "intraorganizational component" or the infrastructure necessary for members to engage in proactive behaviors associated with goal achievement. Also, individuals must have the desire for increased control and trust in the organization if change is to occur (Foster-Fishman and Keys 1997). Even within a single organization, empowerment may mean different things to different people, depending on personal backgrounds involved; and empowerment may also proceed in different ways, depending on an organization's past experiences with empowerment (Foster-Fishman et al. 1998).

In the Practicum design work described in the "Learning to Support Novices" case, the same path was designed for all mentor teachers to follow. Explicit attention was not paid to whether each mentor had the appropriate background and experience to carry out identified tasks. Subsequently, the Partner Classroom work is taking a different approach, starting with the more experienced mentors and proceeding with others more gradually.

Organizations, too, have unique histories that reflect their members' multiple realities (Bond and Pyle 1998). At times, the context in which collaboration occurs can create barriers to success if there is a history of inter-group tensions, narrow role definitions, or resource constraints (Foster-Fishman, Perkins, and Davidson 1997). Subcultures within organizations (old-boys' networks, stereotyping, etc.) can become barriers to change as well (Bond and Pyle 1998). Alternatively, there may be unanticipated opportunities for empowerment to succeed within one or more subcultures, even if the larger organizational system is disempowering (Foster-Fishman and Keys 1997). Recognizing and building upon "small wins" can be one way to foster empowerment in specific, local contexts (Weick 1984, cited in Foster-Fishman and Keys 1997, 364).

Conclusion: the centrality of learning

In chapter 5, we introduced the concept of critical Discourse to emphasize a particular type of interaction that promotes learning. We argued that without it, transformative ends are less likely to be achieved. One approach to foster such learning is empowerment evaluation—a process designed to help people engage in self-evaluation and reflection so they can help themselves improve their own programs (Fetterman 2002). Through a three-step process—establishing a mission, taking stock, charting a course that is repeated in a cyclical manner—evaluation becomes institutionalized and internalized, a means for promoting a culture of learning with the associated potential of becoming a powerful force for change (Fetterman 2002). However, in evaluation partnerships, it is also important to understand individuals' epistemologies (underlying assumptions about how knowledge is generated), as well as to acknowledge who is responsible for knowledge generation. Epistemologies and role identities typically influence how participants react to the collaborative process (Foster-Fishman, Perkins, and Davidson 1997).

While empowerment and co-empowerment processes and outcomes do not always include formal attempts to conduct empowerment evaluation, our experiences suggest that the process of creating cultures of learning is accelerated by promoting cycles of reflection and action; discovering participants' untapped knowledge and skills; and creating safe spaces to hear multiple voices. At the same time, efforts in this regard are impeded if insufficient attention is paid to contextually-influenced issues of power and reciprocity. Toward that end, success is often contingent on the frequency, intensity, and quality of critical Discourse, all of which is enabled when participants value inquiry and formalize it as a means to seek betterment. When that happens, they not only enter into relationships for the purpose of seeking mutual understanding, they also treat their stories of engagement as texts to be shared, examined, and critiqued.

In the next chapter, the issue of what it means to foster empowerment and co-empowerment is explored with specific reference to the matter of working toward transformative ends.

References

Ansley, F. L., and J. Gaventa. 1997. Researching for democracy and democratizing research. *Change* Jan/Feb:46–53.

Bartunek, J. M., P. G. Foster-Fishman, and C. B. Keys. 1996. Using collaborative advocacy to foster intergroup cooperation: A joint insider-outsider investigation. *Human Relations* 49(6):701–731.

Bartunek, J. M., and M. R. Louis. 1996. Insider/Outsider team research. Thousand Oaks CA: Sage Publications.

Blake, R. R., J. S. Mouton, and R. L. Sloma. 1965. The union-management intergroup laboratory: Strategy for resolving intergroup conflict. *Journal of Applied Behavioral Science 1*:25–57.

Bond, M. A. 1999. Gender, race and class in organizational contexts. *American Journal of Community Psychology 27*(3):327. Retrieved May 24, 2005, from Questia database. http://www.questia.com.

Bond, M. A., M. F. Belenky, and J. S. Weinstock. 2000. The listening partners program: An initiative toward feminist community psychology in action. 1. *American Journal of Community Psychology 28*(5):697. Retrieved May 24, 2005, from Questia database. http://www.questia.com.

Bond, M. A. and C. B. Keys. 1993. Empowerment, diversity, and collaboration: Promoting synergy on community boards. *American Journal of Community Psychology* 21(1):37–57.

Bond, M. A., and J. L. Pyle. 1998. The ecology of diversity in organizational settings: Lessons from a case study. *Human Relations 51*(5):589–623.

Campbell, M., B. Copeland, and B. Tate. 1998. Taking the standpoint of people with disabilities in research: Experiences with participation. *Canadian Journal of Rehabilitation 12*(2):95–104.

Casey, K. 1995-6. The new narrative research in education. *Review of Research in Education 21*:211–253.

Chavis, D. M. 1999. Building community capacity to prevent violence through coalitions and partnerships. *Journal of Health Care for the Poor and Underserved 6*(2):234–245.

Chavis, D., and P. Florin. 1990. *Community development, community participation.* San Jose CA: Prevention Office, Bureau of Drug Abuse Services.

Cochran, M., and C. Dean. 1991. Home-school relations and the empowerment process. *The Elementary School Journal 91*(3):261–269.

Cornell University Empowerment Group. 1989. *Networking bulletin: Empowerment and family support 1*(1):October.

Darling-Hammond, L. 1991. The implications of testing policy for educational quality and policy. *Phi Delta Kappa* 73(3):220–225.

Darlington, P. S., and B. M. Mulvaney. 2002. Gender, rhetoric, and power: Toward a model of reciprocal empowerment. *Women's Studies in Communication 25*(2):139+. Retrieved May 24, 2005, from Questia database. http://www.questia.com.

Dewey, J. 1904/1964. The relation of theory to practice in education. In R. D. Archambault, ed. *John Dewey on education.* Chicago: Univ. of Chicago Press.

Dewey, J. 1916. *Democracy and education.* New York: Macmillan.

Elbow, P. 1986. Methodological doubting and believing: Contraries in inquiry. In *Embracing contraries: Explorations in learning and teaching.* New York: Oxford Press.

Fawcett, S. B., A. Paine-Andrews, V. T. Francisco, J. A. Schultz, K. P. Richter, R. K. Lewis, E. L. Williams, K. J. Harris, J. Y. Berkley, J. L. Fisher, and C. M. Lopez. 1995. Using empowerment theory in collaborative partnerships for community health and development. *American Journal of Community Psychology* 23(5):677+. Retrieved May 24, 2005, from Questia database. http://www.questia.com.

Fetterman, D. M. 2002. Empowerment evaluation: Building communities of practice and a culture of learning. *American Journal of Community Psychology* 30(1):89+. Retrieved May 24, 2005, from Questia database. http://www.questia.com.

Foster-Fishman, P. G., and C. B. Keys. 1997. The person/environment dynamics of employee empowerment: An organizational culture analysis. *American Journal of Community Psychology* 25(3):345+. Retrieved May 24, 2005, from Questia database. http://www.questia.com.

Foster-Fishman, P. G., D. Perkins, and W. Davidson. 1997. Developing effective evaluation partnerships: Paradigmatic and contextual barriers. *Nalise Psicologica* 3(15):389–403.

Foster-Fishman, P. G., D. A. Salem, S. Chibnall, R. Legler, and C.Yapchai. 1998. Empirical support for the critical assumptions of empowerment theory. *American Journal of Community Psychology* 26(4):507+. Retrieved May 24, 2005, from Questia database. http://www.questia.com.

Giroux, H. A. 1988. *Teachers as intellectuals: Toward a critical pedagogy of learning.* Granby MA: Bergin and Garvey.

Gomez, M. L., J. C. Stone, and J. Kroeger. 2004. Conversations on teaching reading: From the point of view of point of view. *English Education* 36(3):192–213.

Greenwood, D. J., and M. Levin. 1998. *Introduction to action research: social research for social change.* Thousand Oaks CA: Sage Publications.

Gruber, J. E., and J. Trickett. 1987. Can we empower others? The paradox of empowerment in the governing of an alternative school. *American Journal of Community Psychology* 15(3):353–371.

Guba, E. G., and Y. S. Lincoln. 1989. *Fourth generation evaluation.* Newbury Park CA: Sage.

Gutierrez, L. M. 1990. Working with women of color: An empowerment perspective. *Social Work* 35:149–153.

Heron, J., and P. Reason. 1997. A participatory inquiry paradigm. *Qualitative Inquiry* 3:274–294.

Hogue, T., R. Clark, A. Bergstrom, D. Perkins, and M. Slinski. 1995. *Collaboration framework: Addressing community capacity.* Columbus OH: National Network for Collaboration.

Itzhaky, H., and A. S. York. 2000. Empowerment and community participation: Does gender make a difference? *Social Work Research* 24(4):225. Retrieved May 24, 2005, from Questia database. http://www.questia.com.

Kennedy, M. 1987. Inexact sciences: Professional education and the development of expertise. In E. Z. Rothkopf, ed. *Review of research in education* vol. 14:133–167. Washington D.C.: American Educational Research Association.

Kennedy, M. 1999. Ed schools and the problem of knowledge. In J. D. Raths and A. C. McAninch, eds. *Advances in teacher education vol 5: What counts as knowledge in teacher education?* Stamford CT: Ablex Publishing.

Kessels, J., and F. Korthagen. 1996. The relationship between theory and practice: Back to the classics. *Educational Researcher* 25(3):17–22.

Labianca, G., B. Gray, and D. J. Brass. 2000. A grounded model of organizational schema change during empowerment. *Organizational Science 11*(2):235–257.

Larson, J., P. G. Foster-Fishman, and C. Keys. 1994. Discussion of shared and unshared information in decision-making groups. *Journal of Personality and Social Psychology 67*(3):446–461.

Lee, J. A. 2001. *The empowerment approach to social work practice: Building the beloved community*. New York: Columbia Univ. Press.

Lewin, K. 1951. *Field theory in social science. Selected theoretical papers*. D. Cartwright, ed. New York: Harper.

Liston, D. P., and K. M. Zeichner. (1991). *Teacher Education and the Social Conditions of Schooling*. New York: Routledge.

McMillan, B., P. Florin, J. Stevenson, B. Kerman, and R. E. Mitchell. 1995. Empowerment praxis in community coalitions. *American Journal of Community Psychology 23*(5):699+. Retrieved May 24, 2005, from Questia database. http://www.questia.com.

No Child Left Behind Act. 2002. Retrieved May 24, 2005. http://www.ed.gov/nclb/landing.jhtml?src=pb

Payne, C. M. 1995. *I've got the light of freedom: The organizing tradition and the Mississippi freedom struggle*. Berkeley: Univ. of California Press.

Perkins, D. D., and M. A. Zimmerman. 1995. Empowerment theory, research and application. *American Journal of Community Psychology 23*(5):569+. Retrieved May 24, 2005, from Questia database. http://www.questia.com.

Peterson, N. A., and M. A. Zimmerman. 2004. Beyond the individual: Toward a nomological network of organizational empowerment. *American Journal of Community Psychology 34*(1–2):129+. Retrieved May 24, 2005, from Questia database. http://www.questia.com.

Rappaport, J. 1995. Empowerment meets narrative: Listening to stories and creating settings. *American Journal of Community Psychology 23*(5):795+. Retrieved May 24, 2005, from Questia database. http://www.questia.com.

Rich, R. C., M. Edelstein, W. K. Hallman, and A. H. Wandersman. 1995. Citizen participation and empowerment: The case of local environmental hazards. *American Journal of Community Psychology 23*(5):657+. Retrieved May 24, 2005, from Questia database. http://www.questia.com.

Reissman, C. K. 1993. *Narrative analysis*. Newbury Park CA: Sage.

Rosaen, C. L., and E. Hoekwater. 1990. Collaboration: Empowering educators to take charge. *Contemporary Education 61*:144–151.

Schön, D. 1983. *The reflective practitioner*. New York: Basic Books.

Schön, D. 1987. *Educating the reflective practitioner*. San Francisco: Jossey-Bass.

Speer, P. W., and J. Hughey. 1995. Community organizing: An ecological route to empowerment and power. *American Journal of Community Psychology 23*(5):729+. Retrieved May 24, 2005, from Questia database. http://www.questia.com.

Speer, P. W., and N. A. Peterson. 2000. Psychometric properties of an empowerment scale: Testing cognitive, emotional, and behavioral domains. *Social Work Research 24*(2):109. Retrieved May 24, 2005, from Questia database. http://www.questia.com.

Stall, S., and R. Stoecker. 1998. Community organizing or organizing community? Gender and the crafts of empowerment. *Gender & Society 12*(6):729–756.

Starhawk. 1987. *Truth or dare: Encounters with power, authority, and mystery*. San Francisco: Harper & Row.

Trickett, E. J. 1994. Human diversity and community psychology: Where ecology and empowerment meet. *American Journal of Community Psychology 22*(4):583+. Retrieved May 24, 2005, from Questia database. http://www.questia.com.

Ulrich, W. 2003. Beyond methodology choice: Critical systems thinking as critically systemic discourse. *Journal of the Operation Research Society 54*(4):325–342.

Villegas, A. M., and T. Lucas. 2002. *Educating culturally responsive teachers: A coherent approach.* Albany: State Univ. of New York Press.

Weick, K. 1984. Small wins: Redefining the scale of social problems. *American Psychologist 39*:40–49.

Wolff, T. J. 1992. Coalition building: Is this really empowerment? Paper presented at the American Public Health Association's Annual Meeting. San Francisco CA.

Zimmerman, M. A. 1995. Psychological empowerment: Issues and illustrations. *American Journal of Community Psychology 23*(5):581+. Retrieved May 24, 2005, from Questia database. http://www.questia.com.

CHAPTER 8

CRITICAL ENGAGEMENT, TRANSFOR-
MATION, AND DEVELOPMENT

As is clearly apparent from earlier chapters of this book, we support Boyer's assertion that "the academy must become a more vigorous partner in the search for answers to our most pressing social, civic, economic and moral problems" (Boyer 1996). Having said that, we believe there is a need to move beyond the matter of problems and answers. In our way of thinking, engagement of the Academy with the citizenry is an enduring, ever-unfolding, and enfolding process of experiential learning that reflects a perpetual stream of meaningful communicative actions. For us, engagement is persistent, critical, reflexive, discursive, inclusive, pluralist, and democratic. It is expressed in populist deliberations: people confronting messy complexities of everyday life in their quest to arrive at consensual, public judgments about—and to enable collective actions to achieve—sustainable betterment. It is not a matter of solving isolated problems by instrumental means—of bringing familiar mechanistic ways of *knowing* and *known* knowledge to "familiar" problems. Rather, it is a persistent and collective endeavor focused on learning how to transform ways of living through profound and dogged participation in life itself.

At engagement's core lies an appeal that echoes a Socratic concern, that is, how we should live our lives as autonomous human beings with assumed responsibilities both for others and, also, for the world about us. As Grayling (2004, 36) has suggested recently, Socrates believed that the life truly worth living is "the considered life . . . . a life which is well informed, has worthwhile goals and is lived discerningly so that one can respond to others well, and live flourishingly for oneself." There are strains here, too, of the ancient Greek notion of *paideia* that the "promotion of self-development and lifelong learning should be the central project of a society"—at least once it has found ways of providing sufficient goods and services (Milbraith 1989, 94).

At this late stage of modernity, however, this is no easy matter; people all over the world struggle to deal with the complexity and vagaries of a "risk society" induced, in part, by the very manner by which we have treated the world about us (Beck 1992). Under these circumstances, as Dietz, Ostrom, and Stern (2003) submit:

> [d]evising ways to sustain the earth's ability to support diverse life, including a reasonable quality of life for humans, involves making tough decisions under uncertainty, complexity, and substantial biophysical constraints as well as conflicting human values and interests.

The search for sustainable transformations in the human condition must be set within a context of collective responsibilities for ecological and socio-cultural integrity, which is at once an ethical, economic, techno-scientific, spiritual, political, and socio-cultural matter. It also dictates that we develop the intellectual and moral capabilities to deal with these responsibilities, as well as the social, cultural, and political freedom to express them. As Sen (1999, 74) argues, such freedom is a primary and paramount condition if we are to choose a life that we *each* have a reason to value. The stark reality is that the complexities of contemporary life are just as characteristic of, and challenging to, individual matters of health and well-being as they are of personal and family livelihoods. Likewise, local community concerns for law and order, environmental quality, and public concerns, in general, stand alongside concerns about national security, trade globalization, or trends in planetary climate. Given that reality, we need to get beyond the notion that issues of pressing concern to the citizenry are social *or* economic *or* moral *or* political. Instead, each is a slice of overarching and interconnected complexities, even the gross uncertainties, of contemporary life—different faces, as it were, of the same messy reality.

These matters are not mere semantics, but essential and systemic challenges to the dominant worldviews and prevailing epistemes of the Academy, as well as to the very paradigmatic nature of the academic activities that reflect them. They also represent challenges to the norms, procedures, and epistemic cultures of a host of other vital social institutions, too, although this issue is hardly ever discussed in engagement circles.

While engagement provides opportunities to bring new perspectives to academic work, we do not wish to diminish the significance of conventional approaches to extension, outreach, service, research, or education. Rather, the central theme of our argument is that novel issues deserve innovative ideas and treatments, and that includes innovative interpretations and formulations of scholarly engagement itself. In this regard, much can be learned from the present and the past about what we should do next to assure "better futures." As the poet T. S. Eliot (*Burnt Norton, Stanza 1, Four Quartets*) has put it:

"Time present and time past,
Are both perhaps present in time future."

Chapter overview

With all of this as background, the reader will find this chapter organized in the following manner: In the beginning, we share our interpretation of the term "critical scholarship of engagement" and discuss why work in this domain is so important. That proposition is followed by a discussion of the practices associated with critical engagement. The case is then made for why it is important to link critical engagement and development. At chapter's end, the strands woven in this essay are pulled together in the form of a conceptual schema for understanding and practicing critical engagement as a form of systemic development.

A critical scholarship of engagement

It is the novel characteristics of life in this era of "late modernity" that provide the essentials for our appreciation of the significance of Boyer's (1996) call for a *scholarship* of engagement. Such a scholarship, we submit, should be both critical and transformative in nature. In the best tradition of pragmatism, we also believe that it should be useful and "free from constraints save conversational ones," as Rorty (1982, 165) would have it.

This particular "take" on the scholarship of engagement has emerged from our own investigations as scholar-practitioners who hail from different disciplines and who have been deliberating critically together on the matter for a number of years. These deliberations have had a distinctly hermeneutic flavor through our on-going, if often disjunctive, "pulsing" between what Bernstein (1983, 41) refers to as the "three traditional moments" of hermeneutics— understanding, interpretation, and application. We have developed (or better said, are continuing to develop) a critical scholarship of engagement through a hermeneutic exploration of the concept of a scholarship of critical engagement. It has been a truly emergent process, transformation*al* and transforma*tive*, pregnant with opportunities to learn how to do differently what each of us has been doing for some time.

But our critical engagement has not been without challenges. The conventional empirical researching culture of the Academy presents one challenge, as does the influence of the orthodoxy of the empirical research traditions and objectivist/reductionist paradigmatic foundations of scientific disciplines. In our own case, there has also been the matter of the sheer unfamiliarity of (and occasional discomfort with) a hermeneutic process that is organically participative in its nature—seamless and persistent—and patently different from our "normal" project-oriented practices.

When working as researchers, our concerns are with an activity, which Checkland (1985) suggests involves three inter-connected elements: a framework of ideas (F); a methodology (M); and an area of concern (A). Thus, in any discrete research project, "[a] particular set of linked ideas F are used in a methodology M to investigate some particular area of interest A" (Checkland and Holwell 1998, 23). In contrast, as critically reflective scholars in hermeneutic search of a critical scholarship of engagement, we have come to focus on Bernstein's three moments—of understanding, interpretation, and application—as three *different* elements of scholarly inquiry and how they play out in practice.

Research is an objectively methodical and explicitly methodological process of inquiry into the nature of nature and/or of the nature of human nature. In contrast, hermeneutics is a process of inquiry into meaning as revealed through the study of texts and other narratives—including the stories that each of us has told. Rorty (1982, 199) has even suggested that being "interpretive or hermeneutic" is not having a special method, but (rather) "simply casting about for a vocabulary which might help." In that tradition—at least as it has been established by Gadamer (1975)—it is a much more organic process in which the different moments are blended together in a manner that essentially defies method. The "action" is the dialectical momentum between understanding and interpretation or between "explanation" and "interpretation," as Ricoeur (1991) prefers to express it, such that explanation and interpretation are "indefinitely opposed and reconciled" (1991, 124).

In the process of our own communal hermeneutic, we have come to recognize important differences between what Malinen (2000) refers to as naïve or surface interpretation, on the one hand, and critical or in depth interpretations, on the other. We have also come to appreciate the significance—and to capture the essence in practice of—what Ricoeur (1991) sees as the "emancipation" of the text from the author's original intentions and the initial cultural foundations of the discourse. Where research is science-in-practice or *praxis*, hermeneutics is a practical philosophy; a *phronēsis,* which also embraces concerns for the value-basis of judgment (Bernstein 1983). This, among other issues, dictates a change in perspective on instrumentalism and on the role of the instrumentalist expert. As Gadamer (1975) emphasized, a focus on phronēsis seeks to actually place science and technology into a different context from that which it has come to assume. The philosophical hermeneutic, he insists, seeks to "correct the peculiar falsehood of modern consciousness," which he argued is characterized by:

> The idolatry of scientific method and of the anonymous authority of the sciences and it vindicates against the noblest task of the citizen—decision making according to one's own responsibility—instead of conceding that task to the expert.

While our own hermeneutic search in critical engagement for understanding, interpretation, and application has certainly embraced the significance of decision making and public judgment together—as "the noblest task of the citizen"—our own position has never been anti-scientific or anti-research. While Gadamer was clear in the distinctions between science and hermeneutics, we have come to identify with the position that Bernstein (1983, 35) adopts. He submits that Gadamer's explication of hermeneutics helps "to deepen our understanding of the natural and social sciences." In this way, we can also relate to Bernstein's claim that "we can also use insights gained from recent investigations of the natural and social sciences to test the limits of Gadamer's conception of philosophic hermeneutics." In this manner, we have come to grasp the significance of what seems to us to be a powerful and dialectic complementarity between hermeneutic processes, on the one hand, and participative action researching practices, on the other. This dynamism pertains, not the least of all, to the multi-dimensional character of participation itself. As our scholarly enterprise has progressed, each of us has experienced both the joys and difficulties of an organically participative endeavor where we seek to make sense out of our collective, experiential reflections, as well as understand the writings of others. The goal all the while is to improve our understanding of ourselves as engaged scholars; the nature of engaged scholarship; the nature of engaged practices; and, not the least of which, our own "inner selves" as engaged persons.

The intensity and richness of this *intra-mural* process of critical engagement has led to an acute awareness of what *extra-mural* engagement could potentially achieve as a medium of practice for transformative development of different ways of living lives. At the same time, we are very conscious of intrinsic differences between our intra-mural work as an epistemic community concerned with scholarly questions about the nature of engagement *in contrast to* our extra-mural work as agents involved with engagement-in-practice with communities. A vital issue here is our appreciation of the role that different lifeworlds—each born of different cultural and ecological experiences—can play in promoting profound inter-community differences that exist between different epistemic cultures (Knorr Cetina 1999), and the difficulties that such dimensions present to the integration, or even an appreciation of, different knowledge networks (Box 1989).

As complex as all of this may seem, there has been something innately integrative about the multi-dimensionalities of our process. Something akin to a "wholeness"—and integrity—has emerged, prompting understanding to emerge from the diversity of our individual talents and experiences; and enabling a more profound sense of participation than might have gained by simply collaborating in a jointly undertaken field project. It has also led to profound collective insights about what critical engagement between academics and citizens might "look" and "feel" like. Because of all of this, we strongly relate to Skowlimowski's (1985) interpretation that:

> Wholeness means that all parts belong together, and that means that they partake in each other. Thus from the central idea that all is connected, that each is a part of the whole, comes the idea that each participates in the whole. Thus participation is an implicit aspect of wholeness.

Rather than conveying a mere literary image or a metaphor of engagement, this view of "participation as wholeness" connotes an ontology—a way of being in the world. It is nothing less than a cosmology of connectedness—of the self participating with others, and with the world at large, and of the participative inter-relationships between the individual and the collective, as well as between nature and society. Most significantly, perhaps, it intimately connects the knower with the known, while extending the notions of knowing and knowledge to incorporate values and emotions, as well as facts and theories. It also provides a fresh, participative perspective on the moments of the hermeneutic as a process of dynamic flux between wholes and parts.

This wholeness or systemic construct on these multiple aspects of participation and intimate inter-connections provides vital clues about the nature of critical engagement, as well as what it means to be a critically engaged scholar. It means to become embedded as an essential part of a whole associated with meaningful action-taking and meaning-making. To "engage" in this manner requires those involved to be prepared to be transformed and, also, to be a participant in transformative processes. In other words, "to engage" is to participate; become immersed; become transformed; and contribute to transformation.

We can engage by participating as a part of an integrated whole group of interacting individuals who are, in turn, engaged as parts of some whole event or systemic experience in the immediate world about them. In this manner, we can act as inter-connected knowing systems within other systems, as it were. Indeed, the conceptual significance of participation from this "parts/whole" perspective lies with the key system's principle that "wholes are different from the sum of their parts" with the corollary that they cannot be known through a study of their parts alone.

Systems are therefore inherently self-transformative in character. The unique properties of whole systems are emergent through the interactions of the different component parts (or subsystems of those systems), with unity thus emerging from diversity. The greater the diversity of those parts and the greater the intimacy of their inter-connectedness, then the greater the chance of their creative synergy contributing to a unique power of the whole.

While engagement demands that we do immerse ourselves in a collective with others, it does not mean that we lose our own identities; surrender what we know and personally value; or abandon our particular epistemological positions or idiosyncratic way(s) of knowing, including familiar ways of doing things. What it *does* mean is that we are consciously committed to *critically* reviewing all of these dimensions, along with the processes by which they were generated, and that we are willing to contextualize them to new (w)holistic circumstances—to amend and transform them, if and when appropriate.

The notion of critical engagement that we are promoting here is firmly grounded in a critical consciousness of our part in "wholeness" and of the systemic integrity that that it calls forth. It also reflects the concept of systemic transformation. Concurrent changes in wholes, in their constituent parts, and in relationships within and between wholes and parts (including those between wholes and the greater wholes), are part of the environments in which they themselves are embedded.

Interestingly enough, the integrity (in the sense of participative wholeness) that has characterized our small group over time has been accompanied by a marked increase in our sensitivity to integrity in the other sense of that word—of moral principle. This transformation has come to express itself through a greatly increased awareness of the ethical dimensions of our practices and, indeed, of the moral scope of all of our everyday activities. It has also highlighted the importance and challenge of integrating moral aspects into public discourse about betterment *with* the same sort of rigor and enthusiasm that mirrors the technical, empirical aspects of academic traditions. This, too, is an innately systemic challenge—with intellectual and moral reasoning being accepted and employed as different, inter-acting parts of a whole system of rationality that ultimately yields judgment (Vickers 1983). As Jackson (2000, 67) asserts:

> An individual's appreciative system will determine the way she sees (reality judgment) and values (value judgment) various situations and condition how she makes 'instrumental judgments' (what is to be done) and takes 'executive action'; in short how she contributes to the social world.

In our own case, as we have been engaged together as a small learning community in critically exploring a scholarship of critical engagement, we have continued to live our lives as participant/researchers in consensus-seeking endeavors within our own domains of interest, plying our practices of engagement with the citizenry. Following and extending Wenger (1999), it might be said that we have developed as a "community of critical practice" that is intent on organizing and sustaining other communities of critical practice. The reality is that we continue to interact with academic colleagues in our own disciplines and fields of interest; work with colleagues who participate with us in additional communities of practice; and share our emerging ideas in public forums. All of these efforts have allowed us to participate actively in and learn from a host of different narratives—among different communities with different interests, with different actors, and expressed through different discourses. Along the way, we have developed a strong accord with Gadamer's (1975) notion that, in the end, the most important narratives to understand are the ones in which we ourselves are engaged—ones into which we "have been thrown," as he described it. Warnke captures the difficulty that such a Gadamerian dynamic presents:

> Not only are we always deciphering the story or stories of which we are part, so that we know how to go on, but also we are always already in the process of going on. To this extent, our understanding of these stories is the understanding from the middle of an on-going narrative. We have to reflect on and understand ourselves in the middle of continuing to act as we have already understood ourselves. Put otherwise, we live or write our lives according to the meanings that

we think they have possessed and understand those meanings according to the way we continue to live and write our lives. (Warnke 2002, 80)

Dennett (1991, 418) has added further to these difficulties in suggesting that "[o]ur tales are spun, but for the most part we don't spin them; they spin us. Our human consciousness, and our narrative selfhood, is their product, not their source." We are parts of the very same whole that, in trying to understand, we change. That dynamic simply triggers the need for more understanding. As Bernstein (1983, 166) emphasizes, we are always in what Gadamer referred to as *media res*: "There are no absolute beginnings or endings. Experience is always anticipatory and open."

The hermeneutic nature of our own deliberations, as well as our own work-in-progress as ethically and critically engaged scholars, has served as a contrast to what it typically means to engage in "normal" scholarly activities as researchers. For an institution so concerned with the intellectual rigor of ideas, principles, explanations, and interpretations—and also one that is so enamored with the critical character of scholarly discourse—there is an amazing imprecision in the Academy about the nature of its own work. There is even a deep ambivalence about what scholars actually do in the name of scholarship, and about what it means to be a scholar or an intellectual; indeed, about how we should live the academic life to meet our moral responsibilities. Even the key concept of *scholarship* itself proves frustratingly elusive with a mélange of disputed definitions that are associated in some manner or another with knowledge, knowing, thinking, thought, theories, principles, reason, rationality, meaning, discovering, creating, researching, learning, and the like. On the one hand, this might be regarded as the greatest paradox of all, namely that a central concern of a critical scholarship is precision in meaning. On the other hand, it can be argued that through disputation of meaning and discursive contestability critical scholarship finds its momentum—and, indeed, its very purpose! Latour (1987, 200) presents an appealing logic in this context. In using words like "paradigm" or "society" he notes that

> [t]hese terms always have a vague definition because it is only when there is a *dispute, as long as it lasts,* and *depending on* the strength exerted by dissenters that words such as 'culture,' 'paradigm,' or 'society' may receive a precise meaning. (emphasis in original)

There is further reason to conclude that the precise definition of concepts misses the mark; the concept of "sustainability" offers an example. As Davison (2001, 213) suggests while "there are no simple, universal, or transparent answers to questions of sustainability," that is one of the strengths of the concept. The sustainability ideal, he argues, raises an agenda of "good, practical questions" that bears directly on the way we should live our lives. Different understandings "do not demand of us categorical certainty but the capacity to articulate what we feel most worthy of being sustained in our lives" (Davison 2001, 213).

In such normative circumstances—where there are neither fixed truths nor totally definitive knowledge—the human condition may indeed be best understood "as a continuous effort to negotiate contested meanings," as Mezirow (2000) has proposed. And, perhaps, scholarship itself is best understood as the conscious, self-reflexive capacity to continuously make meanings about, and take meaningful actions in, the world about us.

The nature of critical scholarship

When used in words like seamanship and leadership, the suffix *–ship* in scholarship connotes a set of attributes and of capabilities that are particular to a certain domain of human endeavors. Questions, however, remain with respect to the precise domains of reference. The irony is that, despite the inherently scholarly nature of the question, an "epistemic frenzy" occurs whenever the prevailing ideas of academic work are challenged—be the origins of such challenges conceptual or contextual. A whole spectrum of responses is usually encountered at such challenge. These range from passionate defenses of the *status quo* of conventional interpretations and their expressions as the "way things are done" within the Academy, right through to energetic attempts to embrace the opportunities that these challenges present for the scholastic innovation. In the midst of this range lies the seductive option of co-opting the new label as a way to re-invigorate, if not legitimize, old activities: not to "see" or "do" things differently, or do different things, but to do the same old thing in the name of some new thing.

Reactions to Boyer's (1996) introduction of the idea of scholarship of engagement have spanned the spectrum of those responses. The situation was exacerbated by Boyer's untimely death; he could not respond to the various reactions. Consequently, questions rather than answers abound:

- Is engagement an intentional dimension of all four of the forms of scholarship?
- Is engagement a meta-concept that involves a particular way of being scholarly?
- Is engagement a particularly scholarly way of discovering, integrating, applying, and teaching? If so, how does it differ from non-engaged discovery, integration, application, and teaching?
- Is a "scholarship of engagement" a fifth form of scholarship? If so, how is it different from the other four that he articulated?

In our own dialectical deliberations, we have unashamedly approached these questions from the naïve, pragmatic perspective: "What it is that we can *do* with these ideas in practice?" Even more significantly, and from a normative perspective: "What it is that we *ought to do* with them?" It is these concerns that drove us to the concept of the criticality of a scholarship of engagement, which must include ethical as well as intellectual dimensions, and also reflect socio-cultural as well as epistemic concerns. And it is these matters that reinforce the emphasis that we place on critical engagement as a medium for systemic trans-formation.

As we have come to see it, critical scholarship for engagement should be a critical activity in all senses of that phrase, including asking reflective questions about the way things are known and understood, as well as about the conditions that prevail in those worlds. A scholarship of critical engagement should focus on relationships among people; between people and "things"; and, in a more ab-stract manner, between ideas and events; reflections and actions; and principles and practices. It needs to be a scholarship *of* action *in* action pertinent for both personal and socio-cultural transformation, in which every process, context, and substantive content is continually subjected to critical review and open to poten-tial adaptation.

Essentially, we have come to conclude that the notion of a scholarship of *critical* engagement presents the Academy with opportunities to be truly innova-tive and transformational in response to new socio-cultural contexts. It presents transforming opportunities to develop and adopt news ways of co-participating in public discourses around issues of everyday concern that are characterized by a plurality of rationalities, ways of knowing, and types of knowledge.

Critical engagement, we submit, reflects profound intentionality—to work with others in ways that are truly participative, critical, transformative, democ-ratic, pluralistic, and systemic or holistic. It involves making sense of and creat-ing knowledge of the world that we experience in a manner that evokes all of the elements of what Bohm (1992, 19) refers to as our "thought system," which "not only includes thoughts, 'felts' and feelings but [also] it includes the state of the body." Importantly, as Bohm saw it, "it also includes the whole of society—as thought is passing back and forth between people in a process by which thought has evolved from ancient times."

Because language is central to this process, "you can think of the totality of a given language as an undivided whole from which the various words and their potential meanings all unfold" (Bohm 1987, 17). This continuous "unfolding" and "enfolding" of meanings, thoughts, "felts," and even intentions and "urges to do things," cannot be anything other than a dynamic, transformational process of individuals and social groupings alike—and, indeed, of the mind itself:

> Thoughts and feelings also enfold intentions. These are sharpened into deter-minate will and the urge to do something. Intention, will, and urge unfold into more action, which will include more thought if necessary. So all the aspects of the mind show themselves as enfolding each other, and transforming into each other through enfoldment and unfoldment. (Bohm 1987, 17)

Accordingly, a scholarship of critical engagement presents us with very significant epistemological challenges, including those associated with the normative and the emotional—as well as the empirical and the rational—aspects of meaning making. It also has us grapple with other epistemic challenges, including the inter-relationships between theory and practice; the objective and the subjective; *praxis* and *phronēsis;* fact and value; and the cognitive, the conative, and the affective. It confronts us with the need to explore the nature of knowledge; the processes of knowing and of learning; and transformative dimensions both for individuals and collectives. It has us seeking connections between individual learning and social learning; and the intellectual and moral development of individual persons and communities. In essence, it brings us face-to-face with our ontological realities and confronts our epistemological capacities.

From this multi-perspective, critical engagement cannot be a catch-all phrase for the panoply of extramural activities of the Academy, a rubric to include all forms of "partnering" or "collaborating" with the citizenry in any form of participation. Instead, it connotes a much more comprehensive, critical, yet tentative construct. First, it is much more complex than the process by which technical experts traditionally extend their knowledge to an essentially unknowing or "scientifically ignorant" lay citizenry through outreach education or extension. Second, it is much more profound in concept than seeking the advice of "participating stakeholders" as the basis for priority-setting for applied research and extension agendas. And, third, it is much more systemic in nature than a linear "reaching out" from the Academy to the citizenry, to partner with them in discrete problem-focused community development projects.

What we argue for is commitment to a critical scholarship of engagement, a way of thinking and practicing that extends the Academy significantly beyond its epistemic conventions and conventional practices. Such a commitment will dictate the need to take seriously a plurality of ways of knowing, types of knowledge, and rationalities as the foundations for making ethically defensible judgments and arriving at actions that are socio-culturally and ecologically responsible. This means there is a need for expanding historic patterns of relationships among higher education, civil institutions, and the citizenry.

Transformation as critical work
Fundamentally, a critical scholarship of engagement should be a scholarship of critical transformation—grounded in an acute appreciation of profound changes in the way people come to understand the world and act meaningfully and responsibly within it. A potent underlying assumption in this context is that meaningful and responsible "acts of development" in the material and social world are functions of the intellectual and moral development of the actors involved (Bawden 2005).

This means that transformations in the way that things are *done* depend on transformations in the way that things are *understood*—in the worldview or perspective assumptions that condition those understandings and in the manner by which meaningful or "mindful" judgments about betterment are formulated. And this way of understanding, in turn, demands the need for "mindful learning," where new information is welcomed; different worldviews and perspectives are appreciated; and new categories of knowing and knowledge are constantly and deliberately created (Langer 1997).

As we are presenting it, a commitment to critical engagement should be a commitment to conditions that facilitate the development and expression of each person's capabilities. As Sen (1999, 87) puts it: "the substantive freedoms that he or she enjoys to lead the kind of life that he or she has reason to value." And that means concerns for opportunities as well as processes, as well as the need to confront the challenges that entrenched, structural, socio-political inequalities so frequently present. As we shall argue later, this invokes emphatic focus on the transformative potential of critical learning processes that dictate the need for the transformation *of* education itself *and* a deliberative focus on learning *as* transformation. In the face of all of these complexities, critical engagement will also demand the development of systemic competencies that come only through epistemic development (Salner 1986).

In a spirit engendered by John Dewey, we seek to promote the notion of critical engagement as a form of transformational work that is as democratic in its processes and practices as it is democratic in its intentions and purposes. We call for sustained discursive connections to be established between academia and the citizenry—as well as with other institutions of the state—in democratic processes through which our shared everyday experiences are collectively transformed into shared meanings and meaningful actions. In this manner, we clearly appreciate the significance of what Dewey (1963) called "social intelligence" and we strongly reinforce the importance he attributed to it "in connection with public opinion, sentiment, and action." Because, like Dewey, our ultimate purpose is the pursuit of freedom and the (re)development of a democracy appropriate to the times, critical engagement is an inherently political enterprise. We therefore embrace what Boyte (2002) has referred to as "the political edge of citizenship," that is, the need to challenge the current concentration of political power and influence. If, as Dewey envisaged, citizens are really to be the co-creators of their social world then, as Boyte submits, there is an urgent need "to spread back out the ownership" of a politics that he defines as "the interplay of distinctive, unique interests and perspectives to accomplish public purposes." The implication here is that national governments should be seen as but a component of a "national governance system" that also includes the considerable degrees of self-governance through "inter-dependent individuals, groups, organizations and institutions that operate at different levels of collectivity" (Allen, Kilvington, and Horn 2002).

Here, then, is a very significant focus for critical engagement as transformation: it speaks directly to its political dimension in its radical challenge to relationships between civil society and the state—and to the Academy with both. There are, of course, powerful influences that work counter to the distribution of governance, forces that reflect the paradox of democracy. While the inclusion of people who have been traditionally excluded from deliberations "could be an important contribution to democratic processes in the world today," this might not "contribute to making 'democracy work' as such" (Howell and Pearce 2002). To the contrary:

> It might actually disrupt the smooth running of government institutions as these groups make more demands, precisely the kind of outcomes that elite political theorists have sought to avoid. However such disruptions might be the only way that some sectors of society can make their voices heard and ensure that their claims are listened to as much as the more powerful groups of society. (Howell and Pearce 2002, 49)

Indeed, there is compelling evidence to suggest that the opposite is happening. Yankelovich (1991) refers to this as "an imperative of our Culture of Technical Control": "All of the advanced industrial democracies of today, especially in the United States, are firmly committed to the control way of life and to using expert-driven technology to achieve it—whatever the cost" (Yankelovich 1991, 9). Yankelovich's position echoes the equally somber view of Toffler (1984, 243) that the entire apparatus of democracy as we know it is not "an expression of some undying mystical human commitment to freedom but of the spread of industrial civilization that began in England 200 to 300 years ago." Unfortunately, and as Toffler argued, the "political technology" that emerged has not been particularly adaptive. There has been, as he put it, "a mismatch between our decisional technology and the decisional environment," which has been characterized by "a cacophonous confusion, countless self-canceling decisions, noise, fury, and gross ineptitude." Toffler believed that improved democratic feedback between the citizenry and governments was an essential feature of reform, but he cautioned that:

> For citizen participation to be effective, it must concern itself increasingly not merely with 'here and now' decisions, but with those more basic decisions that influence the long-range future. In fact, participation without future consciousness is not democracy at all; it is mockery of democracy. (Toffler 1984, 248)

This means that a concern for "future consciousness" and for "anticipatory democracy" must be included in an understanding of critical engagement, especially so as we think about this concept in relationship to transformations needed in the current (and "late stage") of modernity.

As emphasized earlier, we do not—and in any way—underestimate the enormous significance of the past traditions of higher education's involvement with society through educational, research, extension, and other "service functions" nor do we suggest that these approaches are either inappropriate or outmoded. We say that because they serve a purpose. We also acknowledge the enormous benefits that modernization, in all of its techno-scientific and socio-economic dimensions, has contributed and will undoubtedly continue to contribute to human betterment. Having said that, we also acknowledge that critical engagement is required as a response to contemporary circumstances, contexts, demands, and imperatives. We also hold that new modes of association are needed—those that express fresh dispositions and are characterized by new discourses that offer novel and profound processes of participation.

A fundamental concern for the unintended, but nevertheless undesirable, consequences and excesses of some of those historical processes is an important element of the current context. And this includes meta-concerns about the impact of the intellectual and moral reasoning that provide the foundations for these processes. As emphasized in earlier chapters, the whole "process of modernization" with its relatively un-reflexive and uncritical commitment to progress to date has brought "bads" as well as "goods" along with it (Beck 1992). The associated dominance of the techno-scientific discourse of modernity, with its foundations in technical reason, has, moreover, tended to extinguish or (at least grossly) diminish other forms of practical reason that are significant to moral, ethical, and aesthetic dimensions vital to improving current situations. As the paradigms that provide the intellectual foundations for this "movement" invariably have their origins within the Academy, higher education is duty-bound to critically investigate them with a view to their potential transformation.

It is not that the linearity, objectivism, and reductionism of techno-science and neo-liberal economics are "wrong," but that they represent a paradigm that is inadequate in the face of the complexities of everyday living and of the values that citizens espouse in everyday lives. Such is the influence of the dominant, "instrumental" form of reason that, as Habermas (1984) argues, is deeply distorted. Questions of *how* things are to be done in society have come to dominate concerns about whether or not they *ought to be done* in the first place. This, Habermas asserts, is a function of the undue influence that is now wielded by the once benign "steering mechanisms" of the social system—those social sub-systems that "co-ordinate action through the media of money (capitalist economy) and administrative power (modern, centralized states)" (Love 1995).

Because Habermas (1984) believes that the lifeworld of modern society—the full range of social actions and institutions that are potentially available to human beings—has been colonized in this manner, an increased emphasis on practical reason in conjunction with technical reason will be, he submits, emancipating. With his theory of communicative action, Habermas (1984) presents the notion of discourse as the medium for mutual understanding between different actors achieved through rational argumentation under conditions that are free from the distorting influences of power. According to Chambers (1995), such immunization against repression and inequality is achieved through "a set of rules that are designed to guarantee equality, freedom, and fair play" that incorporate practical (generally valid moral principles) as well as pragmatic (means/ends issues) and ethical (self understanding) discourses. He writes:

No one with the competency to speak and act may be excluded from discourse; everyone is allowed to question and/or introduce any assertion as well as express her attitudes, desires, and needs; no one may be prevented, by internal or external coercion, from exercising these rights. (Chambers 1995, 238)

From this it follows that both the substantive issues of the day—and the discourses that are used to explore them—deserve critical attention, not by the Academy in isolation from the citizenry or from the institutions of the state, but in direct concert *with them*, indeed, as a component part of an ever unfolding and enfolding discourse system. In this regard and with respect to context for instance, we have earlier submitted that responses to the pressing problems of the day ought to reflect a systemic appreciation for the "hybrid" nature of many contemporary issues. In all of their complexity and dynamics, uncertainties, vagaries, and ambiguities, they are often better seen as a compound, multi-faceted problematique, where the quest ought to be for improvements to messy situations rather than solutions to neatly discrete problems. These "imbroglios," as Latour (1993) has labeled them, call not for simple technical resolution by experts, but for responsible judgments generated collectively by communities of citizens that will perforce include members of the Academy.

In critical engagement, these collective judgments come down to the demand for democratic decisions by people who seek to better their own livelihoods in ways that are *as* socially just, ecologically responsible, and spiritually sensitive *as they are* technically effective and economically desirable. This calls for the acceptance of a way of knowing and judgment making that recognizes and appreciates relationships between and among diverse knowledges, experiences, lifestyles, and livelihoods. It is not just a matter of citizens participating in the discourse, but also of them having what Visvanathan (2005, 92) refers to as their "cognitive representation and empowerment" respected. He calls for *cognitive justice* as "the constitutional rights of different systems of knowledge to exist as part of dialogue and debate." This demand, he suggests, does not represent an anti-science or anti-technology agenda, but "the right for different forms of knowledge and their associated practices and ways of being to coexist, and to carry weight in the decisions that affect people's lives."

The essential focus here must be on rights *and* responsibilities and on freedom *with* accountability. Included must be the freedom for everyone concerned to have the opportunity to speak in their own manner; to assume the responsibility to also listen; and to accept accountability for justifying their positions on issues at hand. Such responsibilities must also include an unequivocal acceptance of the need to *listen* to "those who cannot speak"—and this category includes both those not yet born as well as the rest of "nature." This has particular application with respect to the growing appreciation of the need to embrace an ethic of sustainability, which dictates a commitment to the notion that the needs of today are to be met in a manner that does not compromise the abilities of future generations to meet theirs (Brundtland 1987).

None of the issues associated with either the context or substance of current situations is therefore straightforward. They do not represent simple problems for which there are incontestably obvious solutions. They do not divorce the observer from the observed; the "expert" from the "lay"; the subjective from the objective; or the moral from the intellectual. To engage with this fresh, critical perspective, then, is to enter a realm of contestation, where the notion of "betterment" itself is open to judgment, as is the very language used as the basis for having a discussion about it. As Dewey (1935) asserted with respect to the conflicts inevitable in social change:

> The method of democracy—insofar as it is that of organized intelligence—is to bring these conflicts out into the open where their special claims can be seen and appraised, they can be discussed and judged in the light of more inclusive interests. (McDermott 1981, 657)

Such deliberations, particularly within a context of contestable and inherently conflictual issues—such as those presented by the quest for sustainable ecological development—invariably add considerably to the complexity of already complex issues. This reveals an important dilemma: while in a democracy it is "unthinkable not to allow public participation" and to accept that "complexity in decision making is part of the cost of democratic politics," we rarely know "if today's decisions are *better enough* to warrant the extra complexity and cost" (Allen et al. 2003, 162). The risk is that both increased complexity and ever-escalating costs might eventually overwhelm the capacity of key public agencies to deliver essential services, and even policies, that pertain to the matters under deliberation. And, yet, it is the sustainability of these very agencies that many accept as "a prerequisite to sustainable environmental management or a sustainable society" (Allen et al. 2003).

Complexity, judgment, and empowerment

In this era of reflexive modernity, judgments have to be made about what criteria are adopted as the basis for betterment and also about who is included in the judgment-making process in the first place. No matter how democratic certain societies have become, and no matter the level of participation that its citizens enjoy, the complexities of the era can oppress—or at the very least disempower—even the most liberated human beings. In this regard, decisions about how individual intentions and dispositions are to be clarified and accommodated become vital aspects of empowering processes. This requires paying attention, especially, to the needs of those who will be influenced in some way or another by the outcomes of decisions, including those who, for one reason or another, may be excluded from the decision making process. These are issues, as Ulrich (1983) submits, that embrace important distinctions: between sources of motivation, control, expertise, and "legitimation"; the ways in which various actors are understood as clients, decisions makers, planners, and witnesses; the role-specific concerns of various actors; and the ways in which influence is mediated by source. These matters, Ulrich argues, represent boundary judgments that need to be critically addressed from the perspectives (following both Kant and Habermas) of two rationalities—the "technical" (*is*) and the "practical" (*ought*).

There is also the matter of the form of the discourses in which those deliberations are conducted. Even the choice of location and the characteristics of the forums of deliberation deserve critical review. Of vital significance is the impact that asymmetric power relationships have on collective deliberations. As at least one writer sees it, ". . . there is no such thing as a powerless people. There are only those who have not seen and have not used their power and will" (Okri 1997, 101); and this must change, too, for "the responsibilities of the unvalued, the unheard, the silent, are greater than ever."

Critical engagement can be nothing less than a critical and conscious commitment to transformation; not just in ways of "doing things in the world about us," but also in ways of "viewing that world" and of "coming to know and understand it" in its complexity. All of this is a prerequisite for responsible action to change circumstances for the better. Under conditions of complexity, transformations in the material world—and in the well-being of those within it—are essentially functions of the capacities to deal with that complexity by those participating in the deliberative process. In this sense, all knowing becomes doing, and as Maturana and Varela (1988) contend, all "knowers" are "doers," but with varying capacities to transform and to be transformed. The crux of the matter becomes the connection between the perceived complexities of the issues under deliberative review and the cognitive capacities of those involved in the reviewing.

A key thesis here is that understanding and dealing with complex issues demands the development of particular states of epistemic cognition (Salner 1986) that are themselves complex evaluative systems (West 2004). The work of Paulo Freire (1970) is especially relevant in this regard. Freire argues that the first stage in epistemic development is "an awakening of critical awareness" or *conscientização,* as he named it. This *conscientização* or conscientization is the process by which those engaged "achieve a deepening awareness of both the socio-cultural reality which shapes their lives. . . and their capacity to transform that reality through action upon it" (Friere 1970, 27). If this first stage oppression in the world is uncovered and a commitment to transformation is made, then in

> . . . the second stage, in which the reality of oppression has already been transformed, this pedagogy ceases to belong to the oppressed and becomes a pedagogy of all people in the process of permanent liberations. (Freire 2003, 54)

At its base, these are essentially paradigmatic matters. Critical engagement from this perspective dictates the need for critical appraisals of prevailing onto-epistemological and axiological assumptions about betterment. As outlined earlier, transformations (as understood here) are profound changes in an aspect or aspects of "being human." Criticality implies the "critique of everything." In systems terms, it is a self-reflexive process by which systems maintain the integrity of states and processes, alike, often in response to changes to the environment in which they are embedded. Critical societal (systemic) transformations involve transformations of individuals and of organizations/institutions; both are functions of the transformation of ways of finding out about the world as well as ways of taking responsible actions in it. Such transformations involve not just changes in the way that knowledge is generated and communicated, but also in the epistemological and axiological assumptions that are adopted as the frames of reference through which such knowledge is interpreted (Mezirow 1991). Moreover, the loci for transformative changes extend even beyond the cognitive and affective. As Jackson (2000, 289) asserts, "[h]umans are still in the grip of unconscious forces and their actions still have unintended consequences."

Praxis and Phronēsis

Critical questions are fundamentally scholarly questions especially those pertaining to the nature of paradigmatic assumptions, including the taken-for-granted and idiosyncratic values, norms, and beliefs that constitute our individual and socialized views of the world (Plas 1986, 7). Scholarship in this context needs to embrace not just the technical reason that is so characteristic of the *praxis* of the Academy, but also to what Gadamer (1975) refers to as "the practical and political reason" as embraced by the Aristotelian notion of *phronēsis* with its ethical and aesthetic overtones. As Gadamer argues, it is not enough to hold abstract notions of "the good." One must also be able to *do* good. While the prevailing interpretation of praxis and its manifestation as "expertise" are both inadequate in this regard, it will not be easy to change matters. As Gadamer (1975) has pointed out, the citizenry, in its "longing for orientation and normative patterns," invests the expert "with exaggerated authority":

> Modern society expects him (the expert) to provide a substitute for the past moral and political orientations. Consequently the concept of '*praxis*' which was developed in the last two centuries, is an awful deformation of what practice is. In all the debates of the last century practice was understood as the application of science to technical tasks. . . . It degrades practical reason to technical control. (Gadamer 1975, 312)

One of the essential impediments to decolonizing the life-world and reinstating greater moral consciousness (and ethical action) with the citizenry is a lack of practice in moral discourse. As Busch (2000) argues, we have spent several centuries secure in the abdication of our individual moral responsibilities, deferring it to the care of what he refers to as "one Leviathan or another," such as Bacon's scientism, Hobbe's statism, or Smith's economism. We have been seemingly content, Busch submits, to place our trust in scientists, monarchs, or the market to tell us what is "good" or "bad." Bacon, Hobbes, and Smith, respectively and over time, "attempted to develop moral, ordered, and affluent societies" as they each believed that "moral responsibility was too dangerous to be left in the hands of the ordinary people" (Busch 2000, 30). Similar arguments can be made for organized religion as individuals abdicate their individual moral responsibilities to a "church." That which is "right and proper" is found in "the good book" or revealed in some other spiritual manner. A moral life on those terms becomes a guided response to revelations.

A call for transformation in terms of critical engagement is based on the belief that there are many instances where faith appears "blind" to contemporary circumstances or where it is being lost without the resumption of moral responsibilities by individuals. One of the reasons for this, it might be argued, is there is confusion about the nature of morals and ethics. Consider the limited attention given to that topic in formal education at all levels. As Scruton (1994, 271) asks:

> Where in the world is morality? Is it a matter (as modern philosophers have assumed) of a certain kind of *judgment*— maybe even of certain 'evaluative' *words*? Is it a matter, as Kant argued, of action and practical reason? Is it a matter of emotion, sympathy, motive, as Hume supposed? Or is it, as Aristotle suggested, a matter of character and moral education?

Singer (1994) notes that the differences between the positions held by Kant and Hume take us to the fundamental question of whether ethics is primarily objective or subjective or, possibly, a synthesis of both positions. The debate, he argues, has been reduced to those who hold the primacy of reason as the source of ethics and to others who, in contrast, promote intuition:

> Different terms have been used to frame this question, but behind it always lies the division between, on the one hand, those that hold that there is somehow a true, correct, or best-justified answer to the question, 'What ought I to do?,' no matter who asks the question, and, on the other hand, those who hold that when different individuals or different societies disagree on ethical issues then there is no standard by which one could possibly judge one answer to be better than another. (Singer 1994, 7)

What constitutes morality—a matter that has engaged some of the finest minds over the millennia—is clearly not close to being resolved. Indeed, given our earlier treatment of contestability, there is strength in conceptual doubt as much as there is weakness. Having said that, conversations about morality seem to focus on an appreciation of and respect for one's relationships with others and with the rest of "nature," as well as with the dialectic between *praxis* and *phronēsis*. The need for a "practical philosophy" highlighted here—and the dialectic tensions that exist between it and technical reason—brings to mind another vital dialectical tension associated with modernization: between what Wallerstein (1996, 471) refers to as the "two modernities," liberation on the one hand, and technology on the other. As he sees it, this constitutes "the central cultural contradiction of our modern world-system, the system of historical capitalism," which is leading, as he suggests, "to moral as well as to institutional crisis." This, in turn, reinforces the need to extend the focus of the *praxis* and technical reasoning-in-action. It must include the *phronēsis* of prudent judgment and practical reasoning through discourse. As Bernstein poignantly submits:

> . . . at a time when the threat of total annihilation no longer seems to be an abstract possibility but the most imminent and real potentiality, it becomes all the more imperative to try and try again to foster and nurture those forms of communal life in which, dialogue, conversation, *phronēsis*, practical discourse and judgment are concretely embodied in our everyday practices. (Bernstein 1983, 229)

This, again, is where critical engagement (as we have discussed it in this book) has value. To engage from a critical perspective is to participate in deliberative, democratic, and critical discourses, the purpose of which is to lead to considered public judgments for responsible, collective actions. These actions not only result in sustainable and inclusive improvements in livelihoods; they also embody freedom of expression of ontological ways of being. At its heart, critical engagement is political because it is concerned with "making democracy work in a complex world," as Yankelovich (1991) puts it in his treatise on public judgment.

In the very first instance, then, even the basic idea of *participation* must be transformed: from the conventional sense of "issue involvement" or of "partnering" between academics and citizens to something more profound, critical, and power symmetric. This way of thinking emphasizes that all "aspirations towards participation, however genuine, take place in the context of existing relations of power and hierarchy" (Crewe and Harrison 2002, 184).

As outlined earlier, when referenced in a transformative sense, engagement has a comprehensive, holistic feel. There is an embeddedness to it, interconnected parts immersed into a whole, with dynamic, ever-transforming relationships—between its diverse parts, the whole, and a higher-order environment of which the whole itself is a part. But just as we attempt to be "as one" with others in our engagement so, too, must we try to capture the wholeness of the full spectrum of our own human competencies in a manner that far extends beyond our scientific conventions and, indeed, the very nature of science itself. Barnes (2000) writes of these connections in the context of explicating Goethe's participatory approach to a science "that strives to enliven and deepen our understanding of nature." He continues:

> Participation of this kind calls for the engagement of human faculties that modern science has hitherto attempted to eliminate from its domain—namely sense perception, imagination, intuition, feeling, and ultimately what we may call our deepest moral sensitivity. (Barnes 2000, 221)

"The Goethean scientist," Bortoft (1996, 271) believes, "does not lose himself or herself in nature, but finds nature within himself/herself in fully conscious experience." Such conscious participation

> is a synergistic condition in which humanity and nature work together in such a way that each becomes more fully itself through the other. Both are enhanced, but only within their working together, because there is *one* occurrence which is the mutual enhancement of *both*. (emphases in original)

There are strong parallels here with the concepts of the holomovement of ever-enfolding and unfolding of the implicate and explicate orders of wholeness developed by the physicist David Bohm (1980). Extending ideas drawn from quantum mechanics, Bohm suggests that the universe and everything in it is constantly in such holomovement, including thought systems and meaning, itself. He asserts that

> . . . meaning is a constantly extending and actualizing structure—it is never complete and fixed. At the limits of what has at any moment been comprehended there are always unclarities, unsatisfactory features, and failures of intention to fit what is actually displayed or what is actually done. And the yet deeper intention is to be aware of these discrepancies and to allow the whole structure to change if necessary. This will lead to a movement in which there is a constant unfoldment of still more comprehensive meanings. (Bohm 1987, 82)

This "holistic" or "systemic" essence of participation—both *as* and *for* transformation—is sometimes captured by existing forms of academic engagement as, for instance, with action research and also with what is often referred to as "development studies" and its application in such arenas as international development. To those topics we now turn.

Action research and critical engagement

Reason (1994, 1) contends that action research is a process by which people "engage together to explore some significant aspect of their lives, to understand it better, and to transform their action so as to meet their purposes more fully." It is

> . . . a participatory, democratic process concerned with developing practical knowing in the pursuit of worthwhile human purposes grounded in a participatory worldview which we believe is emerging at this historical moment. It seeks to bring together action and reflection, theory and practice, in participation with others, in the pursuit of practical solutions to issues of pressing concern to people and more generally the flourishing of individual persons and their communities. (Reason and Bradbury 2001, 1)

Action research is an essentially self-reflective exercise undertaken by participants in social situations "to improve the rationality and justice of their own practices, their understanding of these practices, and the situations in which the practices are carried out" (Carr and Kemmis 1986, 162). Such *co-operative inquiry*, as it is often called, emphasizes the systemic or holistic significance of developing new and creative ways of looking at things. This can be the foundation for transforming the way things are understood and done (Reason and Heron 1985). As these two authors have more recently claimed:

> [i]f the primary focus in co-operative inquiry is on action, on transformative practice that changes our way of being and doing and relating, and our world, then it follows that the primary outcome of an inquiry is just such a transformation, that is, our practical knowing, our transformative skills and the regenerated experiential encounters to which they give rise, together with the transformations of practice in the wider world with which the inquirers interact. (Heron and Reason 2001, 184)

Captured by Heron and Reason in that statement are the key features of action research: the dual importance of knowing and acting; the attendant relationship between theory and practice; the significance of the transformation of each to the other with changes in each informing and being informed by the other; and the mutuality of relationships between individuals and the wider world of social reality. In this motif, no individual is either a free agent or a passive subject (Giddens 1979). As Habermas (1992, 26) has put it, "no individuation is possible without socialization, and no socialization is possible without individuation." That said, Habermas also insists that while the social world is created by the interactions of individuals, that creation is not always obvious to them. This possibility reinforces the need for transformation, even the transformation of consciousness itself.

Toward that end, Grundy (1982) and Carr and Kemmis (1986) reinforce connections between action research and Habermas' work by making distinctions in technical, practical, and emancipatory forms of action research—distinctions that reflect the eponymous categories of knowledge and human purposes that Habermas (1971) described in his earlier work. Thus, in concert with the emphasis being placed here on engagement "as" and "for" critical transformation, action research is often explicitly emancipatory in its deliberate intention to contribute to democratic social change (Greenwood and Levin 1998). With that notion there is a shift in emphasis from research undertaken conventionally: "where conventional researchers worry about objectivity, distance, and controls, action researchers worry about relevance, social change, and validity tested in action by the most at-risk stakeholders" (Brydon-Miller, Greenwood, and Maguire 2003).

Whatever form it takes, action research has an emancipatory immanence through its emphasis on *learning*—both for and from action, and by all of those who participate in the process as "co-researchers." When conducted effectively, there are four essential learning outcomes of action research that set the stage for democratic action: increased understanding by the participants of the area of interest or situation under review; improvement in the situations from the perspective of participants; increased understanding among participants of the process or methodologies of action research as a discourse for change; and improvement in the capacities of the participants to conduct action research efforts in the future.

There is a particular tradition of participative research—referred to as Participatory Research (PR), Participatory Action Research (PAR), or even Participatory [Action] Research (P[A]R)—where there is explicit concern with emancipation, and also with empowerment and freedom, in ways that respect the significance of multiple ways of knowing and recognize the importance of language. As one of its founding principals has commented recently:

> Besides establishing a rigorous pertinent science, we also wanted to pay attention to ordinary people's knowledge; we were willing to question fashionable meta-narratives; we discarded our learned jargon so as to communicate with everyday language even with plurivocal means; and we tried innovative cognitive procedures like doing research work with collectives and local groups so as to lay sound foundations for their empowerment. (Fals Borda 2001, 28)

The first World Symposium of Action Research held at Cartagena in Colombia in 1997 proved to be a defining moment for P[A]R. Conferees endorsed the notion that P[A]R would be understood as much more than a research methodology based on public participation. It would also be "a *vivencia* necessary for the achievement of progress and democracy" (Fals Borda 2001, 31). This philosophy of life "carries a liberating, political accent" of promoting political awareness and action, and is a means for working with people to promote their "empowerment for changing their immediate environment—social and physical—in their favor" (Rahman 1991, 16).

While action research "has largely focused on passively explicating the implicit theories of actors and decision makers," participatory research has "sought to serve as enlightenment strategy for raising the consciousness of citizens with common interests and concerns" (Fischer 2000, 173). Accordingly, participatory research has explicitly "emphasized the political dimensions of knowledge production and the role of knowledge as an instrument of power and control."

These *praxial* outcomes have particular significance in circumstances where there is clear evidence of the need for emancipation in the face of unequivocal oppression, where people (for whatever reason) are denied their basic rights. In this manner they can, at a minimum, represent the first stage—critical awareness—of Freire's (2003, 54) "pedagogy of the oppressed," where "the oppressed unveil the world of oppression and through the praxis commit themselves to its transformation." The pedagogy of the first stage must deal with consciousness of the oppress*ed* and of the oppress*or*.

It is such a compendium of ideas that underlies the conceptualization of the "engagement interface" as it is understood here. In a Habermasian sense, the interface is much more than a space where Academy and society meet; it is a space dedicated to undistorted communication and critical learning. This notion draws particular inspiration from Habermas' (1990) ideas of the linkages between communicative *action* and communicative *ethics*. To his earlier concepts of mutual understanding and non-coercive consensus (Habermas 1984), he subsequently added the notion of making "communicative space" where people are brought together around topical (pressing) issues (Habermas 1990).

This latter concern was a matter central to the work of Kurt Lewin, to whom the term "action research" is attributed, as well as the well-known and oft-cited aphorism, "There is nothing as practical as a good theory." As Marrow (1969, xi) reports, the major focus of Lewin's work was the search for "deeper explanations of why people behave as they do and to discover how they might learn to behave better." Lewin's approach was quintessentially experiential; grounded in ideas of field theory and phenomenology; and undertaken as a form of cooperative inquiry—social action guided by informed understanding of issues as experienced in situ. Analysis was a crucial aspect in his approach:

> This analysis must be a 'gestalt-theoretical' one, because the social situation, like the psychological situation, is a dynamic whole. It means that a change in one of its parts implies a change of the other parts. (Lewin 1948, 17)

Unsurprisingly, this sense of "wholeness" has drawn a number of systems theorists and practitioners in the quest to explore connections between transforming systems and action research processes. For example, using what they refer to as "systems thinking," Checkland and his colleagues at the University of Lancaster in England have adopted action research approaches to find "ways of dealing holistically with messy real world problems" (Checkland and Holwell 1998). This work has led to the development of Soft Systems Methodology (SSM), an action research methodology "that aims to bring about improvements in areas of social concern by activating in the people involved in the situation a learning cycle which is ideally never-ending" (Bülow 1989, 35).

A central aspect of the work with SSM that has relevance here is the emphasis it places on the connection between transformations and the *Weltanschauungen* or worldviews that qualify them. In essence, every transformation—every expression of improvement agreed to by a collection of individuals as socially desirable and cultural feasible—is a reflection of the world views of those who have generated that expression. Much like beauty, betterment lies in the minds' eyes of the participating beholders. The clarification of *Weltanschauungen,* and of their impact on judgments, is thus a vital aspect of this and other participative, systemic approaches to social change.

Critiques of approaches like SSM, which are based on perceived inadequacies to accomplish "real" social change, have led to the emergence of a new generation of systemics—a new wave of systems thinking and participative practices that assumes a far more critical stance and embraces a number of different dimensions (Midgley 2000). As Jackson (1991) argues, critical systems thinking combines a concern for socio-cultural conditions, human well-being, and emancipation *with* awareness of the strengths of different systemic methodologies; a commitment to methodological complementarism; and a parallel commitment to what he refers to as "theoretical complementarism." Schecter (1991) takes a similar line in defining critical systems thinking by accentuating its commitments to a critique of all schools of thought, to the emancipation of human beings with respect to the realization of their potentials, and to pluralism of approaches. And to this—within a context of reflective action research—can be added critical reflections about a series of aspects to do with the individual and collective learning of those who participate in particular initiatives.

From all of this it is concluded that participation is not just a necessary methodological requirement in action research—something that accommodates the need for "people to research together" for a common purpose. More fundamentally, it is a moral and aesthetic imperative. To deny participation

> . . . not only offends against human justice, not only leads to errors in epistemology, not only strains the limits of the natural world, but is also troublesome for human souls and for the *anima mundi.* (Reason and Bradbury 2001, 10)

With a commitment to the fundamental principles of critical scientific inquiry, and with foundations that clearly reflect the quintessentially American philosophical tradition of pragmatism, it might be anticipated that action research would be the dominant form of social science inquiry within the Academy. However,

> . . . action research is anything but dominant in the academic world. Universities do not privilege action research because they have built themselves into self-isolating, autopoietic structures dominated by disciplinary departments, colleges, and the coercive behavior of professional academic societies and their journals and presses. (Levin and Greenwood 2001, 112)

Cause or effect, it can be argued that these dynamics have also led to an institutional reification of particular discourses, which further exacerbate self-isolated structures—not just of the Academy—but of all other institutions too. As mentioned earlier, different epistemic cultures (Knorr Cetina 1999) and knowledge networks (Box 1989) have arisen that privilege different ways of knowing that come to be expressed in different discourses. Habermas (1971, 1979) writes of the significance of different "speech acts" that have come to shape distinctly different approaches to social intervention, each with its own discourse (Midgley 2000). Habermas speaks of the *constative* speech acts of "the external world" (validated from the perspective of truth); the *regulative* speech acts of the "social world" (validated as to the truthfulness or trustworthiness of the speaker); and the *expressive* speech acts of "an individual's inner world" (the validity claim of which lies primarily with rightness and the sincerity of the speaker). Meanwhile, as he also emphasizes, there is an overall requirement that speech acts "are intelligible" such that speaker and listener can understand each other.

If the Academy is to commit itself to encouraging and facilitating critical engagement, attention must be paid to the nature of speech acts within discourses. This means, as Ulrich (1983, 123) submits and consistent with Habermas' interpretation, all potential participants in a discourse must:

- have a chance to speak
- have the same opportunity to employ constative, regulative, and expressive speech acts
- be truthful about their intentions and capable of accounting for these intentions
- have the freedom to move from a given level of discourse to a more "radical" one that, say, raises questions about fundamental paradigmatic assumptions.

These are daunting criteria that might expand how some might interpret "participation" within the context of engagement. At the same time, these criteria represent precisely what needs to happen if engagement is to be something more than—and also different from—conventional processes of extension, outreach, or service.

Further leads to this distinctiveness are offered when engagement and action research are connected in the domain of "development studies," especially when applied in the practice of "participatory development." There are encouraging signs, especially in work associated with international development. As Brydon-Miller et al. (2003, 23–24) submit:

> [w]hile action researchers situated within university settings may be having a rough time getting our message about action research heard in university forums, we do seem to have had a modicum of success impacting international development assistance or donor agencies and NGOs.

A paradigmatic shift is in play—one that is slowly transforming approaches to participatory development—a shift with foundations in critical scholarship and social critiques that resonate strongly with what we believe; they lie at the heart of the current call for critical engagement. More than anything else, perhaps because of scale, diversity, and the inherently complex issues at hand, it is not surprising that international development is at the leading edge of thinking and work in this regard. That is what makes this domain so interesting and relevant for critical engagement.

Development and transformation

The scale of international development is vast, and has become an extremely complex matter involving intricate (and often loosely-coupled) networks of relationships among national, regional, and local governments; a host of international and other non-government agencies; commercial business and transnational corporations; research, development, and educational institutions; and, to greatly varying degrees, the citizenry. By definition, international development is about intentional transformation. Having said that, what we are beginning to witness in international development is a meta-transformation: profound change *from* a central focus on economic growth of nations *to* expressions of freedom of individuals within nations "to live the life that they choose to live" and in a manner that is both responsible and sustainable. In this sense, development—as Sen (1999, 298) so passionately observes—is indeed "a momentous engagement with freedom's possibilities."

The traditional approach to international development (one that has prevailed for most of the past half century or so) has been based on adoption of the tenets of "modernism," influenced by theories of modernization, industrialization, and dependency (Escobar 2000). The overarching goals have been the transformation of nations through economic growth and by the modernization principles of technological innovation and managerial efficiency. The methods employed have emphasized scientific and technical education of expert counterparts, technical infrastructure enhancement, and enhanced social control achieved through institutional bureaucratization and regulatory governance. The dominant paradigm of modernization, to which the Academy has lent strong intellectual and methodological support, became an expression of an instrumental logic of "productionism" with foundations unashamedly in technical rationality and mechanistic reductionism.

Norgaard, prominent among critics of the current orthodoxy, calls for a fundamental reconstruction of the character of development such that it embraces a paradigm of co-evolution "of social and environmental systems" and a "co-evolutionary cosmology that stresses the communal nature of knowing" (Norgaard 1994, 99). While criticizing the pre-eminent role that has been given to atomistic science and technology in the development process, his argument is not for their rejection. Rather, he argues for reorientation in a way that "admits, helps us see, lends legitimacy to, and identifies the advantages of a diversity of ways of knowing, valuing, organizing, and doing things." Uphoff (1992) takes a similar line in arguing for a reorientation of mechanistic scientific thinking in development:

> If we cannot eliminate straightaway all material and mental obstacles to human fulfillment, we can begin by revising our scientific and day-to-day thinking along the lines that various disciplines are charting.

Uphoff does not believe we have to abandon all of our present thinking and ways of doing things, but he does believe we need to:

> . . . dethrone those methodologies that restrict positive-sum outcomes in the name of rigor, by equating the closed systems we create analytically through

our minds with the multiple open and overlapping systems that exist all around us. (Uphoff 1992, 289)

The methods and practices that have been adopted in international development historically reflect a *Weltanschauung* of exploitation and manipulation of nature. "Development" became an international phenomenon when the self-titled "developed nations" of the Western world extended their influence into the "under-developed" or "less-developed" nations following the end of their formal colonization by those former countries. The intention was to produce an "ever-increasing flow of standardized goods and services" on a truly global scale and to create "a massified consumer society to absorb them" (Korten 1984). In this manner, the ideals of modernity were to be extended universally across societies and, indeed, across the entire globe, to transform "the heretofore slow and precarious course of human progress onto a fast track" (Norgaard 1994).

Modernity promised control over nature through science, material abundance through superior technology, and effective government through rational social organization. Modernity also promised peace and justice through a higher individual morality and superior collective culture to which all, free of material want, would ascend. (Norgaard 1994, 1)

For all the benefits that have unquestionably accrued though international development efforts, it has become clear that the processes of modernization have not brought universal nirvana. While some individuals, communities, and even whole societies have certainly achieved material abundance, inequities in wealth distribution within and between communities and societies have actually grown larger with the passing of time. Moreover, structural and embedded problems—poverty and starvation, destitution and disempowerment, and tyranny and corruption, among them—are endemic in numberless states across the world. Paradoxically, as democracy has spread, it has been accompanied by an increasing powerlessness by the public sectors in capitalist and socialist nations to meet the social contract with citizens for the provision of health, education, and other basic services (Norgaard 1994). Furthermore, while modernization has certainly resulted in significant "control of nature" to ends that suit human needs and wants, it has also released a host of consequential environmental and social risks and hazards, the like and scale of which have never before been seen (Beck 1992). The quest for material abundance has come at the cost of resource depletion and environmental degradation on a truly global scale. Under these circumstances it impossible to disagree with Beck's claim that many of the problematic issues that we currently face in the world "result from techno-economic development itself." In essence, then, the conventional paradigm of international development—with its emphasis on "perpetual economic growth in industrialized countries and convergence toward the rich country model in poorer countries" (Raskin 2000)—is proving to be fundamentally unsustainable. To some, this represents nothing less than a betrayal of progress brought about through the power of the prevailing paradigm:

> Modernism betrayed progress by leading us into, preventing us from seeing, and keeping us from addressing, interwoven environmental, organizational, and cultural problems. (Norgaard 1994, 2)

As Norgaard argues, five epistemological and metaphysical beliefs—atomism, mechanism, universalism, objectivism, and monism—have become so embedded in our public discourse that they have excluded other beliefs "which are more appropriate for understanding the complexities of environmental systems and which are more supportive of cultural pluralism" (Norgaard 1994, 62).

A new and critical scholarship would seem warranted. In this regard, Norgaard reinforces the arguments of Habermas and others: that the most culpable aspect of the techno-economic stance of modernism has been the rise to dominance of instrumental-rationalist knowledge over others ways of knowing. There are, he suggests, very significant constraints being imposed on the process of development through the "narrowness of accepted patterns of thinking in the modern world" with techno-science thoroughly embroiled at the heart of the matter:

> Western science figures prominently in this critique, not with respect to how scientists go about trying to understand, but with respect to how society accepts particular scientific ways of understanding and tries to act rationally on these understandings to the exclusion of other ways of knowing, both scientific and traditional. Scientists, in turn, become entangled in science's misuse. (Norgaard 1994, 9)

The instrumentalist hegemony has been accompanied by the elevation of scientists to positions of social dominance as "public decision makers" by virtue of their status as experts. While such an elevation might well indeed reflect "the idolatry of scientific method and of the anonymous authority of the sciences," as Gadamer (1975) asserted, there is little doubt that some scientists have exploited this "peculiar falsehood of modern consciousness." Examples are legion of situations where experts "tacitly and furtively impose prescriptive models of the human and the social upon lay people, and these are implicitly found wanting in human terms" (Wynne 1996). This has all led, as some see it (e.g.,Yankelovich 1991) to a climate of *cognitive authoritarianism* where "the rationality of thinking for oneself diminishes as society's knowledge gathering activities expand to the point of requiring a division of cognitive labor into autonomous expertises" (Fuller 1988).

There have certainly been a number of transformations over recent decades in the nature of science, with evidence of the very paradigmatic revolutions of which Thomas Kuhn (1962) talked. Yet, the orthodox techno-science of development still firmly retains its positivistic/reductionistic essence and its insistence on "value-neutrality." This persists in spite of the fact that, as Reason and Heron (1986) contend, it is not at all difficult to take issue with at least six presuppositions associated with that orthodoxy:

1. There is one reality "out there."
2. Reality can be known objectively.
3. Knowledge is identical for all knowers.
4. Knowledge is expressed in propositions that are validated empirically.
5. The whole may be explained solely in terms of the sum of its parts and that the aim of inquiry is to discover more and more fundamental elements and processes.
6. Explanation is sought in terms of linear, energetic cause and effect.

Perhaps the most unfortunate additional deficiency of the orthodox development paradigm is its explicit exclusion of normative dimensions. As Goulet (1995, 2) submits: "Development is above all else a question of human values and attitudes, goals self-defined by societies, and criteria for determining what are tolerable costs to be borne, and by whom, in the course of change." There is, as he and others have come to emphasize, a profound "ethics of development," which presents a radical challenge to the conventional development paradigms on a number of different fronts. There is also the matter of ethics in development. In this vein, Gaspar (2004) proposes a three-stage model. Stage one is similar in essence to Freire's *conscientização* as it relates to experiential realization that some issues in development do, indeed, carry ethical consequences. In stage two, these realizations are transformed into concepts and theories through a process that not infrequently starts with the clarification of values and assessments of value choices. The third stage of development ethics "is the ethics of policy planning and professional practice, devising and negotiating and trying to execute value-sensitive action" (Gaspar 2004, xii).

There are some very significant issues of critical scholarship to be considered here particularly, as St. Clair (2005) argues, with respect to the need to "explicitly address the intrinsic linkages with both experience and perceptions (stage one) as well as with the elaboration of concepts and theoretical approaches (stage two)." As she sees it, the task of development ethics includes addressing a range of epistemic constraints as they relate to our abilities to grasp "what is happening around us," as well as challenging "the value assumptions and hidden values of the knowledge and policies for development of global institutions" (St. Clair 2005). And, of course, this matter relates as much to the ethical issues *within* development practice as it does to the overall ethics *of* development practice.

Criticisms of existing approaches to development are therefore perfectly justified under epistemically-constraining circumstances where moral judgment has seemingly been eliminated from prevailing concepts of rationality as far as they are actually manifested in the techno-scientific paradigms that currently prevail (Ulrich 1993). There is no room in them for axiologies beyond those deeply held assumptions about the value of truth and the objectivity of techno-scientific knowledge.

In contrast, neo-liberal economics has taken the opposite stance by presenting itself as "a social and moral philosophy" in which "the existence and operation of a market are valued in themselves" and "where the operation of a market or market-like structure is seen as an ethic in itself, capable of acting as a guide for all human action, and substituting for all previously existing ethical beliefs" (Treanor 2004). Yet, as Sen (1988) argues, there is little evidence for the claim that the maximization of self-interest provides the best approximation of human behavior or that it leads necessarily to optimum economic conditions. In addition, Sen does not believe that the concept of "utility," which currently prevails within economics, captures the richness of its traditional associations with "happiness" or with "pleasure" in utilitarian economics:

> In modern use of 'utility' in contemporary choice theory, its identification with pleasure or desire-fulfillment has been largely abandoned in favor of seeing utility simply as the numerical representation of a person's choice. (Sen 1999, 67)

There are others who rue this numerical emphasis within economics—from those who believe that the "mathematization" of the discipline is an attempt to "dress up their imprecise ideas in the language of the infinitesimal calculus" (Weiner 1964, 89) to those who believe that the strength of mathematics in economics is intended "to restate more rigorously, economic truths arrived at by more intuitive ways of thinking" (Daly and Cobb 1994, 33). The essential difficulty with economics in this context, however, is fundamentally epistemic, relating to what Whitehead (1929) referred to as the "fallacy of misplaced concreteness," namely, the asymmetric accord of privilege to abstraction over concrete reality. As Daly and Cobb (1994, 43) observe:

> Recognizing the fallacy of misplaced concreteness is particularly important to establishing economics for community, because community is precisely the feature of reality that has been most consistently abstracted from in modern economics. The need is not for one more theorem squeezed out of the premises of methodological individualism by a more powerful economic press, but for a new premise that reinstates the critical aspect of reality that has been abstracted from—namely, the community.

With all of these limitations, it is difficult to understand and accept the "centrality of economic institutions and the paramountcy of economic rationality" in the orthodox development paradigm (Harmon 1984). There is a paradox here: the basic assumptions of this paradigm are seen as "mostly right headed and inescapable and generally uncritically accepted" (Harmon 1984, 16) despite obvious inadequacies, including the epistemic limitations neo-liberalism presents to the development paradigms.

The momentum for critical engagement in international development comes precisely as a challenge to the uncritical acceptance of such premises, while the imperative for a *scholarship* of critical engagement reflects the contestable epistemic foundations of development orthodoxy—from intellectual and moral, as well as from *praxial* and *phronētic,* perspectives. Under such circumstances, the changes in the way that "development is done" represents nothing less than a Kuhnian shift of paradigms—triggered by a recognition that "nature has somehow violated the paradigm-induced expectations that govern normal development," to paraphrase Kuhn's position on normal science and scientific revolutions (Kuhn 1962).

Transformative development and critical engagement

A number of social and intellectual factors are contributing to the emerging meta-transformation of international development—forces that compel critical engagement. Of particular relevance is the privilege that is being accorded to participation in all of its diverse manifestations. As Wilson and Whitmore (2000) put it, participatory approaches are being introduced "as part of a complex counter to the dismal failure of the past several decades of world 'development' efforts in improving conditions of the poor." The growing recognition that current approaches are failing to fulfill their promises is giving rise to questioning the rationality of development (Escobar 2000) and the processes of modernization itself (Beck 1992). At the same time, fresh intellectual perspectives are emerging with reference to the development process (e.g., Sen 1999) and to the ethics of development (e.g., Crocker 1991); and new conceptual frameworks are being developed to guide development assistance efforts (e.g., Groves and Hinton 2004). This work is thematically connected to an emphasis on "people-centered" (Korten and Klaus 1984), "rights-based" (Pettit and Wheeler 2005), and "participatory" (Crocker 2003) development—all of which are grounded in the *Weltanschauung* that Sen (1999) promotes, namely, development as freedom.

Such assertions highlight the significance of moral consciousness as a critical feature of "transforming development." Such moral sensitivity is central to calls for "active citizenship" (Gaventa 2004) and "deliberative democracy" (Crocker 2003) and are crucial features of the "new development." A further aspect of the unfolding transformation is the increasing focus on broader forms of accountability "which enable multiple partners to hold institutions and policy makers to account, and which involve social accountability as well as legal, fiscal, and political forms" (Gaventa 2004, 16). With this, there is an increasing need to address issues that Gaventa refers to as "both sides of the equation"— the citizenry, on the one hand, and social institutions, on the other:

As participatory approaches are scaled up from projects to policies, they inevitably enter the areas of governance, and find that participation can only become effective as it engages with issues of institutional change. As concerns about good governance and state responsiveness grow, questions about how citizens engage and make demands also come to the fore. (Gaventa 2002, 1)

Talk of accountabilities and responsibilities raises the further vital aspect of their implications for relationships between people and nature—or "the environment," as it is now most commonly conceptualized within development circles. The impetus for adoption of sustainability as a particular perspective for development arose from concerns about the exploitation of environmental resources and, in particular, on the constraining impacts that that might have on future generations (Brundtland 1987). In this way, it is a perspective on development that brings together resource questions concerning both inter- and intra-generational equity (Dresner 2002) and draws attention to the "nature of nature" and its conservation, which in and of itself as a moral issue. Consider Leopold's (1949, 224) interpretation: "A thing is right when it tends to preserve the integrity, stability, and beauty of a biotic community. It is wrong when it tends otherwise."

While these moral commitments might appear at first glance to be quite straightforward ways to frame development policies and methodological approaches, the situation in practice is complex and compounded by intellectual confusion, epistemic distinctions, and socio-political realities. For example, Redclift (1987, 199) argues that the concept of sustainable development "draws on two frequently opposed intellectual traditions: one concerned with the limits which nature presents to human beings, the other with the potential for human material development, which is locked up in nature." He also pointed out that the problem with achieving sustainable development pertains to overriding structures of the international economic system, "which arose out of the exploitation of environmental resources" in the first place, and which frequently operate "as constraints on the achievement of long-term sustainable practices." Sustainable development, he concluded, presents a perspective that recognizes "that the limits of sustainability have structural as well as natural origins."

While sustainability and sustainable development remain contestable constructs (Davison 2001), they are central aspects of emerging approaches to what we might we refer to as "post-industrial" paradigms of development that combine the fresh features mentioned above. Foundational to all of these is an emphasis on "participation," the processes of learning and of discourse, and of communication in its broadest sense. As the authors of a recently published report from the Department for International Development in the UK submit, "rights will become real only as citizens are engaged in the decisions and processes which affect their lives" (DFID 2000).

In essence, then, the newly emerging participatory, rights-based, freedom-oriented and sustainable approaches to international development all share key characteristics that are clearly reflected in what we describe as critical engagement. With such assertions comes the vital need for developing a scholarship of critical engagement, much of which has yet to be clarified with respect to principles, tenets, policies, and practices of transformative development. To paraphrase Milbraith (1989), progress in this regard will result from *learning our way out of* the modernist dilemma and *learning our way into* transformative participatory processes—people learning with, from, and through others to improve circumstances in which they find themselves or anticipate finding themselves in the future. This form of learning, "social learning" as Cornwall and Guijt (2004, 166) call it, "entails more than simply group-based learning, but rather bringing together a range of unlikely comrades in multi-stakeholder processes of fact-finding, negotiation, planning, reassessing, and refocusing."

These notions reinforce an important claim being made in this chapter, namely, that responsible and sustainable acts of material and social development in a complex world—at whatever scale of human endeavor—compel the moral and intellectual development of the actors involved. This outcome will only be achieved through and with transformative learning.

Participatory development and social learning

David Korten was one of the first to highlight the connection between participation and social learning in development; he also pointed out the significance of that connection in conjunction with the paradigmatic migration from production- to people-centered development. In this regard, Korten argues for the relevance of engagement practices that

> . . . feature forms of self-organization that highlight the role of the individual in the decision process and call for the application of human values in decision-making. Its knowledge-building processes are based on social learning concepts and methods. (Korten 1984, 300)

Many others have followed Korten's lead, such that numerous approaches over the past two decades or so have adopted as a common theme "the **full** participation of people in the processes of **learning** about their needs and opportunities, and in the **action** required to address them" (Anon. 2004, emphasis in the original). Respect afforded to indigenous knowledge systems (Brokensha, Warren, and Werner 1980) in the development is a manifestation of that claim.

Scholarly inquiries into the nexus between participatory development and knowledge—and also into the nature of the processes of knowing and learning—have resulted in the establishment of important intellectual foundations, including theories and principles that are supported enthusiastically by practitioners in an array of development domains and institutions. This is especially so in agricultural and rural development, which is not at all surprising given the number of people who live in "underdeveloped nations." For example, the nature and significance of indigenous knowledge—Rural People's Knowledge (RPK) as it has come to be known within rural development circles—has become a particular focus of this scholarship. Scoones and Thompson (1994, 17) submit that there are three contrasting approaches (and discourses) with respect to this subject: RPK is "primitive," "unscientific," and basically "wrong" and needs to be "corrected"; RPK is a valuable and underutilized resource, and needs to be studied and incorporated into development practices; and because neither RPK nor Western science can be regarded as unitary bodies or stocks of knowledge, a case can be made for synthesis. Of special note here is that in the third option there are opportunities for *epistemic synergy*—an attractive alternative given the complexity of our contemporary problematique.

Consider the relevance of epistemic synergy in relationship to the complex reality context in agricultural and rural development. For example, in the foreword to a relatively recent monograph on "Knowing and Learning for Change in Agriculture," the chairman of the French National Institute for Agricultural Research observed that participatory learning processes that were supported by

> . . . recent advances on the forms of collective and organised action. . . appear to provide appropriate means for backing the necessary adaptation of farmers to the new and diversified stakes with which they are encapsulated in the concept of 'multifunctionality of agriculture.' (Hervieu 2000)

The prevailing worldview of agricultural development is shifting, Hervieu claims, from emphasizing food production capacities primarily (if not exclusively) to emphasizing issues that pertain to an array of agricultural and rural "goods," including the safety and quality of food, the maintenance of rural employment opportunities, the quality of rural communities and rural lifestyles, and the preservation of rural landscapes and natural resources, among other things. Also relevant is the fact that food shortages that characterize some parts of the world are more likely to be caused by factors outside the food system—warfare and civil unrest and insurgency, political instability and abuses of the power of social privilege, preventable diseases, and poverty, among them—than by limitations in production capacity or distribution.

This "complexification" demands new ways of thinking about development, as well as innovative ways of acting in the pursuit of sustainable development—by scientists and citizens alike (Bawden 1991). Accordingly "agriculture. . . emerges as an exemplary field of action for recasting the relations between science and society" (Hervieu 2000). This recasting comes in the form of a convergence between two, heretofore loosely defined bodies of work—science and technology studies, and development studies (Leach, Scoones, and Wynne 2005). The need for further scholarship at this multi-disciplinary interface, including further synthesis of presumably different "discourses" and "epistemic cultures," is in order:

> . . . although it has been recognized sporadically over the years, the emerging correspondence between the concerns and perspectives of science and technology studies under the 'democratization of science' in developed societies on the

one hand, and the focus of development studies on citizen participation in expert-led development programmes and policies on the other, remains to be developed and exploited. (Leach, Scoones, and Wynne 2005, 5)

Such scholarly collaboration is certainly to be applauded and greatly encouraged, for there can be no doubt that each has much to offer the other. The key issue, of course, is how all of this translates into development practices in situations where epistemic distinctions between citizens and scientists are likely to be far greater than the distinctions among scientists, even when scientists represent different disciplines. And the matter is further complicated by the involvement in development by a host of agents and agencies, each with distinctive cultures and epistemes, intentions, and ideologies. In these circumstances, a focus on social learning must involve a synthesis of different kinds of knowledge. Might this synthesis be a prerequisite for progress in development? And should it also be a key feature of what we call critical engagement?

The emphasis here on the *mutuality of synthesis* is of signal importance, for one set of knowledge has much to offer to others, as do different ways of knowing and valuing, and judging and acting. Furthermore, contemporary circumstances present challenges to all forms of "knowing orthodoxies"—be they instrumental or communicative, reductionistic or holistic, expert or lay, profane or sacred, and rational or intuitive. The danger, however, as has been consistently argued here is that one form of knowledge—one way of knowing—can dominate others and, in so doing, colonize all lifeworlds. Multiple *knowings* represent crucial dimensions to be integrated into a synergistic "epistemological pluralism." The alternative to be avoided is having knowings obliterated in the face of a domineering monistic epistemology that colonizes ways of understanding and doing *with* little awareness or critical acceptance of that happening.

Witness, for instance, the submission by Yankelovich (1991, 8) with regards to the "pervasive march" of the "Culture of Technical Control" and its empiricist/instrumentalist epistemological foundations; where such control is exercised "through the application of expert thinking in science, technology, economic enterprises, government, the policy sciences, and large organizational structures"—and all with the willing acquiescence, and indeed the scholarly support, of the Academy:

> This cultural imperative generates little controversy. The only controversy lies in calibrating its human costs. Its devotees minimize the costs or shrug them off as the price one pays for progress. Its critics complain about its dehumanizing tendencies, but except for a brief period in the 1960s, no one pays them much heed. Little thought has been given to strategies for preserving the benefits of the Culture of Technical Control while at the same time curbing its excesses. (Yankelovich 1991, 9)

The issue of "preserving the benefits" needs emphasis here—not only for the positive aspects of a Culture of Technical Control, but also for desirable features of what was referred to earlier as a "cosmology of connectedness." Such circumstances suggest something important: if social learning is to be a central focus of transformation in development, it needs to adopt both an appreciative stance as well as a critical perspective, while maintaining and further cultivating epistemological pluralism. For this reason, multi-stakeholder participation is obviously a fundamental requirement of critical social learning for development, which is far from saying that all forms of participation inevitably lead to critical social learning! Indeed, the very notion of participation itself is a contestable concept that has come to mean whatever people want it to mean. Pretty (1995, 173) is among those who have developed typologies of different perceptions and consequent forms of participation in development programs. He distinguishes a spectrum that ranges from "passive participation" of people (as spectators of the development process) to "self-mobilization" where "people participate by taking initiatives independent of external institutions."

It is no wonder that, as one writer recently put it, "the polyvalence of the term has given rise to contrasting beliefs and assumptions, and a number of paradoxes and contradictions" (Cornwall 2002). Perhaps the most serious of these is the co-option of the word, such that it means essentially opposing things. As (Pretty 1995) observes:

> One views community participation as a means to increase efficiency, the central notion being that if people are involved, then they are more likely to agree with and support the new development or service. The other sees community participation as a right, in which the main aim is to initiate mobilization for collective action, empowerment, and institution building. (Pretty 1995, 168)

These are cautionary words for those of us who promote the significance of "engagement," especially when it comes to considering connections with "development," "transformation," and "learning." They are also centrally relevant to both sides of Gaventa's (2002) "equation," as cited earlier, of the citizenry on the one side and social institutions (including the Academy) on the other. In the past, these differences have been seen as irreconcilably different "coins" rather than as different, but potentially complementary, faces of the "same coin." And this bifurcated way of viewing things has special significance in formal development organizations where, in the past, differences have represented opposing paradigmatic stances:

> Each perspective has often perceived the other as inadequate, with one warning that consultation without attention to power and politics will lead to 'voice without influence,' and the other arguing that reform of political institutions without attention to inclusion will only reinforce the status quo. (Gaventa 2002, 1)

The task for critical engagement in this context is to transcend differences by challenging the foundations of *both* perspectives and, then, being prepared in the face of a fundamental conflict—a conflict that perfectly exemplifies Maturana and Varela's (1988) notion of "mutual negation"—"to move to another domain where co-existence takes place":

> Hence, the only possibility for co-existence is to opt for a broader perspective in which both parties fit in the bringing forth of a common world. . . .The knowledge of this knowledge constitutes the social imperative for a human-centred ethics. (Maturana and Varela 1988, 246)

In this "knowledge of knowledge" there is "knowledge that compels." This insight helps turn our attention from dwelling on differences between "people's knowledge" and Western science, for instance, to exploring epistemological matters concerned with *knowing about knowledge* and *knowing about the processes of knowing*. To return to the hermeneutic, we must also attempt a metaphysical "understanding of understanding," for as Bernstein (1983, 113) insists: ". . . if we are to understand what it is to be human beings, we must seek to understand understanding itself, in its rich, full, and complex dimensions."

By extending the focus from "knowing" and "understanding" to embracing learning, we also need to investigate learning about what can be learned as well as learning about learning. Of special interest here are issues of "learning *for* development" and "learning *as* development," as well as the vital interconnections between the two as they pertain to participative development as multi-dimensional transformation.

Knowing, learning, and transformation

At its base, all learning is transformational in one way or another, even though the nature of such transformations is often quite unclear. As Bateson (1972, 283) has postulated, "the word 'learning' undoubtedly connotes *change* of some kind. To say *what kind of change* is a delicate matter" (emphasis in original). One essential reason for this "delicacy," he suggested, is that learning is a complex matter of different "logical types" or different "levels" at which different types of change can occur. Because learning is a process of change, it itself is also subject to change; and as that "meta-change" is also a process it, too, is subject to change. Bateson saw these changes as "errors of correction" and, thus, the higher orders of learning as "errors of correction of errors of correction."

In the context of a scholarship of critical engagement that is particularly concerned with connections among learning, transformation, and development, Bateson's position reinforces the significance of change as "transformation." To "engage" is to enter "a learning state," which is both transformative in terms of the nature of the learning process and transformational in terms of changes to "matters of concern." To translate this into potential arenas for transformation in practice, we reintroduce the three-dimensional argument that was rehearsed earlier in chapter 4, namely, that we can learn about: a matter at hand; matters at hand; and epistemological limits to how we can come to know and do both of these.

Argyris and Schön (1996), analysts who are also interested in an error-detection perspective on learning, have introduced the concept of difference between *single-loop* and *double-loop* learning. As they see it, most learning (single loop) focuses on strategies for detecting and correcting errors. Double loop learning, on the other hand, focuses on the values and knowledge that inform the nature of the single-loop processes. As Ison et al. (2000, 45) explain, double loop learning "is learning which results in a change in the values which inform the judgments upon which single-loop learning relies." Others, including Flood and Romm (1996) and Isaacs (1993), have added a "triple loop" to this sequence which, as seen by the latter writer, focuses on what it is that provides the "predisposition to learn in any particular manner."

Kitchener (1983) has presented a three-level hierarchy that adds considerable substance and utility to the concept of a hierarchy of "levels of learning." It also provides an intellectual framework for investigating learning as development—even though her focus is on cognitive processing and not learning *per se*. She distinguishes among cognition, meta-cognition, and epistemic cognition as a sequence through which individuals monitor the way by which they conduct their own basic cognitive tasks, like reading and acquiring language. This is undertaken through a meta-cognitive process, which is itself monitored by a process of epistemic cognition that concerns itself with the nature of the problems and the truth values of alternative solutions:

> At the first level, individuals compute, memorize, read, and comprehend. At the second level, they monitor their own progress and products as they are engaged in first-order cognitive tasks. . . .The third level. . . must be introduced to explain how humans monitor their problem-solving when engaged with in ill-structured problems, i.e., those which do not have an absolutely correct solution. Epistemic cognition has to do with reflection on the limits of knowledge, the certainty of knowledge, and the criteria for knowing. (Kitchener 1983, 230)

Contained here are matters that are of crucial significance to arguments that relate to the need for "different ways of knowing" and "higher ways of knowing" for addressing the ill-structured problematic issues of contemporary life—the problematique. Furthermore, when reframed in terms of *learning*, Kitchener's model is enormously meaningful to a scholarship of critical engagement. In the first place, Kitchener provides a theory that supports Bateson's conceptual scheme of different levels of learning. First, with each "higher" level providing the context for the level(s) below, learning at one level can markedly influence the nature and character of learning at other levels. Second, and following from the first point, the model hints at the manner through which each of the different levels can, in practice, be accessed, critically analyzed, and—if appropriate— transformed in one way or another. This has practical significance with respect to learning about epistemic issues that have to do with the nature and character of epistemologies, and for learning about the processes of learning. Finally, in presenting the claim that under appropriate conditions epistemologies are transformed along a developmental sequence, Kitchener's theory provides a conceptual framework for critical explorations of connections among epistemic learning, intellectual and moral development, and the types of developments in the material and social world that are the concern of those who participate in development. In this context, the connection she makes between epistemic development and the maturity of reflective judgment is of profound importance to a scholarship of critical engagement.

Foundational to Kitchener's conceptual work is the empirical research of Perry (1968) into the ethical and intellectual development of college students. From his longitudinal research on undergraduates, Perry postulated that there appears to be a sequential developmental pattern, which over the course of their studies, was reflected in changes in the manner by which these young people "addressed themselves to challenges." At each step in the sequence of what he saw as "structural transformations," Perry argued that "the student sees himself, his instructors, and even truth itself in very different terms." While identifying nine such steps or phases in the sequence, the essence of his findings was that the students progressed from an initial developmental state of epistemological *dualism,* passed through a state of *multiplicity*, and eventually reached a state of *contextual relativism* that finds expression in *commitment.* He writes:

> In its full range the scheme begins with those simplistic forms in which a person construes his (*sic*) world in unqualified polar terms of absolute right–wrong, good–bad; it ends with those complex forms through which he undertakes to affirm his own commitments in a world of contingent knowledge and relative values. The intervening forms and transitions in the scheme outline the major steps through which the person appears to extend his power to make meaning in successive confrontations. (Perry 1999, 3)

As Perry recognized, there is a strong hermeneutic flavor to this process: an epistemological quest for understanding and explanation that "transcends a mere effort to reduce all of life's incongruities to pat logic," as he put it. Ultimately, he concluded, "our scheme chronicles the course of an aesthetic yearning to apprehend a certain kind of truth: the truth of the limits of man's certainty" (Perry 1999, 63). Development along this sequence—which in Perry's opinion did not occur without considerable challenge in the learning environment—represented one of the major potential cognitive accomplishments of undergraduate students.

Kitchener (1983) extended these ideas on epistemological development within a broader context of reflective judgment. She identified seven developmental stages and submitted that the structure of each level of development "appears to underlie some superficially unrelated beliefs, including the validity of authorities' claims, the way beliefs can be justified as better or worse, and understanding of bias and interpretations." The general movement that she proposed was from dogmatism, through skepticism, and toward rationality, a movement that closely mirrors Perry's epistemological schema of dualism, through multiplicity, and toward relativism and commitment.

A number of other, significant theories about intellectual and moral development have been proposed—for childhood (Piaget 1969; Kohlberg 1963; Hoffman 1970) and for adulthood (Perry 1968; Gibbs 2003). While details of these schemas differ somewhat, the central theses are remarkable congruent regarding the epistemological, ontological, and axiological development through childhood, adolescence, early adulthood, and beyond. Given the similarities, it is useful to apply the phrase *epistemic development* to embrace development with respect to all three as the central inter-connected elements that constitute our worldviews or *Weltanschauungen*. It is through engagement with the epistemic level of learning—both through individual critical self-reflection and discursive social critique—that learners can come to *know* worldviews and also come to appreciate the significance of the often profound differences that are typically present among different people within the same community or working group.

Perry's work explicitly emphasized vital connections between epistemological and ethical development. Kohlberg (1964) and Hoffman (1970) pursued similar interests, although with moral development as the primary focus. Both were concerned about pre-adolescent development—Kohlberg from a perspective of how children develop a sense of "right," and Hofffman from a perspective of how children develop a sense of "good." In a recent text, Gibbs (2003) reviews and then extends the work of both Kohlberg and Hoffman by exploring ontological connections between moral development and reality. He concludes that "acts that wrong and harm one individual. . . ultimately wrong and harm us all." Other researchers, including Belenky et al. (1986), Baxter Magolda (1992), and King and Kitchener (1994) have further enriched understandings of epistemic developments in young people and, in some cases, have extended the work to include lifelong epistemic development (Kitchener and Fisher 1990).

West (2004) contends that all of these studies seem to agree on four essential propositions. First, different stages are qualitatively different structures that "allow knowers to continue the same functions as they develop." Second, the stages follow an invariant sequence. Third, each stage "forms a structured whole based on an internally consistent logic." And, finally, "the stages are hierarchically integrated, such that the structure of each successive stage differentiates and reorganizes the knowledge constructed as the previous stage." With regard to this last proposition, Colby and Kohlberg (1987) suggest that the nature of the hierarchy is additive rather than purely transformational. As West (2004) points out, that means "the insights from earlier stages are included within new structures":

> In this model, knowledge from earlier stages remains accessible at later stages, although it may be used in different ways. . . . Hierarchical integrations that are

> additive rather than transformational allow for the simultaneous manifestation of ways of knowing from more than one stage. (West 2004, 66)

This particular notion of additive integration provides a useful response to those who dispute the "unilinearity" of cognitive development or reject the sequential compartmentalization implicit in the idea of "discreet stages" or disavow the irreversibility of the sequence. West promotes an organic, systemic perspective that finds easy comparison with the "enfolding/unfolding" "holomovement" of Bohm's (1992) "thought systems," with the autopoietic dimensions of cognition promoted by Maturana and Varela (1980) as well as with the "multi-linearity" of Kolb's (1984) experiential theory of development. Furthermore, there is nothing in her propositions that would deny holistic interpretations of cognition that embrace the affective and the moral along with the intellectual, for which Kolb (1984), among others, argue.

Most of the workers in this field of cognitive development agree that progression from one epistemic state to another is rarely achieved without a combination of *social participation* and *sustained experiential stimuli*. As Salner (1986) has argued, learners "must have the opportunity to experience the epistemological dilemmas that characterize each stage as his or her own personal dilemmas." Furthermore, they must be "emotionally able to contend with the temporary stress induced by such dilemmas or mental blocks that are unconsciously erected to slow the pace of cognitive change." In process terms, the development of epistemic competencies is most likely to occur "when mild pressure in the environment toward movement is consistently present so that the student cannot conveniently escape the kinds of confrontations that produce growth" (Salner 1986). In essence, it would seem that epistemic advancements have elements that, on the one hand, are invariant and universal while, on the other hand, rely in part "upon the self's particular and somewhat unique experience" (Kohlberg and Ryncarz 1990). In both cases, experiential stimuli are indicated and this indicates the importance of a "meta-learning" focus—on the process of learning about learning.

Experiential learning and human development

For a variety of reasons, the work of Kolb (1984) on experiential learning is of direct relevance here. Kolb suggests a way of connecting learning with transformation, human experience, and development; offers a theoretical and conceptual foundation for learning as a process of transformation; and provides a meta-level model of learning relevant for what occurs in concrete development situations. Kolb, in patent contrast to those who see learning as the acquisition of knowledge, presents it as "the process by which knowledge is created through the *transformation* of experience" (Kolb 1984, 38). From this experiential perspective, knowledge is continuously being created, recreated, and "used" by individuals as they seek to make sense and meaning of their experiences in the ever-changing world about them—an essential prelude to taking informed action. As Kolb sees it, an essential motivation for such a learning process is adaptation to change: for learning, indeed, is *the* major process of human adaptation" (Kolb 1984, 32). Kolb insists that experiential learning is a "holistic process" that involves constant transactions "between the person and the environment" in a manner that engages "the integrated function of the total organism – thinking, feeling, perceiving, and behaving."

Drawing especially on the scholarship of John Dewey, Jean Piaget, and Kurt Lewin, Kolb presents experiential learning as a profoundly dialectical process— "a tension- and conflict-filled process. . . [where]. . . new knowledge, skills or attitudes are achieved through four modes of . . . learning," which comprise two "sets" of "dialectically opposed modes of adaptation to the world"— concrete and abstract, on the one hand, and reflective and active, on the other hand. If experiential learners are to be effective, Kolb argues, they need to develop four different kinds of abilities that correspond with these different modes, namely, Concrete Experience abilities (CE), Reflective Observation abilities (RO), Abstract Conceptualization abilities (AC), and Active Experimentation abilities (AE). As Kolb describes it:

> That is they must be must be able to involve themselves fully, openly, and without bias in new experiences (CE). They must be able to reflect on and observe their experiences from many perspectives (RO). They must be able to create concepts that integrate their observations into logically sound theories (AC), and they must be able to use these theories to make decisions and solve problems (AE). (Kolb 1984, 30)

What Kolb describes is a quintessentially participative and transformative process with powerful overtones of "engagement," together with a flavor of what it takes to contribute to wholeness through participation. It is a case of the transformative power of both the whole and its parts. This not only leads to possibilities for different transformations within each of the four different modes but, also, to transformation in at least three domains of the whole: in the *situation*; in *engaged learners*, and in the *process* of engaged learning. Put another way, we can conceive of learning as a continuous, transformative flux between "finding out" and "taking action"(Checkland 1981) in both concrete and abstract modalities—with each modality capable of influencing and of being influenced by the other. There is reciprocity, then, between *what we experience and do in the world* and *what we think about the nature of that world*. What we do in the world is a function of how we go about seeing that world which, in turn, is a function of how we go about doing in the world. In this manner, experiential learning has the essence of both Empiricism and Rationalism without being identifiable specifically within either or the other of these epistemological categories. Indeed, as Malinen (2000) argues, experiential learning is a sort of compromise that reflects Kant's attempts to provide a third alternative to Rationalism and Empiricism—of importance to a scholarship of critical engagement—

that embraces the systemic advantages of epistemic pluralism and multi-rationalities.

The overall process of experiential learning can be taken to be the transformation of experience into knowledge. But each of the four modes—the "parts," as it were—is also a potential site for engagement and transformation. Learners can engage in various ways: with the concrete through their experiences of the world about them; with reflections in the abstract; with conceptualizations in the abstract; and with actions back in the concrete. At each "step" in what Kolb presents as a cycle of learning, learners can both transform that with which they are engaged, as well as be transformed by it, in some manner or another. In this way, experiential learning as he sees it is a profoundly transformative and transforming process.

Kolb (1984, 134) also argues that "from the dialectics of learning comes a human development progression marked by increasing differentiation and hierarchic integration of functioning." He suggests that this human development process "is divided into three broad development stages of maturation—acquisition, specialization, and integration," which, together, represent a hierarchy of ever-higher "orders of learning." Briefly put, at the level of acquisition the self is undifferentiated and merely immersed in the world. The self is also "content," that is, in a state of interacting with the world. Finally, at the level of integration, the self is "process," that is, in a state of transacting with the world. Learning, as Kolb concludes, "is thus the process whereby development occurs" in the manner by which we come to be-in-the-world. There is, as Kolb sees it, a vital inter-connectivity between the internal characteristics of individual learners and the external circumstances of the social worlds of those individuals.

Development in this way of thinking is a function of mutually influential transactions, namely, "between personal knowledge and social knowledge." As a consequence "the course of individual development is shaped by the cultural system of social knowledge." Borrowing from Vygotsky, Kolb (1984, 133) claims that "human beings create culture with all its artificial stimuli to further their own development." The highest goal of such development for Kolb "is a fully integrated personality with an integrative consciousness of its structure" (Malinen 2000, 89).

While Kolb's work on experiential learning focuses essentially on what we are referring here to as meta-learning (that is, learning about learning), others have focused explicitly on the epistemic dimensions of learning and its relevance to transformational learning. As Kegan (2000, 48) argues, "genuinely transformational learning is always to some extent an epistemological change rather than merely a change in behavioral repertoire or an increase in the quantity or fund of knowledge—learning that is sometimes called "informational learning." A key distinction between the outcomes of these forms of learning lies with their differential impact on the frames of reference (or minds) that we use in structuring our knowing. Thus, as Kegan sees it, "[b]oth kinds of learning are expansive and valuable, one within a preexisting frame of mind and the other reconstructing that very frame." Such "frame reconstruction" is the central pre-occupation of Mezirow in his work on Transformation Theory (Mezirow 1991) and its expression in adult education practice. He, too, is concerned with learning as an experiential process. However, where Kolb focused on learning as the transformation of experience into knowledge, Mezirow presents it as "the process of using prior interpretation to construe a new or revised interpretation of the meaning of one's experience" (Mezirow 1991, 12).

Transformative learning and development action

With a self-acknowledged debt of inspiration to Freire and Habermas, Mezirow is interested in what makes learning emancipatory:

> The emancipation in emancipatory learning is emancipation from libidinal, epistemic, institutional, or environmental forces that limit our options and our rational control over our lives but have been taken for granted or seen as beyond human control. (Mezirow 1991, 87)

Mezirow emphasizes frames of reference—"the structure of assumptions and expectations through which we filter sense impressions," which involve cognitive, affective, and conative dimensions. Mezirow explicitly identifies this focus as an illustration of Kitchener's epistemic domain of cognition, believing that a frame of reference is composed of two dimensions, what he calls "habits of mind" and the "resulting points of view." This leads him to the conclusion that learning occurs in one of four ways: by elaborating existing frames of reference; learning new frames of reference; transforming points of view; and transforming habits of mind:

> . . . we transform frames of reference—our own and those of others—by becoming critically reflective of their assumptions and aware of their context—the source, nature, and consequences of taken-for-granted beliefs. Assumptions on which habits of mind and related points of view are predicated may be epistemological, logical, ethical, psychological, ideological, social, cultural, economic, political, ecological, scientific, or spiritual, or may pertain to other aspects of experience. (Mezirow 2000, 19)

Mezirow introduces the term "meaning perspective" as an analogue of frame of reference to illustrate its epistemic character in providing a context for making meaning. He also identifies meaning schemes as the essential components of meaning perspectives. Mezirow sees a *meaning scheme* as "the particular knowledge, beliefs, value judgments, and feelings that become articulated in an interpretation." A *meaning perspective*, on the other hand, is a "habitual set of expectations that constitutes an orienting frame of reference" that serves as a "belief system for interpreting and evaluating the meaning of experience" (Mezirow 1991, 42). He continues: "Meaning perspectives determine *the essential conditions for construing meaning for an experience*. Each meaning perspective *selectively orders* what we learn and the way we learn it" (Mezirow 1991, 43 emphasis in original).

With these distinctions, Mezirow (1991, 93) restated his four ways of learning:

- *Learning through meaning schemes*: This form of learning typically includes "habitual and stereotypical responses to information," such as recipe learning or rote learning, where one behavior becomes a stimulus for another. "The only thing that changes within a meaning scheme is a specific response."
- *Learning new meaning schemes*: In instrumental mode, we learn how to take tests; and in a communicative mode, we learn how to play a different role. "New meaning schemes may be assimilated consciously or unconsciously in the course of socialization."
- *Learning through transformation of meaning schemes*: This learning involves reflections on assumptions, typically under circumstances when (for one reason or another) points of view are perceived as dysfunctional and "we experience a growing sense of the inadequacy of our old ways of seeing and understanding meaning."
- *Learning through perspective transformation:* Learning this way means "becoming aware, through reflection and critique, of specific presuppositions upon which a distorted or incomplete meaning perspective is based, and then transforming that perspective through a reorganization of learning."

For Mezirow there are therefore two major dimensions to transformative learning—the transformation of meaning schemes and of meaning perspectives, respectively. Critical reflection is central to each of these forms. In the specific context of problem solving, Mezirow sees the need for reflection on the content, the process, and the premises, which in interpretation resembles Kitchener's three-level model of cognitive processing. Reflection, Mezirow argues, is not simply being aware of experience or being aware of that awareness. Process reflection involves "reflection and critique of how we are perceiving, thinking, judging, feeling, and acting," while premise reflection "involves awareness and critique of the reason why we have done so" (Mezirow 1991, 106).

> The transformation of meaning schemes is integral to the process of reflection. As we assess our assumptions about the content or process of problem solving we create new ones or transform our old assumptions and hence our interpretations of experience. This is the dynamics of everyday reflective learning. When occasionally we are forced to assess or reassess the basic premises we have taken for granted and find them unjustified, perspective transformation, followed by major life changes, may result. (Mezirow 1991, 192)

While incomplete, this review of Mezirow's understanding of transformative learning has important implications for better understanding the connections among learning, transformation, and development, as well as for its relevance to the scholarship and practice of critical engagement. In this regard, attention to the *praxis/phrōnesis* of critical engagement deserves particular attention because, by its very nature, critical engagement involves both critical reflections and acts of critical transformations. In essence, while critical reflection is an essential prerequisite for transformative learning to occur, it is not by itself sufficient—even when it explicitly addresses all three of the dimensions that were mentioned earlier, namely, *social context* (particularly as it relates to the distribution of both power and opportunities), *boundary judgments*, and *epistemic assumptions* within frames of reference. As Brookfield (2000) professes:

> Critical reflection is certainly a necessary condition of transformative learning, in that existence of the latter depends on the former. However, it is not a sufficient condition; in other words, just because critical reflection is occurring does not mean that transformative learning inevitably follows. (Brookfield 2000, 142)

For Brookfield, transformative learning connotes "an epiphanic, or apocalyptic, cognitive event—a shift in the tectonic plates of one's assumptive clusters," which leads to fundamental questioning and reordering of how one thinks or *act*s (Brookfield 2000, 139, Bawden emphasis). Transformative development demands critical actions *as well as* critical thinking and, indeed, as Freire argues, their synthesis into critical praxis is vital:

> The insistence that the oppressed engage in reflection on the concrete situation is not a call to armchair revolution. On the contrary, reflection—true reflection—leads to action. On the other hand, when the situation calls for action, that action will constitute an authentic praxis only if its consequences become the object of critical reflection. (Freire 2003, 66)

To further extend this notion into the context of transformative development, learning transformation itself is of little consequence *unless* it results in transformative, sustainable, and responsible improvements to problematic situations that people are facing *in situ*. And that outcome can have just as much to do with freedom from institutional suppression of opportunities and environmental resource constraints as it has to do with conscientization and allied epistemic transformations. Sen (1999) insists that a focus on development as freedom must embrace opportunities, as well as processes, for human "functionings." In similar vein, de Beauvoir (cited in Freire 2003) emphasizes that changing the consciousness of the oppressed does little unless it is accompanied by changing the situation that oppresses them. Clearly, the more the oppressed become adapted to existing conditions, they more they are likely to be dominated!

Efforts to contribute to the transformation of the dominant frames of references of those within development agencies—at whatever scale—becomes a primary focus for critical engagement. And while that might seem to represent a challenge of apocalyptic proportions, the foundations for transformation already exist. Thus, as Sen puts it:

> A variety of social institutions—related to the operation of markets, administrations, legislatures, political parties, nongovernmental organizations, the judiciary, the media, and the community in general—(already) contribute to the process of development precisely through their efforts on enhancing and sustaining individual freedoms. (Sen 1999, 297)

That stated, we should never underestimate or disregard cultural influences in development, and the impact which those influences have on the structure of frames of references, the character of the "lifeworlds" of people and institutions, and the impediments they can present to self-development. Nor must the matter of language be ignored, for there is a host of ways of expressing meaning, just as there are multiple pathways to making meaning itself:

> Art, music, and dance are alternative languages. Intuition, imagination, and dreams are other ways of making meaning. Inspiration, empathy, and transcendence are central to self-knowledge and to drawing attention to the affective quality and poetry of human experience. (Mezirow 2000, 6)

Freire (1970) recognized that a range of socio-cultural conditions—including differences in language, personal motivations, and priorities, and levels of consciousness—can contribute to situations that confront people of the "Third World," especially. This recognition led to the realization that a pedagogy of the oppressed needs to be extremely sensitive to cultural-determined differences in both awareness and preparedness for social action. As Mezirow has claimed: the "who, what, when, why, and how of learning may only be understood as situated in a specific cultural context" (Mezirow 2000, 7).

A critical engagement must take all of these features into consideration. Adding further complexity to this matter is mutuality between individuals and the broader culture of which they are part. "Cultures 'r' us," as it were, and the dialectic between the personal and the social is of profound importance with respect to social learning, collective action, and participatory development. One of the most consistent criticisms of the experiential learning theories and conceptual models offered by analysts, such as Kolb and Mezirow, is that they refer essentially to the individual learner. As others see it, learning is a social activity rather than an activity confined to the individual mind (Luckett and Luckett 1999).

Malinen provides a useful perspective in this regard by drawing attention to the distinctions between first- and second-order experiences. First-order, first-person experiences are transformed into personal knowledge, whereas second-order, social experiences often lead to social re-constructions in the face of epistemological, ethical, and existential challenges. Indeed, "an individual equipped with personal experiential knowledge *needs* social interaction in order to "better" the epistemological parts of his (*sic*) knowing" (Malinen 2000).

> The social situation provides both an epistemological and existential environment for the individual learner. These dimensions modify the social process of dialogue. As a consequence, the other participants' experiences provide possibilities for varied forms of second-order experiences. (Malinen 2000, 138)

Therefore, social situations are an essential aspect of individual learning. They are arenas for social learning, staging grounds for collective communicative actions, and practice fields for developing critical consciousness and epistemic competencies.

Connections between critical learning of individuals and the social learning that occurs within (and by) communities and organizations is accomplished through the negotiation of meanings. This is a central tenant of Wenger's (1999) notion of "communities of practice," what we might now call *communities of critical praxis/phronēsis*. Connectedness is also fundamental to the "overlapping networks of democracy," which Busch (2000) promotes as essential vehicles for social re-engagement with moral issues—the deliberative democracy that Dewey and others envision:

> What networks of democracy can do is to put before us the key problems of the day in a manner in which they may be addressed by informed citizens. They can help citizens become informed through participation in the networks. They can ensure that all citizens have the opportunity (without being forced) to engage in deliberation, discussion, and debate about the issues affecting their lives. (Busch 2000, 187)

This notion of democratically deliberative networks can be extended to embrace entire cultures, which as Hejl (1993) suggests, can be seen as networks of socially constructed realities—which may or may not be homogeneous within a culture. Thus, in some circumstances:

> Instead of one knowledge system there are many networks that lack articulation among each other. The lifeworlds of the participants, or their values, norms and interests differs so greatly that they do not allow for communication and interaction between the parties. (Box 1989, 167)

Fundamentally, networks of democracy and communities of practice are learning communities or learning systems (Bawden 1994): coherent collectives of individual learners who collaborate to "learn their way forward" in the face of the pressing issues of the day that they share in common. Their purpose is to transform their own circumstances in a holistic and experiential manner. In so doing, they also learn how to transform the way that they learn how to deal with those pressing issues; including how and why prevailing and contested world-views may become impediments to negotiated meanings, shared reality constructions, and consensual, appreciative judgments for action. They also can learn about the impediments associated with the "whole" in which they are embedded and, also, about the impact of the inequalities of power on the self-replicating nature of social order:

> The use of power in interaction involves the application of facilities whereby participants are to generate outcomes through affecting the conduct of others; the facilities are both drawn from an order of domination and at the same time as they applied, reproduce that order of domination. (Giddens 1976, 122)

This, again, reinforces the need for a systemic appreciation of the complexities of situations that so commonly confront people seeking transformation of the circumstances of their lives. It also calls attention to the insistence of Habermas (1984) on the fundamental need to assure communication undistorted by power.

Kolb, Mezirow, Freire, Wenger, and Malinen all agree on the "holistic" nature of experiential learning in the sense of the inseparability of the individual as the "part" of a social "whole"—between the internal (subjective) and the external (objective). There are other points of convergence, as well, including dynamic connections between reflection and action, and learning and development; and between the existential and experiential, the ethical and empirical, and the rational and emotional. The *essence of wholeness* that this conjures up has been a *leitmotif* that, along with claims about the advantages of a "systemic consciousness," characterizes the profundity of the concept of "epistemic transformation" that we are arguing lies at the very heart of critical engagement.

And it is to matters of holistic appreciation and systemic competencies—and their application to critical engagement—that we now turn in an attempt to provide a conceptual framework for integrating the diverse issues of learning, transformation, development, and cognition that have all been treated here. The general thesis to be explored is this: to deal systemically with complex issues in the world about us we must collectively develop to a stage of epistemic maturity, a stage that reflects complex cognitive structures and "thought systems." From this perspective, any talk of wholeness and integrity, bounded-ness and embeddedness, inter-connectedness, and "emergence" will only make sense to those who have achieved such a state of epistemic development. If we are to act in the world in manner that is systemic in its appreciation of the complexities of the challenges that we face, we need to develop meaning perspectives and epistemic competencies that provide cognitive support for our development practices. To restate a claim made earlier: to more successfully come to public judgment about what needs to be done to deal with the complex, holistic issues of the contemporary problematique, citizens and scholars alike need to develop "systemic" or "systems" capabilities—to collectively learn how to put systems principles, concepts, theories, and philosophies into practice. In essence, we need to learn how to engage systemically.

Critical systemic engagement

The most fundamental systems idea is that parts both contain each other and express aspects of the whole (Flood 1996). An example is what Norgaard (1994) refers to as a "co-evolutionary approach to international development," which involves the conjunction of social and environmental (natural) systems. He elaborates:

> To emphasize coevolutionary processes is not to deny that people directly intervene in and change the characteristics of environments. The coevolutionary perspective is merely the next step, how different states of the environment alter the selective pressures and hence relative dominance of species and relationships between species thereafter. (Norgaard 1994, 36)

Addressing development systemically runs counter to the formal orthodoxy of development practice and confronts entrenched meaning perspectives and epistemic positions in the scientific community. Ironically, it likely represents an approach that is more likely to be appreciated by indigenous people who have lived in cultures of connectedness. It may well be that those who live in close communion with the natural world—and those whose lifeworlds have not been subjected to colonization by techno-scientific reductionism—have achieved a state of epistemic maturity that Western paradigms of modernization deny, impede, or even extinguish. It might also be that some people are just born with an innate, if naïve, sense of wholeness and holistic way of knowing, which under historical circumstances has been a cultural norm, even if accepted uncritically. The challenge, then, is to introduce systemic development methodologies that represent improvements on the way things are currently done—in the face of the prevailing techno-centric paradigm of modernism, on the one hand, and the often cognitively non-critical paradigm of traditionalism, on the other, even when the latter is an expression of an innate sense of holism.

A first issue is the matter of what it means to act systemically. To act in a systemic manner is to act in a way that reflects epistemic assumptions about the nature of integrated "wholes" and about the character and influence of patterns of inter-connectedness and inter-relationships. To address issues in a systemic manner is to approach them in "three dimensions," that is, to appreciate the significance of the nature and dynamics of the sub-system parts that are embedded simultaneously within whole systems and environmental supra-systems. To adopt a systemic ethos in practice is to anticipate that unique and unpredictable properties will emerge through the interactions of the "parts" within the "wholes" and the "wholes" with their [w]holistic environments.

The argument here is that all three of these features demand explicit attention to issues of epistemic development. As Salner (1986) contends, "for systems learning. . . epistemic competence may be the most critical competence of all." Systems competence, she argues, is characterized by and dependent on "the combination of a contextualizing sensibility with flexibility in epistemic strategies" (Salner, 1986). Basing her arguments on Perry's submission that intellectual and moral developmental maturation typically proceeds from a position of dualism eventually to contextual relativism, Salner posits that systemic capabilities only come with advanced epistemic development. In other words, until and unless people reach a stage of epistemic development equivalent to an epistemological position of contextual relativism and reflective judgment of rationality, they are unlikely to be able to develop praxis appropriate for either the sort of critical engagement that we have been promoting here or to the systemic approaches to learning and development for which Bawden (1994) has appealed.

This radical proposition provides a whole set of new dimensions to those approaches to participatory development that currently embrace learning, participation, and transformation as their central features. It places emphasis on the need for epistemic consciousness and development, and provides essential guidelines for those who wish to take systemic development seriously. Most significantly, it indicates a set of fresh features for the scholarship of critical engagement and additional imperatives for critical engagement in practice. And it introduces a further dilemma with respect to tensions between non-distorting democratic participation, on the one hand, and deliberate intervention, on the other.

The central motivation is to intervene with deliberate strategies to nurture epistemic development. This will inevitably involve epistemological confrontations and even prompt paradigmatic conflicts. The essential aim is to help people collectively learn how to *think* and *act* systemically through learning how to *be* systemic: when people engage critically about an issue of pressing concern and give attention equally to *praxis* (as theory-informed action) and *phronēsis* (as judgment-informed action).

It is the logic of different levels and/or logical types of learning, and of a nested hierarchy of embedded levels of cognitive processing, which provide the beginnings of a systemic framework for *scholarly engagement* with the process of learning itself. Learning is at the heart of transformational change of self, of collaborating selves, and of the relationships between self, selves, and the world of collectively shared everyday experiences. The learning to which we refer is a critical, self-interrogating, embedded process, where learners (acting both as individuals and as collectives), consciously pursue the nature and consequences of their knowledge at and across different levels of cognitive processing. As knowledge is generated in the context of each specific level, it has the capacity to trigger transformative changes at that level, which then—following systemic premises of interconnectedness—also has the capacity to trigger changes at other levels within the cognitive system.

The idea of "critical systemic engagement" follows the logic of "phased cognitive development" and draws on a range of theories from the different systems schools of thought—or different waves of systems thinking (Midgley

2000) that prevail within the systems movement. From this perspective, "engaged communities," as communities of *praxis/phronēsis,* are construed as dynamic, coherent "critical learning systems" (Bawden 2005)—self-conscious, self-organizing, self-critiquing, self-transforming, and self-developing social entities—that are capable of acting as agents of transformation of the environments in which they are embedded and with which they are "structurally coupled" (Maturana and Varela 1988). With this [w]holistic image in mind, we present a conceptual scheme as a tentative model for the development of critical engagement.

The development of critical engagement—a conceptual scheme

It is heuristically useful to present the conceptual development of critical learning systems as a recursive sequence of seven steps, stages, waves (we shall call them stages here) that enfold and unfold in response to both *internal* dynamics and *external* stimuli. It is neither essential nor invariant that the process starts at Stage I and moves in linear fashion without deviation to Stage VII.

Stage I: Wholeness consciousness—Engagement with Others

Reflecting the appeal of Skolimowski (1985) that "participation is an implicit aspect of wholeness," the sensation of the holomovement of Bohm (1980), and a commitment to the communicative action of Habermas (1984), participants in an engaged community come to a collective consciousness of their own coherence as a bounded critical learning system of interacting and interdependent parts that seeks to act as a coherent whole. Other vital features at this stage include awareness of possible power asymmetries and consequent tensions between experts and citizens (Wynne 1996) and of the impeding impact that this can have on deliberative democracy (Crocker 2003) and consensual public judgment (Yankelovich 1991). Of equal importance is the extension of "wholeness consciousness," that is, of self as an amalgam of many different features of being human that include emotions, values, beliefs, assumptions, knowledge, and behaviors (Dewey 1935, Kolb 1984). Participating in this holistic manner allows a constructive dialectic between self-identity and the identity of the whole system, and between individual and collective capabilities. It also enables the exploitation of the mutuality of the influences of each on the other. Paraphrasing the arguments that Scruton (1994) has developed, it might be said that critical learning systems are formed through agreements between rational individuals, while rational individuals are formed through critical learning systems.

Stage II: Boundary judgment—Engagement with Issues of Collective Concern

Reflecting the notion of boundaries as critical human judgments (Ulrich 1983, Midgley 2000), and judgments themselves as products of appreciation (Vickers 1983), a critical learning system comes to appreciate that the selection of a particular pressing issue to address involves exclusions as well as inclusions—of people and issues alike. These judgments are *critical* because exclusions and inclusions have instrumental and normative consequences. In selecting the bounded issue to be considered, critical learning systems essentially become cognitive and appreciative sub-systems embedded within the system of concern that they themselves have designated. The observers become part of the observed, which is a second-order cybernetic. These sub-systems also recognize that any system that is so designated is itself embedded within a higher-order environmental supra-system, which has the potential to have a very marked influence on the system being observed and the sub-systems doing the observing. The supra-system is, in turn, open to influence from both. Awareness of this mutuality of influences and of associated risk impacts of change (Beck 1992), highlights the need for ethical and aesthetic sensibilities, of what should be as well as what could be.

Stage III: Emancipation—Engagement with a Responsible Development Ethos
Following the notions of conscientization (Freire 1970), arguments for emancipation as a knowing interest (Habermas 1970), and the logic and purpose of emancipatory systems approaches (Jackson 2000), critical learning systems come to consciously adopt a position of development as freedom (Sen 1999). This translates as a critical concern for opportunities as well as for processes within a context of "suspicion of prevailing socio-cultural and particularly institutional conditions" (Jackson 2000)—and a preparedness and capability to transform them, if and when this is considered appropriate. It also further emphasizes a normative imperative of what *ought* to be done in the name of sustainable improvements, as well as what *could* be done (Ulrich 1983).

Stage IV: Meta-learning—Engagement with the Process of Learning
Drawing on the ideas of meta-cognition (Kitchener 1983), the nature and design of inquiring systems (Churchman 1971), learning as the transformation of experience (Kolb 1984), the nexus between transformation and *Weltanschauungen* (Checkland 1981), and meaning perspectives (Mezirow 1991), critical learning systems come to concentrate on critical reflections of their own learning processes. Where the spirit of "cognitive justice prevails" (Visvanathan 2005), multiple ways of knowing and different knowledge networks (Box 1989) are both acknowledged and accommodated. "Learning to learn" assumes an important focus of activity of the critical learning system. This, in turn, demands attention to both individual and collective critical reflections on process—before, during, and after deliberations on learning about matters at hand.

Stage V: Epistemic learning—Engagement with Epistemological Issues
Reflecting the concept of epistemic cognition (Kitchener 1983), meaning schemes and perspectives (Mezirow 1991), and the systemic relationship between transformation and *Weltanschauung* (Checkland 1981), critical learning systems come to an epistemic awareness of the nature of worldviews and meaning perspectives. They explore, understand, explain, and apply principles of

epistemological, ontological, and axiological pluralism as they relate to the quest for consensual actions for desirable, feasible, responsible, and sustainable changes in the systems of concern.

Stage VI: Epistemic development—Engagement with Intellectual and Moral Development

Consistent with the cognitive development theories of Perry (1968), Kohlberg (1963), Hoffman (1970), and Gibbs (2003), critical learning systems come to both appreciate the significance of epistemic development and explore its character in practice. In this manner, epistemic developmental concerns are included in the discourse of the system as it seeks to characterize the potential diversity of epistemic states that are internal and which it confronts through external relationships. Finally, critical learning systems take deliberate actions to develop their own state of epistemic maturity and epistemic competencies.

Stage VII—Systemic competencies— Engagement with Systemic Development

Reflecting the calls of Norgaard (1994) for the co-evolution of environmental and social systems, the claims of Salner (1986) with respect to the nexus between epistemic competencies and systemic capabilities, the submission of Jackson (2000) with respect to the nature of systemic pluralism, and the thesis of Bawden (1994, 2005) with respect to the nature of critical learning systems, critical learning systems now reach a stage of true self-understanding of their own nature and, indeed, of the stages of their development that has preceded this final state of maturity. It is with this realization that critical learning systems can now achieve advanced, systemic capabilities for dealing with the complexities of the contemporary problematique.

Summary

Critical engagement leads to transformation

- at Stage I from participating as individual selves to participating as members of a coherent and self-conscious "critical learning system"
- at Stage II from focusing only on problematic issues "out there" to becoming a cognitive/affective learning system
- at Stage III from understanding the concept of development as external to self and through material progress to understanding development as internal to self and as an expression of freedom; and from understanding the concept of learning as the acquisition of instrumental knowledge to understanding learning as an expression of emancipation
- at Stage IV from giving singular attention to the designated system of concern to embracing the meta-issue of "learning to learn"

- at Stage V from learning only about "the matter at hand" to learning "about learning about those matters"
- at Stage VI from grasping matters through less complex epistemic states to interpreting matters with increasing complexity
- at Stage VII from relying on dualist/reductionist perspectives to embracing contextual/holist onto-epistemologies and, with that, showing increasing capacity to address complex situations in their complexity.

Not until Stage VII do engaged communities of actors recognize the essentials of *being systemic* and, thus, truly appreciate the significance of why it is valuable to improve their systemic capabilities.

Interpretation

This framework was received initially in our faculty learning community as impenetrably theoretical and dense. However, with time it not only spoke plainly to one member, it helped that member better understand the dynamics taking place in an especially difficult episode of community engagement. For more than a year, this colleague had been embroiled in a public discussion about future directions of work in a community's nonprofit sector. Although many around the table felt that things should not continue as they had previously, it was difficult for them (for a variety of reasons, including politics and community history) to move forward together. "Progress" seemed like taking two steps forward, three steps sideways, and two steps backward—and frustration was growing.

While almost to a person those involved were committed civic leaders— persons driven by an ethic of doing what is best for the community—it was becoming increasingly clear to members that they were floundering. Success would require a new way of being together, a way based on high levels of trust, patience, the ability to listen and learn from each other and, perhaps most importantly, being open and willing to go "to a new place" without knowing in advance what or where that place might be.

Step by step the collective began making decisions that enabled the group to "live their way into a new way of thinking." Although words like "critical learning systems" and "development as freedom" were never spoken, it was clear to most members that something different and important was happening; and, because of that, they stayed committed to the process during the most turbulent of times. Especially important in the evolution of this group's experience was its capacity to embrace matters with increasing sophistication and understanding. Rather than bring the problem to a level that could be managed with available tools, techniques, and approaches, they continually framed and re-framed the problem in ways that extended beyond immediate grasp, as "high hanging fruit" as one member put it. Time and time again, there was evidence of the willingness and capacity to up-shift thinking.

While an easy and natural explanation for describing what happened is to say that the group had "good leadership," the reality is that different people were at the helm; there were rotating point persons with different backgrounds, community roles, leadership capabilities, and (in some cases) philosophies. What they shared—and this attribute was reinforced by almost all members—was a desire (over time) to engage critically. It was clear that wherever this road might lead, traveling it would take time. And, with time, it was clear that this would not be a familiar road.

The faculty member involved in this effort was in this wave of change, not above it. He gained two important lessons from the experience. First, he learned that "being at sea" represents a transformative opportunity. Rather than be "lead dog"—the one to which others turn for guidance—he became co-learner, collaborating in a jointly designed and implemented inquiry process. Second, he recognized that others evaluated his contributions largely in terms of how he conducted himself. Attributes like integrity, honesty, trustworthiness, conscientiousness, caring, empathy, and discernment, among other things, really did matter.

Closing observations

The essential message of this chapter is that the Academy has a moral imperative to *engage critically* with the citizenry in addressing the current complex problematique. It must do so in a manner that is characterized by (while concurrently contributing to) a deliberative, moral, democratic, and systemic discourse. The process of critical engagement is not an end unto itself—a focus for evaluating academic work away from the campus—but a means to make democracy work.

From this development perspective, the aim of critical engagement is nothing less than transformation at all levels—individual, communal, societal, and global. It includes the transformation of worldviews and meaning perspectives; of ways of knowing and being; of learning and learning about learning; and of consciousness itself. It also embraces profound changes in institutions and in the meta-institutional discourses that set the manner of the ways things are done, including governance, commerce, security, and development practice.

The essential promise of such a *learning turn* at the engagement interface is the development of a critical, self-confrontational discourse that promotes meta- and epistemic-learning (and the transformation of both) in ways that lead to the emergence of collective systemic competencies. And this represents a profound and urgent focus for an Academy that seeks to truly engage both with the citizenry and with other institutions in the pursuit of a universe of human discourse in a risk society and in an era of reflexive modernization. Such a discourse will have foundations in both instrumental rationality and communicative action; and it will be a discourse that is transformative in intent. In the spirit of the philoso-

phy of pragmatism, it will need to embrace different ways of knowing and valuing, and be dedicated to transforming experience in a collective quest for betterment. It will also represent a relevant alternative to prevailing science-based,
reductionist approaches to development-as-modernization; to the character of
scientific research as the mechanistic search for "the truth"; to the ethos of policy as the expression of expert opinion; and to the focus of education and extension as the transmission of instrumental knowledge. Finally, and most importantly, critical engagement does not seek material progress at the expense of the
epistemic colonization of the lifeworlds or promote a "democracy" that is in-
visibly cloaked in cognitive authoritarianism.

References

Allen, W., M. Kilvington, and C. Horn. 2002. *Using participatory and learning-based approaches for environmental management to help achieve constructive behaviour change.* Landcare Research Contract report LC0102/057. Ministry of Environment. Wellington: New Zealand.

Anon. 2004. Editorial statement. *Participatory learning and action.* No. 50. London: IIED.

Argyris, C., and D. Schön. 1996. *Organizational learning II. Theory, method, and practice.* Reading MA: Addison-Wesley.

Barnes, J. 2000. Participatory science as the basis for a healing culture. In R. Steiner, ed. *Nature's open secret: Introductions to Goethe's scientific writings.* Trans. John Barnes and Mado Spiegler. Anthroposophic Press.

Bateson, G. 1972. *Steps to an ecology of mind.* London: Paladine.

Bawden, R. J. 1991. Systems thinking and practice in agriculture. *J. Dairy Science* 74:2362–2373.

Bawden, R. J. 1994. Creating learning systems: A metaphor for institutional reform for development. In I. Scoones and J. Thompson, eds. *Beyond farmer first: Rural people's knowledge agricultural research and extension practice.* London: Intermediate Technology Publications.

Bawden, R. J. 2005. Systemic perspectives on community development: Participation, learning, and the essence of wholeness. *Perspectives on Community Development in Ireland* 1:45–62.

Baxter Magolda, M. B. 1992. *Knowing and reasoning in college: Gender-related patterns in students' intellectual development.* San Francisco: Jossey-Bass.

Beck, U. 1992. *Risk society: Towards a new society.* London: Sage Publications.

Belenky, M. F., B. M. Clinchy, N. R. Goldberger, and J. M. Tarule. 1986. *Women's ways of knowing: The development of self, voice, and mind.* New York: Basic Books.

Bernstein, R. J. 1983. *Beyond objectivism and relativism: Science, hermeneutics, and praxis.* Philadelphia: Univ. of Pennsylvania Press.

Bohm, D. 1980. *Wholeness and the implicate order.* London: Routledge.

Bohm, D. 1987. *Unfolding meaning: A weekend dialogue with David Bohm.* London: Ark Paperbacks.

Bohm, D. 1992. *Thought as a system.* A transcription of a seminar held at Ojai CA from Nov. 31 to Dec. 2, 1990. David Bohm, ed. London: Routledge.

Bortoft, H. 1996. *The wholeness of nature: Goethe's way toward a science of conscious participation in nature.* New York: Lindisfarne Books.

Boyer, E. L. 1990. *Scholarship reconsidered: Priorities of the professoriate.* The Carnegie Foundation for the Advancement of Teaching. San Francisco: Jossey-Bass.

Boyer, E. L. 1996. The scholarship of engagement. *Journal of Public Service and Outreach* 1:11–20.

Box, L. 1989. Knowledge, networks and cultivators. In N. Long. *Encounters at the interface: A perspective on social discontinuities in rural development.* Wageningen studies in Sociology 27. The Netherlands: Wageningen Univ.

Boyte, H. C. 2002. A different kind of politics: John Dewey and the meaning of citizenship in the 21st century. Dewey Lecture, Univ. of Michigan. Nov. 1, 2002. http://www.ia.imich.edu/publications/archives/BoyteDeweyLecture. (Accessed 6/25/05)

Brokensha, D., D. Warren, and O. Werner. 1980. *Indigenous knowledge systems and development.* Maryland: Univ. Press of America.

Brookfield, S. D. 2000. Transformative learning as ideology critique. In J. Mezirow and Associates *Learning as transformation.* New York: Jossey-Bass.

Brundtland, G. H. ed. 1987. *Our common future: Report World Commission on Environment and Development.* Oxford: Oxford Univ. Press.

Brydon-Miller, M., D. Greenwood, and P. Maguire. 2003. Why action research? Editorial. *Action Research* 1: 9–29.

Bülow, I., von. 1989. The bounding of a problem situation and the concept of a system's boundary in soft systems methodology. *Journal of Applied Systems Analysis* 16:35–41.

Busch, L. 2000. *The eclipse of morality.* New York: Aldine de Gruyter.

Carr, W., and S. Kemmis. 1986. *Becoming critical: Education, knowledge and action research.* 3rd ed. London: Falmer Press.

Chambers, S. 1995. Discourse and democratic practices. In S. K. White, ed. *The Cambridge companion to Habermas.* Cambridge: Cambridge Univ. Press.

Checkland, P. B. 1981. *Systems thinking, systems practices.* Chichester: John Wiley and Sons.

Checkland, P. B. 1985. From optimizing to learning: a development of systems thinking for the 1990s. *Journal of the Operations Research Society* 36: 757–767.

Checkland P. B., and S. Holwell. 1998. *Information, systems and information systems: Making sense of the field.* Chichester: Wiley.

Churchman, C. W. 1971. *The design of inquiring systems.* New York: Basic Books.

Colby, A., and L. Kohlberg. 1987. *The measurement of moral judgment: Vol. I. Theoretical foundations and research validation.* Cambridge: Cambridge Univ. Press.

Cornwall, A. 2002. Locating citizen participation. *IDS Bulletin* 33:49–58.

Cornwall, A., and Guijt. 2004. Shifting perceptions, changing practices in PRA: From infinite innovation to the quest for quality. *Participatory Learning and Action* 50:160–167.

Crewe, E., and E. Harrison. 2002. *Whose development? An ethnography of aid.* 3rd Imp. London: Zed Books.

Crocker, D. 1991. Towards development ethics. *Word Development* 19:457–483.

Crocker, D. 2003. *Participatory development: The capabilities approach and deliberative democracy.* Working paper. Institute of Philosophy and Public Policy. Institute of Public Affairs: Univ. of Maryland.

Daly, H. E., and J. B. Cobb, Jr. 1994. *For the common good: Redirecting the economy toward community, the environment, and a sustainable future.* Boston: Beacon Press.

Davison, A. 2001. *Technology and the contested meanings of sustainability.* New York: State Univ. of New York Press.

Dennett, D. C. 1991. *Consciousness explained.* London: Little, Brown, and Co.

Dewey, J. 1963. *Liberalism and social action.* Originally published in 1935. New York: Capricon Books.

DFID. 2000. *Realising human rights for poor people: Strategies for achieving the international development targets.* London: Department for International Development.

Dietz, T., E. Ostrom, and P. C. Stern. 2003. The struggle to govern the commons. *Science* 302:1907–1912.

Dresner, S. 2002. *The principles of sustainability.* London: EarthScan Publications.

Escobar, A. 2000. Beyond the search for a paradigm? Post-development and beyond. *Development* 43:11–14.

Fals Borda, O. 2001. Participatory (Action) research in social theory: Origins and challenges. In P. Reason and H. Bradbury, eds. *Handbook of action research: Participative inquiry and practice*. London: Sage Publications.

Fischer, F. 2000. *Citizens, experts, and the environment: The politics of local knowledge*. Durham NC: Duke Univ. Press.

Flood, R. L, and N. R. A. Romm. 1996. *Diversity management: Triple loop learning*. Chichester: John Wiley.

Freire, P. 1970. *Pedagogy of the oppressed*. New York: Herder and Herder.

Freire, P. 2003. *Pedagogy of the oppressed*. 30th Anniversary Ed. New York: Continuum.

Fuller, S. 1988. *Social epistemology*. Bloomington IN: Indiana Univ. Press.

Gadamer, H. G. 1975. Hermeneutics and social science. *Cultural Hermeneutics* 2:307–316.

Gaspar, D. 2004. *Ethics and development: From economism to human development*. Edinburgh: Edinburgh Univ. Press.

Gaventa, J. 2002. *Exploring citizenship, participation and accountability*. IDS Bulletin 33:1–11.

Gaventa, J. 2004. Participatory development or participatory democracy? Linking participatory approaches to policy and governance. Participatory learning and action. No. 50. 150–159. London: International Institute for Environment and Development.

Grayling, A. C. 2004. What is the good life? *Journal of the Royal Society for the Arts* July 2004:36–37.

Gibbs, J. C. 2003. *Moral development and reality: Beyond the theories of Kohlberg and Hoffman*. London: Sage Publications.

Giddens, A. 1976. *New rules of sociological method*. London: Hutchinson.

Giddens, A. 1979. *Central problems in social theory*. London: Macmillan.

Goulet, D. 1995. *Development ethics: A guide to theory and practice*. New York: Apex Books.

Greenwood, D. J. and M. Levin. 1998. *Introduction to action research: Social research for social change*. Thousands Oaks CA: Sage Publications.

Groves, L., and R. Hinton, eds. 2004. *Inclusive aid: Changing power relationships in international development*. London: EarthScan.

Grundy, S. 1982. Three modes of action research. *Curriculum Perspectives* 2: 23–34.

Habermas, J. 1971. *Knowledge and human interests*. Trans. Jeremy Shapiro. Boston: Beacon Press.

Habermas, J. 1979. *Communication and the evolution of society*. Trans. Thomas McCarthy. Boston: Beacon Press.

Habermas, J. 1984. *The theory of communicative action*. Trans. Thomas McCarthy. *Vol. 1. Reason and rationalization; vol 2. Lifeworld and systems: A critique of functionalist reason*. Boston: Beacon Press.

Habermas, J. 1990. Discourse ethics: Notes on a program of philosophical justification. S. Benhabib and F. Dallmayr, eds. *The Communicative Ethics Controversy*. Cambridge MA: MIT Press.

Habermas, J. 1992. *Postmetaphysical thinking: Philosophical essays*. Trans. William Mark Hohengarten. Cambridge MA: MIT Press.

Harmon, W. H. 1984. Key choices. In D. C. Korten and R. Klaus, eds. *Contributions toward theory and planning frameworks*. Hartford CT: Kumarian Press.

Hejl, P. M. 1993. Culture as a network of socially constructed realities. In A. Rigney and D. Fokkema. *Cultural participation: Trends since middle ages.* Amsterdam: John Benjamens Publishing.

Heron, J., and P. Reason. 1985. *Whole person medicine: A co-operative inquiry.* London: British Postgraduate Medical Foundation.

Heron, J., and P. Reason. 2001. The practice of co-operative inquiry: Research 'with' rather than 'on' people. In P. Reason and H. Bradbury, eds. *Handbook of action research: Participative inquiry and practice.* London: Sage Publications.

Hervieu, B. 2000. Foreword. In M. Cerf, D. Gibbon, B. Hubert, R. Ison, M. Paine, J. Proost, and N. Röling, eds. *Cow up a tree: Knowing and learning for change in agriculture case studies from industrialized countries.* Paris: INRA.

Hoffman, M. L. 1970. Moral development. In P. H. Mussen, ed. *Carmichael's manual of child psychology.* Vol. 2. 3rd ed. New York: John Wiley.

Howell, J., and J. Pearce. 2002. *Civil society and development: A critical exploration.* London: Lynne Reiner Publishers.

Isaacs, W. N. 1993. Taking flight: dialogue, collective thinking, and organisational learning. *Organizational Dynamics* 22:24–39.

Ison, R. L., C. High, C. P. Blackmore, and M. Cerf. 2000. Theoretical frameworks for learning-based approaches to change in industrialized-country agricultures. In M. Cerf, D. Gibbon, B. Hubert, R. Ison, M. Paine, J. Proost, and N. Röling, eds. *Cow up a tree: Knowing and learning for change in agriculture case studies from industrialized countries.* Paris: IRNA.

Jackson, M. C. 1991. *Systems methodologies for the management sciences.* New York: Plenum Publishers.

Jackson, M. C. 2000. *Systems approaches to management.* New York: Kluwer Academic/Plenum Publishers.

Kegan, R. 2000. What "form" transforms? A constructive-developmental approach to transformative learning. In J. Mezirow and Associates *Learning as transformation.* New York: Jossey-Bass.

King, P. M., and K. S. Kitchener. 1994. *Developing reflective judgment.* San Francisco: Jossey-Bass.

Kitchener, K. S. 1983. Cognition, meta-cognition, and epistemic cognition: A three level model of cognitive processing. *Human Development* 26:222–232.

Kitchener, K., and K. W. Fisher. 1990. A skill approach to the development of reflective thinking. *Contributions to Human Development* 21: 48–62.

Knorr Cetina, K. 1999. *Epistemic cultures: How the sciences make knowledge.* Cambridge MA: Harvard Univ. Press.

Kohlberg, L. 1963. The development of children's orientation towards a moral order. 1. Sequence in the development of moral thought. *Vita Humana* 6:11–33.

Kohlberg, L. and R. A. Ryncarz. 1990. Beyond justice reasoning: moral development and consideration of a seventh stage. In C. N. Alexander and E. J. Langer, eds. *Higher stages of human development: Perspectives on adult growth.* New York: Oxford Univ. Press.

Kolb, D. A. 1984. *Experiential learning: Experience as the source of learning and development.* Englewood Cliffs NJ: Prentice Hall.

Korten, D. C. 1984. People centered development: Toward a framework. In D. C. Korten and R. Klaus, eds. *Contributions toward theory and planning frameworks.* West Hartford CT: Kumarian Press.

Korten, D. C., and R. Klaus. 1984. Introduction. In D. C. Korten and R. Klaus, eds. *Contributions toward theory and planning frameworks.* West Hartford CT: Kumarian Press.

Kuhn, T. 1962. *Structure of scientific revolutions.* Chicago: Univ. of Chicago Press.

Langer, E. 1997. *The power of mindful learning.* Reading MA: Adison Wesley.

Latour, B. 1987. *Science in action.* Cambridge MA: Harvard Univ. Press.

Latour, B. 1993. *We have never been modern.* Harvard: Harvester Wheatsheaf.

Leach, M., I. Scoones, and B. Wynne. 2005. Introduction: Science, citizenship and globalisation. In M. Leach, I. Scoones, and B. Wynne, *Science and citizens.* London: Zed Books.

Leopold, A. 1949. *A Sand County almanac.* New York: Oxford Univ. Press.

Levin, M., and D. Greenwood. 2001. Pragmatic action research and the struggles to transform universities into learning communities. In P. Reason and H. Bradbury, eds. *Handbook of action research: Participative inquiry and practice.* London: Sage Publications.

Lewin, K. 1948. Resolving social conflicts. In G. W. Lewin, ed. *Selected papers on group dynamics.* New York: Harper and Brothers.

Love, N. S. 1995. What's left of Marx? In S. K. White, ed. *The Cambridge Companion to Habermas.* Cambridge: Cambridge Univ. Press.

Luckett, S., and K. Luckett. 1999. *Developing 'reflective' development practitioners through an action learning curriculum: Problems and challenges in a South African context.* Unpublished manuscript. Pietermaritzburg: Univ. of Natal.

Malinen, A. 2000. *Adult experiential learning.* Finland: SoPhi. Univ. of Jyväskylä.

Marrow, A. J. 1969.*The practical theorist: The life and work of Kurt Lewin.* New York: Basic Books.

Maturana, H. R., and F. J. Varela. 1980. *Autopoeisis and cognition: The realization of the living.* Dordecht: D. Reidel Publishing Company.

Maturana, H. R., and F. J. Varela. 1988. *The tree of knowledge: The biological roots of human understanding.* Boston: New Science Library.

McDermott, J. J. ed. 1981. *The philosophy of John Dewey.* Chicago: Univ. of Chicago Press.

Mezirow, J. 1991. *Transformative dimensions of adult learning.* San Francisco: Jossey-Bass.

Mezirow, J. 2000. Learning to think like an adult: Core concepts of transformation theory. In J. Mezirow and Associates *Learning as transformation.* New York: Jossey-Bass.

Midgley, G. 2000. *Systemic intervention: Philosophy, methodology, and practice.* New York: Kluwer Academic/Plenum Publishers.

Milbraith, L. W. 1989. *Envisioning a sustainable society: Learning our way out.* New York: State Univ. of New York Press.

Norgaard, R. B. 1994. *Development betrayed: The end of progress and a co-evolutionary revisioning of the future.* London: Routledge.

Okri, B. 1997. *A way of being free.* London: Phoenix.

Perry, W. G. 1968. *Forms of intellectual and ethical development in the college years.* New York: Holt, Rinehart and Winston.

Perry, W. G. 1999. *Forms of intellectual and ethical development in the college years.* Reissued. San Francisco: Jossey-Bass.

Pettitt, J., and J. Wheeler. 2005. Developing rights? Relating discourse to context and practice. *IDS Bulletin* 36: 1–8.

Piaget, J. 1969. *Judgment and reasoning in the child*. M. Warden, trans. Original work published in 1928. Totowa NJ: Littlefield Adams.

Plas, J. M. 1986. *Systems psychology in the schools*. New York: Pergamon Press.

Pretty, J. N. 1995. *Regenerating agriculture: Policies and practices for sustainability and self-reliance*. London: EarthScan Publications.

Rahman, M. A. 1991. The theoretical standpoint of PAR. In O. Fals Borda and M. A. Rahman, eds. *Action and knowing: Breaking the monopoly with participatory action research*. New York: Apex Press.

Raskin, P. D. 2000. Bending the curve: Toward global sustainability. *Development* 43:67–74.

Reason, P. 1994. Introduction. In P. Reason, ed. *Participation in human inquiry*. London: Sage Publications.

Reason, P., and H. Bradbury. 2001. Introduction: Inquiry and participation in search of a world worthy of human aspiration. In P. Reason and H. Bradbury, eds. *Handbook of action research: Participative inquiry and practice*. London: Sage Publications.

Reason, P., and J. Heron. 1986. Research with people: The paradigm of experiential inquiry. *Person-Centered Review* 1:457–464.

Redclift, M. 1987. *Sustainable development: Exploring the contradictions*. London: Methuen.

Ricoeur, P. 1991. *From text to action: Essays in hermeneutics. II*. Trans. by K. Blamey and J. Thompson. Evanston IL: Northwestern Univ. Press.

Rorty, R. 1982. *Consequences of pragmatism*. Minneapolis: Univ. of Minnesota.

Salner, M. 1986. Adult cognitive and epistemological development in systems education. *Systems Research* 3:225–232.

Schecter, D. 1991. Critical systems thinking in the 1980s: A connective summary. In R. L. Flood and M. C. Jackson, eds. *Critical systems thinking: Directed readings*. Chichester: Wiley.

Scoones, I., and J. Thompson. 1994. Knowledge power and agriculture. In I. Scoones and J. Thompson, eds. *Beyond farmer first: Rural people's knowledge, agricultural research and extension practice*. London: IIED.

Scruton, R. 1994. *Modern philosophy*. London: Sinclair-Stevenson.

Sen, A. 1988. *On Ethics and economics*. Oxford: Basil Blackwell.

Sen, A. 1999. *Development as freedom*. New York: Anchor Books.

Singer, P. 1994. Introduction. In P. Singer, ed. *Ethics*. Oxford: Oxford Univ. Press.

Skowlimowski, H. 1985. The co-operative mind as a partner of the creative evolution. *Proceedings of the First International Conference on the Mind-Matter Interaction*. Brazil: Universidad Estadual de Campinas.

St. Clair, A. L. 2005. *Third stage development ethics: Global institutions, scientific uncertainty and the politicization of moral worth*. Paper presented at International Conference and Workshop on Ethics and Development: The Capability Approach on Practice. Michigan State Univ. April 11–13.

Treanor, P. 2004. *Neoliberalism: Origins, theory, definition*. Internet Publication: http://web.inter.nl.net/users/Paul.Treanor/neoliberalism.html.

Toffler, A. 1984. Introduction on future-conscious politics. In C. Bezold. *Anticipatory democracy: People in the politics of the future*. New York: Vintage Books.

Ulrich, W. 1983. *Critical heuristics of social planning: A new approach to practical philosophy*. Bern Switzerland: Haupt.

Ulrich, W. 1993. Some difficulties of ecological thinking considered from a critical systems perspective: A plea for critical holism. *Systems Practice* 6:584–609.

Uphoff, N. 1992. *Learning from Gal Oya: Possibilities for participatory development and post-Newtonian social science.* Ithaca NY: Cornell Univ. Press.

Vickers, G. 1983. *Human systems are different.* London: Harper and Row.

Visvanathan, S. 2005. Knowledge justice and democracy. In M. Leach, I. Scoones, and B. Wynne, *Science and citizens.* London: Zed Books.

Wallerstein, I. 1996. *Open the social sciences.* Report of the Gulbenkian Commission on the restructuring of the social sciences. Stanford: Stanford Univ. Press.

Warnke, G. 2002. Hermeneutics, ethics and politics. In R. J. Dostal, *The Cambridge Companion to Gadamer.* Cambridge: Cambridge Univ. Press.

Weiner, N. 1964. *God and Golem Inc.* Cambridge MA: MIT Press.

Wenger, E. 1999. *Communities of practice: Learning, meaning and identity.* Cambridge: Cambridge Univ. Press.

West, E. J. 2004. Perry's legacy: Models of epistemological development. *Journal of Adult Development* 11:61–70.

Whitehead, A. N. 1929. *The function of reason.* Boston: Beacon Press.

Wilson, M., and E. Whitmore. 2000. *Seed of fire: Social development in an era of globalism.* Halifax: Fernwood Publishing.

Wynne, B. 1996. May the sheep safely graze? A reflexive view of the expert–lay knowledge divide. In S. Lash, B. Szerszynski, and B. Wynne, eds. *Risk, environment and modernity: Towards a new ecology.* London: Sage Publications.

Yankelovich, D. 1991. *Coming to public judgment: Making democracy work in a complex world.* Syracuse NY: Syracuse Univ. Press.

PART III:
MAKING SENSE OF IT ALL

CHAPTER 9

COMING TO CRITICAL ENGAGEMENT: PERSONAL IMPLICATIONS

As we complete this effort, it is interesting to look back on what has transpired over the years of joint learning. As noted in chapter 1, we deviated from what we thought would happen—synthesizing understanding in the form of principles of effective practice—embarking, instead, on a journey of learning, discovery, and personal transformation. With every intent to better understand the *it* of engagement *only*—and to share that understanding with others—we found ourselves also exploring the "*me and we*" of engagement. Because of that evolution, writing this book has helped us understand our work (individually and collectively) in fresh and indelible ways. Because of that, it is fair to conclude that *this book has written us* as much as we have written it.

What have we learned? This simple, yet provocative, question is the focus of Part III. In this chapter, we explore the question in personal terms, sharing thoughts that emerged during a dialogue session that took place after we had read and reflected on the previous eight chapters. In chapter 10, we tackle the question in intellectual terms, seeking to better locate ourselves in the multifaceted territory of engagement.

In reflecting on the question of what we learned, we recall a distinction made in our earliest writing together, a distinction expressed also in this book: that is, our learning journey represents the perspective of *faculty* who seek to more deeply understand what it means to participate at the engagement inter-face—in a range of organizations and communities and in a variety of settings. We do not describe, speak to, or represent an *institutional* perspective and offer, instead, one (of many possible) interpretations of what it means to engage in conjunction with faculty responsibilities. As faculty members, we learned—first and foremost—that our journey together has been an exploration of core episte-mological questions, including: What do we know? How did we come to know it?

With that in mind, we discuss what learning has meant to us and where we think that learning has led us. We do that by considering *what* it means to en-gage; what it means *when* we engage; and, finally, what it means to learn *how* to engage. We intersperse quotes from our dialogue in the text, spoken words drawn from the transcript of our conversation (*presented in italics*). Although these contributions stimulate shared understanding, it is important to know that shared understanding *always* began with independent voices, offered by people with different backgrounds, experiences, and points of view. Although this book was written together, how we collaborated in its writing surprised us: it is writ-ten in a way that accentuates the unique perspectives and qualities of each au-thor. As Frank observed:

> *It's not intended to be written where we're all agreeing on everything . . .*
> *There's enough we share in common, but there are also points of emphasis that*
> *each of us has. There's enough here that cuts across, but there are also ideas,*
> *thoughts, and points of emphasis that are unique to each of us. I think the test*
> *of this book will be whether or not we've achieved a balance.*

The conversation on which this chapter is drawn took place in Cheryl's of-fice on an extraordinary day—a campus-wide power outage. Luckily, the phone system worked, enabling Richard to join us by telephone from Australia. But, without electricity, it was impossible to tape record our conversation with the equipment at hand. Thankfully (and quite by accident), Pennie had a battery-powered digital recorder in her purse. Just enough daylight streamed into the room for those present to make eye contact, even though (without air condition-ing or much of a breeze coming through an open window) it was quite stuffy on this humid, August afternoon. Despite these environmental challenges, we ea-gerly dove into the conversation, anticipating new learning from spending time together.

Discovering a cycle of learning

We began the conversation by reflecting on our metamorphosis as a group—how we had shifted after a few months from describing and analyzing project experiences (with an *instrumental* character to the conversation) to learn-ing how to engage each other in discourse (with a *hermeneutic* character to the conversation). For example, in the early years of our collaboration, we co-authored a manuscript that included a framework for conducting community-based research methods. The framework, derived from in-depth analysis of community-based projects, was not accepted for publication. Our initial disappointment—griping about what the reviewers had "missed" or "didn't get"—evolved into sustained and critical review of the manuscript's substance. We asked: What *is it* that we *really* have to say—if anything—in this piece?

By shifting from an instrumental to a hermeneutic stance, literally everything we talked about became subject to interpretation and reinterpretation through critique. Included in discourse were admissions of failure and regret, including the delicate circumstances, missteps, and embarrassments that colleagues often hide from one other. We started asking probing questions, seeking to examine critically what we had done (and not done) and why. From that inquiry emerged a practice routine. Frank recounts:

> *Pennie's work is a good example. She engaged with us in discourse and then applied that learning in the field. Then, she engaged in discourse with her field colleagues based on their experiences. Pennie brought that learning back to us. We engaged in more discourse and then wrote about all of it. What a dynamic process!*

This, we discovered, was a cycle of learning—trying out new practices based on nascent insights; reflecting on them; and asking normative questions. Prominent in all of this was the writing. Cheryl observed:

> *Writing matters! If we think this work is about learning, then it's not about just talking about learning. The conversation is good but the writing pushed us to a different level. It enabled us to do one thing, which is to treat our ideas as text to examine, critique, elevate. Without the writing process piece of it, I think we'd be in a very different place.*

Pennie agreed, and talked about how the writing process influenced her work as it unfolded:

> *One of the things that I was struck by as I wrote up my cases was that while the cases unfolded during the time we worked and I was kind of intentional in my thinking about discourse, the layers of discourse I was not fully aware of until I reflected on the case. That was very powerful for me. And it really told me the importance of setting aside time to write and reflect on my work in the community, my engagement work. There were hidden discourses that were present that I was not so fully cognizant of, even though I was trying to be intentional in attending to discourse in my work.*

As Richard put it, "*You are continually questioning not just what you are doing and writing, but the narrative of which you are a part as it unfolds.*" Thinking that way allowed us to better understand that the text, subtext, and context of this work are connected inextricably. There is a *story* in each episode; there is a *storyline* evolving (both dimensions in autobiographical and contextual terms); and there are overlapping *frames of reference*—a local frame of reference associated with every instance of engagement, and a disciplinary frame of reference associated with how engagement is understood as a field of study and practiced over time.

Drawing on a distinction made by Kaplan (1964;1998) and discussed in chapter 3, embracing this stance enabled us to fashion commentaries about engagement that we think align more with logic-in-use (how this work actually unfolds) than with reconstructed logic (what this work looks like in idealized form). For us, logic-in-use meant exploring and reexploring the intricate connections among the text, subtext, and context of engagement. As Frank interpreted it:

> *One of the things that struck me about reading chapters 5–7 is that the stories presented aren't expressions of reconstructed logic. They are about logic in use. And that's terribly important in this work, especially so because there is a political backdrop—the political need to show that you are in control, that what you're doing is successful. As I reflect on Part II, one of the themes is that this is really difficult work and that there is a sense of being vulnerable, of finding yourself in a pickle. What am I going to do now? Anybody who has experienced engagement knows that feeling.*

Taking this approach required focusing increasingly on the messy, complicated, and less-than-perfect accounts of difficult work—of the challenges and failures, as well as the successes. The work was examined; then critiqued and revised; and eventually tested against ongoing experience. Moreover, as we subjected our stories and ideas to analysis, interpretation, reinterpretation, and critique, we began to ask fundamental, normative questions: Does the work matter? If it does matter, to whom does it matter? And, how do we know? Cheryl characterized it as *both a process and a stance toward one's work,* and Richard mused about how he now makes explicit what he had previously underplayed:

> *The way I see it is that here's an opportunity in the world with new needs. So rather than just using a new word for old processes, let's really rethink this whole notion of engagement in terms of recasting not just the role of universities, but us. What do we mean by scholarly activity and practice where truth is under question and where the normative now becomes incredibly important? And that for me was another lesson. The idea of (in the past I've seen) the normative as something outside my scholarship. I've had to deal with it, in my case through notions of appreciation and so on, but I've always been a bit sort of cavalier about it. Now I see this as profoundly important with the whole idea of the normative having to be embraced by scholarship and scholarly activities. And that itself is open to critique: How do you critique your positions and values? It's quite a new phase for me.*

Once we stepped into the territory described here, we saw that our joint work was more about asking questions than arriving at answers. Cheryl expressed the difference this way: *"The learning piece is much more prominent and the showcasing of what we know is much less prominent."* In addition, just as we learned to be intentional about examining the ideas and stories we were sharing, we also learned to examine explicitly the learning processes we were experiencing. Richard commented about that this way:

> *It seems to me that, again, what our book is illustrating quite profoundly: the significance of a group like ours in terms of an opportunity for that meta-discourse that we've talked about and I think comes through in the book. In other words, we go out, we do our work as one would in a normal academic discipline-based department or even a multidiscipline-based department, but instead of coming back and talking about the projects themselves, we don't. We did that early on and talked about our cases. But, for me, doing that was just background. The foreground was the meta-discourse. It was this constant un-raveling of meaning and meaning making. And it only takes a couple of hours a week or less in terms of the process that people do within their departments. So it's not anywhere near as time consuming as people imagine, but it's absolutely vital, I think, to the idea of reconstructing the way we operate in the world.*

Slowly, but surely, we reasoned that this way of thinking and approaching engagement was too important to be *only* matters for faculty consideration. So, critical Discourse (as we described in chapter 5) soon became a staple of our engagement practices. We reasoned it this way: If it has helped to ask each other probing questions, why not examine questions jointly with our community partners? This was not done without risk, though. With pressure to get things done, will people tolerate what some may perceive to be "wasteful" episodes of *thinking about* engagement rather than devoting attention to *doing* engagement? But that fear was overplayed, largely because there is a polarity between thinking and doing only if one prefers to see it that way. Whether it was a matter of the type of work we do, the people with whom we work, or our conviction to the importance of critical discourse, the reception was positive, seen as opportunities to "cut through" to the heart of matters—an enhancement to practice rather than a distraction from it. As Pennie discovered:

> *It was incredibly useful for me to take our cycle of inquiry and apply it to my work. It's a framework that you can so easily take and ask: Am I asking these questions? What am I doing to help people do this kind of work?*

As we thought about the reception in the field, we considered how much some people thirst for transformation. They often want to think differently and to live their lives in profoundly different ways. When they find like minded persons, they are more likely (rather than less likely) to participate actively. As we thought about this outcome, it seemed to make sense in terms of what we know about change—that transformation in organizational and community settings is more likely to take place when there is openness to personal transformation.

Lessons from the swamp

While we have emphasized that our work (and this book) is about a learning journey— cycles of inquiry and critical Discourse guided by analysis, interpretation, and critique—we also gained important insights about the work itself, particularly in terms of how to better understand our role in it and what it means in terms of our scholarship. Clearly, our interpretation of this work emerges from what Schön (1987) referred to years ago as the "swampy lowlands." Although it is complex and messy work, the journey of and to critical engagement enables understanding. You will find one interpretation (ours) in Figure 1. In this rendition, situated learning through critical Discourse is seen as a necessary element in transformation at multiple levels, and there is dynamic interplay between developing social capital and co-empowerment.

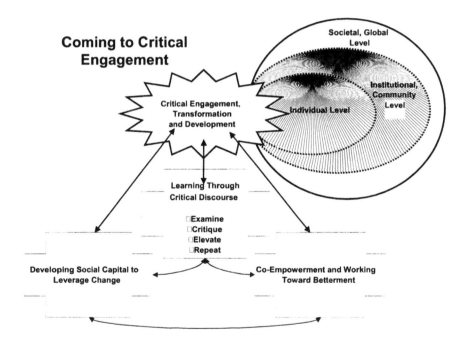

Figure 9–1: Coming to Critical Engagement

So, what is our role in all of this? Although academics, alone, do not and cannot "make" critical engagement happen in organizational and community work, we believe that academics can help (and can also disturb) the conditions necessary for it to happen. To do that, academics must find ways to balance sharing what they know with learning from, with, and through others, *especially* learning from, with, and through *everyday* people. Frank elaborates:

I think it was in chapter 1, but it may have been the Introduction, we talked about the importance of learning with, from, and through others. And I think we can think of plenty of examples where you learn with others in a collaborative effort. I also think we can think of plenty examples when we learn from others where someone has an experience and shares that experience and you learn from it. But one that is more vague, most vague, is the learning through others, and through not just what one has learned as a commodity, so to speak, but the emotionality, the cross currents—the whole package, everything that goes into what learning is about. And I think that's been one of the most important things for me—not just learning with and from others, but learning through others, through the aspirations, the churning in your stomach, and the way you get through the tough times—especially the times when you goof or flat-out fail.

Engagement, as we see it, abrogates arrogance and stimulates humility. Put bluntly, the things we abhor about elites and elitism—the penchant for exclusivity, dominance, and unilateral exercise of power—are replaced by inclusivity, collaboration, and participation. Simply stated, creating the conditions for critical engagement requires academics to model attributes that endear humans to one another. Anything less jeopardizes the journey to critical engagement, for academics and all others, and mocks the very pillars on which engagement rests. By exhibiting the values of engagement and working with others in like ways, the lived experience of engagement is profoundly democratic, emancipative, and empowering—precisely what engagement in civil society needs to be.

Ironically, hardly any of this is the stuff that comes to mind when we think about what it means to be an academic and to do academic work. But that may be just the point: change is needed and engagement may be a portal of change. For that reason we suppose, an early and frequent topic of conversation for our group was the matter of what it means to be scholarly. In being scholarly, academics seek to understand subject matter deeply; and knowledge is revisable, always subject to change. Wherever scholars may be at any point in time in their thinking about a subject or issue, the hope is that current understanding will illuminate the day-to-day unfolding of events; provide a direction and vision for the work; and render improvement of society in some way. And when scholars use concrete examples to illustrate or build theory, the "grand conversations" they often have among each other are rarely undertaken as self-contained episodes. On the contrary, cycles of inquiry are constant occurrences, endemic to the incessant effort to improve theory through research and practice; improve research through theory and practice; and, ultimately, improve practice through theory and research. Scholar*ly* (the adjective), then, refers to "how" scholars do what they do. Scholar*ship* (the noun) refers to the "it" of those endeavors.

What meaning does this have for engagement? We believe engagement is scholarship in popularized form. There is nothing that organizational and community partners do (and what we do with them) that is fundamentally different from what "scholars" do as we have just described. Partners may not do it as formally as academics and they may not call what they do "research" or "theory," but they are testing and retesting all the time; learning from experience constantly; and endlessly trying to understand better and do whatever they do, better. Consequently, we no longer use the term "colleague" to refer to "our fellow academics" only. Today, we use the term to refer to all those involved in engagement. And we engage in the same form and fashion with all colleagues and in virtually all endeavors, which is simply another way of saying what we said in chapter 3: that is, engaged learning is a set of practices that takes place in a variety of settings, on-campus and off-, and cuts across various forms of academic work—teaching, research, *and* service.

But the challenge is incorporating all of this into the rubric of "normal, typical, and expected" scholarship. Without question, we are not always at ease talking about our approach in the Academy. We feel, and in some ways are, different. While ours may be an "alternative way," we frequently find support for it in the field even when there is tepid response on campus. Richard describes his experience:

> It's interesting that even within our own university, in fact within our own department, Frank, somebody always seems to say: 'Oh, that's all so grandiose.' But when I'm in India it's like a stampede of people saying: 'Of course, that's what we should be doing! And, yes, we should be reconceptualizing and rethinking in a scholarly way about what all that means.' That to me goes back to the work of Paulo Freire in Latin America all those years ago, who was essentially saying the same sort of thing, but not from a university base.

What does it mean "to learn" to do this work?

Engaging in meta-discourse—beyond talking about individual projects—is an avenue to learning. A key feature of our collaborative work was a disposition to transformation of self. For different reasons and without realizing it at the beginning, each of us was open to and inviting of change. We participated viscerally, not just intellectually, and expressed deeply felt emotions—frustration, anger, puzzlement, excitement, and joy, among them. Along the way, we discovered that self-exploration with an openness to change is an important aspect of "learning how to learn" from this work.

We also learned that spending time with faculty from diverse backgrounds is not merely an "enjoyable" thing to do, although it certainly was that. It is a vital part of learning. Examining themes grounded in experience helped us probe issues from different vantage points. Moreover, there was collegial encouragement to try out new ideas and approaches in the field, as well as group interest in learning from the experimentation. With plenty of collegial support, the culture of our group stimulated, among other things, risk taking and dynamic communication, and also gave members the strength and courage to innovate. Very importantly, it became a safe space, an oasis of sorts. Pennie elaborates:

I think this process of meeting together with other faculty who have done the work is quite powerful. One of the risks for a novice is that when you face those obstacles, which there are plenty of, it is easy to stop because you're worried the outputs that are valued and prioritized won't emerge. How am I going to get my data or my publication if I'm spending all my time helping people come to some agreement on what goals they're talking about? So I think having a discourse process with colleagues is very useful. In some ways, our book is a model of how to learn together as faculty. What we're saying is examine your own work, critique it, elevate it, and repeat the process.

Venturing out to share what we were learning (first) at conferences was an important step in enriching our time together. We received important feedback from others, especially in terms of how *they* framed or interpreted our work, including the meaning (for them, if any) that it had. We learned that many colleagues are interested in going beyond "getting things done" or receiving a pre-digested list of bullet points about effective strategies. When we probed more deeply in that regard, we gained an important insight: there are colleagues who work alone or in small groups; tend to think and feel apart from the mainstream; and are not always connected consistently in networks of like-minded colleagues. Listening to what we had to say was reinforcing, if not comforting, to them—knowing that they were "not alone."

Having said that, the conclusion offered here is not meant to contradict the observation shared in chapter 1, namely, that there are simultaneous responses to this sort of work, not just one; and affirmation, anger, and puzzlement are among them. Although those words may not fully capture the range of interpretations, the plain fact is that this is controversial, if not contested, work. We experienced that, personally, when we would go directly from one of our conference sessions to a plenary address, wondering how the sessions could possibly be on the agenda at the same conference, let alone offered back-to-back.

Because our approach is different, a recurring question we received from colleagues is: "How did you ever get the administration to support you to do this?" Many were stunned when we told them (as described in chapter 1) that we undertook this as an overload effort. Although there was support at the unit level for our involvement, the project did not replace or substitute for a class or any other academic endeavor. Central administration graciously supported us with travel funds, assistantship support, and money for other operating items, including underwriting the publication costs associated with this book. In exchange, departments and administrations gained credit for our scholarly productivity and could follow our progress to see if this approach had any value, institutionally, in replicated or adapted form.

Without question, institutional characteristics help explain some of this: Michigan State is a large research university where there is space to undertake what we did. Yet, it is important to point out that not all of us will receive similar credit in our respective units for writing this book. In fact, one of us will likely receive no credit at all: refereed articles in specific journals are the currency of the realm in that department. On the other end of the continuum, another co-author needs to receive credit for this book to substantiate the significant expenditure of time on a project not exclusively connected to that colleague's professional domain.

Obviously, these are not unimportant matters, especially when one of us went through the promotion and tenure process during the writing of this book and another co-author will be going up soon for promotion to professor. Those circumstances, shared by others we know, have prompted a frequently heard question during conference sessions: "Is it possible for untenured faculty to get credit for this work?" That is another way of asking whether or not critical engagement is the exclusive territory of forty-something (and older) academics with professorial standing. Our response is simple and direct: it cannot possibly be if this work is to prosper and if the field is to thrive. The paradox of change is also an opportunity for institutional transformation, namely, that the approach described in this book is (we feel) reflective of what we interpret as the ethos of engagement. It is that very ethos, we believe, which higher education needs to embrace more deeply and pervasively.

Another way of answering this question is to be a bit more strategic: to pay explicit attention to documenting the processes, outcomes, and learning that emerge. This is another way of saying that emphasis needs to be placed on products, outcomes, and results (Driscoll and Lynton 1999). Rather than simply interpreting this as a way "to keep doing the work," we also see it as a way to improve the work. Pennie described such an experience:

> Did you (Cheryl) do that presentation with me and [another colleague] to the deans on campus in which we were trying to introduce them to the concept of engagement? Anyway, part of what [my colleague] had me do [because she was worried that the deans would view this as fluff because it doesn't produce the stuff that will help their units get rated, to be honest with you] was to take a somewhat instrumental approach, which actually got their attention. She had me create a table that showed what work I was doing in one column; what conference presentations I got in another column; and what money I generated and what publications I had produced in yet another column. Oh, and I also had a column on what has been changing in the community. Showing the mutuality of the work was very powerful for them. And some of the deans came up and said: 'We didn't know that this work could be this good for the community and good for the university.'

Being able to demonstrate that a project *really made a difference* (in community-based and academic-based terms) should not be a contested matter, especially for those who aspire to be engaged scholar–practitioners.

Concluding thoughts

As we gathered to leave the room at the end of our dialogue session on that steamy August day, we knew there was one chapter left to write. Years ago, each of us came to the table armed with literature that we believed would be a good starting point to talk about this joint effort. What literature makes the most sense now? And, more so, where might we locate ourselves intellectually in the vast possibilities of engagement scholarship? It is to intellectual questions we now turn attention.

References

Driscoll, A., and E. A. Lynton. Eds. 1999. *Making outreach visible: A guide to documenting professional service and outreach*. Washington, D. C.: American Association for Higher Education.

Kaplan, A. 1964. *The conduct of inquiry: Methodology for behavioral science*. Scranton PA: Chandler.

Kaplan, A. 1998. *The conduct of inquiry: Methodology for behavioral science*. New Brunswick NJ: Transaction Publishers.

Schön, D. 1987. *Educating the reflective practitioner*. San Francisco: Jossey-Bass.

CHAPTER 10

COMING TO CRITICAL ENGAGEMENT: INTELLECTUAL IMPLICATIONS

In this chapter we shift the lens, moving the focus from the personal to the intellectual. How (if at all) are we different, intellectually, having taken this journey together? First of all, it is clear to us that critical engagement is different from instrumental engagement, the latter with its primary emphasis on getting things done. That is not at all to say that critical engagement is impractical; it simply means that its value extends beyond the necessary objective of accomplishing things "out there." For us, the primary value is the effect it has on participants: helping them think intentionally and deeply about themselves, their work, and how they approach their practice. The outcomes can be transformative in the way that Tobin Hart (2001) interprets transformation:

> To transform is to go beyond current form. This means growth, creation, and evolution, an expansion of consciousness. When education serves transformation, it helps take us beyond the mold of categories, the current limits of social structure, the pull of cultural conditioning, and the box of self-definition; in thus going beyond, we ride the crest of the wave of creation, a wave that constantly collapses and rises into new forms. (2001, 149)

Transformative or not, critical engagement by design influences the quality and impact of the work undertaken. It does so by emphasizing the exercise of mindfulness in terms we discussed at the beginning of chapter 3. Mindfully engaged, those involved pay close attention to the "me, we, and it" of the work. As amply illustrated in the case examples shared in chapters 5–7, participants exit episodes of engagement thinking and feeling differently from the way they entered scenarios. Clearly, critical engagement is not about implementing steps, conforming to principles, or mimicking practice routines. Instead, it is an ethic—a commitment to constantly deepen understanding and improve practice. As an ethic, critical engagement is a lived, revelatory phenomenon.

The value of critique

Revelations certainly emerge from taking the time to reflect on practice. But reflecting on practice is a necessary but insufficient element in critical engagement: *critique* is what makes engagement critical. Critique enables seeing the world with fresh eyes—seeing things that were heretofore blocked or obscured from view and reframing reality in surprisingly new and meaningful ways. The value of critique is how it helps people *reinterpret* taken for granted, commonly accepted ways of thinking and acting; and how it enables people to evaluate the "facts and truths" presented by others.

The stark reality is that many aspects of life are accepted just as they appear without being given much (if any) thought. A good share of what we accept as "normal" represents acculturated features of everyday life, ways that people ordinarily think and act and, just as importantly, how people expect others to think and act. Take, for example, notions of "good leadership." In Western society, boldness and decisiveness are commonly associated with what it means to lead well. "Good leaders" are expected to beat the competition, if not be "number one," in whatever is the business at hand. However, being bold, decisive, and competitive is not the same as being participative, collaborative, and engaged. In fact, those inclined in the later directions might be judged to be "weak leaders," overly dedicated to process rather than to outcome.

Yet we rarely take the time to think about this: the prevailing conception of leadership represents a worldview of a particular sort—valuing assertiveness, if not aggressiveness, with priority given to completing tasks and achieving goals. There are many circumstances in which another worldview—grounded in the value of relationships, community building, and a caring ethic—is more appropriate to circumstances. The point here is not to say or conclude that one worldview is right and the other notion is wrong, or to say that the two conceptions are necessarily incompatible. The points to be made are these: (1) There is value in being attentive to multiple interpretations and possibilities; (2) One should not assume that there is only one way or a best way; and (3) It is important to be discerning about how options apply to the circumstance at hand.

Then there is the matter of being able to *trust what others say* and to have *faith in the sincerity of their intentions.* Along those lines, Princeton philosopher Harry Frankfort (2005) makes a strong case for why it is important to pay attention to what is happening in everyday life. In *On Bullshit,* Frankfort decries what he sees as pervasive attempts in modern society—emanating from virtually all sources—to manipulate people to think and act in certain ways. While he believes that most people are generally confident of their ability to recognize manipulation and to avoid being taken in by it, Frankfort thinks bullshit is being propagated skillfully these days. "Bullshitters" do not necessarily speak mistruths; instead, they portray "reality" in ways that *appear* compelling. The endgame is to influence others to affirm as valid what is being portrayed: for the propagator "to get away with what he says" (2005, 56).

What Frankfurt says about "bullshit in society" is similar to what organizational learning specialist Peter Senge and co-authors convey—more politely and perhaps more profoundly—in *Presence* (2004). Senge and colleagues assert that it was once safe to assume that the primary issue was getting from A to Z, in their words, *pursuing the unanswered question*. But contemporary circumstances demand that we evaluate what is being presented to us—to interpret and analyze, to consider and decide—and not to take what is being presented at face value. Consequently, Senge and colleagues contend that watchwords today are, in their words, *avoiding the unquestioned answer*.

Critique, therefore, is a way to counter the "spin" of partisan interpretations that are increasingly common place, not only in the media, but is also in society, generally, and in institutional life as well. And while critique may seem to be an elevated practice, available only to those with highly developed intellectual skills, the plain fact is that critique—often characterized by different labels—is one of the primary outcomes expected from going to college. From research on the undergraduate experience, we know that many students enter college as "absolute knowers," that is, they frequently defer to what authorities have to say about matters and also tend to believe there are simple "right and wrong" answers to complicated questions. The collegiate experience is supposed to help students transition from being absolute, dependent thinkers to becoming more complex, independent thinkers. The transition process involves being able to sift and sort through knowledge claims so that, over time, students discover—and then trust—their own voices. Educational researcher Marcia Baxter Magolda (2001) has an attractive way of referring to this transition—*self-authorship*, which (among other things) includes "viewing knowledge as relevant to a context" and assessing "knowledge claims as better or worse based on evaluation of relevant evidence" (2001, xvii).

But critique is not only a mental process or regimen, although it is certainly that. In our coming to critical engagement we found enormous value in a distinctive literature, that is, the literature dedicated to critique. While some of that literature is the outcome of critical analysis of higher education (e.g., Washburn 2005), there is an historical strand of literature, Critical Theory, which we found to be especially relevant because it is theoretically and conceptually rich. That literature includes the work of such analysts as Michel Foucault (1980); Antonio Gramsci (1995); Herbert Marcuse (1969); Jurgen Habermas (1987); Erich Fromm (1956); Miles Horton (1990); Cornell West (1998); belle hooks (1994), and John Dewey (1938), to name a few. We are also very much influenced by contemporary writers who have taken that literature and used it as interpretive frame of reference for considering contemporary matters, including Harry C. Boyte (2004) in community affairs; William M. Sullivan (2005) in professional education; and Gerald Delanty (2001) in the history of higher education. A special place in this regard is Stephen D. Brookfield's (2005) elegant translation and application of Critical Theory. The chapter headings of that book, *The Power of Critical Theory*, represent important mooring points for our evolving understanding of what it means to engage critically: challenging ideology; contesting hegemony; unmasking power; overcoming alienation; learning liberation; reclaiming reason; learning democracy; racializing criticality; gendering criticality; and teaching criticality.

How has Critical Theory influenced our thinking, specifically? While we believe (and hope) the answer to that question will be evident throughout this chapter, here is an example. With contemporary emphasis on higher education-community partnerships, civic engagement, and the need for universities to prove their value and earn their keep, it seems less necessary to make a case for engagement. Just the opposite rings true today: many persons (including academic administrators) embrace its value and are eager to implement it. *Is that a good thing*? What appears to be an odd question is anything but distracting. To pose the question is to stimulate critique, the purpose of which (in our case) is to stimulate the ability to engage mindfully, not to obstruct progress.

It is in this regard that observations made by Max Horkheimer (1947) decades ago seem applicable. Horkheimer warned of circumstances where thinking and reason become "instrumentalized." According to Brookfield (2005), that happens when answers and actions become disconnected from overarching questions and interpretations. With that outcome, thinking becomes "subservient to practical utilitarian ends" (69). In extreme form—and we believe there is some evidence to suggest this is happening in conjunction with the "Engaged Institution" movement—the instrument becomes a fetish, that is, an object of hyperactivity. Although the use of word "fetish" conjures up images of inappropriate behavior, that is certainly not the intention here. The purpose is to emphasize possible implications of hyperactivity, one of which is single-minded emphasis on engaging in the act or possessing the object and, with that outcome, closing off or limiting the need to think much about the phenomenon of attention. Thinking tends to be minimized when the object is perceived to have—in Brookfield's words—"innate worth" (71).

With hyperactivity, the focus is on answering *instrumental* questions. In engagement's case, those questions might include: How can we get more faculty members involved in engagement? How might we better organize and structure engagement efforts on our campus? While there is no doubt that questions like these are often posed and answered thoughtfully on our campuses, at issue for critique is whether instrumental questions crowd out *non-instrumental* questions. In the case of engagement, that means whether questions like these are posed: Is our campus beholden (over-engaged) to certain stakeholders and less involved (under-engaged) with others? If so, what explains the outcomes? What are the implications? What (if anything) might we do in response?

Again, posing questions like these does not subvert engagement, although instrumentally-focused colleagues might contest that point. Rather, the purpose is to elevate the level of discourse, that is, to enrich (if not ennoble) activities undertaken in engagement's name. In critical engagement, emphasis shifts from focusing exclusively on "what and how" questions to also considering "why, for whom, for what purpose, and so what" questions.

Frames of engagement

It is not as though we came together the first night compelled and committed to the value of critique. That is about as far from the truth as it can be. It is the journey that led us to critique. And, surprisingly, it was not the intellectual portion of that journey that "closed the deal" about critique's value: it was what we experienced and observed. It became clear to us over time that our interpretation of engagement was not the only interpretation and, more so, was not the predominant way, even though we believe our interpretation is compatible with how the father of engagement, Ernest Boyer, understood it. In a classic manuscript on the scholarship of engagement (cited in chapter 3), Boyer (1996) wrote:

> I have this growing conviction that what's needed is not just more programs, but a larger purpose, a larger sense of direction . . . . Increasingly, I'm convinced that the scholarship of engagement . . . means creating a special climate in which the academic and civic cultures communicate more continuously . . . what . . . Geertz describes as the universe of human discourse and enriching the quality of life for all of us." (1996, 20)

"Not *just* more" suggests that engagement is fundamentally more than the programs that carry its name; and that doing more and more engagement is not a fundamental feature of Boyer's point of view. For him, engagement is about a "larger purpose" and "sense of direction." It requires the creation of a "special climate" and lives in continuous communication and discourse among collaborators from higher education and civic society. We see Boyer's conception as visionary, relational, and transformative.

What also strikes us—intellectually and emotionally—about Boyer's conception of engagement is that it speaks to our sense of calling in ways that feel vocational. And we also notice how society-centered his definition is: Boyer does not define engagement in Academy-centered terms using language of the Engaged Institution; and we like that. Instead, he articulates a vision of engagement that (we think) has profound implications for what an engaged institution might be: it is more than higher education offering knowledge for society's benefit.

By comparison—not for the purpose of criticism but solely for the sake of critique—here is a second definition of engagement. It is offered by a higher education association, the American Association of State Colleges and Universities (2002, 7):

> The publicly engaged institution is fully committed to direct, two-way interaction with communities and other external constituencies through the develop-

ment, exchange, and application of knowledge, information, and expertise for mutual benefit.

This definition does not have the same feel to us as Boyer's interpretation. First of all, it is institution-centered. Second, it uses categorical language to describe partners (e.g., engaged institution, external constituencies). Third, it portrays engagement as an instrumental exchange—knowledge, information, and expertise to be generated, brokered, and used.

Certainly, the purpose of making those points is not to say that (in our eyes) Boyer "gets it" and the Association "does not"; or even to say that we prefer Boyer's interpretation, although in truth we do. The purpose is to illustrate what we gain from exercising critique, namely, *an understanding that engagement is more fluid than fixed.* In taking that position, we make a simple point: it is not unusual for the same word to carry different meanings, that is, to be interpreted differently by different people for different purposes. Take, for example, the word "freedom":

> Harvard sociologist Orlando Patterson (2005). . . contends there are at least two versions of what freedom means. In one version—the classic version rooted in liberal social philosophy—matters of 'civil liberty, public participation, and social justice' are emphasized. Legal systems have been built on that interpretation of freedom. There is also a second version of freedom, more contemporary in origin Patterson asserts, that is embraced by many people in everyday life. It is a 'radically privatized' interpretation of freedom, he says, one that conceptualizes freedom as a 'personal matter having to do with relations with others and success in the world.' In this interpretation of freedom, being free means being able to 'do what one wants and get one's way.' Whereas the first version of freedom informs matters of personal and civic engagement, the second notion speaks to personal autonomy and independence. (Fear and Avila, Forthcoming)

Exploring the possibility that engagement may be interpreted in multiple ways led us to the "framing" literature. Frames, accordingly to Berkeley scholar George Lakoff (2004, xv), are "mental structures that shape the way we see the world." Frames not only influence the way we think "they shape the goals we seek, the plans we make, the way we act, and what counts as a good or bad outcome of our actions." Putting this understanding into practice helps us understand why Boyer sees engagement in one way; why we interpret it as we do; why an association of higher education institutions defines engagement as it does; why (from chapter 1) Scott Peters thinks about engagement as public scholarship; and why Mark Wood (also from chapter 1) talks about it as transformed non-conformism. Each frame of engagement (using Lakoff's words) represents a way of "seeing the world." Thus, while critique is the center of gravity in our frame, there is no hint of it in the Association's definition. And because each frame influences "the goals we seek" (again, drawing on Lakoff's words), Peters sees engagement as distinctive scholarly work whereas Wood sees engagement as a way to achieve a just and equitable society. Certainly, these are not incompatible conceptions, but—by the same token—it would be a mistake to fly past distinctions and concentrate on "implementing engagement" only. With different frames there are also different outcomes in mind.

Exploring the politics of engagement: Discourses in, of, and about engagement

There is also a *social dynamic* to framing that we believe needs to be considered; and understanding that dynamic was an important outcome of our journey to critical engagement. When frames become compelling expressions to a sufficient number of people they become embellished as *discourses* (a concept discussed in the Introduction). Educational theorist James Gee and colleagues (1996, 10) interpret a discourse as a way "of talking . . . acting, interacting, believing, valuing . . . so as to display or to recognize a particular social identity." Another way of saying this is that those affiliated with a discourse take a distinctive (if not unique) stance about a phenomenon; declare that stance publicly; and dedicate activity to honing the clarity, coherence, and compelling nature of their stance.

When a sufficient number of like-minded people share a discourse they become members of a *discourse community* and engage each other in a variety of activities, including seminars-workshops-conferences, professional associations, and courses-degree programs. Activities in some discourse communities become professionalized, thereby offering positions, titles, and professional identity to members (service-learning is an example). Other discourse communities are thematic in nature (public scholarship is an example): affiliates incorporate the discourse in the work they do and in the roles they play. In both instances, discourse communities have distinctive ways of thinking and practicing. Members develop agendas for discussion and action in ways that galvanize community attention; and establish routines to guide understanding and behavior (e.g., principles of good practice). Over time, norms of thinking and behaving become habitual, that is, taken for granted as "the way," rarely questioned *inside* the discourse. Of course, it is not uncommon for persons *outside* the discourse to point out deficiencies and flaws they perceive in others' discourses, as was illustrated in the Peters–Wood exchange presented in chapter 1.

What are the discourses of engagement? That question represents fertile ground for scholarly inquiry and work in this regard is underway. For example Derek Barker (2004) a Rutgers political scientist, has discussed what he considers to be five practices in the scholarship of engagement, including public scholarship and participatory research. And, Stephen Bowen (2005), a senior fellow with the Association of American College and Universities and an administrator at Bucknell University, has differentiated among "four related but different ways" of framing engagement with respect to undergraduate student involvement.

Although work of this sort is vital for building an intellectual foundation in engagement, also needed we believe is exploration of what might be called *the politics of engagement* (Fear et al. 2004), that is, investigating engagement as a contested (rather than as a monolithic) expression. For example, it is not unusual to find multiple discourses about the same phenomenon as different people enunciate distinctive "takes" on a topic of shared interest. Consider community organizers and college-university presidents. If community organizers and presidents do not share a common discourse of engagement, which is often the case we suspect, then that is probably because they come from different backgrounds, work in different circumstances, have different responsibilities, and face different issues. This interpretation helps explain why discussions of the same phenomenon can differ across discourse communities, meaning why engagement in Extension and engagement in Service-Learning, for example, may not be discussed in exactly the same way; and why certain public gatherings (conferences, for example) are often organized with a particular "slant" on engagement.

Making the point that there are different discourses *of* engagement (discourse as noun) is not the same as talking about the importance of discourse *in* engagement (discourse as verb). For example, it is clear from what we have written in this book (consider the discussion in chapter 5) that discourse *in* engagement is an indelible feature of our discourse *of* engagement. While true in our case, discourse (the verb) is not a fundamental feature of *all* engagement discourses. For evidence of that conclusion, re-read the Association's definition of engagement. But rather than view the existence of multiple discourses as problematic (e.g., we are not all on the same page), distinctions serve an important scholarly function: inviting those who frame engagement differently to participate in discourse *about* engagement. That way, engagement becomes a *subject* of scholarly attention, not just an *object* of instrumental attention.

For these reasons, we find it useful to differentiate among three interpretations of discourse:

- Discourses *of* engagement (there are multiple discourses of engagement)
- Discourse *in* engagement (there is discourse in engagement), and
- Discourse *about* engagement (engagement is a subject of discourse).

Engagement: From liberal modernity to discursive post-modernity

We believe that framing discourse in multiple ways opens the door to discussing engagement issues that otherwise might not be considered. For example, in addition to lauding philanthropy's investments in engagement, a question for critique is this: When philanthropists take a specific stance on engagement, what are the implications (indeed, the constraints) on higher education and for communities—as resource-starved as they are? And, in addition to applauding the subtle or overt pressure put on higher education by legislators to engage, also at issue is this: What are the consequences if public officials make demands on higher education to engage in particular places, on particular topics, with particular groups, and for particular purposes?

Perhaps the most important outcome of engaging in discourse about engagement is when the lens of critique focuses on the institution of higher education itself. That happens when we engage in discourse (the verb) regarding engagement (the noun). We were assisted in that task by reading Gerald Delanty's insightful book, *Challenging Knowledge: The University in the Knowledge Society* (2001). Historical and sociological in approach, Delanty helps readers understand the socio-cultural circumstances that have influenced various "ideas of a university" as they have emerged in different national contexts and across time.

The rise of the modern university came during a time (approximately from the French Revolution to the end of the nineteenth century) when higher education gained secular identity and gained cosmopolitan character. Delanty calls this era, *liberal modernity*. An example of university development during this time is the distinctly German interpretation of higher education promulgated by Wilhelm von Humboldt in the nineteenth century. Perhaps best known for affirming the research function and, with that, influencing the rise of the research university, the core of von Humbold's idea of a university was a preferred relationship between higher education and society at large. In exchange for performing fundamental social purposes—including serving as a training ground for professionals and helping to cultivate the moral character of society—von Humboldt sought autonomy for the university from institutional influences (the government and Church in particular) and also from societal influences, in general. von Humboldt's vision for the university was for it to "protect culture from society" (Delanty 2001, 46). For that to happen, he wanted the university to evolve as an institution more "on its own terms" than in response to external demands and dictates; and he also believed that the university needed to have the freedom to operate as a cultural agency and agent. With von Humboldt's idea in place, the university evolved in important ways. For example, a range of disciplinary specialties emerged and student development was undertaken in secular terms.

The idea of higher education changed dramatically in the twentieth century during a time that Delanty calls *organized modernity*—when knowledge was generated and controlled by experts. Far from being separated from society, higher education's value became rooted in how well it served society, most notably in conjunction with the industrial and scientific revolutions. It is in this regard that Etzkowitz and Leydesdorff (1997) write about the "triple helix" of university, industry, and government—giant monoliths co-evolving in connected fashion with each institution serving the others' needs.

The university in this environment was valued for the uses it had and the users it served. Clark Kerr, a leading mid-century voice, wrote eloquently about a purpose-driven university in his provocative, *The Uses of the University*

(1963). While Kerr believed that "use" was the idea of a university in American terms, he found the reference to "university" restrictive and inaccurate. The American idea was not about *uni*ty he reasoned; it was about multiplicity of intentions, expressions, and contributions. The *multiversity,* as Kerr coined it, served a variety of purposes, masters, and outcomes. But Kerr was not an enthusiast for the multiversity as much as he was a realist regarding its place in the American socio-cultural context. He wryly concluded that this institution became, in very practical terms, what it needed to become. In a haunting passage, Kerr wrote:

> The Idea of Multiversity has no bard to sing its praises; no prophet to proclaim its vision; no guardian to protect its sanctity. It has it critics, its detractors, its transgressors. It has it barkers selling its wares to all who listen—and many do. But it also has its reality rooted in the logic of history. It has an imperative rather than a reasoned choice among elegant alternatives. (Kerr 1963, 6, as quoted in Delanty 2001, 55–56)

In Delanty's view, we have been migrating out of organized modernity since the 1980s—entering a new (yet to be defined) era, a time when higher education's place in society is likely to be redefined in fundamental terms. The migration is the result of a variety of pushes and pulls—pushes coming largely in the form of negative reactions to the ill-effects of organized modernity ("big science," "big government," and "big industry," most notably) and pulls coming largely from the democratization of knowledge and the movement to organizational forms that are less hierarchical, linear, and authority-based than the prevailing institutions of organized modernity.

Delanty believes that higher education has contributed to the pushes *and* pulls, and has done so in its uniquely contorted way. In what it stands for, enables, and does, higher education *simultaneously* supports and subverts the dominant paradigm; conventional and progressive work co-exist, functioning side by side, in the same institutional environment. This both–and existence also applies, as Delanty sees it, to how higher education is responding to its possible transformation as an *institution* serving society in a post-modern environment. While there are many and varied initiatives underway that suggest that transformation is inevitable, at issue is whether these are widespread expressions of new institutional values and priorities, apart from the myriad work faculty, staff, and students undertake as *personal* expressions *in* institutional settings.

Delanty believes it is clear where the institutional matter settles: the university aids and abets organized modernity, both as proponent and apologist. Consider, Delanty asserts, how the university mimics the quintessential system of organized modernity—the market—in terms that Slaughter and Leslie (1997) call *academic capitalism.* Operating very much like capitalists do in financial markets, administrators, faculty, and professional staff act as entrepreneurs (state-supported in the public sphere) in a competitive academic environment, competing for students, funding, and market share.

One way to explain academic capitalism is to portray it as means of survival: necessary for the university as a system, and for the people in it, to remain viable in a turbulent, hostile environment. While that is certainly true—and readily apparent to even the casual observer of everyday university life—it would be a mistake to portray the university as victim. It is also instigator. A creation of organized modernity, the modern university (particularly the research university) is now *an engine of it*. Because of that, the university has a significant stake in maintaining (if not strengthening the grasp of) organized modernity. Slaughter and Leslie elaborate:

> The postindustrial technological revolution depends on universities. Universities provide the training necessary for the increasing numbers of professionals employed by corporations to invent, maintain, and innovate with regard to sophisticated technologies and products. In a growing number of cases universities are the sites where new technologies and products are developed, often in partnership with business, through funding provided in part by the state. (Slaughter and Leslie, 1997, 27 as quoted in Delanty 2001, 122)

In Delanty's view, market-driven academic capitalism is the dominant mode by which the university performs *external* activities. For *internal* affairs, Delanty sees the university mimicking another embellishment of organized modernity, the bureaucracy. The preferred form of bureaucratic engagement is *the new managerialism* (2001, 106), a form that undermines higher education's collegial culture:

> As a new managerial ethos is pervading the university, deans and heads of departments are coming more to resemble managers than academic figures. University presidents were once trained to be moral leaders, but in the transformation of higher education over the past few decades they are increasingly forced to become entrepreneurs. . . . Reform through managerialism becomes a strategy of academic management (Currie and Vidovich 1998). Power becomes centralized in the hands of a few senior managers who make decisions quickly. Academic self-governance is not time-efficient and consequently it is eroded in a world of corporate style decision-making. (Delanty 2001, 107)

With Delanty's critique in mind, a question looms large: *Is engagement as promulgated today an expression of organized modernity? Or is it a manifestation of the post-modern era, perhaps higher education's "new idea?"* Circumspect in judgment, we believe that higher education is being pulled in both directions: engagement is both protective of the status quo (as an artifact of late-stage organized modernity) *and* pushing the boundaries of change (as an expression of early-stage post-modernity).

We think about that conclusion each and every time we hear about or witness a new "engagement" project. Many of these efforts seem to be outreach-as-engagement—engagement used communicatively (as a language expression) to convey a university connection with an off-campus audience: "We are engaged." But other efforts cannot be explained that way; in those efforts, engagement seems more than a new word for a traditional activity. It is non-traditional activity when the work undertaken is more than "universities bringing to bear knowledge on problems." That interpretation feeds into Delanty's analysis of knowledge in post-modern perspective. "The university is no longer the primary site of knowledge production, having been challenged by a range of knowledge producers" he writes (2001, 3).

Drawing on Michael Gibbons et al. (1984) seminal work, Delanty believes a new model of knowledge, Mode 2, is replacing Mode 1 of organized modernity. In Mode 1, knowledge is produced by experts who conduct their work in privileged sites—notably in university settings—using sanctioned routines to produce valid outcomes. In Mode 2, knowledge outlets proliferate and more people have access to knowledge and engage as actors in knowledge creation, evaluation, and application.

Mode 2 is illustrated in four features of contemporary life. First, living in a "network society" (Castells 1996) not only enables people to exchange information and knowledge with each other, it is easy to access information and knowledge through the World Wide Web and other technology-supported instruments. Second, because formal education is more accessible to the public, more people than ever before are capable of acquiring, evaluating, and acting on information. Third, there is a renaissance of sorts going on: people acknowledging and respecting "the wisdom" of local knowledge as contextually and substantively rich. And, fourth, professionals in various fields (public health, for example) are helping the public learn how to organize, conduct, and apply research (e.g., undertaking a community health audit).

For these and other reasons, the transition to Mode 2 represents the *democratization of knowledge* where democratization means the "participation of more and more actors in the social construction of reality" (2001, 6). With all this in mind, Delanty argues that

> We are living in a knowledge society in the sense that social actors have ever greater capacities for self-interpretation and action (Giddens 1990, 1991; Melucci 1996). Professional knowledge and lay knowledge are less separate then they used to be. The idea of a knowledge society refers also to something more basic. the opening up of new cognitive fields which have a reflexive relation to knowledge. (2001, 5)

Of course, those with expert status may choose to criticize Mode 2 knowledge, rendering it inferior—something less than "knowledge" (unevaluated information, perhaps), and not to be trusted. But Delanty believes that defending an exclusive path to knowledge will prove fruitless, largely because a "major epistemic/cognitive shift" (2001, 5) in society has already occurred: many people do not believe that knowledge is or should be the *exclusive* province of experts and institutions, especially with respect to matters in the social and cultural domains. In the name of deliberative democracy and to protect themselves against untrustworthy agents, many people prefer to sift and sort through issues and come to their own conclusions.

All of this serves as a threat to and as an opportunity for the university. To seize the opportunity, the university will need to set aside its claim to knowledge primacy and, instead, take up another knowledge-related role. Here is how Delanty sees it:

> The university today. . . *can be the most important site of interconnectivity* in what is now a knowledge society. There is a proliferation of so many different kinds of knowledge that no particular one can unify all the others. The university cannot re-establish the broken unity of knowledge, but it can *open up avenues of communication between these different kinds of knowledge*, in particular knowledge as science and knowledge as culture. Of what would a communicative concept of the university consist? (2001, 6, italics added)

If the university does this, it will embrace a "new idea"—an idea as relevant for our time as were the previous ideas of a university. What might we call this idea? Let's call it *discursive post-modernity*. The university will specialize in creating discursive opportunities among various knowledge systems and actors. Rather than seek answers only, universities will encourage people to seek understanding, especially with regard to the most contested, politicized, and problematic matters of the day.

This way of thinking, we believe, contextualizes in contemporary reality Boyer's conception of engagement, making it much more than a preference among multiple interpretations of engagement. Instead, it becomes an absolute necessity—a tool for the times.

Of course, what we propose as vision is already happening. At issue, only, is whether it will become the valence point of the Engaged Institution. Will the Engaged Institution be a place where engagement is a communicative expression, an activity, a thing people do? Or, will it also be a place where engagement is a communicative practice, an ethic, a mode of living?

Critique of the Engaged Institution

It is for these reasons that we cannot accept uncritically the Engaged Institution discourse so prominent in today's literature and conversation. Although the title is so appealing to us, we are not sure what it means and how adherents are using the term. If, in using it, the intention is to sustain and embellish organized modernity, we want no part of it. Consequently we are cautious in approach, concerned that engagement will be dragged into the prevailing paradigm and become—in Foucault's (1980) words—a "regime of truth," accepted unequivocally as "the way." If that happens, engagement as transformation is doomed, its heart and soul cut away. It will have been co-opted by the prevailing paradigm, reinterpreted to suit its purposes.

Stimulated by Delanty's analysis, two issues for critique are considered here in relationship to the Engaged Institution discourse. First, there is the matter of recognizing that institutional behaviors are *always* influenced, in part, by self-interest. At issue, then, is how and in what ways (not whether) self-interest is expressed by higher education through engagement? That means taking seriously the issue that higher education may sometimes use engagement as an instrument to achieve self-serving ends. When is engagement valued primarily as a means to generate valued system inputs (external revenue) and outputs (publications)? Are there instances where "preferred" collaborators—persons, groups, and entities with access to influence and resources—are favored over others? Do institutions have a special interest (if not a stake) in promoting certain engagement initiatives because they serve the institutional good?

The relevance of posing these questions was underscored recently in comments made by Richard Freedland (2005), president of Northeastern University. Freedland wrote in *The Chronicle Review* (of the *Chronicle of Higher Education*) that he believes the "most significant and positive effects of universities on cities" have been "byproducts of efforts to strengthen our institutions," "defensive actions taken to protect our institutions," and initiatives that cities "demand of the university as a quid pro quo." And based on his study of higher education engagement in a variety of urban locations and by different types of higher education institutions—from Philadelphia and the University of Pennsylvania to San Francisco and San Francisco State University—Dave Maurrasse (2001) summed up his analysis with these unsettling words:

> Colleges and universities should not be concerned solely with their self-interest, but if their missions are furthered by partnerships with local communities, all the better, as long as communities are not harmed in the process. (2001, 194)

The second matter for critical analysis is this: the Engaged Institution initiative is being framed largely by elites, that is, by those inside and outside higher education who occupy positions of authority, have access to and leverage financial resources, and wield considerable influence. For example, university presidents and chancellors authored reports associated with the influential Kellogg Commission on the Future of State and Land-Grant Universities, which was funded by The W. K. Kellogg Foundation and sponsored by the National Association of State Universities and Land Grant Colleges (1999). There is nothing inherently wrong with actions like that: networks of like-minded CEOs can make important reforms in literally any industry. Having said that, there are implications associated with elite interactivity: first, when elites engage each other over an extended period of time they are likely to develop a discourse on whatever is the topic of attention; and, second, because they are in positions of privilege they have the ability to act on shared beliefs, perhaps even using their power to counter or mitigate the influence of competing discourses.

A special concern is when elite engagement becomes *hegemonic*. Associated historically with the work of Italian economist Antonio Gramsci (1995), hegemony is a particularized expression of ideology by an elite group. In unvarnished and non-hegemonic form, elites exercise power directly, trying to get others to do what they prefer. Hegemony, on the other hand, is anything but unvarnished: it is a subtle, indirect expression of power. It occurs when non-elites *internalize* the preferences of elites, such that elite preferences pervade everyday life. Brookfield (2005) observes:

> The important thing to remember about hegemony is that it works by consent. People are not forced against their will to assimilate ideology. They learn to do this, quite willingly, and in the process they believe that this ideology represents their best interests. Hegemony works when people actively welcome and support beliefs and practices. . . . (2005, 95)

An insidious expression of hegemony in higher education, generally, and an in engagement, particularly, is when elites "do the thinking" for others, concluding (for whatever reason) that X is "the right and proper way" of thinking about engagement. The situation worsens when a preferred way of thinking is converted into a set of practice guidelines. With thinking done for others (especially when controversial issues are presented in uncontested terms) and with implementation strategies laid out, what might otherwise be a complex matter is presented straightforwardly, akin to "painting by the numbers." Habermas (1987) warns that practices like these can lead to what he calls the "colonization of the lifeworld"—when preferred thoughts and routines of the elite become routinized in the way that everyday people think about and live their lives. Colonization is stimulated when non-elites acquiesce to elite preferences by seeking benefits that are available by going along with elite preferences and prescriptions. Non-elites can act assertively, if not aggressively, in the quest to secure benefits. Recognizing that possibility, a commonplace practice among elites is to encourage non-elites to "run with the ball," that is, to implement ideas advanced by elites. When done publicly and seen by others, that tactic affirms and validates what the prevailing power structure has in mind and seeks to accomplish.

While all of this takes place frequently before our very eyes—and we believe it happens all the time—it is not always easy to see. It happens beneath the veneer because its successful application *demands* that it remain imperceptible to the majority. And while it is dangerous to impute motives (with the corresponding risk of "seeing what is not there"), there is the matter of detecting patterns. This happens when certain activities and behaviors take place in the same setting, and when a pattern is detected across settings.

But to attribute all of this to intentional, strategic behavior is a mistake. First of all, not all of what we have described is done with manipulative intent. Some of what we have observed over the years seems to be (1) a function of unconscious behavior; (2) explained away by people "just doing what they need to do" to survive and thrive in contemporary situations; and (3) seen by some as "good leadership." Furthermore, as Foucault (1980) points out, because "power over" is so prevalent in society, there are numerous instances where everyday people simply do what they think others expect of them. This phenomenon, which Foucault calls "self-surveillance," involves self-policing, that is, everyday people governing *their own* thinking and behavior so that it conforms to expectations.

Is it possible to counter possible hegemonic influences in the Engaged Institution discourse? Yes. Rather than talk about engagement exclusively through the filter of an Engaged Institution, focus instead on the essence of engagement—in philosophy, in theory, and in practice. Then (and only then) pose the question: Given these understandings, what are the implications for creating Engaged Institutions? Another strategy to "contest hegemony" (using Brookfield's words) is to convene conversations among people who represent *different* discourses of engagement. The purpose is not to privilege a particular discourse (the noun), but to enhance understanding about engagement through discourse (the verb).

We propose these approaches for a simple reason: we believe that focusing the conversation—first and foremost—on institutional matters not only changes the fundamental nature of the conversation (e.g., what you talk about), it privileges the voices of those who have fiduciary responsibility for running institutions. To counter that, we recommend putting emphasis on exploring and understanding the phenomenon—engagement—a phenomenon owned by everybody and controlled by nobody (at least in concept).

Angst and collegial professionalism

So much of what we say cuts against the grain of commonly accepted thinking. It is not easy for us to put these thoughts on paper; people might think we have an ax to grind. Because of that, co-author Bawden urged us to include a treatment of our *angst* in this chapter. In making his case, here is what he wrote to his co-authors:

> In the autoethnographic narrative that we have developed, the two key points of our departure are the impact of theories and experiences on ourselves, and our emphasis on the scholarly aspects of engagement. But it ain't easy being critical!

Critique is not meant to be—and should not be taken as—destructive criticism. Critique explores issues from multiple angles. Destructive criticism, on the other hand, diminishes and demeans others.

Know that we come to critique not out of bitterness or arrogance. We are not disingenuous, self-absorbed, or "anti-university." We do not want to "bite the hand that feeds us." We are neither passive aggressive nor disloyal. We do not see ourselves as "renegades" or "saviors." And we have no desire to either disrupt or derail important work.

Having said all of that, we do not believe the engagement movement can prosper unless there is robust consideration of issues. What surprises us more than anything else is how little we see of that, except with respect to instrumental matters. More discourse is needed for at least two important reasons. First, vetting issues broadly is a sensible first step in selecting reasonable courses of action. Second, exploring matters from various angles is a routine practice in academic life. Engagement, it would seem, can only benefit from critique.

For example, while it is inarguable that there is an engagement movement underway in higher education (it is, for example, the theme of a recently published book edited by Kezar and Associates 2005), at issue is this: What are movements about? As Tony Chambers (2005, 4, 5) rightly declares, movements are populated by people who are "engaged in a collective enterprise to establish a new order of life" (Blumer 1939); and movements "consist of informed networks of actors engaged in a conflict for the control of material or symbolic stakes on the basis of shared identities" (Diani 1992). While not quibbling with those interpretations (they are spot on), we ask: Are those words applicable to engagement? We ask that question for a reason.

Brookfield (2005) warns that words can "become tools that are stripped of layers of meaning and dislocated from their history of social use" (71). A good example of that is "transformation," a word used so glibly these days that it is becoming devoid of essential meaning, namely, referring to profound change (e.g., Mezirow and Associates 2000). Given that concern, we raise this question: What are the implications when movements are championed—as is engagement—primarily *from within* the institutions that are the targets of change?

Palmer (1997; 1999) reminds us that social movements are populist initiatives undertaken *against* institutions—that is, struggles against the prevailing power structure—not as initiatives undertaken *by* institutions. He writes:

> Movements start when individuals who feel very isolated in the midst of an alien culture come in touch with something life-giving. . . . They make one of the most important decisions a human being can make, which I have come to call the decision to live "divided no more," the decision to no longer behave differently on the outside than one knows one's truth to be on the inside. I call it "the Rosa Parks decision" because she is emblematic of the historic potentials of a decision that might seem to be "merely inward". . . . It was a lonely decision being made in the inwardness of many people's lives for which Rosa Parks became the icon and exemplar—and it was a decision that changed the lay and the law of the land. (Palmer 1999, 31)

Think of movements in our society worth noting, those associated with matters of racial and gender equality; environmental justice; and corporate rightdoing, to name a few. In those (and other cases), the charge for change is led by people of all walks of life—including those affiliated with other institutions—who, fed up with business as usual, decide to take action. That is not to say that outsiders act alone. They are often joined by institutional insiders, many of whom are probably "tempered radicals," as discussed in chapter 3. But, at issue, is this: If championed primarily from within, what would be the outcomes? We speculate that it would be achieving just enough change to mitigate external pressure and/or to direct change in self-serving ways. As noted in chapters 6 and 7, the point of developing social capital and aiming toward co-empowerment is for citizens to be in charge of improving their own lives.

Politically, it makes sense that insiders want to be in charge in times of change, and there is no question that well intentioned insiders often work aggressively to change the way business is done. But does that option always serve the greater good? And even if it does, what is that change about? One way of answering the first question is to conclude that—yes—the engagement movement IS generally about serving the greater good, and we are better off for it. An answer to the second question—a more difficult and contested question—is that the engagement movement may be a revolution designed to change higher education in fundamental ways. If it is, then we need to acknowledge that the engagement movement is *not* the only movement afoot in higher education. There are other movements underway, including (to name only a few) the sustainability movement in higher education (e.g., Blewitt and Cullingford 2004); the spirituality movement in higher education (e.g., Chickering et al. 2005); and the learning college movement (e.g., Tagg 2003). Even when core ideas associated with other movements reinforce engagement, the politics of having multiple movements in play simultaneously means this: different partisans (from inside and outside higher education) seek to make their ideas center stage in what higher education is and does. Even if they see each other as kindred spirits, they are still likely to maintain focus on their agenda—to have a significant say, if not *the* say, about higher education's future. The outcome, which happens *all the time* in literally all domains of institutional life, is a "shoot out at the OK Corral," a political contest waged among partisans. We have seen all of this happen so many times before—with the power plays, strategic positioning, winning over of funding sources, and soliciting of support that goes with it—all designed to change the system in essential ways, and a good share of it with noble intent.

And while all of this is happening, business as usual—the dominant discourse—typically tightens its grip on the way things are done, finding ways to deflect the winds of change. One way the dominant discourse maintains control—as we pointed out in chapter 3 (from Barr and Fear 2005)—is through co-optation. The dominant discourse *accepts* a new idea, but it accepts it on *its* terms—subtle redefining, diluting, or (worse yet) corrupting it—so that essential characteristics of the dominant discourse are preserved.

All of what we have just described is nothing more than a storyline from a *very* old book—using age-old rubrics to determine who will be the "king or queen of the hill." As we see things, it is time to say "Enough!" As an alternative, we prefer exploring *a pathway that in philosophy and method is consistent with the ethos of engagement.* A good example is expressed by John B. Bennett in his *Academic Life: Hospitality, Ethics, and Spirituality* (2003). Bennett's storyline is that engagement is a lived experience where—in everyday efforts (on-campus and off)—core virtues are in evidence, including hospitality, integrity, perseverance; and core capabilities are exercised, such as discernment, humility, attending to others, and seeking self-knowledge. Engagement, then, is a *way of being* with an associated set of practices.

This way of thinking has profound implications for the engagement movement. What it means is that engagement is not simply an institutional platform or a vision for society—even if that platform or vision speaks to our hearts and compels our energies. It is more than that: it is about *what is inside us, and how that "inside-ness," is expressed in the platforms and visions we espouse and embrace.* This is nothing more than another way of expressing Gandhi's oft-quoted aphorism: "You must be the change you wish to see in the world" (http://www.sfheart.com/Gandhi.html). Although that sounds simple in theory, it is challenging to put into practice because it requires that change be an authentic expression of personhood: You *are* (become) the change you seek. That requires abandoning what Bennett calls "insistent individualism," which he believes corrupts institutions (not just individuals) through its emphasis on self-promotion, hierarchy, and ego-rewards. "The disposition to behave in self-absorbed and self-protecting ways and to put narrow self-interest of the welfare of others or a broader common good is widespread," writes Bennett (2003, 21).

Bennett's counterpoint to insistent individualism in academic life is what he terms *collegial professionalism*, an emphasis on "connectivity, and imaginative empathy. . . and dedication to the. . . needs of the other" (2003, 37, and also see Bennett 1998). In collegial professionalism, power is exercised through relationships *with* others, not exercised by having power *over* others:

> In this relational view, the concept of power is transformed. It no longer means only the unilateral exercise of force to achieve one's objectives in relationship to the other. Power is now recognized as the capacity to be influenced and affected as well as to influence and affect—it involves both giving and receiving. In Loomer's (1981, 149) words, "the size and worth of an individual or a group is measured and created by the range, intensity, and concreteness of relationships that can be sustained. (Bennett, 2003, 41)

The portal to sharing power with others comes when we fully embrace what Bennett describes as the virtue of *hospitality*. In one of the most elegant passages in the book—and we believe the entire engagement literature—Bennett writes:

> To practice hospitality is to share with others in ways that involve receiving. . . Truly to share is to invite others into our world, eventually allowing their strangeness and unfamiliarity to affect and engage us. Sometimes the other is literally a stranger, but it may also be someone in our midst whom we have ignored. In either case, hospitable engagement can be threatening as well as enriching—challenging our comfortable truths, but also enlarging them and compensating for limitations in our understanding. . . . A newly, jointly constructed

world may then emerge. In its fullness, hospitality bears the fruit of reciprocity, an ongoing dialectic of the host and guest. (2003, 48)

Our group has thought of this jointly constructed world as the engagement interface—a place neither "in here" nor "out there"—but, rather, as a shared opportunity for rich interaction.

A cornerstone of Bennett's collegial professionalism is *conversation*. Bennett makes a case for what he calls "hospitable conversations" (2003, 109) that "lack hierarchies," have "no prior order of standing among the voices," and where there "is no master of ceremonies," "no keeper of the gate," or "bouncer who examines credentials." Conversations of this sort need to be ones (borrowing from Oakeshott (1989, 98) where there is "no chairperson" or "predetermined course," and where quality "springs from the qualities of voices which speak" and value "lies in the relics it leaves behind in the minds of those who participate." Conversations like these need to occur on campus, and not just off, Bennett asserts: "Engaging in, rather than avoiding, courageous conversation about the raveled edges of contemporary higher education can rejuvenate initial enthusiasm and provide hope for the future" (2003, 135). But rather than having these exchanges be ad hoc, episodic happenings, Bennett sees the need for conversation as an indelible characteristic; and, with that, he calls for reframing higher education as "conversationally defined institutions" (145) where "conversation is true dialogue, not sequential or seriatim monologues." He continues:

Marked by respect toward participants as well as subject matter, it is neither controlled nor controlling. Indeed, conversation requires that participants put at risk the routine and other familiar presumptions and suppositions in which they dwell. Then, something new can happen. . . . It can revive purpose-defined institutions. (2003, 146)

Engaging in this way makes possible what Bennett sees as *covenantal institutions* and *a covenantal society*. His conception of "covenant" is how we see engagement, especially as it takes place in the engagement interface. A covenant

. . . is rooted in member's commitment to each other in public pursuit of the common good. Covenants are public vows, declarations, or pledges to each other. They are created and maintained through the promises of each member to others—the promises of practicing hospitality, of being open in sharing and receiving, and of committing to mutuality and reciprocity. The covenantal community is both internal and external to its members, cherished privately and visible publicly. (2003, 157)

The irony to us in sharing this extensive interpretation of Bennett's thinking is that his work was not on our initial reading list. Its value emerged through our coming to critical engagement—as we went though the sifting and sorting of what really mattered to us and, with that, in discovering our voice. The path we followed (and still follow) is not unlike the road to *self-authorship* that Baxter Magolda (2001 and cited earlier in this chapter) believes is experienced by many young adults. That journey includes the subtle and delicate interrelationships among epistemological evolution, sense of self, and the influences of significant others. In discussing the issue of "becoming the author of one's life" among young adults Baxter Magolda uses words that apply equally well to our coming to critical engagement:

> Becoming the authors of their own lives involved *reshaping what they believed* (epistemology), their sense of self (intrapersonal), and their relationships with others (interpersonal). Participants shifted from 'how you know' to 'how I know' and in so doing began to choose their own beliefs. They *acknowledged the inherent uncertainty of knowledge* and *took up the challenge of choosing what to believe in context.* They also *attempted to live out their beliefs* in their work and personal lives. At the same time, 'how I know' required determining who the 'I' was. *Intense self-reflection and interaction with others helped participants gain perspective on themselves and begin to choose their own values and identity.* This emerging sense of self *required renegotiation of existing relationships that had been built on external approval at the expense of personal needs and the creation of new mutual relationships consistent with the internal voice.* (2001, 119–120, emphasis added)

Parker Palmer (2004) discusses the evolution to self-authorship in a similar vein in his most recent book, *A Hidden Wholeness*, but uses a different reference point (as discussed earlier in our consideration of movements): "the journey toward an undivided life." In that analysis, Palmer speaks directly to a matter that is especially relevant to us: how evolving understandings affect one's relationship with, and stance toward, institutions:

> As we move closer to the truth that lives within us—aware that in the end what will matter most is knowing that we stayed true to ourselves—*institutions start losing their sway over our lives.* This does not mean we must abandon institutions. In fact. . . *we gain the courage to serve institutions more faithfully,* to help them resist their tendency to default on their own missions. (2004, 21, italics added)

Serving institutions faithfully often means having to live with angst, knowing that you need to cross boundaries constantly—moving back and forth between the world you prefer and participating in worlds dedicated to other matters, including (sometimes) matters to which you once attended. That happened to co-author Fear as he was writing this chapter. Dedicated to the concept and practice of engaged learning that emerged during the writing of this book, Fear now involves diverse colleagues in a variety of settings (on campus and off) in engaged learning experiences. As described in the Introduction and illustrated in chapter 2, many of those experiences are organized as communities of practice, just as was this book-writing project.

In the example to be considered here, Fear worked with campus visitors to organize a community of practice during their year-long fellowship experience at Michigan State. Although framed as a "leadership development" experience, this is obviously leadership development of a certain kind, certainly not leadership development undertaken through conventional means (delivering leadership programs in workshop settings using modules on such topics as negotiation, strategic thinking, and public speaking.) Not too many years ago that is how Fear delivered most of his outreach programs. Today, he engages participants in discourse about issues relevant to their shared experiences.

This is a different way of approaching leadership development, palatable to some and unfathomable to others. And although the administrator of record for this program and his staff are comfortable with the communities of practice approach—and the evaluations from participants warrant its continuing use—on this day there is very different challenge: the Federal administrator who funds the program is visiting campus. It is clear from past conversations that there is not a good degree of fit between how that administrator sees leadership development and what happens in communities of practice. Because of the politics involved, those at MSU (including Fear) wonder what will happen if the administrator responds unfavorably to seeing the group function as a community of practice. So, on this day, the Federal administrator observes a hired trainer (not Fear) conduct a workshop for participants on a specific leadership skill.

The story just told compels people like Fear to cross borders nimbly, knowing when it is appropriate (and safe) to exercise roles through critical engagement. Co-author Bawden has had the same experience. A good example is his work in the late 1970s, when he (as dean) with colleagues launched a radical approach to undergraduate education at Hawkesbury Agricultural College—a long-established, small, autonomous, publicly-funded institution located in Sydney, Australia. The institutional changes pursued were undertaken in response to a source of institutional anxiety: there was genuine concern among the academics about Hawkesbury's institutional reputation, which had been steadily eroding over preceding decades in contrast to the institutional reputations of other institutions of higher education for agriculture across the nation and in the state of New South Wales (NSW).

Bawden was recruited to Hawkesbury from another state institution with the charge to design and enact curricular reform. Somewhat unconventionally, he began by enjoining the faculty to investigate the actual conditions "on the ground" in rural NSW. They did that by exploring anxieties that people on farms and in broader rural communities felt about their own futures "on the land," as well as to tap their opinions about the state of that land. The information gathered would be crafted in the form of an "official institutional position" on the status and outlook for NSW agriculture and would also set the stage for curricular reform.

Study findings revealed a disturbing mismatch between the everyday experiences and concerns of rural people and interpretations made by experts in the educational, research, and policy institutions of NSW. One of the most telling aspects of this lacuna was the level of antagonism that each "side" held for the other. Rural people generally felt that institutions were not only "missing the point," but were actually exacerbating the problem: for example, they perceived research to be narrow in focus and the help received from extension to be limited in scope. The experts had a different take on the circumstance. They held an "efficiency will out" mind-set with the belief the "fittest farmers" would be able to respond best in the face of economic and other realities. A key difference between the two perspectives was the issue of complexity. Rural people felt that the issues were increasingly complex and, because of that, demanded a complex response. The experts, on the other hand, tended to reduce issues to parts. They reasoned that if the parts could be understood and managed well enough then the whole could be tended to acceptably.

It is important to know that farming in Australia has always been a particularly anxious enterprise for those involved in the business: the climate is harsh; the weather is variable; the soils are generally poor; surface water is scarce; and markets are often remote and quintessentially uncertain. By the mid-1970s, a host of new issues emerged, including concerns about the possibility of agricultural contamination from the chemical pesticides. There was also widespread "die-back" of trees in the countryside and the landscape was being irreparably altered by land clearance programs. In the face of these circumstances, environmentalists began mounting media campaigns designed to draw the public's attention to the loss of biodiversity and to the misuse and abuse of the water resources, among other matters. At about the same time, health professionals were talking about the dangers associated with the extensive use of antibiotics and other synthetic growth promotants in animal production; animal liberationists were grabbing headlines with talk about cruelty to animals; and voices were calling attention to plight of the aboriginal population, who some felt had been effectively dispossessed of their land rights.

In the face of all of this, the Hawkesbury faculty made three decisions that not only triggered curricular reform, but would (over time) change the character of the entire institution. First, systems theories, philosophies, and practices were used to address the inherent complexity of the circumstances faced in agriculture and rural development. Second, experiential (rather than lecture-based) pedagogies were used to immerse students and faculty in the problematique, enabling them to live in rural communities and work side-by-side with farmers. Third, dialogue and discourse would be used as a means to engage diverse parties in the quest to enhance the development of shared meaning, understanding, and solutions.

Looking back, more than thirty years ago Bawden and his colleagues put into place an institutional platform enabling critical engagement. Using language from this book, Hawkesbury faculty committed themselves to new and different discourses (than had been in place) about rural and agricultural development, and just as importantly, about undergraduate education. It was an example of what Fairclough (1992) calls discourse as a mode of action. Among other things, it facilitated the creation of new forms of social relationships between people; and contributed to the construction of new knowledge systems about pressing matters at hand.

This was a radical approach, especially for the time. And even though the approach was inarguably successful in terms of what was envisioned, the unconventional approach was difficult to sustain. The integration of Hawkesbury in 1989 with two other previously autonomous (non-agricultural) colleges into a comprehensive university proved to be a turning point. Critical engagement, including the discourse that it requires, soon became a source of angst among the faculty. That led to the eventual demise of the initiative, and with it, an invitation to have Bawden join the Michigan State faculty as a distinguished professor.

In reflecting on the story just told, Bawden wrote the following message to his book co-authors:

Throughout my life as an academic I have found myself in positions of profound discomfort (of angst) even when I have been in positions of authority. The basis for this angst, I came to slowly understand, was my rejection of the hegemony and monopoly within my discipline of agriculture, of techno-scientific rationality—of the instrumental technical reason that I was later to learn about from reading Habermas and others. . . . This is not an easy position to hold when you are an aggie—and even less when you are a dean of agriculture. I was seemingly born a critical theorist.

Engagement as leadership for the public good

Bawden's story demonstrates that coming to critical engagement is not simply a matter of sharpening intellectual understanding. It is intensely personal—a lived, revelatory—experience, exactly as we described it at the beginning of this chapter. As a habit of the mind with a pathway to the heart, coming to critical engagement clarifies the essential characteristics of one's personhood.

The reason we resonate so strongly with Boyer's framing of engagement—"creating a special climate in which the academic and civic cultures communicate more continuously"—is that it speaks to us intellectually *and* viscerally. In our terms and language, it requires exercising *leadership for the public good* (Fear 2005; Kezar et al. 2005). Leading for the public good as we see it entails the exercise of personal integrity and requires crossing organizational, political, and ideological boundaries; participating with diverse others on shared initiatives; and committing (in spirit and substance) to actions that embody "the high road." To participate in engagement that way calls for statesperson-like behaviors—seeing the bigger and more complex picture; being trusted as a credible and competent partner; and eschewing intransigence and rejecting narrow mindedness.

We believe that leading for the public good, and the statespersonship it connotes, are sorely needed in today's society. Leading for the public good seems to be often trumped by advancing the private good, that is, by-passing the interests of the many and (instead) serving the interests of a few. Engagement, it seems to us, is an antidote to these tendencies. As a profoundly civilizing enterprise it stands against disturbingly un-civilizing attitudes and behaviors—rampant self-interest, ideological rigidity, unethical comportment, derisiveness, and divisiveness.

While the circumstances to which we speak apply generally in society, and specifically (as most might presume) to the private sector, they also have prominence in public affairs and institutional life, generally. Consider Christine Todd Whitman's (2005) experience during her tenure as director of the U.S. Environmental Protection Agency. Although she well understood the political environment in which she worked, she was struck by how narrowly "acceptable thinking" was defined and how allegiance to that position was expected unconditionally. And while this outcome might be expected in party politics, Theda Skocpol (2003) asserts that there is evidence of its existence in the non-profit sector, too. Skocpol describes the evolution of associational groups in the U.S. What had been undertaken primarily among networks of citizens who engaged each other face-to-face is now frequently undertaken and orchestrated by national membership associations. These entities are led by professionals; managed from central locations; and fueled by the financial contributions of elites.

When there are dynamics like these, public institutions and civic organizations sometimes act more like *industries* than enterprises dedicated to and for the public good. The tell-tale sign of malaise is when organizational self-interest becomes the locus of attention—when *running a place like a business* becomes the driveshaft of everyday organizational life—and budgets, personnel management, market development, "branding," competitive positioning, and the like, get the spotlight. When that happens, matters of mandate and mission get displaced by obsession with business operations; and organizations advance goals and measure progress in predominately self-serving (to the organization) terms.

Overemphasizing internal matters leads to embellishing good management as leadership. Conflating the meaning of leadership (the visionary function) is common these days: a "good leader" is often seen in managerial terms, as one who manages budgets well; de-structures and re-structures appropriately; deploys personnel effectively; raises funds successfully, and generally tends to all the other matters that keep the system operating efficiently and effectively. This tendency produces settings that are "over-managed and under-led," a term we borrow from President Jim Votruba of Northern Kentucky University. In its extreme form, over-managed organizations become production systems.

What happens when higher education becomes a production system? At some schools, the primary driver is the quest for prestige, meaning improving an institution's position in the hierarchy of competing schools. Improving one's position means ramping up the production system—increasing inputs (e.g., grant money) and producing more outputs (e.g., publications). While there is no doubt that higher education institutions undertake vitally important public work, say, by conducting research on life-threatening diseases, it is possible for colleges and universities to focus excessively on the organizational benefits that accrue from that work. Higher education becomes an industry when system inputs and outputs become foci of organizational attention. If that happens, higher education might value engagement more for its instrumental value and extrinsic merit—for the funding, political value, and media attention it brings—than for its relevance in performing a mission-related responsibility—serving the public good.

Reversing the normal and democratic imagination

One way of addressing the malaise is to think differently about the way business is done typically. That includes considering alternative ways of envisioning and undertaking change. For one thing, it may be time to question commonly accepted strategies for planned change. Consider, for example, the outcome that often follows from making frontal assaults on systems. In their analysis of various twentieth century movements, Anderson and Ray (2000) found that movements had relatively limited impact on the general population when they followed either a strongly political path or required radical lifestyle changes (137). On the other hand, new ideas are often easier to accept for a broader population when they are disassociated from politics and uncoupled from extraordinary ideas and practices. For example, vegetarianism (a well-established life expression for a number of people in our society) is unlikely to become a predominant practice. However, ideas embraced by vegetarians, such as selecting food choices mindfully and engaging in healthy eating habits, appeal to many people and are becoming routinely manifest in mainstream society.

Another change alternative that merits attention is the kind Malcolm Gladwell discusses in his provocative book, *The Tipping Point* (2002). Fascinated by several social outcomes of significant proportions, including the decline in New York City's crime rate, Gladwell began investigating outcomes by asking reasonable questions: Who was responsible? What policies were enacted? What programs were put in place? Instead of finding a trail of bread to a single source or to a coordinated effort among parties, Gladwell found evidence of many people doing many things, not always in concert, to make an impact. As he studied the dynamics more closely, he recognized that the patterns of change more closely resembled the way infections spread through a population during a public health epidemic. Gladwell drew on his findings to fashion a networked-based theory of change with different people playing different roles as they engage each other over time. In some (but not all cases) —with time, perseverance, and interactive intensity—circumstances can reach a "tipping point" of change.

Gladwell's tipping point theory makes political sense, too. If a proposed change is really transformative and represents a paradigm shift, it is also likely to threaten those who wield power currently. Because of that, less aggressive approaches—even covert actions—might prove to be more effective as change means than "rushing the castle to take over the kingdom."

However, no matter what means are used to achieve transformative, para-digm-shifting change—conventional or alternative—the outcome is always the same. Robert Chambers (1997) has a compact way of putting it: *reversing the normal*. A necessary step in that reversal involves shedding prior assumptions about why and how things are done. Doing that enables (or at least promotes) learning new ways of performing roles. For example, Fear and others (2003) have written about their transition from using a conventional approach to teach-ing a course to participating in engaged learning as learning collaborators. A necessary, early step in this transition was releasing prior assumptions about what "a good class" looks like.

How does all of this apply in our journey to critical engagement? Of first order was our letting go of the assumption that academic knowing is *the* superior way of knowing. We see it today as *a* way of knowing, among many ways, even though we recognize it is our primary way; and also understand it as a privileged way of knowing—a way that gives us considerable standing in society. For one thing, it enables people like us to view ourselves as experts and to be viewed by others as experts. In coming to critical engagement, we also understand that—as academics—we occupy elite status and, because of that, *we* can be agents of he-gemony. That happens when we use elite status to privilege our voices above others' voices. Through story telling we recounted instances of our own behav-iors in that regard.

To help replace the assumption of privilege, we read provocative literature about what it means "to be smart." A good example is Mike Rose's elegantly written, *The Mind at Work* (2004). Rose, an award-winning UCLA education professor, investigated intelligence by studying an unlikely group: workers who engage in everyday activities, including waitresses, hair stylists, plumbers, car-penters, and welders; that is, people not often seen by the public (or by them-selves) as exhibiting high levels of intelligence. By collecting data through ob-servations and interviews, Rose was introduced to the complexities associated with how people in those fields learn their respective crafts and, then, "get good" at their work. As the study proceeded, Rose found no evidence of "com-mon laborers" who were ill-equipped to do complex work. Instead, he found evidence of people mindfully engaged in advanced and sophisticated work. Rose talks about what he learned as his subjects engaged in work:

> When seriously engaged—the traditions and values one acquires and the com-plex knowledge and skills developed—give rise to the virtue of practice, an ethic and aesthetics, and a reflectiveness intermixed with technique. Further-more. . . all of this becomes part of the construction of one's sense of self. (2004, 102)

Rose's work has profound implications—and relevance—for thinking about en-gagement and our roles as faculty members. In one of the most compelling pas-sages in the book, he writes: "If we think that whole categories of people—

identified as class, by occupation—are not that bright, then we reinforce social separations and cripple our ability to talk across current cultural divides" (2004, 216). Rose implores readers to see the value of a "model of the mind" that "*befits the democratic imagination*" (216, emphasis added).

The words, "democratic imagination," resonate with us because it is an inherently populist concept. Along that line, we find great value in James Surowiecki's (2004) recent book, *The Wisdom of Crowds*. Of the first order, he debunks the myth that only elites have answers and are unilaterally wise. Drawing on extensive research conducted in a variety of fields, he shows that wisdom is ubiquitous: found in everyday actions; undertaken by everyday people, who engage in everyday life. To be "wise," he found, requires aggregations of people with opinion diversity; personal independence; decentralization; and a method for aggregating opinions. Characteristics like diversity of opinion guarantee multiple perspectives; and independence mitigates the prospects that a group will be swayed by a single opinion leader.

Rather than trying to "chase the expert," Surowiecki argues that we need to pay closer attention to the "wisdom of the crowd." In one sense, Surowiecki (in his own words) "describes the world as it is." But, in another way (again, in his own words), he portrays a world "as it might be" through engagement:

> One of the striking things about the wisdom of crowds is that even though its effects are all around us, it's easy to miss, and, even when it's seen, it can be hard to accept. Most of us, whether as voters or investors or consumers or managers, believe that valuable knowledge is concentrated in a very few hands (or, rather, in a very few heads). We assume that the key to solving problems or making good decisions is finding that one right person who will have the answer. Even when we see a large crowd of people, many of them not especially well-informed, do something amazing like, say, predict the outcomes of horse races, we are more likely to attribute that success to a few smart people in the crowds than to the crowd itself. . . . The argument of this book is chasing the expert is a mistake, and a costly one at that. We should stop hunting and ask the crowd (which, of course, includes the geniuses as well as everyone else) instead. Chances are, it knows. (2004, xv)

Surowiecki's treatment addresses a knotty and contested epistemological question: *Who knows what?* The plain truth is that it is too easy to look at higher education as a center of knowledge and, with that, to view colleges and universities as places that create, transmit, and apply knowledge. While that it is certainly true, there are limits to that truth because it depends on what you mean by "knowledge." In one form—what the late Donald Schön (1995) called "technical rationality" (as discussed in chapter 3)—higher education does bring expert knowledge to the table. Daniel Yankelovich (1991) speaks to that form in his book, *Coming to Public Judgment*. The core of his argument is that, for too long, modern society has considered factual information "real knowledge" and judgment as not. Because of that belief, Yankelovich sees what he calls a culture of technical control, which is a manifestation of the doctrine of objectivism, namely, a preference for "hard facts," a position that "excludes values and norms and opinions and judgments because these express subjective preferences that cannot be scientifically verified in the way that factual assertions can." And while no one can (or should) deny the importance and impact of knowledge defined in objectivist terms, there are also limits and dysfunctional consequences. Yankelovich elaborates:

> The quest for knowledge enjoys enormous prestige in our society and scientific technical-factual information has hegemony over other modes of seeking knowledge. Those who possess it—the experts—lord it over those who do not. Experts play a dominant role in public life because they are presumed to have the knowledge that ordinary folk lack. Nor is our culture likely to diminish its high regard for experts in the future because their type of knowledge has contributed so much to our success in extending longevity, creating affluences, and using technology to make life more comfortable, convenient, and stimulating. The trend is to entrust the experts with ever more power and influence. (1991, 197)

To achieve another reality—that which we see as the promise of engagement—is not easy. An objectivist philosophy is not only baked into society, it is the mainstream academic epistemology *and* the primary source of higher education's status and prestige. Because of those factors, for transformation to happen a "reversal of the normal" (in Chambers' terms, 2005) of significant proportions is required.

Co-intelligence and what it means to act wisely

Reversal of the normal is inherent in a tenant of engagement: *knowledge emerges from being at the table with everyday people.* Thomas Atlee (2003, 3) offers such a vision in what he calls *co-intelligence,* which he defines as "the ability to generate or evoke creative responses and initiatives that integrate the diverse gifts of all for the benefit of all." Co-intelligence requires collective intelligence and, with that, reframes intelligence from an individual trait to what *groups* know, understand, and are capable of doing. Because of that, co-intelligence is a profoundly populist expression. Consider Atlee's core assertion:

> Given a supportive structure and resources, diverse ordinary people can work together to reach common ground, creating wise and deliberate policy that reflects the highest public interest. (2003, xv)

The glibness of Atlee's words masks considerable depth of meaning. In saying that this requires *a supportive structure and resources,* Atlee implies that this work needs to be enabled. In other words, a vitally important contribution of any institution, agency, group, or person is to help others engage; it is not sufficient just to "do the work." By declaring that *diverse ordinary people engage* means that they must have the opportunity to do so. That seems obvious on the surface, but it means disdaining and countering attempts to disable the exercise of community voice. And implicit in Atlee's interpretation of *reaching common ground* is the understanding that common ground is rarely, if ever, a starting point. The stark reality is that many engagement episodes seek traction in circumstances that are wracked with conflict; where there is a history of mistrust; and when people do not see eye to eye.

Creating wise and deliberate policy is a compound reference. To be wise means a number of things, including weighing options and thinking through consequences; paying attention to matters of justice (who wins and loses); and taking the long view into consideration (because wisdom is never short-sighted). All of this emphasizes the importance of being deliberate, systematic, and planful—the ingredients that go into being thorough. And note that Atlee uses the word "policy" not programs. That suggests rules are needed to compel observance, ensure permanency, and secure stability. That is another way of saying that forces exist that may either keep engagement from succeeding or might sweep away its gains.

Finally, in saying that co-intelligence *reflects the highest public interest*, the target for Atlee is unwavering and elevated—not high or higher, but highest. While that may seem unrealistic, even child-like in aspiration, the writers of this book can think of circumstances where our roles in community affairs were just that: an obligation exercised on behalf of people—many of whom we did not know and would never meet—but people who depended on our perceptivity, acumen, judgment and, in some cases, courage. When thought of that way, acting on behalf of the public interest seems less like a vision and more like an everyday expectation.

Atlee makes it clear that co-intelligence means more than possessing facts and knowing about issues—as important as are those capabilities. It also includes *understanding* and what it means to *act wisely*. These attributes are central to the way Tobin Hart (2001) discusses learning and education in his absorbing book, *From Information to Transformation*. Hart's contribution is grounded in a framework that includes "six interrelated layers":

> At the surface layer, *information* is given its rightful place as currency for the educational exchange. Information can then open up into *knowledge*, where direct experience often brings together the bits of information into the whole of mastery and skill. Knowledge opens the possibility of intentionally cultivating *intelligence*, which can cut, shape, and create information and knowledge through the dialectic of the intuitive and the analytic. Further down lies *understanding*, which takes us beyond the power of intelligence to look through the eye of the heart, a way of knowing that serves character and community. Experience then has the possibility for cultivating *wisdom*, which blends insight into what is true with an ethic of what is right. Ultimately, the depths lead to the possibility of *transformation*. (2001, 2, emphasis in the original)

There are enormous implications for engagement in what Hart asserts. So much of formal education is about acquiring *information*. Hart sees acquiring information as the lowest, although foundational, matter in the learning quest. With the influence of experience in domains of interest, one converts information into combinations and wholes—schemes, frameworks, models, and the like—in the form of *knowledge* that is meaningful and has value to the user. And as important as it is to say confidently, "I know!" Hart sees a higher level— *intelligence*—that involves more than combining information bits and mastering skills. Through intelligence, we "put our signature" on what we know; we do that through the interplay of the logical mind and the interpretive spirit. Hart explains:

> The analytic and the intuitive play off each other: the analytic grasps and holds, while the intuitive opens and embraces; the analytic has purpose, while the intuitive plays; the analytic measures and calculates, while the intuitive appreciates; the analytic builds, cuts, and controls, while the intuitive remains open-ended and is characterized by movement; the analytic is contained and directed by the ego and the will, while the intuitive tends toward self-transcendence and arises spontaneously; the analytic is willful, while the intuitive is willing; the analytic fosters self-separateness, while the intuitive sees interconnections; the analytic is bound to subject-object distinctions, while the intuitive transcends boundaries; the analytic tends toward linearity and moves step by step, while the intuitive meanders and leaps. In dialectic, these ways of knowing generate a plurality of knowledge and a depth of intelligence. To what extent do we invite one or the other, both or neither, in our educational practices? (2001, 72)

What strikes us most about Hart's interpretations is what it means in terms of our contributions to engagement as faculty members. Through immersion in a variety of educational experiences, including our doctoral experiences, we have acquired an enormous amount of information. Through the mentoring we received by principals in our respective fields and from our collaborations with many and diverse academic partners—not to speak of the years and years of experience of doing this work—we have become knowledgeable (quite clever in fact) in piecing together ideas to magnify what is known about this or that subject. All of that is at the core of what we bring to our students, undergraduate and graduate. "To know" and to help others know are traits we admire in ourselves (and in which we take great pride); they are also traits that are affirmed regularly (and expected, too) by our engagement partners.

But, as Hart asserts, there is a difference between knowing and being intelligent. Like many others, we suspect, we assume that to know things at elevated levels is, ipso facto, to be intelligent. Not so, argues Hart. Why? As academics, our strength is inarguably in the analytic domain of intelligence. But the intuitive domain is different. And that is probably why it took so many years, trials, and challenges for us to discover and (then come to) critical engagement. That is not to say that we were un-intuitive; but it is to say that we needed to nourish and engage intuitiveness so that it could be in balance with analysis. Because intuition was probably less developed during our formative years, it is not surprising then that many "insights" today either emanate from the intuitive domain or emerge from the dialectic with analysis (like the blend of gasoline and oil, together, make for running an automobile). The "Eureka!" comes in this form: "Gosh! Sure! *Why* didn't we see that before?" The answer, we think, is quite straightforward: life cannot possibly be lived solely in the mind, no matter how well-developed the mind might be.

Saying all of this makes it clear that "being smart" in engagement includes, but extends far beyond, the knowledge that we (as faculty members) bring to the table. But, in Hart's view, the learning quest extends beyond the dialectic with intuition. *Understanding* is also required; the nurturing attributes that we commonly refer to as "heart." Understanding "is cultivated through empathy, appreciation, openness, accommodation, service, listening, and loving presence," Hart writes (2001, 89). Without caring, compassion, and attentiveness, there can be no understanding; and without understanding, engagement is a cold, lifeless activity that comes only in the form of projects with milestones and objectives. But in Hart's mind, understanding not only activates a caring ethic, it helps form individual character and nurtures the conditions necessary for establishing and sustaining strong communities. Understanding is so important in Hart's view that he sees it as an antidote to violence—a shocking, but heartfelt and logical, conclusion:

> The most insidious sources of violence are the ideologies of objectivism and materialism, which treat the other (person, object, the natural world, or even some disowned parts of self) as an object to possess, measure, or control. Such non-relational knowing creates environments that lead to a basic sense of insecurity and isolation. Without a solid relational ground and basic sense of trust and security, basic anxiety develops and is manifest in personality struggles that include 'moving away,' 'moving toward,' and 'moving against' others (Horney 1950). Much of our social concern these days involves the level of violence, the moving against another; much of our educational concerns involve the moving away, the isolation and numbness that stares back at us or simply drops out altogether. The moving toward implies an external dependence and lack of autonomy and individuation. . . . We never experience the other's subjectivity; the other remains merely an object. . . (Hart 2001, 115)

For Hart, "being smart" and "heartful" are only stage-setters for the ultimate challenge, that is, being able to *act wisely*, especially in complex, contested, and conflict-ridden circumstances where it is unclear what ought to be done or what is the right thing to do. Because different people—with different takes and stakes on a matter—may prefer different outcomes, Hart argues that wise action requires filtering what might be done in intensely personal terms. One does that by making interpretations using a moral code, an inner truth, a set of guiding principles, or a value system—to name just a few of the things that serve as filters—to decide what is appropriate, best, and prudent.

Because Hart believes that developing wisdom is fundamental to the educational enterprise, he concludes that it needs to be given the attention accorded to information and knowledge. But that is a contested matter, too; and even when it is accepted as a need, the matter of *how* to cultivate wisdom is an issue of debate. Hart addresses that topic head on: "A culprit. . . is not the lack of moral guidance. . . . It is, instead, in part, our habit of relying on external moral or intellectual authority. . . (2001, 132). For Hart, the solution is not concluding that external authority has no place. Rather, it involves developing capacity to anchor one's judgments in ways that are personally authentic, meaningful, and life-serving. Hart refers to this capacity as "discernment" (135), and rejects approaches where

> . . . truth and morality are imposed from the outside, doled out in the cafeteria line of values, prepackaged and processed rather than grown organically from our deep roots in dialogue and exchange with the outside. When our own profundity is not permitted space, we do not learn to center ourselves in wise counsel. When we recognize that. . . [we]. . . have a. . . capacity for innate wisdom, we may no longer think of the task of education as simply downloading 'truths'; instead we may recognize the task as helping to bring forth the wise self. (140)

Perhaps the ultimate value of critical engagement is the way it serves wisdom. The most powerful engagement experiences in our lives have been circumstances where the exercise of wisdom was a first-order requisite; those experiences pushed us hard in unimaginable ways as did, for example, Fear's experience working with public officials and citizens to explore possibilities for siting a low-level radioactive waste facility in Michigan. But as personally influential as are those experiences, more pertinent to the analysis here is what all of it means for questions like these: Should we simply assume and expect that faculty members are "heartful" and wise? Do graduate programs help aspiring faculty members develop their intuitive qualities? Are we sure that all faculty members are able to collaborate in responsible, respectful, and non-hegemonic ways?

These are important questions. If we define engagement as "bringing facts and knowledge to bear on problems and issues," the odds are that faculty members can do that and do it well. But conceiving engagement in that way positions it closely with service and outreach. As Bawden argues in chapter 8, there is a "turn" that makes engagement unique; its exercise requires more than what most faculty members are well-prepared and know how to do. Consequently, spreading engagement in higher education demands more than making it easier for faculty to engage, such as rewarding faculty better for doing this work and making more resources available to them. Although those (and similar) goals are important and necessary, there is a more fundamental question: *Are we, as faculty, generally ready for engagement?*

Asking that question reminds Fear of a comment once shared with him by a county Extension director. The problem for that director, as he told it, was not securing faculty assistance; it was keeping out faculty members who did not know how to engage.

The point here is that engagement is a subject matter unto itself, a "discipline" so to speak. If we act as though that is not true and that the primary issue is to "get faculty out there to do engagement," then by our own hands we disable engagement. It renders engagement a trivial pursuit, something that either everybody knows how to do or can learn to do by following a checklist. Avoiding that outcome requires making a fundamental admission: many faculty members are *not* well-equipped to engage. Education, training, and ongoing support will be necessary for faculty members to participate competently in something that is new to many of them.

As important as is this conclusion when speaking about the matter of individual faculty involvement, its importance is magnified when collective interventions are undertaken, that is, when departments, schools, and even entire institutions "adopt" or target resources to develop communities. The co-authors' institution did that in the case of Benton Harbor, Michigan; Boston University did it in the case of Chelsea, Massachusetts; and Bawden's former institution did it in New South Wales. What was learned from those interventions? How might we apply learning to enhance prospects that engagement will be done responsibly and well?

But there is another point to make in this regard, perhaps an even more important point, drawn from the co-authors' interpretation of Hart's framework. It is the matter of what faculty gain from and by engaging. To raise that issue is to blow right past the elitist assumption that civic society has much to gain by engaging with faculty. While that is often true, Hart's interpretation of intelligence, understanding, and wisdom leads us in the opposite direction, namely, asking *what faculty members gain—as human beings—from engaging.* It can be, and often is, a profound learning experience where (as discussed earlier in this book) participants can learn new things (and not always attractive things) about themselves. An example of what we mean can be said no more plainly than by repeating these words from chapter 9:

> *Engagement, as we see it, abrogates arrogance and stimulates humility. Put bluntly, the things we abhor about elites and elitism—the penchant for exclusivity, dominance, and unilateral exercise of power—are replaced by inclusivity, collaboration, and participation. Simply stated, creating the conditions for critical engagement requires academics to model attributes that endear humans to one another. Anything less jeopardizes the journey to critical engagement, for academics and all others, and mocks the very pillars on which engagement rests. By ex-*

hibiting the values of engagement and working with other in like ways, the lived experience of engagement is profoundly democratic, emancipative, and empowering—precisely what engagement in civil society needs to be.

Public work and engaged learning

It should be clear by now that we see engagement as a means to (1) counteract elitist influences and approaches; (2) democratize knowledge; and (3) strengthen populist resolve. A brilliant exposition in all three dimensions is found in the recently published *Everyday politics: Reconnecting citizens and public life* (2004) authored by Harry C. Boyte, founder and co-director of the Center for Democracy and Citizenship at the University of Minnesota. In the book, Boyte expounds on the concept of *public work*, which he believes

> . . . leads to people seeing themselves as the co-creators of democracy, not simply as customers or clients, voters, protestors, or volunteers. To highlight the creative, educative, and productive dimensions of politics, public work can be best defined as *sustained effort by a mix of people who solve problems or create goods, material, or culture, of generable benefit.* Public work is work that is visible, open to inspection, whose significance is widely recognized, and which can be carried out by people whose interests, views, and backgrounds may be quite different. (2004, 5, italics added)

For Boyte, public work as an expression of what he calls "everyday politics," an amalgam that fits the both–and environment of today's postmodern era, blending community *and* politics and interest-group actions *and* civic ideals (2004, 15). There is no question about the locus of this work (it is about people in community); and there is no question about the professional role required (it is to enable this work. . . more about that later). As Boyte sees everyday politics: "It relocates politics primarily in face to face horizontal interactions among people. . . . It has as its first premise, a respect for the intelligence and talents of ordinary, uncredentialed citizens" (35).

For sure, public work is one among many discourses of engagement. Yet, it is impossible for us to think about engagement without thinking about it as public work. For starters, public work is community-based, not Academy-centered. It is about community capacity building with higher education invited to assist. Public work is also emancipatory in intent, a medium for converting community environments from cultures of disconnectedness and blame into cultures of relationality and responsibility. People mobilize at the grassroots around issues of shared, public concern. Through public work, people with limited voice (and perhaps insignificant influence) create opportunities to gain both.

As we saw in Part II, as people take charge of their lives a number of important things happen. First, they learn important personal and social skills. Second, they convert hope into tangible outcomes. Third, they gain confidence in their ability to make a difference. And, when undertaken successfully, public work leaves a positive residue—on people and on community culture. Participants can apply learning in subsequent organizing opportunities; and communities have a frame of reference for how to design and enact productive, grassroots endeavors. At a minimum, public work is a vehicle of reform—an effort to fix what is wrong, including redressing injustices wrought by the inappropriate or uncaring exercise of power. At its best, public work is a vehicle of transformation—both for the people involved and for community circumstances. Transformation occurs when lives are changed fundamentally and when ways of doing business locally (including underlying systems, structures, standards, and processes) are altered substantially or replaced with protocols that are defined to be more liberating and just. At its core, we see public work as *collaborative, deliberative,* and as an outcome of *self-directed, situated learning.*

Collaborative: Exemplary public work is characterized by constructive conservations among community members. People feel that they can express themselves freely and openly with everyone's voice heard. In these best cases there is shared and rotating leadership: certain people come forward to take the lead at one time and other people come forward to take the lead at other times. Persons with formal titles and positions do not control the agenda. Rather, they serve as enabling leaders—making everybody feel comfortable, inviting participation, and accommodating differences of opinion even when opinions are expressed emotionally. In these ideal situations, groups develop a culture of democratic leadership in contrast to environments where leadership is personalized in heroic form.

Deliberative: Public work requires a significant amount of deliberation. People spend time around the table discussing issues, goals, and approaches—the conversation goes back and forth as participants sift and sort through information; consider the pros and cons of alternative interpretations and courses of action; and arrive at judgments about what to do, how, when, where, and by whom. This "going back and forth" falls apart if authority and power is exercised inappropriately or if judgments are based on misinformation or faulty interpretations. Thoughtful consideration is required to evaluate circumstances, weigh options, and consider appropriate actions. The credibility of every grassroots group demands measured consideration of facts and circumstances, as well as the ability to select wise courses of action.

Self-directed, situated learning: When people organize around an issue of common concern they often find themselves in situations that require learning. They not only become knowledgeable about the matter at hand, they also apply that knowledge in a specific setting. To do that, those involved in public work engage in self-directed, situated learning—figuring out what needs to be learned, organizing for learning, acquiring knowledge, contextualizing that knowledge, and rendering judgments about wise courses of action. Gaining access to and grasping technical information—scientific, medical, and legal, for example—is typical as activists address an issue of collective concern, say, pertaining to public health. The scope and quality of this learning is often quite impressive. Activists often develop a level of understanding that enables them to engage in informed conversations with professionally-trained experts. They must be able to base judgments on solid understanding, and must also confront experts from time to time who hold discordant values, beliefs, or intentions.

Collaborative, deliberative, self-directed, and situated learning is a form of *engaged learning* as described in chapter 3 (Fear et al. 2002). We use the word "engaged" because people *feel* engaged in the emotive sense and *are* engaged in the active sense. Engaged learning is what happens when a group of people organize around an issue or topic of common concern. They interact collaboratively and deliberatively for the purpose of creating and enacting a shared learning agenda. Then, they apply what they learn to ameliorate situations in their community. In the words of the title of a report produced by the American Association of State Colleges and Universities (2002, cited earlier in this chapter), they act as "stewards of place."

Engaged learning elevates public work to the level of social virtue because a democratic society is impossible without it. The political energy created by blending the voices and actions of similarly affected people functions as an antidote to efforts undertaken by elites to control people and circumstances. Political outcomes of engaged learning can range from counteracting hegemony ("keeping them honest") to redefining the political landscape in populist terms. When seen this way, engaged learning blends the three ways of knowing that Habermas (1971) describes: *instrumental* (getting something accomplished), *communicative* (enhancing shared understanding of different points of view), and *emancipatory* (helping to uncover manipulative intentions). For those things to happen, first, there must be open access to engaged learning—anybody and everybody is invited to participate. Second, engaged learning must be undertaken in a way that accentuates the *might of we.* Through engaged learning, people need to be able to create ad hoc forms that they manage and in which they participate voluntarily. Third, there should be no predetermined blueprint; everything needs to be a matter of negotiation and a product of group imagination and creativity. Fourth, norms of engagement need to be co-created by participants democratically.

When these four aspects are in place, engaged learning is a lived experience that unfolds in real-time as people learn their way into the future. Engaged learning is a profound example of what Meg Wheatley (2002) calls "turning to one another." She writes: "When a community of people discovers that they share a concern, change begins. There is no power equal to a community discovering what it cares about" (22).

Civic Professionalism

With so much emphasis on the citizen role, it is easy to overlook the vitally important contributions to be made by professionals and institutions. But those contributions are diminished when citizens *only* play voluntary and philanthropic roles organized for them by professionals; and the contributions are diverted when professionals and institutions take primary or exclusive responsibility for work that takes place in the public domain. Boyte calls this the "professionalizing impulse" which, at its worst, is an ideology of domination, stifling the robust expression of public work. With that, Boyte calls for the "de-professionalization" of public work (2004, xi) an observation with which Skocpol (2003, cited earlier) concurs. She ruefully asks: "What will happen to democracy if participatory groups wither, while civic involvement becomes one more occupation rather than every citizen's right and duty?"

To avoid that fate, balance needs to be achieved between what professionals and institutions do and oversee; and what citizens own and undertake. Achieving that balance requires reframing professional expectations and institutional obligations—from professionals taking the lead and getting the credit to professionals *enabling citizens* to succeed in the work that citizens undertake—a necessary reframing if we are to have cultures of civic engagement where democracy flourishes. When that happens, the outcome is nothing more or less than what Baxter Magola (2001) describes as self-authorship—a phenomenon which, like parenting, authority figures can and should enable, but cannot and should not produce.

To convey an understanding of the enabling function, Baxter Magolda uses the metaphor of the tandem bicycle, where there is a first rider, the captain, and a second rider, the stoker: "The captain steers the bicycle and shifts the gears. The stoker's role is to contribute to the forward motion by pedaling" (2001, 331). For self-authorship to occur, professionals need to move from the captain's to the stoker's seat and, in doing so, release control. This will make it possible for professionals to "offer guidance and advice as appropriate," with the public taking the lead "in directing and managing the journey" (332).

Playing professional roles in this way is exactly what William Sullivan (2005) of the Carnegie Foundation describes as *civic professionalism*, which he believes is a necessary matter for professional reform in today's world. Civic professionals view themselves—in Steven Brint's (1994) term—as "community trustees," an understanding that *once* was predominant in American life, influenced by the thinking of noted Progressives, such as Jane Addams, John Dewey, and Charles Peirce. For Pragmatists, a goal was "developing social capacities by which interdependent but disperse and anonymous citizens could recognize each other and themselves as members of a public and so organize to achieve a rich shared form of social life." The role of professionals in that regard, according to Sullivan, was "to assist and support the nascent publics in developing the understandings and institutions that could make the modern public viable" (2005, 136).

But Sullivan believes that the "entrepreneurial spirit" has eroded—if not corrupted—that interpretation. With so many "opportunities" to be had, the meaning of a "good professional" has now migrated from that of enabling public engagement to achieving self-serving objectives, such that professionals understand *clearly* what it means to "achieve success in a highly competitive marketplace." Because of that, Sullivan calls for a "new professionalism" in the form of an ethic that is outward- (to society) looking; an ethic that "reinvigorates the civic purposes of professional life" (2005, 193). Doing that

> . . . requires that professionalism be understood as a public good, a social value, and not the ideology of some special interest. To make good on this claim, the positive features of professionalism must be extended to all work in the modern economy. By combining the dignity and security of occupational identity with the integrity and competence of social function, professionalism can be a major source for rebuilding not just a dynamic economy but a viable public order as well. (159-160)

The implications for higher education are obvious and considerable. At issue is this: *What is higher education educating and training professionals to do and be?* To answer that question with engagement in mind, higher education needs to understand that undergraduate, graduate, and professional programs

> . . . set the protective social context within which the goals of professionalism can be nurtured, understood, and passed on as a collective asset that defines a sense of common purpose within an occupation. When this larger institutional context is missing, or allowed to decay, the result is nearly textbook anomie: loss of morale and purpose that leaves individuals, and groups such as professional firms, highly vulnerable to the opportunistic path of least resistance. Such outcomes represent institutional failure as much as individual corruption. They also raise the difficult question of how the essential purpose of professional work can be sustained amid the conflicting pressures of the contemporary environment. (Sullivan 2005, 50)

This interpretation reinforces a point made early in this book, namely, that engagement is a cross-cutting function, not an activity that exists only as a new way of talking about "service." What that means is there are interconnections and relationships across mission-related domains. For engagement to flourish, higher education not only needs to participate by "doing engagement," it must enable participation, including getting serious about readjusting the way students are prepared to play professional roles. It is in this regard that we believe Sullivan's calls for reform represent a clarion call for higher education. Because higher education is both accomplice in the modern project (e.g., college is a pathway to financial success) and a reactor to it (e.g., living a life is as important as making a living), at issue is how this tension will play out.

Conclusion

This book has been about locating our voice. In finding that voice we have been influenced by others' voices. A good example is what Terry Tempest Williams (2004) has to say in *The Open Space of Democracy*. She sees engagement as

> Flesh-and-blood encounters. . . grounded in real time and space with people we have to face in our own hometowns. It's not altogether pleasant and there is no guarantee of the outcome. Boos and cheers come in equal measure. (23)

Not only does Williams' writing speak directly to our experience, it also speaks directly to our convictions: "I do not believe we can look for leadership beyond ourselves. . . for someone or something to save us. We are in need of a reflective activism born out of humility, not arrogance." She continues: "Reflection, with deep time spent in the consideration of others, opens the door to becoming a compassionate participant in the world" (2004, 88).

Think about a world ripe with reflective activists who exercise personal diplomacy with compassion. Do not believe that this is a world you or we might create; it is our world that already exists, a world that invites our participation. Some call this world (as Williams does) the open space of democracy; others call it public work, engaged learning, collegial professionalism, stewardship of place, working toward a larger purpose, co-intelligence, or collegial professionalism. Although different people use different terms, the reference point is the same—engagement—a virtue accessible to all, not reserved for a few. Engagement speaks of caring, hope, commitment, enablement, and resolve; and it not only stimulates and provokes, it also inspires and helps people "aspire to."

In giving ourselves to others, we gain so much for ourselves, with self-understanding being perhaps the greatest gift of all. That point is made beautifully by Paulo Coehlo's in his metaphysical narrative, *The Alchemist* (1988). Santiago—an Andalusian shepherd boy—travels from his homeland of Spain to the Egyptian desert in search of a treasure he believes is buried in the Pyramids. Along the way, Santiago comes in contact with many people who help him (directly or indirectly) in his quest, including an alchemist. The alchemist offers Santiago this advice: "Remember that wherever your heart is, there you will find your treasure. You've got to find the treasure, so that everything you have learned along the way can make sense" (116-117). After a seemingly endless journey, Santiago reaches the desert. He believes what the alchemist told him, so he listens closely to what his heart has to say. But he finds that his heart says many things, not just one thing, and he is not sure what that means. Unsettled about a direction or course of action, Santiago presses ahead, hoping that clarity will come. If not, he will not only fail in his quest, he will also be lost in the desert. As he "climbs yet another dune, his heart whispers: *Be aware of the place where you are brought to tears. That's where I am, and that's where your treasure is"* (159, emphasis added).

Engagement is all of these things: it is our treasure; it is in our hearts; it helps us make sense of things; and it brings us to tears. But, more than anything else, it fuels passion for our work in ways that Kay Redfield Jamison (2004) describes as *exuberance*: "It spreads upward and outward, like pollen toted by dancing bees, and in this carrying ideas are moved and actions taken" (4). When you are exuberant you are alive, full of energy and hope. People want to be around you and you want to be around them—to participate and do things together. You look forward to, relish being with, and glance fondly back on. That is how we feel with engagement, and there is nothing else like it. But, as Jamison points out emphatically, exuberance is not enough:

> Without a counterweight or discipline, it can be dazzling scattershot: excitement without substance, fizz and no gin. When enthusiasm lacks a fuller emotional or intellectual context, it lends credibility to those, more circumspect, who contend that high spirits and unrelenting optimism are intrinsically shallow. . . . (249)

That brings us full circle, back to critical engagement. If discovered and embraced it is a traveling companion that makes the journey meaningful, enriching, and worthwhile.

"If discovered and embraced. . . . " Important words, indeed.

References

American Association of State Colleges and Universities. 2002. *Stepping forward as stewards of place.* Washington D.C.: American Association of State Colleges and Universities.

Ray, P., and S. Anderson. 2000. *The cultural creatives: How 50 million people are changing the* world. New York: Harmony Books.

Atlee, T. 2003. *The Tao of democracy: Using co-intelligence to create a world that works for all.* Cranston RI: The Writers' Collective.

Barker, D. 2004. The scholarship of engagement: A taxonomy of five emerging practices. *Journal of Higher Education Outreach and Engagement 9*(2): 123–138.

Barr, R., and F. Fear. 2005. The Learning Paradigm as bold change: Improving understanding and practice. In C. McPhail, ed. *Establishing and sustaining learning-centered community colleges.* Washington D.C.: The Community College Press.

Baxter Magolda, M. 2001. *Making their own way: Narratives for transforming higher education to promote self-development.* Sterling VA: Stylus.

Bennett, J. 1998. Collegial professionalism: The Academy, individualism, and the common good. Phoenix: The Oryx Press (for the American Council on Education).

Bennett, J. 2003. *Academic life: Hospitality, ethics, and spirituality.* Bolton MA: Anker Publishing.

Blewitt, J., and C. Cullingford. 2004. *The sustainability curriculum: The challenge for higher education.* London: Earthscan Publications.

Blumer, H. 1939. Collective behavior. In R. Park, ed. *An outline of the principles of sociology.* New York: Barnes and Noble.

Bowen, S. 2005. Engaged learning: Are we all on the same page? *Peer Review* (Winter) http://www.aacu.org/peerreview/pr-wi05/pr-wi05 feature1.cfm

Boyer, E. 1996. The scholarship of engagement. *The Journal of Public Service and Outreach 1*(1):11–20.

Boyte, H. C. 2004. *Everyday politics: Reconnecting citizens to public life.* Philadelphia: Univ. of Pennsylvania Press.

Brint, S. 1994. *In an age of experts: The changing role of professionals in politics and public life.* Princeton: Princeton Univ. Press.

Brookfield, S. D. 2005. *The power of critical theory: Liberating adult learning and teaching.* San Francisco: Jossey-Bass.

Castells, M. 1996. *The rise of the network society.* Oxford: Blackwell.

Chambers, R. 1997. *Whose reality counts? Putting the last first.* London: ITDG Publishing.

Chambers, A. 2005. The special role of higher education in society: As a public good for the public good. In A. Kezar, A. Chambers, J. Burkhardt, and associates, eds. 2005. *Higher education for the public good: Emerging voices from a national movement.* San Francisco: Jossey-Bass.

Chickering, A., J. Dalton, and L. Stamm. 2005. *Encouraging authenticity and spirituality in higher education.* San Francisco: Jossey-Bass.

Coelho, P. 1988. *The alchemist.* San Francisco: HarperSanFrancisco.

Currie, J, and L. Vidovich. 1998. Micro-economic reform through managerialism. In J. Currie and J. Newson, eds. *Universities and globalization: Critical perspectives.* London: Sage.

Delanty, G. 2001. *Challenging knowledge: The university in the knowledge society.* Buckingham England: The Open Univ. Press.

Dewey, J. 1938. *Experience and education.* New York: Collier Books.

Diani, M. 2000. Towards a network theory of new social movements. *European Journal of Social Theory* 3(4): 387–406.

Etzkowitz, H., and L. Leydesdorff. 1997. *Universities in the global economy: A triple helix of university, industry, and government relations.* London: Cassell Academic.

Fairclough, N. 1992. *Discourse and social change.* Cambridge: Polity Press.

Fear, F. 2005. Guest essay: Apply tsunami-type efforts to everyday needs. *Rochester NY. Democrat and Chronicle* (Jan. 21, 2005).

Fear, F., and M. Avila. Forthcoming. Frames and discourses: Exploring the meaning of engagement. *Perspectives on community development in Ireland 1*(2). http://www.democratandchronicle.com/apps/pbcs.dll/article?AID=/20050121/OPINI ON02/501210398/1039/OPINION.

Fear, F., R. Bawden, C. Rosaen, and P. Foster-Fishman. 2002. A model of engaged learning: Frames of reference and scholarly underpinnings. *Journal of Higher Education Outreach and Engagement* 7(3): 55–68.

Fear, F., N. Creamer, R. Pirog, D. Block, L. Redmond, with M. Dickerson, S. Baldwin, and G. Imig. 2004. Higher education-community partnerships: The politics of engagement. *Journal of Higher Education Outreach and Engagement* 9(2): 139–156.

Fear, F., C. McCarthy, A. Diebel, S. Berkowitz, L. Harvey, and C. Carra. 2003. 'Turning the all around upside down': The graduate classroom as an alternative, self-organizing setting. *Encounter: Education for meaning and social justice* 16(2): 34–39.

Foucault, M. 1980. *Power/knowledge: Selecting interviews and other writings, 1972–1977.* New York: Pantheon Books.

Frankfurt, H. 2005. *On bullshit.* Princeton NJ: Princeton Univ. Press.

Freedland, R. 2005. Universities and cities need to rethink their relationships. *The Chronicle Review, the Chronicle of Higher Education* (May 13, 2005). http://chronicle.com/temp/email.php?id=3wxcxq6fnqrp2io9am522b12ohg7oxbm.

Fromm, E. 1956. *The sane society.* London: Routledge.

Gee, J., G. Hull, and C. Lankshear. 1996. *The new work order: Behind the language of the new capitalism.* Boulder CO: Westview Press.

Gibbons, M., C. Limoges, H. Nowotny, S. Schwarzman, P. Scott, and M. Trow. 1984. *The new production of knowledge.* London: Sage.

Giddens, A. 1990. *The consequences of modernity.* Cambridge: Polity Press.

Giddens, A. 1991. *Modernity and self-identity.* Cambridge: Polity Press.

Gladwell, M. 2000. *The tipping point: How little things can make a big difference.* Boston: Little, Brown, and Company.

Gramsci, A. 1995. *Further selections from the prison notebooks.* D. Boothman, ed. and trans. Minneapolis: Univ. of Minnesota Press.

Habermas, J. 1971. *Knowledge and human interests.* Boston: Beacon Press.

Habermas, J. 1987. *The theory of communicative action, Vol. 2: Lifeworld and system—a critique of functionalist reason.* Boston: Beacon Press.

Hart, T. 2001. *From information to transformation: Education for the evolution of consciousness.* New York: Peter Lang.

hooks, b. 1994. *Teaching to transgress: Education as the practice of freedom.* New York: Routledge.

Horkheimer, M. 1947. *Eclipse of reason.* New York: Continuum.

Horney, K. 1950. *Neurosis and human growth. The struggle toward self-realization.* New York: W. W. Norton.

Horton, M. 1990. *The long haul: An autobiography.* New York: Doubleday.

Jamison, K. 2004. *Exuberance: The passion for life.* New York: Vintage Books.

Kellogg Commission on the Future of State and Land-Grant Universities. 1999. *Returning to our roots: The engaged institution.* Washington D.C.: National Association of State and Land-Grant Universities.

Kerr, C. 1963. *The uses of the university.* Cambridge MA: Harvard Univ. Press.

Kezar, A., A. Chambers, J. Burkhardt, and associates, eds. 2005. *Higher education for the public good: Emerging voices from a national movement.* San Francisco: Jossey-Bass.

Lakoff, G. 2004. *Don't think of an elephant: Know your values and frame the debate.* White River Junction VT: Chelsea Green Publishing.

Loomer, B. 1981. Theology in the American grain. In J. B. Cobb and W. W. Schroeder, eds. *Process philosophy and social thought.* Chicago: Center for the Scientific Study of Religion.

Marcuse, H. 1969. *An essay on liberation.* Boston: Beacon Press.

Maurrasse, D. J. 2001. *Beyond the campus: How colleges and universities form partnerships with their communities.* New York: Routledge.

Melluci, A. 1996. *Challenging codes: Collective action in the information age.* Cambridge: Cambridge Univ. Press.

Mezirow, J., and associates. 2000. *Learning as transformation: Critical perspectives on a theory in progress.* San Francisco: Jossey-Bass.

Oakeshott, M. 1989. *The voice of liberal learning.* New Haven: Yale Univ. Press.

Oakeshott, M. 1991. *Rationalism in politics and other essays.* Indianapolis: Liberty Press.

Palmer, P. 1997. *The courage to teach: Exploring the inner landscape of a teacher's life.* San Francisco: Jossey-Bass.

Palmer, P. 1999. The grace of great things: Reclaiming the sacred in knowing, teaching, and learning. In S. Glazer, ed. *The heart of learning: Spirituality in education.* New York: Tarcher/Putnam.

Palmer. P. 2004. *A hidden wholeness: The journey toward an undivided life.* San Francisco: Jossey-Bass.

Patterson, O. 1992. The speech misheard around the world. *The New York Times* (Jan. 22, 2005) at http://www.nytimes.com/2005/01/22/opinion/22patterson.1.html?ex=1107397249& ei=1&en=c7a3fbb7203c6f34

Rose, M. 2004. *The mind at work: Valuing the intelligence of the American worker.* New York: Viking.

Schön, D. 1995. Knowing-in-action: The new scholarship requires a new epistemology. *Change (Nov–Dec):* 27–34.

Senge, P., C. Scharmer, J. Jaworski, and B. S. Flowers. 2004. *Presence: Human purpose and the field of the future.* Cambridge, MA: The Society for Organizational Learning.

Skocpol, T. 2003. *Diminished democracy: From membership to management in American civic life.* Norman, OK: Univ. of Oklahoma Press.

Slaughter, S., and L. Leslie. 1997. *Academic capitalism: Politics, policies, and the entrepreneurial university.* Baltimore: The Johns Hopkins Univ. Press.

Sullivan, W. 2005. *Work and integrity: The crisis and promise of professionalism in America.* San Francisco: Jossey-Bass.

Surowiecki, J. 2004. *The wisdom of crowds: Why the many are smarter and how the collective wisdom shapes business, economies, societies, and nations.* New York: Doubleday.

Tagg, J. 2003. *The learning paradigm college.* Bolton MA: Anker Publishing.

Washburn, J. 2005. *University, Inc.: The corporate corruption of American higher education.* New York: Basic Books.

Wenger, E., R. McDermott, and W. Snyder. 2002. *Cultivating communities of practice.* Boston: Harvard Business School Press.

West, C. 1998. Cornell West. In G. Yancy, ed. *African-American philosophers: 17 conversations.* New York: Routledge.

Wheatley, M. 2002. *Turning to one another: Simple conversations to restore hope to the future.* San Francisco: Berrett-Koehler.

Whitman, C. T. 2005. *It's my party, too: The battle for the heart of the GOP and the future of America.* New York: Penguin.

Williams, T. T. 2004. *The open space of democracy.* Great Barrington MA: The Orion Press.

Yankelovich, D. 1991. *Coming to public judgment: Making democracy work in a complex world.* Syracuse NY: Syracuse Univ. Press.

ABOUT THE AUTHORS

Frank A. Fear is Professor of community, agriculture, recreation, and resource studies at Michigan State University where he is also faculty member in the Liberty Hyde Bailey Scholars program. He has served in a variety of administrative roles, most recently as acting senior associate dean, College of Agriculture and Natural Resources. A sociologist with background in organization and community development, he writes and teaches about extraordinary change—people who by situation or temperament envision and engage in out of the box change. His work focuses primarily on extraordinary change in higher education and extraordinary change in society resulting from collaboration with higher education.

Cheryl L. Rosaen is Associate Professor of Teacher Education at Michigan State University and a faculty Team Leader in a five-year Teacher Preparation Program. She teaches courses in literacy methods and teacher education and also conducts research on learning to teach literacy and the role technology plays in supporting teacher learning. Dr. Rosaen collaborates with colleagues in research and the development of video case materials for use in literacy teacher preparation and professional development.

Richard J. Bawden is a Visiting Distinguished University Professor at Michigan State University and a Professor Emeritus of the University of Western Sydney in Australia, where he served as dean of agriculture and rural development. The main focus of his current work is the practical application of critical systems principles to rural development with emphasis on the changing role of the Academy in the process of development. He has extensive experience in developing countries with a spectrum of stakeholders, from citizens to academics to policy makers.

Pennie G. Foster-Fishman is Associate Professor of Psychology at Michigan State University and the leader of an empowerment evaluation team on campus. She teaches courses in qualitative research methods, comprehensive community change, and university/community collaboration; and conducts research on comprehensive community and systems change and the role of social planning, social action, and multiple stakeholder collaboration in fostering change. Dr. Foster-Fishman collaborates with partners in many community settings, engaging with them in capacity building and transformative change endeavors.

Patricia P. Miller, book editor, is a writer, editor, and outreach professional at Michigan State University. She has served as technology transfer manager, Hazardous Substance Research Center; and in various roles in University Outreach and Partnerships, MSU Extension, and the Institute for Health Care Studies. She is the author of numerous academic and journalistic manuals, articles, essays, poems, and book chapters.